Firefighter Exam
FOR
DUMMIES®

by Stacy L. Bell, Tracey Vasil Biscontini, and Lindsay Rock

WILEY
Wiley Publishing, Inc.

Firefighter Exam For Dummies®

Published by
Wiley Publishing, Inc.
111 River St.
Hoboken, NJ 07030-5774
www.wiley.com

About the Authors

Stacy L. Bell is the executive vice president and co-owner of Fire & Police Selection, Inc. (FPSI), a leading consulting firm that specializes in the development and validation of testing instruments used in the protective services industry. Stacy holds a bachelor's degree in psychology from California State University, Sacramento, and a master's degree in industrial/organizational psychology from Capella University.

Stacy is responsible for the test development and validation of all pre-employment and promotional products offered by FPSI, including written tests, physical ability tests, structured interviews, and personality inventories. She has 14 years' experience in providing selection tools to human resources and public safety departments across the country.

Stacy currently resides in beautiful Northern California. In her "spare time," Stacy enjoys spending time with her family, riding bikes, hiking, and being outdoors. When she's not mothering her 9-year-old son, she's mothering one of her two Golden Retrievers or her Bernese Mountain Dog.

Tracey Vasil Biscontini is the founder, president, and CEO of Northeast Editing, Inc., a company specializing in the creation of test-preparation products. She holds bachelor's degrees in education and mass communications from King's College and a master's degree in English from the University of Scranton. Recently named one of the Top 25 Women in Business in Northeast Pennsylvania, she is a former educator, journalist, and newspaper columnist whose award-winning writing has appeared in national magazines. Since founding Northeast Editing, Inc., in 1992, she has managed educational projects and authored test-preparation and library-reference content for some of the largest publishers in the United States.

Northeast Editing, Inc., is located in a former rectory in Jenkins Township, nestled between Wilkes-Barre and Scranton in northeastern Pennsylvania. Tracey's company boasts a relaxed work environment that serves as her staff's home away from home. When they're not hard at work, the editors and writers at Northeast Editing, Inc., enjoy breaks in a large backyard and welcome hugs from Prince, a stray cat that showed up one day and never left. Tracey lives in Avoca, Pennsylvania, with her husband, Nick; son, Tyler; and daughter, Morgan.

Lindsay Rock is a former volunteer firefighter with the Mt. Zion Bicentennial Volunteer Fire Department (MZFD) in Harding, Pennsylvania. She earned a certificate of attainment in Pennsylvania Essentials of Firefighting and completed a structural burn session at the Schuylkill Fire Training Center in Frackville, Pennsylvania, in 2004. In addition to proudly serving her community through the fire department, Lindsay wanted to prove that she could "keep up with the boys" — a brother, Nick, and an uncle, Seth, who also were firefighters. She briefly served as president of MZFD in 2005.

Lindsay is the managing editor of Northeast Editing, Inc., where she has written and edited test-preparation and trade books since 2003. She holds a bachelor's degree in journalism with a minor in English from the Pennsylvania State University and is a member of Phi Beta Kappa, an academic honor society.

Lindsay currently resides in Exeter, Pennsylvania. She spends much of her free time continuing to prove that she can keep up with the boys. If she's not riding her bright yellow quad through the woods, you may find her on the golf course or watching Penn State and Pittsburgh Steelers football.

Dedication

To the men and women of the fire service — who put their lives on the line every day.

Authors' Acknowledgments

Special thanks to Tracy Boggier, our acquisitions editor, who got the ball rolling; Vicki Adang, our incredible project editor, who offered advice and guidance every step of the way; our wonderful copy editor, Danielle Voirol; and our technical editors, Chad Abel and Jeff Seaton.

Finally, more special thanks to everyone at Northeast Editing, Inc., who devoted countless hours of research and writing to help create this book.

Publisher's Acknowledgments

We're proud of this book; please send us your comments at http://dummies.custhelp.com. For other comments, please contact our Customer Care Department within the U.S. at 877-762-2974, outside the U.S. at 317-572-3993, or fax 317-572-4002.

Some of the people who helped bring this book to market include the following:

Acquisitions, Editorial, and Media Development

Project Editor: Victoria M. Adang

Acquisitions Editor: Tracy Boggier

Senior Copy Editor: Danielle Voirol

Assistant Editor: David Lutton

Technical Editors: Chad Abel, Jeff Seaton

Editorial Manager: Michelle Hacker

Editorial Assistants: Rachelle S. Amick, Jennette ElNaggar

Art Coordinator: Alicia B. South

Cover Photo: © iStockphoto.com/ryasick

Cartoons: Rich Tennant (www.the5thwave.com)

Composition Services

Project Coordinator: Patrick Redmond

Layout and Graphics: Carl Byers, Carrie A. Cesavice, Joyce Haughey, Mark Pinto, Brent Savage

Proofreaders: Laura Albert, Betty Kish

Indexer: Estalita Slivoskey

Publishing and Editorial for Consumer Dummies

Diane Graves Steele, Vice President and Publisher, Consumer Dummies

Kristin Ferguson-Wagstaffe, Product Development Director, Consumer Dummies

Ensley Eikenburg, Associate Publisher, Travel

Kelly Regan, Editorial Director, Travel

Publishing for Technology Dummies

Andy Cummings, Vice President and Publisher, Dummies Technology/General User

Composition Services

Debbie Stailey, Director of Composition Services

Contents at a Glance

Table of Contents

. . . .

Introduction

Chances are that if you're reading this book, you've thought about pursuing a career in the fire service. Good for you! Firefighting is an exhilarating career. Sure, it involves some risk, but for the most part, firefighters consider what they do honorable, rewarding, and essential for public safety. Firefighters rescue people from all manner of emergencies, including wildland fires, structure fires, floods, motor vehicle accidents, and more. They work to keep the public safe from harm.

Perhaps you want to become a firefighter because you like the thought of helping people each day. Maybe you like the idea of an ever-changing work environment or you want a job that keeps you active all the time. Whatever your reason, we applaud your choice and want to help you get hired.

The firefighter hiring process is unlike that of any other job. It's much more than a job application, a resume, and an interview. It involves numerous tests and evaluations designed to ensure that you're ready to begin training to become a firefighter. No need to worry. We wrote *Firefighter Exam For Dummies* for people just like you. Consider us the tour guides on your career path; we'll lead you from application to academy.

About This Book

The firefighter hiring process has many elements, including a number of exams, interviews, and evaluations, each pushing you one step closer to proving that you have what it takes to begin firefighter training. *Firefighter Exam For Dummies* guides you through every step of the process with detailed descriptions and information.

This book begins with a general overview of what firefighters do and then moves on to the specifics of the exam process, including detailed chapters on each element of the written exam, the physical ability test, the oral interview, the medical exam, and the psychological evaluation. We provide four full-length practice tests to help you prepare for the written exam, as well as tips for interviewing and staying in shape.

Although this book is likely to catch the attention of career firefighter hopefuls, volunteers may benefit from the information, tips, and advice within its pages, too. Volunteers often have to undergo the same training as paid firefighters, and with the number of volunteer departments transitioning into paid fire companies on the rise, employment testing may change from "option" to "requirement." We're certain that if this occurs, *Firefighter Exam For Dummies* can help.

Conventions Used in This Book

The following conventions are used throughout the text to make things consistent and easy to understand:

- We use the term *applicant* to refer to a person who applies for a firefighting job by signing up to take the written exam. We use the term *candidate* to refer to a person who has been screened as qualified and invited to participate in the recruitment process.

- All Web addresses appear in `monofont`.

- New terms appear in *italics* and are closely followed by easy-to-understand definitions.
- **Bold** is used to highlight keywords in bulleted lists and the action parts of numbered steps.

Foolish Assumptions

Everyone knows what happens when you assume, but while writing this book, we decided to live dangerously and make the following assumptions about you:

- You're interested in becoming a firefighter, and you want to know more about the job and the hiring process.
- You want to take some firefighter practice tests so you know what to expect and where to focus your studying.
- You want to prepare yourself for each step of the firefighter hiring process to help ensure your chances of overall success.
- You understand that successfully completing all exams, interviews, and evaluations means that you qualify to *begin* training to become a firefighter. You know that actually rushing into burning buildings doesn't occur until after you've received extensive training at an academy or some other training program.
- You can read, speak, and understand the English language reasonably well. (Writers of firefighter exams assume this, too.) If you need to brush up on your vocabulary and grammar skills, you may want to review Chapter 5.

How This Book Is Organized

This book is divided into five parts and 24 chapters. The table of contents outlines the specifics, but the following is an overview of what you can expect to see.

Part I: So You Want to Be a Firefighter? Get Ready!

If you're curious to know exactly what firefighters do and where they work, or if you'd like to know more about the various exams you have to take to begin training to become a firefighter, turn to Part I. Chapter 1 explains a firefighter's typical duties and career path, and Chapters 2 and 3 describe the screening process and the exams.

Part II: Gearing Up to Take the Test: The Written Exam

If the written exam makes you a bit nervous, turn to Part II, where you find details about and practice questions for the various subject areas typically found on written firefighter exams.

Part III: Demonstrating Physical, Mental, and Emotional Fitness with Interactive Tests

If the physical ability test, oral interview, medical exam, or psychological evaluation has you stressed, open to Part III. Chapter 12 describes the elements of a physical ability test, Chapter 13 explains what to expect in the oral interview, and Chapter 14 presents an overview of the medical exam and psychological evaluation.

Part IV: Practice Firefighter Exams

Want to try your hand at taking a written firefighter exam? Part IV includes four practice exams, including two general exams, an exam based on the National Firefighter Selection Inventory test, and an exam based on the New York City Fire Department's written exam.

Part V: The Part of Tens

The Part of Tens is a standard element of *For Dummies* books. Chapter 23 contains some helpful tips for succeeding on the various firefighter exams. Chapter 24 describes some things every firefighter (or future firefighter) should do.

Icons Used in This Book

To make this book easier to read and simpler to use, we include some icons that can help you find key ideas and information. Keep an eye out for them.

The Example icon draws your attention to sample questions and answers that help you understand the concept we're explaining.

This icon appears next to information that could benefit you during the various steps of the hiring process. This information can save you time and effort.

When you see this icon, you know the information that follows is especially important to the various firefighter exams.

This icon highlights information that could pose a threat to your success on the firefighter exams.

Where to Go from Here

The great thing about *For Dummies* books is that you can start wherever you want and still find complete information. Want to know how you'd perform on a written firefighter exam without any preparation? Open up to Chapter 15 and take a practice test. Then check your answers in Chapter 16 to see how well you did. Interested in what happens after you've passed the written test? Go to Chapters 12 to 14 to get the skinny on the non-written exams such as the oral interview and the physical ability test. The point is that you don't have to read this book from cover to cover. You can start wherever you think you need the most work.

If you're not sure where to start, we suggest Part I, which explains what firefighters do and where they work, along with a detailed description of the hiring process and an overview of the different exams.

Part I

So You Want to Be a Firefighter? Get Ready!

The 5th Wave · By Rich Tennant

"Are you sure firefighting is the right career choice for you?"

In this part . . .

Has it been your lifelong dream to jump into a shiny, red fire engine with screaming sirens and flashing lights and race to someone's rescue? Do you want to make your dream a reality? First things first. Before you can leap into that fire engine, check out the process for becoming a firefighter.

We know you're eager to get started, but take a few minutes to read Part I. This part provides information about careers in the fire service, the firefighter hiring process, and the various pre-employment firefighter exams. The more you know about the hiring process and the exams, the more prepared you'll be for each stage down the road.

Chapter 1

Getting the Lowdown on the Job of Firefighter

* *

In This Chapter

▶ Understanding firefighters' duties and work environment

▶ Realizing the risks associated with firefighting

▶ Identifying the levels of fire departments' occupational hierarchy

▶ Pinpointing where to find firefighting jobs

▶ Looking ahead at the occupational outlook for firefighters

* *

*W*hy does a career in firefighting appeal to you? Do you enjoy the physical demands of the job? Do you cherish the opportunity to save a life? Do you like the feeling that your job gives something back to the community? Many career firefighters believe that they didn't choose the job — the job chose them. Perhaps you've experienced a similar calling, or maybe you're inspired by the good work you've seen other firefighters do. Regardless, before you become a firefighter, you need to understand exactly what the job entails.

In this chapter, we give you information about careers in firefighting, such as salaries, employment outlooks, work environments, ranks within fire organizations, and risks associated with the job. Although firefighter exams won't likely test your knowledge of this information, it's still important to know what you're likely to encounter if you plan to make firefighting your career.

Understanding What It's Like to Be a Firefighter

Firefighting has certainly changed from the early days of bucket brigades and horse-drawn fire trucks. Today's firefighters must be prepared to not only fight fires but also respond to crises ranging from traffic accidents and medical emergencies to natural disasters, water rescues, and sadly, even terrorist attacks. Before entering a career in the fire service, it's important that you understand what firefighters do and where they work, as well as the risks associated with the job.

Knowing your role

Movies and television would have you believe that you'll spend most of your time tracking down serial arsonists or racing out of a burning building, an unconscious victim draped over each shoulder, just as the structure behind you explodes into a huge fireball. Although such scenarios do happen on occasion, you'll more often respond to rush-hour fender benders and activated fire alarms caused by overcooked pot roast. The following sections cover some of the roles you may play, both at the station and away.

Responding to emergencies

As a firefighter, you'll be responsible for a number of duties. Most obvious among those duties is fighting fires, but you'll also respond to a variety of other emergencies, from minor nuisances such as a fallen tree blocking a roadway to major incidents such as gas leaks, traffic accidents, vehicle rollovers, plane crashes, building collapses, and floods.

When disasters occur, firefighters often are the first responders. As a result, many departments require firefighters to be trained as emergency medical technicians (EMTs) so they can provide first aid and perform other life-saving medical procedures on victims. Most departments require only the most basic EMT certification (EMT-Basic), but many are moving toward requiring more advanced training (EMT-Intermediate or EMT-Paramedic).

As a firefighter EMT, you'll likely be the first person to encounter victims experiencing medical emergencies such as heart attacks, strokes, burns, broken bones, shock, blocked airways, bleeding, and more. Firefighting is *not* for the squeamish or the faint of heart. When you respond to an emergency, you never know what you might find when you arrive. Our best advice is to be prepared for anything and everything.

Other responsibilities include rescues, not only from burning buildings but also from hard-to-reach places, such as lakes or rivers or even steep cliffs. You may have to help clean up hazardous materials. For example, when a truck hauling oil overturns on a highway, fire departments are often called to block roadways, prevent fire, clean up the oil, assist injured victims, and more. During floods, you may have to notify people to evacuate their homes or help them pump water from their homes after flood waters begin to recede.

Firefighters often work in conjunction with other emergency services, including police departments, other fire departments (for example, a state- or county-run wildland firefighting team), and paramedics and ambulance personnel. When working with other emergency services, you'll follow the direction of your superiors, who are responsible for coordinating with other units.

Working back at the station and in the community

Here are some of the tasks firefighters fulfill when they're not on an emergency call:

- **Household chores:** Firefighters in many departments, especially small or rural departments, have a lot of downtime between calls, which they spend at the station. There, you'll take care of everyday tasks such as laundry (firefighting's a dirty job), cooking (shifts are long; you'll need food keep your motor running), and cleaning (treat the station like your home away from home).

- **Training and preparation:** As a new firefighter, training and preparation will make up most of your job. After you've gotten a few years of service under your belt, you'll likely use downtime to review new skills, read fire science literature, study for upcoming tests, run practice drills, prepare written reports, work out, and assist new firefighters with their training.

- **Equipment maintenance:** You may be asked to assist in performing maintenance on fire apparatuses — that is, firefighting vehicles such as fire engines, ladder trucks, and tenders (sometimes called tankers, depending on the region in which you live) — or to clean and maintain other equipment. For example, you may have to refill empty air cylinders, which provide the air you breathe in your self-contained breathing apparatus (SCBA), or you may have to wash lengths of hose and hang them to dry.

- **Fire inspection:** Firefighters specially trained as fire prevention inspectors may take time to enter structures and assess sprinkler systems, extinguishers, exits, and fire escapes to make sure they comply with fire codes. Those trained as fire investigators may revisit a fire scene to determine the fire's cause.

- **Other programs:** Some firefighters may be responsible for activities related to public relations — how the public views the fire department and its role in the community — such as public speaking engagements and creating and teaching fire prevention programs for schools.

Looking at shifts: Timing is everything

Firefighting is a time-consuming occupation. Fire departments are on call 24 hours a day, 7 days a week, and firefighters must be ready to respond to an emergency at a moment's notice. This doesn't mean that you have to strike family vacations from the calendar forever; however, it does mean that you should expect to work rotating shifts (a combination of day and night shifts), put in overtime hours, and give up some holidays here and there.

A typical shift for a firefighter may be 24 hours on the clock followed by 48 hours off the clock. Another department may require you to work three 10-hour days, followed by three 10-hour nights, followed by three days off. Shifts largely depend on the size and location of your department. Another thought to keep in mind: When emergencies occur, "quittin' time" goes out the window. You'll be expected to work until the job is done.

Picturing your work environment

As a firefighter, your work environment will generally alternate between the fire station and emergency scenes. The fire station is a relatively static work environment, but emergency scenes constantly change and evolve.

On a call

Firefighters respond to all types of emergency calls. The following are just a few:

- Structure fires
- Wildland (forest) fires
- Gas leaks
- Traffic accidents
- Vehicle rollovers
- Plane crashes
- Building collapses
- Fallen trees and natural disasters

Because emergency scenes vary so much — the weather alone can vary from hot, humid, and sunny to freezing, cloudy, and icy — it's impossible to know exactly what your working environment will be like at each call. One day you may find yourself knee deep in floodwater. The next day you may respond to a car accident on a busy interstate highway. Another day you could be trekking through a forest.

Emergencies occur anywhere and anytime, but certain types of emergency scenes generally have the same type of environment. For example, at traffic accidents, you'll likely be surrounded by moving traffic, so you always have to stay alert. During floods, your environment will likely include deep water, washed-out roadways, thick mud, and slippery surfaces. Emergency scenes involving structure fires could involve extremely high temperatures, thick smoke, and falling debris. Our best advice is to stay alert.

At the station

One part of your working environment that shouldn't change too much is the fire station. As a firefighter, you won't always be responding to calls and fighting fires. Depending on the size of your department and the area in which you live, you'll probably spend much of your time at the station, preparing for the next emergency situation.

Fire station components and layouts vary greatly from one department to the next. Departments in large metropolitan areas have to accommodate more firefighters and are likely much larger than municipal departments in smaller communities. Certain areas are essential to all fire stations, however, and the following is a list of facilities that you may encounter in a fire station:

- **Apparatus room/garage/workshop/storage area:** This room often serves as a combination garage and tool shed. You'll find fire engines, brush trucks, tanker trucks, and ladder trucks parked here. You'll also likely find a variety of tools and equipment.

- **Conference room/classroom:** This room is likely equipped with either a large conference table and chairs or several smaller desks. Here, you'll undergo training or take part in meetings with fellow firefighters.

- **Dormitory area:** The dormitory area is where firefighters try to catch some z's between calls. It's usually equipped with beds or cots so firefighters have a place to rest.

- **Exercise facility/gym:** This room contains exercise equipment, such as a weight bench, free weights, and a treadmill. Here, you can work out and maintain your physical fitness.

- **Kitchen/dining area:** Because firefighters are often on duty for extended shifts of 10 to 24 hours, they need a place to cook and eat meals. Often the whole crew will gather for meals in the kitchen/dining area at the same time.

- **Laundry facility:** Firefighting is a dirty job. Firefighters crawl on their knees through soot and other debris. They encounter liquids such as floodwater, oil, natural gas, and blood. In the laundry facility, you can clean your gear and make sure it's ready for the next call.

- **Lounge:** Many stations have a lounge area where firefighters can kick back and relax — when they can actually find a minute to do so.

- **Office:** Most fire stations have an office where the chief or other senior officers create schedules, make phone calls, and fill out paperwork.

- **Restrooms/shower facilities:** When you return from a call, you'll probably want to get cleaned up. Most stations have a restroom/shower facility or a locker room where you can shower and change clothes.

Considering risks on the job

Nearly every call that firefighters face in the line of duty — whether a house fire, car accident, or tanker truck rollover — involves some degree of risk. Firefighters consistently put themselves in risky situations to save people's property and, more important, their lives.

The following are some examples of the risks firefighters face on a regular basis:

- **Flames:** Obviously firefighters will encounter fire at some point. Fires are unpredictable, and firefighters always run the risk of getting burned.

- **Smoke and fumes:** Fires produce byproducts including smoke and soot, and burning objects — a plastic chair or the stuffing from a couch cushion, for example — can release noxious fumes. If firefighters aren't properly wearing SCBAs, they may end up inhaling these harmful products of combustion and damaging their lungs.

- **Hazardous materials (hazmat):** Firefighters may encounter any number of hazardous materials such as poisonous, flammable, or explosive gases; toxic chemicals; medical waste; and radioactive materials. Large trucks often haul these materials on the nation's highways, and when one of them rolls over or gets into an accident, these materials can leak out, creating danger for everyone involved — including the firefighters who help clean up the mess.

- **Collapsing walls, ceilings, floors, and buildings:** As fire spreads throughout a building, it weakens walls, ceilings, and floors. This puts firefighters at risk because a wall or ceiling could collapse on them or a floor could cave in beneath them, leaving firefighters trapped or injured.

- **Traffic accidents:** Fire trucks often travel at high speeds to reach fires and other disasters as quickly as possible. Although other cars and trucks are supposed to yield to emergency vehicles, not all do, and this can result in collisions between fire trucks and other automobiles. A high volume of traffic and excessive speeding can also result in accidents.

- **Long-term health risks:** A leading cause of death among firefighters is heart disease, which can result from high blood pressure, overexertion, and exposure to extreme heat. In addition, firefighters encounter numerous blood-borne pathogens, such as HIV, hepatitis B, and hepatitis C, at emergency scenes. Exposure to certain toxins in the air can lead to an increased risk of developing certain forms of cancer. For example, exposure to asbestos, a material often found in old buildings, may lead to the development of a form of lung cancer called mesothelioma.

As a firefighter, you could encounter any of these hazards — and more — on any given day, and they could result in injury or even death. Our goal in sharing these risks isn't to scare you into forgetting your dream of becoming a firefighter. Rather, we want to adequately prepare you for your future career so you know exactly what to expect — both the risks and the rewards.

Handling the highs and lows

Firefighting can take a toll on your psyche because of all the highs and lows firefighters face. The rewards of firefighting are numerous — making an amazing rescue, saving a family's home, working as a team, bonding with other firefighters. Such scenarios can make you feel like you're on top of the world. But some parts of the job may weigh on your mind and lead to psychological stress. For example, witnessing death and injury, losing co-workers, dealing with guilt after a failed rescue, coping with family issues, and facing angry members of the public can lead to stress.

In the past, many departments used a response approach to help firefighters deal with psychological stress — for example, intervening after a firefighter turned to alcohol or drugs to deal with his or her stress. Today, however, departments have begun to focus on stress management and prevention. Departments may set up education programs or workshops to teach firefighters stress-management techniques and methods for identifying signs of stress. Firefighters and their families may take part in such programs. In addition, fire departments may offer mentoring programs and spiritual guidance or recommend mental health experts to help firefighters deal with the psychological stress of the job.

From Firefighter to Fire Chief: Climbing the Fire Department Ladder

As a firefighter, you'll work with all kinds of ladders: wall ladders, roof ladders, extension ladders, and so on. One more ladder you may want to consider is the occupational ladder. A fire department's occupational ladder has many rungs. If you plan to make firefighting your career — which we assume you do, because you're reading this book — chances are that you'll want to start climbing that ladder someday.

In addition to the department positions we list in the following sections (which represent just one of the many rank structures used by fire departments throughout the country), other jobs within the firefighting industry include fire apparatus driver/operators, communications personnel, fire police personnel, airport firefighters, hazardous materials technicians, fire and arson investigators, and public fire and life safety educators.

Starting on the bottom rung

The saying goes, "The only job where you can start at the top is digging a hole." In firefighting, you'll have to start on the bottom rung of the career ladder. That means beginning your career as a recruit or probationary firefighter fresh out of a training academy and ready for some real, on-the-job training and, over time, working through the ranks to become a fire chief.

Firefighter

Firefighters respond to medical emergencies and activated fire alarms. They extinguish fires, ventilate buildings, perform salvage and overhaul duties, and remove people from danger. They also perform inspections. A firefighter's salary may be between $30,000 and $55,000 per year.

Engineer

Engineers may perform standard firefighter duties, but they're also responsible for training new firefighters and driving and operating heavy-duty fire apparatuses. They may also discuss fire safety regulations with the public. An engineer may earn $48,000 to $62,000 each year. (An engineer should not be confused with a fire engineer, also known as a *fire protection engineer* or a *fire safety engineer,* who has a fire engineering degree and would likely work outside the fire department in areas such as fire suppression system design, building design and layout, or risk analysis.)

Moving to middle management

Firefighters and engineers who want to be promoted to middle management often take exams that show their growing knowledge of the field. They may have to demonstrate their knowledge of building construction, equipment management, emergency medical practices, and public speaking.

Fire lieutenant

A fire lieutenant coordinates the operations of his or her company during emergencies. He or she may be responsible for regular equipment maintenance and developing training standards. The fire lieutenant may also participate in hiring new recruits and creating personnel schedules. The salary for a person in this position is between $50,000 and $62,000.

Fire captain

The fire captain of a department may be responsible for communicating with the public, overseeing the use and maintenance of department equipment, and maintaining personnel records. He or she may also participate in training and employee development. In some departments, captains are responsible for maintaining an individual station and its equipment. A fire captain's annual salary may range from $60,000 to $72,000.

Battalion chief

The battalion chief creates a link between an assistant fire chief (see the next section) and a fire captain. He or she may supervise the fire captain in goal-setting and planning, budget preparation, and personnel management. A battalion chief may also create departmental policies. In many departments, battalion chiefs serve as shift commanders, who direct firefighters at emergency scenes. Battalion chiefs earn between $66,000 and $81,000.

Becoming the top dog

Depending on the department, advancing to positions beyond battalion chief may require a bachelor's degree. If a degree is required, it'll most likely be in the areas of fire science or public administration.

Assistant/Division chief

The assistant chief reviews and evaluates department/company personnel. He or she researches and plans community activities and appearances for the department, investigates causes of fires, and inspects buildings for fire hazards. The assistant chief may also assist in developing training programs and maintaining department records. The annual salary for this position is $65,000 to $83,000.

Deputy chief

The deputy chief's responsibilities are similar to the assistant chief's duties. If both positions exist in a department, the deputy chief may share the assistant chief's tasks. He or she may handle administration, participate in training and hiring, and oversee financial records. The deputy chief may also be responsible for disciplining those who break department rules. The annual salary for this position is $69,000 to $88,000.

Fire chief

The fire chief commands all emergency scenes through the delegation of responsibilities, priorities, and tasks. He or she makes final decisions regarding budget and personnel issues and may create and maintain safety regulations. A fire chief provides communication between his or her department and other agencies. A fire chief earns between $78,000 and $105,000 annually, depending on location, department size, and experience.

Finding Firefighters: Who They Work For

Where do firefighters work? If you plan to pursue a career in firefighting, you should know where to look for a firefighting job. Firefighters work in both the public sector and the private sector; we discuss both in the following sections.

In the public sector

Most paid firefighters work in fire departments in the public sector. Departments in the public sector — as you may have guessed — are responsible for taking care of the general public. Their main goal is to protect families, homes, businesses, and wildland areas.

Firefighters who work in departments in the public sector are usually employed by local governments. These departments may cover regions ranging in size from small towns to large cities or entire counties. According to the U.S. Bureau of Labor Statistics, about 91 percent of firefighters work for local governments. In addition, the U.S. Fire Administration estimates that approximately 74 percent of paid career firefighters who work in the public sector protect cities or towns with a population of 25,000 or more people. Therefore, your best chance for becoming a career firefighter is in a large metropolitan area.

A small percentage — less than 9 percent — of paid firefighters in the public sector may work for federal or state governments, such as those who work at airports or for government agencies such as the U.S. Forest Service, the National Park Service, or the Bureau of Land Management. The remaining paid firefighters work in the private sector.

In the private sector

Some private companies, especially those with a high potential for hazards such as the oil and chemical industries, have their own fire departments that respond to emergencies. These departments employ a small number of paid firefighters known as *industrial firefighters*.

Industrial firefighters receive highly specialized training to deal with emergency situations common to the industry in which they work. For example, firefighters who work for a department in the oil industry are skilled in handling fires, hazardous materials releases, emergency medical responses, and rescues. The goal of private industrial firefighters is to protect companies, factories, products, and employees. Among the many important jobs of industrial firefighters are routine inspections of company facilities to ensure that all precautions are in place to prevent a fire from starting.

Predicting the Future: How Many Firefighting Jobs Will There Be?

You're in luck! According to the U.S. Bureau of Labor and Statistics (BLS), the number of firefighting jobs available in the decade between 2008 and 2018 is expected to grow by 19 percent, which is an increase of about 57,500 jobs. The BLS also expects that the majority of paid firefighting jobs will come from volunteer positions transitioning to paid positions.

Although the outlook for firefighting jobs in the next few years is good, competition for those positions is fierce. The number of applicants for firefighting jobs far surpasses the number of available positions, and the BLS cites several reasons for this:

- A career in firefighting is both challenging and rewarding.
- Firefighters usually need only a high school diploma or its equivalent to enter the fire service (although those who have completed additional firefighter education classes or have achieved other certifications may have an edge).
- Most firefighters have the opportunity to retire and earn a pension after 25 years of service.

Don't let the competition scare you away, though. You've already taken an important first step in preparing for a career in firefighting by picking up this book. In the chapters that follow, we prepare you for each step along the path toward firefighting career success. The key is persistence. Most applicants don't get hired on their first pass through the firefighter hiring process, so don't give up. With preparation and determination, we have no doubt that you'll succeed.

Chapter 2

Throwing Your Hat in the Ring: Applying to Be a Firefighter

In This Chapter

▶ Filling out the application and submitting a resume, a cover letter, and references

▶ Familiarizing yourself with the various interviews and exams in the screening process

You've probably spent time researching what firefighters do. Maybe you've spent time at the local fire department meeting career firefighters and asking about their day-to-day lives. Perhaps you're already a volunteer firefighter who wants to transition to a full-time, paid firefighting career. Whatever your reason, you've made the decision to become a firefighter. So what's the next step?

For most occupations, you fill out an application or submit a resume and a cover letter and then undergo an interview to determine whether you're the right fit for the job. The firefighter screening process, however, includes many more steps. It involves a lot of paperwork, numerous tests, an interview, and more. Each step in the process is designed to weed out those who don't quite make the cut and narrow down the choices to the best and brightest candidates.

In this chapter, we explain how the hiring process works, from obtaining the job announcement or bulletin to filling out the application to undergoing the medical and psychological exams that are part of a conditional offer of employment. You'll know exactly what you have to do to become a firefighter.

Finding and Applying for a Job

Though fire departments in different municipalities may vary the structure of the screening process, most departments generally include the same elements, and most have the same or similar requirements for employment. In the following sections, we explain how to apply for a firefighting job, including info on where to find job listings, what kinds of paperwork you may have to submit, and more.

Understanding job requirements

The following are some criteria that you have to meet to become a firefighter:

▶ **Age:** Age limits vary and often depend on a department's pension (money paid upon retirement) system, but most departments require candidates to be at least 18 to take the exam and be hired as a full-time firefighter. Some departments have maximum age limits, but others base eligibility on physical ability and health.

- ✔ **Background check:** Most departments conduct a background check to verify your education records, employment history, driving history, police record, and so on. They may require you to record this information on a background data collection form. The background check is *very* important to the hiring process and may even require you to take a polygraph (lie detector) test to verify information. Departments eliminate many candidates from the screening process because they fail to disclose or lie about past indiscretions.

- ✔ **Education:** Most departments don't require candidates to have a college degree, but they do require a high school diploma or proof that you passed your General Educational Development (GED) test.

- ✔ **Citizenship:** To become a firefighter, you must be a U.S. citizen and both speak and understand English. You may need to produce a birth certificate, a passport, or naturalization documents to prove that you're a citizen of the United States.

- ✔ **Residency:** Most departments require that you reside in the area where you're seeking employment. For example, if you're applying for a position in the county fire department, the department will likely require that you live within the county. Don't rule out applying to fire departments in other areas, however; most give you six months to a year to move to the area if you're hired.

- ✔ **Driver's license:** You must have a valid driver's license. You may need to submit a copy of your driver's license with your application, which those in charge of hiring will use to identify you throughout the screening process.

- ✔ **Drug screening:** Most departments require candidates to pass a drug screening.

- ✔ **Medical and psychological requirements:** Medical standards for firefighters are high, so the job or exam announcement may include a list of medical qualifications for candidates to consider before applying. Firefighters must meet physical fitness standards and be free of serious medical conditions that could hinder their ability to perform their job and cause injury to themselves or others. Firefighters also have to be mentally able to handle the pressures of the job.

  Temporary or correctable conditions such as drug use, pregnancy, or being overweight or underweight can disqualify you from becoming a firefighter until the condition is corrected. Other, more serious medical conditions may permanently disqualify a person from becoming a firefighter. These types of conditions include anemia, diabetes, epilepsy, gastrointestinal disorders, heart disease, high blood pressure, and lung disease.

  Following a written exam, physical ability test, and oral interview, you may have to pass a medical exam and a psychological evaluation as part of a conditional offer of employment. We discuss these evaluations later in this chapter.

If you meet these criteria, you're ready to apply to be a firefighter.

Obtaining information about the exam and the position

The competition for firefighting positions is fierce — some departments receive more than 3,000 applications to fill just two or three job openings! You have to be on top of your game if you want to succeed. This means taking a proactive approach by knowing which departments are hiring and when testing will occur.

The Internet is tremendously helpful in finding info about the exam and available firefighting jobs. For example, at www.nationalfireselect.com, you can sign up for the National Fire Select Program, which allows you to take one written test online and have your scores considered by fire departments throughout the United States and Canada. For a monthly fee, www.firerecruit.com sends you e-mail notifications about job openings in departments across the United States. You can expand your search from the rare opening at your local fire department to hundreds of available positions nationwide.

Becoming a Stronger Candidate

Firefighting is a competitive field, but you can do a number of things to strengthen your resume and turn yourself into a top candidate. Most departments require firefighters to have a high school diploma, but it never hurts to continue your education. Consider taking some firefighting classes. A little Internet research can help you locate classes at community colleges, local universities, and local fire departments. Many teach skills such as first aid and CPR (cardiopulmonary resuscitation), which firefighters have to know. Others may offer courses in essentials of firefighting or emergency vehicle operations. Eventually, you'll learn these skills at a fire academy, but why not give yourself an advantage and get a head start?

Volunteering is another way to improve your resume. By volunteering with a local fire department, you can familiarize yourself with fire department operations, firefighting gear and equipment, and fire apparatuses. You also get to see exactly what happens at emergency scenes. Volunteering gives you valuable firsthand experience in the field. If you're under strict time constraints, at the very least consider talking to some experienced firefighters about what the job entails, how they got their start, and what advice they can offer to a newcomer. For more ways to improve your chances of success, read Chapter 23.

Fire departments also post announcements about job openings and the exams that you have to take to be considered for those positions on their Web sites or at public locations such as the fire department, the post office, or the library. Some fire departments may keep mailing lists of people interested in becoming firefighters and send announcements to specific candidates. They may post announcements in local newspapers, and trade magazines such as *Fire Engineering*, *Firehouse*, and *FireRescue* run job announcements from departments across the country, which they update on a monthly basis.

In many cities, fire departments don't do their own hiring. Rather, the human resources (HR) department of the local government screens candidates and conducts testing. However, it doesn't hurt to call both the local government's HR department and local fire stations to find out as much as you can about the test.

The job announcement includes information such as

- ✔ A job description, salary, and eligibility requirements
- ✔ Important dates for submitting your application
- ✔ Instructions for filling out specific forms
- ✔ Information about the written exam, including testing dates

Think of this announcement as a cheat sheet that provides you with the information you need to know about the firefighter selection process.

When applying for firefighting jobs, we recommend applying everywhere and applying often — even if you haven't quite finished a firefighting class you signed up to take or if you're still working on sculpting your physique. The more you apply, the more chances you'll have to take the written exam and the more experience you'll get in the overall hiring process.

Filling out the application

The first step after receiving the exam or position announcement is filling out an application to take the examination. The application asks you to supply personal information such as your name, address, and Social Security number. It usually contains questions about your education, prior work experience (generally up to ten years, if applicable), criminal background, driving history, family, and more.

The exam announcement gives you directions on how to obtain and submit the application. Sometimes a nonrefundable fee accompanies the application process. Some fire departments may request that you fill out and submit the application online, and others ask that you fill out the application and mail it back or return it in person.

When completing the application, make sure you fill out every question. Leaving a question blank can hurt your chances of landing a job. Use the following tips when filling out the application:

- ✔ **First, read the instructions.** Little mistakes on the application can cost you the job. For example, if you fill out the form in red ink, the fire department may toss your application because the instructions specifically state that you should use blue or black ink to fill out the form. Using red ink suggests that you can't follow directions.

- ✔ **Write neatly and legibly.** Your writing reflects what type of person you are. If you submit a sloppy application, it sends the message that you don't care about the position.

- ✔ **Check with references before adding them to your application.** Before adding a person as a reference, make sure you have his or her approval. People appreciate the heads-up so they can prepare what they want to say if someone calls to ask about you.

- ✔ **Ensure that all dates, addresses, and phone numbers are correct.** If you're unsure of specific information, such as a phone number for a reference or a former employer, make every effort to find it and make sure it's correct.

- ✔ **Check your grammar and spelling, paying close attention to names.** Use a dictionary or grammar book if necessary.

- ✔ **Answer all questions on the application accurately and honestly.** Telling the truth on the application is vital. Not only will this information be verified by an investigator, but it will also be used during your oral interview later in the hiring process. Many departments even require polygraph testing to verify information. Dishonest answers can cost a candidate the job — even after he or she has been hired!

Submitting resumes, cover letters, and references

In addition to the application for examination, some fire departments may require you to submit a resume, a cover letter, and references. Don't fret over this step. A resume and a cover letter are great opportunities to sell the department on your skills and qualifications, and references back up this information. A resume summarizes your education, experience, work history, and community involvement. A cover letter states why you're the right person for the job and emphasizes your strengths and accomplishments. (If you need help writing a resume and cover letter, check out *Resumes For Dummies* [Wiley] by Joyce Lain Kennedy.)

References are people who will provide unbiased information about you, such as your work history or your character. Carefully consider the people you choose as references. Whom do you trust to give honest and sincere information about you? Most departments place restrictions on whom you can list as a reference, which means Mom, Dad, Grandma, and Grandpa are out of the question. Some departments will not accept relatives or friends as references; rather, they prefer the names of former employers, teachers, or neighbors. Some departments also put restrictions on the length of time a reference must have known you. For example, you may be asked to list only references who have known you for at least three years.

Noting special considerations

Some people may qualify for special considerations when taking the written or physical portions of the firefighter exam. Certain religious practices, learning disabilities, or physical disabilities could impact a test-taker's ability to take the exam. Another special consideration is awarding extra points to those who served in the military. In New York City, a candidate also may receive points if he or she lost a parent or sibling in the line of duty as a police officer or firefighter.

If circumstances warrant that you should receive special consideration, contact the specific fire department to which you're applying to ask about its policy for these types of situations. Fire department procedures for handling special cases vary, but most departments request that candidates submit this information separately from the application. In addition, they may require the candidate to present the information in person or in writing.

The Road to Landing a Firefighter Job

The road to becoming a firefighter isn't an easy one. It's long and tedious, and around each bend is a road block that you must clear to reach your destination. Candidates are eliminated at each step, which means restarting the whole process. Dedication is key. A candidate who successfully completes each step on the first try may be hired in less than a year, but others may find that it takes several years to get hired. Therefore, after you submit your application, you should start to prepare for the host of exams you have to take. These exams and interviews include the following:

✔ A written exam

✔ A physical ability test

✔ An oral interview (sometimes more than one)

✔ A medical exam

✔ A psychological evaluation

The order of these exams and interviews may vary by department, but laws prohibit departments from conducting medical and psychological exams early in the process, so these are typically part of a conditional offer of employment. If you pass them, you'll be able to enter a fire academy, where you receive essential firefighter training. Each exam and interview has different requirements, but as long as you adequately prepare yourself for each one, you'll perform well. Throughout this book, we provide detailed information about each exam, but the following sections give you a general idea of what to expect from each one.

Throughout the screening process, always act professionally. Be open and honest when giving information. Be polite and courteous toward those in charge, and show respect for fellow candidates. Arrive for the various exams at least 15 minutes early and be ready to go. Bring extra pencils and scratch paper to the written exam, and wear comfortable clothes and sneakers to the physical exam. Be ready to answer questions about your background at the oral interview. In each step of the process, show that you are honest, confident, reliable, and respectful.

The written exam

Most departments begin the screening process with the written exam. After you apply to take the exam, you can expect to receive a notification telling you where and when the exam will take place.

The written exam tests a variety of skills, but the most common subject areas include reading comprehension, verbal expression, observation and memory, spatial orientation, judgment and reasoning, mathematics, and mechanical aptitude. (For detailed information about the written exam, review Chapters 4 through 10.)

The written exam usually takes at least three-and-a-half hours to complete. Most written exams contain between 150 and 200 multiple-choice questions. Some written exams also include true/false and fill-in-the-blank questions. Some exams, such as the National Firefighter Selection Inventory (NFSI), are standardized tests. The NFSI test includes 105 multiple-choice questions and 50 behavioral questions designed to assess stress tolerance, attitude, teamwork, and motivation, and it takes two-and-a-half hours to complete. (For more information on the NFSI, see Chapters 11 and 21.) Keep in mind, however, that the NFSI is just one of dozens of standardized tests used by departments throughout the country.

If you fail the written exam, don't fret. You can take it multiple times until you pass, so find another testing site and sign up again.

The physical ability test

Firefighting is a physically demanding and dangerous job. You have to carry heavy loads while wearing cumbersome gear and battling heat, water, and smoke. Although laws prohibit hiring practices based on age or physical fitness for most jobs, firefighting is a different ballgame. Because the job is so strenuous and involves the safety and health of others, candidates for firefighting positions must be physically fit and mentally sound and must pass physical ability, medical, and psychological tests.

Many fire departments follow the written exam with the physical ability test, or PAT. The PAT is designed to measure candidates' fitness and determine whether they can handle the highly physical nature of firefighting. Like the written exams, the physical exams can vary, but many incorporate exercises that imitate the actual work of a firefighter. For example, you may have to

- Drag hoses
- Climb flights of stairs
- Raise, extend, or climb a ladder
- Navigate an obstacle course
- Use a variety of tools to mimic firefighting operations such as forcible entry, search and rescue, or roof ventilation

Some departments rely on standardized physical ability tests, such as the one administered by Fire & Police Selection, Inc. (FPSI), but others create their own tests. They may require candidates to complete fitness tests such as a 1.5-mile run, sit-ups, push-ups, and weight lifting. In some departments, the physical requirements of the fitness test vary for men and women, based on anatomical differences between the genders. In addition, some standards are dependent on age. Candidates may have to obtain a medical release from a doctor before they are allowed to complete the test. (For detailed information about the physical ability test, see Chapter 12.)

The oral interview

Candidates who pass the written exam and the physical ability test usually undergo an oral interview. For many departments, the oral interview is the last stage before candidates receive a conditional offer of employment. During the oral interview, a panel of interviewers asks you a variety of questions. Your responses to these questions allow interviewers to get a feel for your attitude, values, personality, and general character. The interviewers may ask you to explain how you'd respond to certain circumstances on the job or describe your greatest accomplishment or life goals. In addition, they may ask you to expand upon information you supplied on your application, such as your education or employment history.

Some departments may require a chief's interview, an in-home interview, or both. During a chief's interview, the fire chief and sometimes one or two other officers meet with you to get to know you better before making the final hiring decisions. During an in-home interview, which may be part of the background check, a few members of the department meet with you at your home and get to know your family, too.

Interviewers may ask about background information you filled out on your application or background-data collection form, so enter the interview prepared to answer any and all questions about yourself and your personal history. (For more information about the oral interview, see Chapter 13.)

The medical exam

After the oral interview, the hiring panel whittles down the list of candidates to the best of the best, and those people receive a conditional offer of employment. What makes it conditional? Before the fire department can hire you, you have to undergo a complete medical examination and a psychological evaluation to make sure you're in tip-top physical and mental health. The fire department, not you, will choose a doctor to conduct the medical exam.

Some conditions have nothing to do with your physical fitness, but they can still disqualify you from becoming a firefighter. For example, hearing problems, allergies, cancer, and even a reliance on glasses or contacts can eliminate you as a candidate. Regardless of whether you can pass the physical ability test, these conditions can hinder your own and others' safety. For example, if you have a hearing disability, you may not be able to hear important instructions or alarms that could save lives.

So, what's involved in the medical exam? During the examination, the doctor checks for a variety of conditions that may put your health at risk. The following are a few of the conditions for which doctors check:

- Heart conditions
- Blood conditions
- Hernias
- Genitourinary conditions (conditions of the reproductive organs and the urinary system)
- Vision and other eye problems
- Hearing and other ear problems
- Muscular disorders
- Skeletal disorders
- Glandular disorders
- Gastrointestinal (digestive system) issues

If you receive the go-ahead from the examining physician, it's on to the psychological evaluation. (For more information about the medical exam, refer to Chapter 14.)

The psychological evaluation

The psychological evaluation is usually the last step in the firefighter screening process. Most departments require candidates to undergo a psychological evaluation because firefighting is a stressful job. Think about it: Day in and day out, firefighters are responsible for saving people's lives and, unfortunately, sometimes lives can't be saved. Departments want to make sure that candidates are mentally prepared to handle the difficult situations they may face as firefighters.

The psychological evaluation usually includes two parts: a personality questionnaire and an interview with a trained psychologist or psychiatrist chosen by the department. The personality questionnaire typically includes statements for which you have to provide a rating of *strongly agree, agree, neither agree nor disagree, disagree,* or *strongly disagree.* It's designed to determine whether you have the right attitude and motivation to be a firefighter.

After you complete the questionnaire, you may have to undergo an interview with a psychologist or psychiatrist, who may ask you why you responded to a certain question in a certain way. He or she also may ask questions about your background, your relationships with family members and friends, or your hobbies and interests. In combination, the questionnaire and the interview give departments a clear picture as to whether you're mentally prepared for a job as a firefighter. (For more information about the psychological evaluation, refer to Chapter 14.)

After you pass the medical exam and the psychological evaluation, your conditional offer of employment becomes official. In other words, you're hired!

Chapter 3

Preparing Yourself for the Firefighter Exam

In This Chapter

▶ Familiarizing yourself with the style of the written exam

▶ Answering questions for which you may not know the answer

▶ Getting ready for the physical, medical, and psychological tests and the oral interview

*O*ne of the first steps toward becoming a firefighter is passing the exams — all of them. As a candidate, you'll most likely have to successfully complete written, physical, medical, and psychological exams, a background check, and an oral interview before you're considered for a position with most fire departments across the country.

Why do you have to take these tests instead of just completing an interview or two? Firefighting is a job that demands intense dedication, responsibility, precision, and drive. Firefighters are responsible for saving lives, so they have to be the best of the best. This combination of exams brings to light the best candidates for the job — the men and women who will put their lives on the line to save others.

In this chapter, we provide an overview of each exam you have to complete to become a firefighter. We also share information about what to expect on each test and tips to help you prepare.

Getting Familiar with the Written Exam

To earn a position in most departments, you have to pass a written exam. Although each department's exam may vary, the format and the types of questions that appear on each test tend to be similar.

Test format

The written firefighter exam is a multiple-choice test. The number of answer choices for each question depends on which test you take. For example, the New York City Firefighter Exam features four answer choices for each question, and the National Firefighter Selection Inventory Exam has four or five answer choices, depending on the question.

 Most written firefighter exams are divided into a number of smaller sections, but this number, as well as the number of questions in each section, can vary from one test to another. We recommend doing some Internet research about the specific exam you're taking well in advance of the test to find out the number of sections, the number of questions in each section, and the time limits for each section and the test as a whole. Check with the department that's administering the test to see whether it offers study sessions or practice tests. If you're taking a nationally recognized exam, consider checking the library for books about the test.

On the day of the test, ask test administrators whether you're allowed to break between sections or whether you have to work straight through to the end of the test. Also, ask whether you're permitted to go back and work on sections you've already completed if you finish another section early. Never assume that you'll be allowed to do either.

Question topics

In the past, firefighter exams received criticism for being too difficult and asking irrelevant questions. Test-takers claimed that some questions on the written portion of the exam weren't appropriate because they required prior knowledge of firefighting skills — knowledge that one acquires only through training or on the job. Today's tests, however, don't include questions that require knowledge of specific tools or tactics, the interpretation of fire laws, or even the rules regarding behavior or operations in departments or companies. Those who create the exams are more aware of the critical abilities the test-taker should possess at the time of hire and have redesigned exams to measure only these abilities on the written test.

Most written firefighter exams include questions in the following subject areas:

- ✔ **Observation and memory:** Though written firefighter exams vary greatly, many begin with memory and observation questions, because this section often includes an illustration or some reading material in a separate booklet. The memory and observation section often presents a picture such as a fire scene or a floor plan. For some tests, you have 5 to 20 minutes to study the image. Then you're instructed to turn the page, and you have to answer 10 to 20 questions about the image based only on what you can recall from memory. For other tests, you may have to attend a two- to three-hour study session in the morning, take a lunch break, and then return to answer the memory questions later in the day. You may encounter a reading passage instead of an image. In such cases, you have a set amount of time to read and study the passage and any materials that accompany it. Then you have to answer the questions from memory. You may not return to the image or the reading material at all during the test. See Chapter 6 for more info.

- ✔ **Spatial orientation:** Another image-heavy portion of the written exam is the spatial orientation (sometimes called *visualization*) section. For this section, you're typically allowed to view the image as much as you want as you answer the questions. Spatial orientation questions test your directional skills. You'll most likely have to look at a map or a floor plan and visualize yourself moving through the defined area, following specific directions or creating routes. Visualization questions ask you to change your original perspective. Oftentimes you have to look at an illustration of an object and then identify the same object shown from a different point of view. To find out more, read Chapter 7.

- ✔ **Reading comprehension:** Reading comprehension questions often appear in sets that accompany passages or lists. The questions test your ability to understand what you've read. Such questions may ask you about main ideas and supporting details or causes and effects. You may also have to make inferences or draw conclusions based on what you read. Chapter 4 has more info.

- ✔ **Verbal expression:** Verbal expression questions test your grammar, spelling, and punctuation skills. As a firefighter, you may have to fill out reports or otherwise communicate with people both inside and outside the fire station. Therefore, you need to demonstrate a good grasp of the English language (for more info, see Chapter 5). On this portion of the exam, you may see questions about

  - Sentence fragments and run-on sentences

  - Parts of speech, including nouns, pronouns, verbs, adjectives, adverbs, prepositions, and conjunctions

- Punctuation marks, including periods, commas, question marks, exclamation points, apostrophes, and quotation marks
- Correctly and incorrectly spelled words

✔ **Judgment and reasoning:** Most written exams include questions that test your judgment and reasoning. These questions typically present scenarios and ask you to choose the correct behavior or verbal response for each situation. Questions may touch on public and interpersonal relations or firefighter operations and procedures. (Don't worry. You don't need a working knowledge of firefighting to answer the fire operations and procedures questions. Answering these questions typically requires a combination of common sense and logic.) This section of the test may also include a few analogies, series, or sequences. Read Chapter 8 to find out more.

✔ **Mathematics:** Some tests include a math section. The math questions typically require a basic understanding of operations such as addition, subtraction, multiplication, and division. In some cases, you need to use basic algebraic or geometric formulas to determine area, volume, or distance. The skill level varies from one test to the next. Chapter 9 has more details about this part of the test.

✔ **Mechanical aptitude:** Most written exams include at least a few questions about tools and mechanical devices. Tool questions may ask you to identify the best tool for a certain task or the reason you'd use a specific tool. Other questions in this section ask about simple mechanical devices, such as gears, pulleys, and levers. None of the questions in this section requires prior knowledge of the fire service industry. Read Chapter 10 for more info.

Tips for the written exam

Although each exam is slightly different, the following tips can help you on any test you take. In addition to these tips, be sure to get plenty of sleep before the day of your exam, and be prepared! Eat a healthy breakfast on the morning of the exam, and bring at least two pencils, an extra eraser, and a pencil sharpener (if allowed) to the test site. If calculators are permitted, toss one of those into your purse or pocket, too.

Using your time wisely

Time can be your friend or your enemy on the written firefighter exam, so know how to manage it correctly. Pay attention to time limits and listen for time warnings. Also, try to pace yourself; don't rush through the exam, but be sure to avoid spending too much time on one or two questions. If you don't know the answer to a specific question, skip it and come back later.

Make sure you take time to read the directions. You can prep all you want before the test, but if you tune out the administrator on the day of the exam, you risk missing vital pieces of information.

Many written firefighter exams take three hours or more to complete. On test day, give yourself adequate time to take the exam. Avoid scheduling appointments or making other time commitments so you can give your full attention to the test.

Looking for key words

Always keep an eye out for key words and phrases that help you understand what the question is asking you to do or find. You find a few lists of key words throughout this book, but some common words to look for are *each, fewer, more, most, in addition, first, next, last,* and *total.* Directional cues in maps or diagrams often indicate important facts, too, so look for words such as *north, south, east,* and *west* when possible.

Using the process of elimination

One of the most important things to do when taking a test is to read every answer choice available to you. If you think you know the right answer, be sure to read the other answer options, just to make sure a better choice isn't available. If you're unsure of the correct answer, eliminate choices that you know are incorrect. If you're allowed to write in your test booklet, draw a line through the answer, put an X next to it, or do whatever you need to do to stop yourself from considering that specific answer choice. Go through this process a few more times until you've narrowed your choices to the two best options. Then choose the one that seems most correct.

Making an educated guess

It's going to happen — you're going to see one or two questions on the exam that completely stump you. You may not know which mathematical operations to use, which information is important, what a particular word means, or even whether using so much time to figure out the answer to one question is worth it in the end. Should you skip the question or guess?

Most tests count incomplete answers as wrong, so it's beneficial to make an educated guess instead of skipping a question altogether. Always make an attempt to answer a question before deciding to guess. Then, if you don't think you can answer a question in a reasonable amount of time, work backward. Instead of trying to find the answer, plug the answer choices into the passage, scenario, or math problem. See which choices make sense. For math problems, if the first choice you try seems too large, try a smaller one. Keep going until you find one that works. Look for context clues if you're struggling to define a word. Skip the question for a few minutes, get it out of your head, and come back to it later. If you really don't know how to answer the question, then by all means, guess.

Preparing for the Non-Written Tests

In addition to the written exam, candidates have to undergo a number of non-written tests, including the physical, psychological, and medical exams, a background check that may include a polygraph (lie detector) test, and an oral interview. Any one of these tests has the potential to disqualify you from a career in firefighting, but knowing what to expect can help you succeed.

1, 2, 3, lift: Prepping for the physical test

The physical portion of the firefighter test requires physical fitness and hours of practice and training. The physical exam doesn't test your ability to perform specific firefighting tactics; rather, it helps departments determine whether you have the flexibility, strength, and endurance that firefighters need to succeed.

Like the written exams, physical exams vary, but some common activities include climbing stairs, dragging and coupling hoses, carrying equipment, raising and climbing ladders, and simulating roof ventilation. You'll also most likely encounter activities related to forcible entry and search and rescue.

You can prepare for the physical ability test in a number of ways. Here are a few ideas:

✔ **Schedule an appointment with your doctor.** Have your doctor conduct a physical to make sure you're healthy enough to begin a workout regimen. Many departments require a medical release from your doctor to participate in the physical ability test anyway, so this is a way to kill two birds with one stone. In addition, your doctor can recommend ways to improve your physical fitness.

✔ **Get your heart pumping.** Any exercise that gets your heart beating faster and the blood flowing through your veins not only improves your overall health but also helps you trim body fat and build muscle. Go for a run or a bike ride, jump rope, or take a cardio-kickboxing class. For more targeted training, toss a few weights in a backpack and run some bleachers to simulate climbing stairs while bearing the weight of fire-fighting equipment. Stick a few bricks or cinder blocks in a duffel bag, tie a rope to the handle, and drag it behind you as you run to practice advancing a charged hose line.

✔ **Lift some weights.** Firefighters have to be strong to haul equipment, lift and carry victims, hoist hoses, and so on. Build up your muscle strength by lifting weights. If you don't have weights at home, consider joining a gym. Most gyms have weight-lifting machines and free weights that you can use to increase your strength.

✔ **Improve your endurance.** You build endurance through repetition — doing the same motion over and over. Exercises such as push-ups, pull-ups, and sit-ups repeatedly use the same groups of muscles for an extended time, and all three exercises can increase both strength and endurance in your arms, shoulders, back, and abdominal muscles. You may also try standing on an elevated platform, such as a deck, and hoisting a duffel bag containing bricks from the ground to your position on the platform. The action simulates hoisting a hose to an upper story of a building. The weight of the bag increases your strength, while the hand-over-hand motion you use to pull the rope improves your endurance.

✔ **Stretch it out.** Firefighters have to be flexible, too. Trying to fit through a hole in a breached wall while wearing turnout gear and an air pack sometimes requires moving in ways you didn't think were possible. To improve your flexibility, begin and end each workout by stretching your muscles. Before workouts, warming up and stretching prepares your muscles for activity. After workouts, stretching gives you time to bring your breathing back in line and cool down.

Try to find out as much as you can about the physical test by contacting the fire or human resources department responsible for administering the test. Some departments offer training programs to help you get in shape before the test, and others require several weeks of training before the day of the test. The following are some other questions you may want to ask: Is the test pass/fail? Does the test have a time limit for each task? How do I score the greatest number of points? Don't be afraid to ask questions; the more you know, the more you can prepare and the better you'll perform on test day. To find out more about the physical ability test, read Chapter 12.

For more information about improving your fitness, check out *Fitness For Dummies* by Suzanne Schlosberg and Liz Neporent, *Weight Training For Dummies* by Liz Neporent, Suzanne Schlosberg, and Shirley J. Archer, or *Stretching For Dummies* by LeReine Chabut with Madeleine Lewis (Wiley).

You don't say: Prepping for the oral test/interview

All firefighter examinations are designed to achieve a similar goal: to determine the men and women best suited for firefighter training. The oral interview is no exception. The interviewers judge everything you say — and even what you don't say. Nonverbal communication — your body language — plays a huge role in interviewers' impression of you.

During the interview, you'll likely face a hiring board that includes skilled firefighters and others such as community leaders or a representative from the city or county human resources department. The interviewers may have your resume or application and a rating sheet to grade your performance, depending on the department and the type of interview. As you answer their questions, they record their thoughts on the rating sheets and later convert those thoughts into points.

Your oral interview may be structured, unstructured, or a mix of both. In structured interviews, the board members are prepared with specific questions they want to ask.

These questions are typically hypothetical and job related, and the board is looking for specific answers based on predetermined criteria — yes or no answers won't cut it. Every candidate is asked the same questions in the exact same order and is evaluated on the same criteria and nothing else. Interviewers usually don't have your resume on hand, as it could bias their opinion of you one way or another. Members of the panel typically aren't allowed to explain questions, and they're usually instructed to show no emotion as you respond. In other words, expect many blank stares and few smiles.

In unstructured interviews, board members ask open-ended questions that also require more than yes or no answers. They may use your resume, application, or the results of your background check to generate questions, so make sure you review this info before you get to the interview. Many times, they ask you to respond to a question using an experience from your past.

Some subjects you'll likely discuss during your oral interview include educational history, interpersonal relations history, and work history. The interviewers also ask you questions that require you to show reasoning and problem-solving skills. Be prepared for questions such as

- ✔ Why do you want to be a firefighter?
- ✔ What are your strengths and weaknesses?
- ✔ What aspect of firefighting do you think will be most challenging for you?

Consider how you would respond to each of these questions. A quick online search for common interview questions will bring up hundreds of additional questions that you can use to practice. (Also see Chapter 13.) Practice answering questions aloud by having friends or family members "interview" you. This gives you a chance to prepare exactly what you want to say. It also allows others to help you identify bad habits, such as slouching, tapping your foot, wringing your hands, or failing to make eye contact — nonverbal cues that may cast you as lazy, worrisome, or lacking confidence.

The interviewers rate you on your behavior during the interview, so keep your cool. Answer the questions concisely and completely, but don't rush; if you appear confused or frustrated, they may award you a low grade. Arrive at the interview prepared with a few personal experiences ready to go when they ask. During the interview, be honest, be friendly, and take your time.

Keeping it clean: Prepping for the background check

Most departments conduct thorough background checks on all candidates at some point during the hiring process. You may have to fill out a background data collection form, but the background check involves a much more thorough investigation into your past. Departments may check anything from your police record to your credit history. Most departments overlook minor problems that occurred many years ago, so it's best to come clean when you have the chance.

The only way to prepare for a background check is to live your life in a respectful, responsible way. Consider the following guidelines:

- ✔ **Don't get arrested.** Live your life responsibly and avoid activities that could tarnish your reputation or lead to a police record. If you drink too much, call a cab or ask a friend to take you home; never drive under the influence of alcohol. Don't use, sell, carry, or otherwise touch illegal drugs. In general, avoid activities that you'll regret for the rest of your life, and follow the law.

- ✔ **Look for the signs.** Be sure to follow all traffic laws when you drive. A lot of tickets or an unusually high number of accidents are red flags, and candidates may be eliminated because of them.

- ✔ **Pay your bills on time.** That's right — even your financial history is up for debate during the background investigation. If a department sees that you're in debt up to your eyeballs and fail to pay bills on time, they may see it as a sign of irresponsibility.

- ✔ **Update your records.** Fire departments are likely to talk to personal references, neighbors, family members, and others to get a well-rounded perspective on who you are. Be sure to keep up-to-date contact information for these people handy, in case the department requests it. Also, try to maintain an accurate work history, including employer names, addresses, and phone numbers for up to ten years. Don't forget to keep accurate records about your education, too. Departments are interested in all schools you've attended from high school forward, as well as credits, certifications, degrees, and so on.

As part of the background check, you may have to take a polygraph test. Our best advice for this test: Tell the truth. A polygraph, after all, detects lies. The department sorts through your past with a fine-toothed comb; nothing slips by them, so it's best to be open, honest, and up front from the get-go.

Take a deep breath: Prepping for the medical test

A number of health conditions can hinder your performance as a firefighter, and it's up to a physician to find them during the medical exam. The medical test is one of the few exams that doesn't require studying, and if you have a predetermined or hereditary condition, you can't exactly make it go away. You can improve your chances of a good report, however, by making smart lifestyle choices, eating right, and exercising daily.

Take the following steps to prepare for the medical exam:

- ✔ **Quit unhealthy habits.** If you smoke or drink, stop right away. These habits can wreak havoc on your physical health and well-being. In fact, some departments require candidates and employees to be nonsmokers.

- ✔ **Get moving.** If you're carrying around a few extra pounds, now's the time to start a daily fitness routine to shed the unwanted weight.

- ✔ **Eat healthy foods.** Avoid junk food that could contribute to health problems down the road. If you need to pack on a few pounds, eat plenty of lean protein, whole grains, and veggies. Be sure to fill up on healthy foods to gain weight.

The medical exam is lengthy and may take several hours, so don't expect a quick in-and-out appointment. When you make the appointment for the exam, find out whether you must follow any special rules. For example, some blood tests require fasting for 8 to 12 hours beforehand, so you may have to stop eating and drinking the night before the appointment. On the day of the exam, dress in comfortable clothes and sneakers. Some of the tests, such as the cardiac stress test on your heart, require you to run on a treadmill, so you'll want to be able to move freely.

When you arrive for your appointment, expect to complete a medical history questionnaire before your medical exam begins. Be honest about any diseases or conditions that run in your family and try to recall important information such as allergies, previously broken bones, and prior surgeries.

Don't hide a medical condition, no matter how insignificant it may seem to you. Be completely honest with the doctor during your medical exam — any information that you omit can be detrimental to your health. In many cases, doctors base their decision about whether to disqualify you on the severity of a condition, not just the presence of one. If a condition is correctable — through surgery, approved medications, and so on — you won't automatically be disqualified.

The physician will most likely test you for glandular and gastrointestinal conditions, hernias and urinary or reproductive conditions, blood conditions, eye and ear conditions, and heart conditions. He or she conducts vision and hearing tests and examines your skin, teeth, skull, and back, along with your entire muscular and skeletal systems.

Before you endure the entire application process, consider asking your family physician to run a full medical exam to make sure you don't have any medical conditions that could disqualify you (for more details about these conditions, read Chapter 14). He or she may uncover a condition, such as high blood pressure, which you can work to correct long before the official medical exam takes place. Also, keep in mind that your family doctor's findings may not disqualify you from the running. The final decision is up to the department-appointed physician.

The information physicians receive about your health helps them form a medical baseline. A medical baseline shows doctors what your body, specifically, looks like and acts like when it's healthy. In the future, if you're injured on the scene or develop a new medical condition over the years, physicians can compare your new condition to your medical baseline. If it differs, they'll be able to link your injuries or illnesses to your occupation, which hopefully will help them develop ways to treat you and others like you.

Don't psych yourself out: Prepping for the psychological test

No one doubts that firefighting is a stressful profession. Firefighters often work in life-threatening conditions, knowing that they're responsible for both their own and others' lives. Therefore, firefighter candidates must demonstrate that they're mentally sound and capable of dealing with these situations. The psychological exam is designed to find those candidates who can mentally handle the stress and pressure that come with the job.

The psychological test, or psychiatric evaluation, is typically the last test/interview you have to complete. If you've made it this far, you have successfully passed your written, physical, and medical exams and your oral interview — so congrats! Similar to the medical exam, the psychological evaluation is a test for which you can't really study. Even if you gather information about the types of questions that you'll be asked, you don't want your answers to sound rehearsed. You'll score better if you answer honestly and avoid overthinking the questions.

The psychological exam, like the other exams, may vary from one department to the next, but many departments give the exam in two parts. The first is a questionnaire designed to bring to light any underlying psychiatric problems that you may not be aware of or that you may not want to talk about with a therapist or psychologist. The questionnaire is long and may seem somewhat repetitive — don't be surprised if you see the same or similar questions multiple times — but departments use it to identify your personality traits and the ways you respond to conflict and stress.

Don't try to figure out what the questionnaire is "really" asking you. Just read the questions, fill in your honest answers, and move on. Don't make attempts to appear healthy or stable. Just take your time, tell the truth, and finish the exam.

After your questionnaire has been reviewed, you move on to the second part of the evaluation: a meeting with a psychologist who interviews you about specific responses you gave on the questionnaire. He or she usually explains the results of the exam and discusses any conclusions he or she has reached about your personality, your coping methods, or your stress levels. The psychologist may ask you about your relationships with your friends and family or your childhood. Regardless of the topic, always be honest and open with the psychologist. In some cases, the psychologist may not have any questions for you at all, so don't be alarmed if he or she sends you on your way without asking anything.

Part II
Gearing Up to Take the Test: The Written Exam

The 5th Wave   By Rich Tennant

"I'll be conducting the observation and memory portion of the firefighter exam. Who's got $10?"

In this part . . .

*T*ake it from us — "eenie, meanie, miney, moe" is not the best way to answer questions on a multiple-choice test. Part of the firefighter hiring process is a written exam, which tests your knowledge in subject areas that include reading comprehension, verbal expression, observation and memory, spatial orientation, judgment and reasoning, math, and mechanical aptitude.

In this part, we break down the types of questions you'll see in each subject area. We also supply plenty of practice exercises to prepare you for the real thing. We even provide a whole chapter about a standardized written exam called the National Firefighter Selection Inventory (NFSI).

Chapter 4

Showing Off Your Reading and Verbal Comprehension

....

In This Chapter
▶ Understanding the reading and verbal comprehension part of the written test
▶ Developing skills to become a better reader and listener
▶ Practicing your reading and verbal comprehension skills

....

Reading and listening — these are simple tasks, right? You read every day — magazines, newspapers, text messages, or e-mails. You may even curl up with a good book at night. You listen every day, too — to the radio, news broadcasts on television, or a friend's lively story. How much of what you read and hear, however, do you truly comprehend? In other words, when you read, do you actively try to understand and absorb the material? When you listen, do you think about the spoken words and consider their meaning?

Many fire departments require candidates to take a written exam as part of their candidate-screening process. These exams may include both reading and listening questions, so if you hope to become a professional firefighter one day, you should brush up on your reading and listening skills. Luckily for you, that's just what we help you do here.

In this chapter, we prepare you for the reading and listening comprehension component of the written exam. We help you hone your reading and listening skills and show you how to answer different types of questions. We even give you some practice activities to get you rolling.

If you're still concerned about the reading and verbal comprehension component of the test after reading this chapter and completing the practice exercises, talk to your local career firefighters. They've all undergone the hiring process and can lead you in the right direction. You can also try contacting the local department or hiring agency to see whether they can recommend any study materials or practice tests that directly reflect the material you'll see on the test. And don't forget about the local library or bookstore — they're certain to have books that teach you more about reading retention and comprehension strategies.

Getting an Overview of the Reading and Verbal Comprehension Component

You may not realize it now, but reading and listening are an important part of a firefighter's job. Reading and listening are requirements for completing recruit school or a fire academy, where you learn the basics of firefighting, and reading is essential for both continuing education and promotional opportunities. As a firefighter, what you find out from reports, manuals, or information about new equipment or procedures may come in handy during future fire calls. Listening to and comprehending a senior officer's orders, your fellow firefighters' descriptions of a fire scene, or even a question from a curious second grader could save a life one day.

The written firefighter exam you take will most likely include reading and verbal comprehension questions. *Reading comprehension* questions test your ability to read information and interpret what it means. *Verbal comprehension* questions assess how well you listen to spoken information and process what you hear.

What is a reading passage, anyway?

Do you remember when you had to take college entrance exams or even just plain old high school English or reading tests? These tests likely included reading passages, which are excerpts from books, stories, poems, or nonfiction articles followed by sets of multiple-choice questions that ask you to recall the details of what you read.

The written exam for firefighter candidates may include similar passage-and-question sets. During the exam, you'll be expected to read the passages and respond to the questions. Some of the passages may relate directly to firefighting activities — rules, procedures, and so on — and others simply present information about a general topic. Regardless of the topic, it's important to read carefully and comprehend the entire passage before you attempt to answer the questions. (See the upcoming section "Processing What You Read and Hear" for details.)

Tuning in to the listening portion

Sure, you hear the news broadcast on the television in the living room. But if someone asked you to explain the story that the anchor just described, could you do it? A big difference exists between *hearing* and *listening*. Hearing doesn't require much effort, but listening requires your full attention so you can absorb spoken information, interpret it, understand its meaning, and in some cases, act on it.

Some written tests assess firefighter candidates' ability to listen. In the verbal comprehension (listening) portion of a written test, the test administrator reads a passage aloud. As he or she reads, you need to listen carefully, process the information, and then answer questions in your test booklet about what you just heard.

Processing What You Read and Hear

We're good, but even we can't predict exactly what you'll see in the reading and verbal comprehension sections of the written exam. Although we can't tell you exactly what to expect, we can give you some comprehension strategies that can help *you* identify the information you'll need to answer the questions.

Unlike other skills you need to be a firefighter, reading and listening don't really have a physical component, other than taking notes. You can't run up and down stairs or handle an ax or even work out the math to arrive at an answer. Most of the processing occurs in your head, so you need to condition your brain to think about what you're reading or hearing. But don't worry if it's been a long time since you last took a reading comprehension test. In this section, we give you practical advice to prepare for this portion of the firefighter exam.

If you encounter difficult words in your reading or listening, write them down. Later, check their definitions in a dictionary and record their meanings in a notebook. This helps you commit them to memory. Boosting your vocabulary skills helps you improve your comprehension skills.

Scanning the questions first

"Pssst. What'd you get for number one?"

Okay, that's one way of answering questions. (It's also a good way to get yourself removed from the hiring process.) A better way — and one of the best strategies to improve your chances of doing well on the reading comprehension part of the written test — is to check out what you need to know *before* you actually read the passage. That's right. Scan the questions to see what information you'll have to locate within the passage. Knowing what the questions ask helps you pinpoint this information as you read. If you're allowed to write in the test booklet, consider underlining key points in the questions so you remember to look for them as you read. If you're not allowed to write in the test booklet, jot down the key points on scratch paper.

A drawback of verbal comprehension (listening) tests is that you probably won't be allowed to scan the questions before you listen to the passage. If you are allowed, however, use the same strategies that you would use for reading passages.

After you've reviewed the questions that accompany a reading passage, quickly scan the passage. Don't read anything carefully at this point. Just look for key words that catch your attention. Again, recognizing what to look for — and where to look for it — can help you maintain your focus as you read. After your scans are complete, return to the beginning of the passage and carefully read the whole thing, watching for key points as you go.

Noting important details

One strategy to improve your comprehension is to jot down essential details as you read or listen. Check with test administrators first, however, to make sure note-taking is permitted. Feel free to use words, phrases, abbreviations, symbols, bullet points, or shorthand — just make sure *you* understand what your notes mean. For reading passages with multiple paragraphs, jot down a few words summarizing each paragraph. The summaries can help you quickly find the information you need to answer a question. Also, the short summaries come in handy when trying to figure out the main idea, whether for a single paragraph or the entire passage.

If you're not sure how to identify essential details, imagine, just for a moment, that you're a reporter instead of a prospective firefighter. Try to answer these questions as you read or as you listen to the test administrator read the passage:

✓ **Who?** Identify the people and organizations.

- Who was the victim?

- Which department responded to the call?

✓ **What?** Identify the event/effect — that is, the result of the cause.

- A car rolled over.

- A fire gutted a kitchen.

✓ **When?** Identify the time and date.

- What day?

- What time?

✓ **Where?** Identify the location.

- What was the address?

- What area was involved?

✔ **Why/how?** Identify the cause (that is, the reason the event/effect occurred).

- A woman swerved to miss a deer.
- A pan of grease on a stove caught fire.

If you can note the answers to these questions, you've absorbed the most important details, and you can probably summarize the entire passage in a single sentence. Some passages may not answer all these questions, but you can still use these questions to your advantage. Keeping them in mind helps you locate the important details.

Figuring out the main idea

One comprehension strategy is to figure out the main idea of a passage. The main idea describes what the *whole passage* is about. A reading passage has a single main idea and several supporting details. As you may have guessed, *supporting details* support the main idea; they provide evidence or clarification to further explain the essential message of a passage.

To determine the main idea of a passage, underline or write down the most important supporting details — the details that are essential to understanding the passage. Don't confuse these with minor details, which still support the main idea but aren't necessarily required to determine the main idea. When you've finished reading or listening, go back and review these details. You'll notice that they likely share a relationship. This relationship is the main idea of the passage.

If you've jotted down a few words to summarize each paragraph, review those notes and make sure the main idea you identify covers all the paragraphs of the passage, not just one. You may also benefit from relying on *who, what, when, where,* and *why/how* questions (see the preceding section) when you're trying to figure out the main idea and the supporting details.

Answering Different Types of Questions

The reading and verbal comprehension component of a written firefighter exam typically includes a series of passages followed by sets of questions related to the passages. Because departments vary so much in their testing procedures, we can't say for sure which types of passages or questions you'll encounter. We can, however, give you an overview of the question formats you may see and show you how to answer different types of questions.

The following are some common question formats on written firefighter exams, along with some tips for each type:

✔ **Multiple-choice:** Multiple-choice questions include a question stem and usually four answer choices. When answering multiple-choice questions, narrow down your answer to the *best* answer choice.

✔ **True/false:** True/false questions present a statement and ask you to decide whether it's accurate (true) or inaccurate (false). When answering true/false questions, watch out for words such as *always* or *never*. These words can make seemingly accurate statements inaccurate by removing the possibility of any exceptions to the rule.

✔ **Fill-in-the-blank:** Fill-in-the-blank questions present incomplete statements. You must use *context clues* (the information the statement does give) to determine what's missing. Fill-in-the blank questions on the written firefighter exam will likely be multiple-choice questions, too. You'll have to select the letter of the word or phrase that correctly fills in the blank.

✔ **Matching:** Matching questions generally present two lists: a list of terms and a list of definitions. To answer matching questions, you have to pair each term with its correct definition. If matching terms relate to a reading passage, you'll likely find both the terms and their definitions within the passage.

In addition to having different formats, the reading and verbal comprehension questions often ask for different types of information. They may test your ability to find details, identify the main idea, determine word meanings, find exceptions, draw conclusions, or analyze charts and tables. This section explains how to handle each question type.

Finding-details questions

Yep, you guessed it! Finding-details questions ask you to find or recall specific details within a reading or listening passage. A name, a number, a place — finding-details questions can pretty much ask about anything you read or heard. In most cases, the answers to finding-details questions are stated directly in the passage. These questions don't usually require you to draw conclusions or use your prior knowledge to find the answer, so rely on the information in the passage when you select your answer choice. Take a look at the following paragraph, and then check out the questions that follow it:

Class B fires involve flammable liquids and gases such as gasoline, kerosene, or natural gas. When fighting fires that involve these materials, firefighters should not use water as an extinguishing agent. Although water can easily douse the flames of a fire involving ordinary combustibles such as wood, paper, or cloth, it can actually splatter the fuel in a Class B fire and cause it to spread.

According to this passage, _____ is a fuel involved in a Class B fire.

(A) wood

(B) paper

(C) gasoline

(D) cloth

The correct answer is Choice (C). You can find this detail in the first sentence of the paragraph.

True/false questions can also test your ability to find details. Consider this question about the same paragraph:

Class B fires involve ordinary combustibles such as wood, paper, or cloth.

(A) True

(B) False

The correct answer is Choice (B). Again, you can find this detail in the first sentence of the paragraph. Class B fires involve flammable liquids and gases, not ordinary combustibles.

When answering finding-details questions, read the question carefully and make sure you understand *exactly* which detail you need to find in the passage.

Determining-the-main-idea questions

The reading and verbal comprehension section of the written firefighter exam may include questions that ask you to determine the main idea of a passage. In other words, you have to figure out what the entire passage is about. Sometimes the main idea is stated directly in the passage as a topic sentence, often at the beginning or end of a paragraph. Other times, it's up to you to piece together the supporting details to determine the central focus of the reading.

Determining-the-main-idea questions don't always come right out and ask, "What is the main idea of this passage?" The question may be phrased in one of the following ways:

✔ What is this passage mainly about?

✔ The best title for this passage is . . .

✔ Which statement best summarizes the passage?

The main idea must apply to the *entire* passage. Incorrect answer choices may give supporting details in the passage.

Questions about new words

Some questions on the reading and verbal comprehension sections of the written exam may ask you about the meanings of words. The passage may define a word directly, or you may have to use context clues to figure out its meaning.

Getting clues from other words in the sentence

Context clues are bits of information in the sentences surrounding the unknown word that help you determine its meaning. The following are a few examples of context clues:

✔ **Definitions:** Definitions are word meanings. Sometimes writers work the definition of a word right into the sentence, as in, "Megan's attempt at short-story writing was hackneyed, showing no creativity at all." The definition in this sentence shows that *hackneyed* means *unoriginal*.

✔ **Synonyms:** Synonyms are words with similar meanings, such as *cold* and *chilly*. Writers often use synonyms to avoid repeating the same word, and if you know the meaning of one word, you can usually figure out the meaning of the unfamiliar word. For example, consider the following sentence: "The stinking garbage pile gave off such a fetid odor that Shaun had to hold his nose when he walked by it." The words *stinking* and *fetid* are synonyms, and although *fetid* might be unfamiliar, you can guess that it means *bad-smelling* based on the word *stinking* — and on the mention of garbage. Although questions on the test probably won't specifically ask, "What's a synonym for . . .?" synonyms can still help you as you read.

✔ **Antonyms:** Antonyms are words with opposite meanings, such as *smooth* and *rough*. Writers often use antonyms to contrast two things, so if you know the meaning of one word, you can assume that the unfamiliar word has the opposite meaning. For example, "Fred doesn't like conjecture; he prefers solid evidence and straight facts." From this sentence, you can tell that *facts* and *conjecture* are opposites; because you know that *facts* are true statements, you can assume that *conjecture* refers to opinions or guesses. Again, although questions won't likely ask you to identify the antonym of a word, antonyms are still helpful context clues.

Breaking a word into parts

Sometimes clues within a word can help you define it. Here are parts of words with meaning:

✔ **Root words:** Root words are word parts that serve as the base of a word, such as *move* (in movement) or *own* (in owner). Table 4-1 contains a list of common root words and their meanings.

- **Prefixes:** Prefixes are word parts, such as *re-* or *dis-*, that are attached to the beginning of a root to create a new word, such as *remove* or *disown*. Table 4-2 lists common prefixes and their meanings.

- **Suffixes:** Suffixes are word parts, such as *-ment* or *-er*, that are attached to the end of a root to create a new word, such as *movement* or *owner*. Table 4-3 contains a list of common suffixes and their meanings.

Tables 4-1, 4-2, and 4-3 aren't exhaustive, and it's not necessary to memorize them; just become familiar with the different word parts. You may run into other roots, prefixes, and suffixes on the actual test, but if you know how to break a word into its parts, you can usually figure out its meaning.

If you encounter an unfamiliar word, try thinking of similar words and make educated guesses about what the different parts mean. For example, consider the word *bilateral*. From Table 4-2, you know that the prefix *bi-* means "two." From Table 4-3, you know that the suffix *-al* means "characterized by." But what about the rest of the word? Think of some similar words, such as *latitude*. You know that lines of latitude run in east and west around the Earth, so you guess that *bilateral* means "characterized by having two directions." Guess what? You're pretty close. According to the dictionary, *bilateral* means "having two sides."

For now, use these tables to practice putting different roots, suffixes, and prefixes together and understanding how the various word parts change word meanings. If you'd like, check the results in a dictionary to see how close your definition comes to the real meaning of the word. For example, the prefix *tele-* combined with the root word *graph* creates *telegraph*. Based on the table, *telegraph* means "far writing." The dictionary definition for *telegraph* is "a device that uses coded signals to communicate at a distance." The two meanings aren't exactly the same, but they're close enough that you can make an educated guess.

Table 4-1	Common Root Words	
Root	*Meaning*	*Sample Word*
alter	other	alternate
amphi	both ends	amphibian
ann	year	anniversary
anthro, anthrop	relating to humans	anthropology
aqua	water	aquarium
arch	chief	monarch
arthro	joint	arthritis
aud	sound	audible
bell	war, bad	bellicose
bibli, biblio	relating to books	bibliography
bio	life	autobiography
brev	short	abbreviate
cap	seize	capture
carn	meat	carnivorous

(continued)

Table 4-1 *(continued)*

Root	Meaning	Sample Word
cede, ceed	go, yield	recede
chrom	color	monochrome
chron	time	chronology
circum	around	circumnavigate
cogn, cogno	know	cognizant
corp	body	corporate
crat	ruler	autocrat
cred	believe	credulous
cruc	cross	crucifix
crypt	hidden	cryptic
culp	guilt	culprit
demo	people	democracy
derm	skin	epidermis
dic, dict	speak	diction
domin	rule	dominate
dynam	power	dynamo
ego	self	egomaniac
equ	equal	equidistant
flu, flux	flow	influx
form	shape	formulate
frac, frag	break	fragment
frater	brother	fraternize
graph	writing	biography
hemo	blood	hematology
hydro	water	hydroplane
junct	join	juncture
liber	free	liberate
log	word	epilogue
lum	light	illuminate
magn	large	magnate
mater	mother	maternity
min	small	minuscule
morph	form	morphology
mut	change	mutate
neuro	nerve	neurology
nom, nomen	name	nominate
oper	work	operate
pac	peace	pacify
pat, path	suffer	pathology
pater	father	paternity

Root	Meaning	Sample Word
pneum	lung	pneumonia
pod	feet	podiatrist
port	carry	portable
press	squeeze	repress
psych	mind	psychic
scrib, script	write	describe
sed	sit	sedentary
sequ	follow	sequel
simil	same	assimilate
son	sound	resonate
spec	see	spectator
spir	breathe	perspiration
tang, tact	touch	tangible, tactile
temp	time	temporary
terr	earth	terrestrial
therm	heat	thermos
tract	pull	traction
vac	empty	vacuum
vit	life	vital
voc, vok	call	revoke
zoo	animal	zoology

Table 4-2	Common Prefixes	
Prefix	**Meaning**	**Sample Word**
a-	no, not	atheist
ab-, abs-	away, from	absent
anti-	against	antibody
bi-	two	bilateral
com-, con-	with, together	combine
contra-, counter-	against	contradict
de-	away from	deny
dec-	ten	decade
extra-	outside, beyond	extracurricular
fore-	in front of	foreman
geo-	earth	geology
hyper-	excess, over	hyperactive
il-	not	illogical
mal-, male-	wrong, bad	malediction
multi-	many	multiply

(continued)

Table 4-2 *(continued)*

Prefix	Meaning	Sample Word
nom-	name	nominate
omni-	all	omnibus
ped-	foot	pedestrian
que-, quer-, ques-	ask	question
re-	back, again	return
semi-	half	semisweet
super-	over, more	superior
tele-	far	telephone
trans-	across	translate
un-	not	uninformed

Table 4-3 **Common Suffixes**

Suffix	Meaning	Sample Word
-able, -ible	capable of	agreeable
-age	action, result	breakage
-al	characterized by	functional
-ance	instance of an action	performance
-ation	action, process	liberation
-en	made of	silken
-ful	full of	helpful
-ic	consisting of	alcoholic
-ical	possessing a quality of	statistical
-ion	result of act or process	legislation
-ish	relating to	childish
-ism	act, practice	Buddhism
-ist	characteristic of	elitist
-ity	quality of	specificity
-less	not having	childless
-let	small one	booklet
-ment	action, process	establishment
-ness	possessing a quality	goodness
-or	one who does a thing	orator
-ous	having	dangerous
-y	quality of	tasty

Looking at a word-defining example

Read the following sentence and answer the question that follows:

Class B fires involve <u>flammable</u> liquids and gases such as gasoline, kerosene, or natural gas.

<u>Flammable</u> most nearly means

(A) odorless.

(B) colorful.

(C) transportable.

(D) burnable.

Flammable means burnable, which is Choice (D). You can use context clues to figure out the meaning of the word. First, the sentence refers to Class B *fires.* You may realize that people burn kerosene and natural gas to heat their homes and burn gasoline when they drive their cars.

Also, the root of *flammable* looks like *flame;* it comes from the Latin *flammare,* meaning "to flame or burn." Last, the suffix *-able* means "capable of." Which of the answer choices means "capable of flame"?

Questions that use NOT or EXCEPT

We're all about staying positive, but some questions on the reading and verbal comprehension test may take a turn toward the negative side. You may see questions that use the words *not* and *except.* These questions ask about details that are not included in or are exceptions to the information in the passage. For instance, look at this passage and the question that follows it:

Class B fires involve flammable liquids and gases such as gasoline, kerosene, or natural gas. When fighting fires that involve these materials, firefighters should not use water as an extinguishing agent. Although water can easily douse the flames of a fire involving ordinary combustibles such as wood, paper, or cloth, it can actually splatter the fuel in a Class B fire and cause it to spread.

All of the following are ordinary combustibles EXCEPT

(A) cloth.

(B) natural gas.

(C) wood.

(D) paper.

The correct answer is Choice (B). According to the passage, natural gas falls into the category of flammable liquids and gases. It is not an ordinary combustible.

Be careful with questions using *not* and *except.* Read them carefully and make sure you understand exactly what they're asking.

Drawing-conclusions questions

Drawing-conclusions questions are tricky because you can't just return to a reading passage to find the answer. The passage may imply the answer, but it doesn't directly state it. To answer these questions, you have to take the details presented in the passage and fit them together like puzzle pieces until the big picture — the conclusion — becomes clear. This "big picture" reveals additional information about what you read. Read the following passage and check out the question that follows:

> For a fire to start and continue to burn, four elements must be present. The first is heat, which may come in the form of a flame, a spark, or some other ignition source. The second is fuel, which is anything that will burn, from dry grass to furniture to certain metals. The third is oxygen. The fourth is a chemical chain reaction.

Based on the passage, what happens to a fire if all available fuel is used up?

(A) The fire will stop burning.

(B) The fire will use more oxygen.

(C) The fire will heat up.

(D) The fire will change direction.

The correct answer is Choice (A). If all of the fuel is gone, the fire will stop burning. In the passage, you discover that four elements — heat, fuel, oxygen, and a chemical chain reaction — must be present for a fire to burn. Therefore, you can conclude that if one of those elements is missing — in this case, the fuel — the fire will stop burning.

Questions about charts and tables

Some questions on the reading and verbal comprehension test may ask you to analyze information in a chart or table. Charts and tables neatly organize data into columns and rows, which are usually labeled with headings or titles that explain what you find in each one. Fire departments often use charts and tables to track things such as equipment checks or maintenance schedules, so it's important that you understand how to read them.

Here are some tips for reading and understanding charts and tables:

✔ **Read the title.** The title gives the "main idea" of the chart or table. Charts and tables are basically summaries of information, and the title clarifies the type of information that the chart or table contains.

✔ **Pay attention to column headings.** Column headings reveal the specific information in each column — in other words, they tell you what the numbers, words, or phrases in each column represent. They usually also explain units of measurement (Does the temperature represent °F or °C? Is the distance measured in feet, meters, or miles?)

✔ **Save time by reviewing the questions first.** Scan the questions to see what information you need. Then look at the chart or table to find this information.

✔ **Look for information that appears directly in the chart or table.** Some reading comprehension questions about charts and tables require you to make basic mathematical calculations, but other information is right in the chart — no math necessary. A quick glance can tell you exactly what you want to know. Always look for stated information before you start performing a bunch of math to figure out the answer to a question.

Look at the following example table and the question that follows it.

Target Heart Rates during Exercise		
Age (Years)	*Target Heart Rate (Beats per Minute)*	*Average Max Heart Rate (bpm)*
20	100–170	200
30	95–162	190
40	90–153	180
50	85–145	170
60	80–136	160

Based on the chart, the average maximum heart rate decreases by how many beats per minute every ten years?

(A) 5 beats

(B) 8 beats

(C) 10 beats

(D) 20 beats

The correct answer is Choice (C). The first column gives you ages in increments of ten years. Now check the last column, Average Max Heart Rate (bpm), and compare the numbers from one row to the next. Every ten years, a person's average maximum heart rate decreases by 10 beats per minute (bpm).

Practice Reading and Verbal Comprehension Questions

The following passages and question sets are designed to help you practice your reading and verbal comprehension skills. Here's how to use them:

- ✔ Set aside three of the six passages in this section to use as listening passages. (Passage five is a table and should be used as a reading passage, not a listening one.)

- ✔ To practice your reading skills, read each passage carefully and answer the questions that follow it. We suggest you scan the questions before reading a passage and underline or write down important details as you read. (For more tips, see the earlier section "Processing What You Read and Hear.")

- ✔ To practice your verbal comprehension skills, ask a friend to read the three passages you set aside aloud. Listen to each passage and take notes. After he or she has finished reading, answer the questions that follow the passage.

For all questions, choose the answer that *most correctly* answers the question.

Passage one

Have you ever tried to transmit or receive a message via a telephone or radio? If so, you probably know that certain letters of the alphabet are difficult to <u>discern</u>. B and V, for example, often sound the same, as do N and M or S and F. To provide clarity to radio and telephone communications, firefighters, police officers, and other emergency response personnel often rely on a special alphabet, which assigns a code word to each letter. For example, A becomes Alpha, B becomes Bravo, C becomes Charlie, and so on. Notice that each code word begins with the letter it represents. This way, when a police officer pulls over a speeding motorist, he or she can report the license plate number ABC-123 with perfect clarity: "Alpha-Bravo-Charlie-One-Two-Three." Likewise, a firefighter responding to a call can accurately interpret the address 123F Main Street: "One-Two-Three-Foxtrot Main Street." This alphabet code, known as the international radiotelephony spelling alphabet, can save time and frustration, which allows emergency personnel to save lives.

1. Based on the information in the passage, what name would you record if you received the following radio transmission: "First name, Juliet-Oscar-Echo, and last name, Sierra-Mike-India-Tango-Hotel"?

   (A) Juliet Sierra

   (B) Oscar India

   (C) Joe Smith

   (D) Juliet Smith

2. Each code word in the international radio-telephony spelling alphabet begins with the letter it represents.

   (A) True

   (B) False

3. As used in the passage, the word <u>discern</u> most nearly means

   (A) write.

   (B) sign.

   (C) speak.

   (D) recognize.

Passage two

You can find a fire extinguisher in a domestic kitchen, in a hallway in a shopping mall, even in the trunks of some cars. Although most people know what fire extinguishers look like, few have probably had to use one. It's a good idea to learn how to operate a fire extinguisher before an emergency situation occurs.

Fire extinguishers may contain a variety of extinguishing agents such as water, carbon dioxide, dry chemicals, or special powder. Each of these agents is designed to fight a different type of fire. All fire extinguishers operate in a similar way. Using a fire extinguisher is not difficult, especially if you remember the acronym PASS, which stands for Pull, Aim, Squeeze, and Sweep. To expel the extinguishing agent from a fire extinguisher, follow these steps:

1. **Pull the pin.** The extinguisher will most likely have a safety pin in the handle. You must remove this pin to make the extinguisher operable.

2. **Aim the extinguisher at the fire.** Don't aim at the tops of the flames. Point the nozzle or hose of the extinguisher toward the base of the fire.

3. **Squeeze the handle.** When you squeeze the handle, the hose or nozzle will expel the extinguishing agent.

4. **Sweep the nozzle or hose from side to side.** As you spray the extinguishing agent at the base of the blaze, move the extinguisher back and forth until you have doused the flames.

4. What is the main idea of this passage?

    (A) instructions for using a fire extinguisher

    (B) differences among extinguishing agents

    (C) the best place to install a fire extinguisher

    (D) the benefit of using a carbon dioxide extinguisher

5. According to the passage, you should spray the extinguishing agent _____ of the fire.

    (A) at the top

    (B) around the edge

    (C) toward the base

    (D) through the middle

6. According to the passage, all of the following are extinguishing agents EXCEPT

    (A) dry chemicals.

    (B) water.

    (C) special powder.

    (D) steam.

7. You can use a fire extinguisher that contains water to put out all types of fire.

    (A) True

    (B) False

Passage three

Wildfires, also called wildland fires, brush fires, or forest fires, occur in rural or woodland areas where dry grass, brush, leaves, trees, and other vegetation are prevalent. These materials provide a seemingly endless fuel supply for the flames, which is why wildfires often spread rapidly and consume large tracts of land. Because wildfires are dangerous and destructive, firefighters have developed several methods to stop them. One common wildfire suppression method is called a firebreak.

A firebreak is an area free of combustible, or burnable, materials that serves as a "break" in the path of a wildfire. Examples of natural firebreaks are rivers and canyons. When a fire reaches the bank of a river or the edge of a canyon, it runs out of fuel and has no place to go. Unfortunately, wildfires can occur in places with ample vegetation, and rivers and canyons are not always available to stop the spread of flames. As a result, firefighters sometimes create firebreaks to prevent wildfires from spreading further.

To create a firebreak, firefighters use machines to clear or plow land. The goal is to remove as much potential fuel — dead trees, dry leaves, fallen brush, and so on — from the path of the fire as possible. Sometimes highways and other roads that traverse woodland areas also serve as firebreaks. Although firebreaks are a good way to fight wildfires, they are not 100 percent effective, especially when strong winds are involved. Wind can carry hot embers across firebreaks and spark forest fires on the opposite side of the break.

8. Based on the information in the passage, which of the following is NOT a firebreak?

(A) a logging road

(B) a lake

(C) a field

(D) an interstate

9. Which statement best summarizes the passage?

(A) Wildfires occur in rural or woodland areas and can spread rapidly.

(B) A firebreak is one way to slow, and possibly stop, a wildfire.

(C) Wind can cause a wildfire to cross a firebreak and continue burning.

(D) Firefighters use machines to clear land to create firebreaks.

10. Traverse most nearly means

(A) cross.

(B) damage.

(C) surround.

(D) weaken.

Passage four

Probably most famous because of a 1991 movie of the same name, a *backdraft* is actually a very serious situation that can result in an explosive, deadly fire. A fire is essentially a chemical reaction that occurs when three elements are present: a heat source, a fuel supply, and oxygen. When a fire in an enclosed area — that is, an area with little or no ventilation — becomes starved of oxygen, the flames may reduce to smoldering embers. The temperature in the enclosed area remains very high, however, and large amounts of combustible gases collect in unventilated spaces — these are the perfect conditions for a backdraft. All the fire needs is a swift intake of oxygen to mix with the hot fire gases, and a backdraft explosion will occur.

Where does the fire get this supply of oxygen? Sometimes firefighters open doors and windows to allow hot gases and smoke to escape from a structure or simply to enter a building. These actions are enough to provide the fire with the oxygen it needs to ignite the hot gases and cause a backdraft.

Before entering an enclosed area by opening a door or window, firefighters can check for a few signs that indicate a possible backdraft. First, if a fire has very little flame or if the smoke appears yellow or brown, the potential for a backdraft exists. Smoke-stained windows are another indication. A third sign is the appearance of small puffs of smoke that exit through small openings and get sucked back into the enclosed area. This "breathing" appearance is a strong indicator of a possible backdraft.

At this point, it may seem like all is lost. How can firefighters battle the blaze if they can't get to it without creating an explosion? To avoid a backdraft, firefighters can vent smoke and gases from the highest point above the fire. For example, they might cut a hole in the roof of a building. This allows hot gases to escape, so the gases are gone when firefighters finally enter the enclosed area through a door or window.

11. According to the passage, all of the following conditions have the potential to create a backdraft EXCEPT

    (A) smoldering embers.

    (B) trapped gases.

    (C) hot temperatures.

    (D) high oxygen.

12. Which of the following is a sign that a backdraft could occur?

    (A) thick, black smoke

    (B) smoke-stained windows

    (C) rolling flames

    (D) low heat in the surrounding area

13. Opening a door or window is one way to vent out gases and prevent a backdraft explosion.

    (A) True

    (B) False

14. What is the best title for this passage?

    (A) Avoiding a Backdraft Explosion

    (B) How Accurate Is the Movie *Backdraft*?

    (C) Locating Backdraft Indicators

    (D) Fire Ventilation Procedures

Passage five

Anywhere, USA — Firefighter Pay Scale		
Position (Ranked Lowest to Highest)	*Starting Salary*	*Maximum Salary*
Firefighter	$31,000	$58,000
Engineer	$48,000	$60,000
Fire lieutenant	$50,000	$61,000
Fire captain	$61,000	$73,000
Battalion chief	$65,500	$84,000
Assistant fire chief	$66,000	$82,000
Deputy chief	$69,000	$88,500
Fire chief	$77,000	$100,000

15. Based on the information in the table, which position has the potential for the greatest increase between starting salary and maximum salary?

    (A) fire chief

    (B) deputy chief

    (C) assistant fire chief

    (D) firefighter

16. Based on the information in the table, which position has a higher starting salary but a lower maximum salary than the position ranked right below it?

    (A) assistant fire chief

    (B) fire lieutenant

    (C) engineer

    (D) fire captain

17. Based on the information in the table, what is the maximum salary a battalion chief can expect to earn in Anywhere, USA?

    (A) $65,500

    (B) $84,000

    (C) $77,000

    (D) $100,000

18. A fire lieutenant has the potential to receive a greater increase in pay than a fire captain.

    (A) True

    (B) False

Passage six

Woven-jacket fire hose, which is fire hose with a rubber lining and one or two woven-fabric jackets on the exterior, requires more <u>maintenance</u> than rubber or hard-suction hoses. Woven-jacket fire hose must be washed and thoroughly dried before it is returned to the fire apparatus or storage unit to prevent the formation of mold and mildew.

When cleaning woven-jacket fire hose, first try to remove dirt and dust by brushing it off. If additional cleaning is necessary, stretch the hose across a long flat surface and use a hose with a powerful stream of clean, clear water to wash the entire length of the hose.

Next, allow the hose to dry thoroughly. Avoid leaving it in the direct sunlight or lying on hot blacktop. A good place to dry woven-jacket hose is in a hose tower, which is a tall structure through which you can weave lengths of hose. A hose tower allows air to circulate around the lengths of hose. This allows the hose to dry faster and prevents mold and mildew from forming.

19. Based on the passage, what can you conclude about rubber or hard-suction hoses?

    (A) They last longer than woven-jacket hoses.

    (B) They can be returned to the apparatus wet.

    (C) They should be stored in a hose tower.

    (D) They are easier to handle than woven-jacket hoses.

20. The root of the word <u>maintenance</u> is

    (A) ten.

    (B) main.

    (C) tenant.

    (D) maintain.

Answers and Explanations

Use this answer key to score the "Practice Reading and Verbal Comprehension Questions" in this chapter. The answer explanations give you a little more insight on how to find the right answers. Remember, the more you practice reading and listening, the more you'll improve these skills.

1. **C.** According to the passage, each code word begins with the letter it represents. To determine the correct name, look only at the first letter of each code word: J-O-E S-M-I-T-H. The correct answer is Choice (C).

2. **A.** The passage states directly that each code word in the international radiotelephony spelling alphabet begins with the letter it represents.

3. **D.** As used in the passage, *discern* means "recognize," so Choice (D) is correct. Choice (C) may seem tempting because the letters are spoken during the communication. Context clues in the article, however, suggest that the alphabet code is a way to provide clarity to letters that sound similar in radio transmissions. Using code words such as Alpha, Bravo, and Charlie helps people *recognize* exactly which letters have been stated.

4. **A.** The correct answer is Choice (A). The entire passage is about learning to use fire extinguishers, including a step-by-step process.

5. **C.** According to Step 2, you should aim the extinguisher at the base of the fire, which makes Choice (C) the correct answer.

6. **D.** The passage gives examples of four types of extinguishing agents: water, carbon dioxide, dry chemicals, and special powder. It never mentions steam, which makes Choice (D) the correct answer.

7. **B.** This is a true/false drawing-conclusions question. The passage tells you that each of the extinguishing agents mentioned is designed to put out a different type of fire. You can conclude, then, that water cannot be used to put out *all* types of fire.

8. **C.** A field is a large grassy area and would likely contain vegetation that a wildfire could use as fuel, so it's not an example of a firebreak.

9. **B.** The whole passage describes types of firebreaks and explains how firefighters use firebreaks to slow or stop wildfires, so Choice (B) is the best answer.

10. **A.** *Traverse* means "to cross." The root of *traverse* looks like *travel*, which has a similar meaning to *cross*. Also consider context clues. The passage discusses natural firebreaks, such as rivers and canyons, which cross the path of a fire to prevent it from spreading. They don't surround the fire, so you can eliminate Choice (C). The words *damage* and *weaken*, Choices (B) and (D), seem irrelevant to the discussion of firebreaks, so you can eliminate these answers, too.

11. **D.** When a fire has a low oxygen supply, high temperatures, trapped fire gases, and smoldering embers, the potential for a backdraft exists. The introduction of oxygen will ignite the hot gases and cause a backdraft.

12. **B.** The signs that a backdraft could occur include thick yellow or brown smoke, smoke-stained windows, and the appearance that the enclosed area is breathing smoke. Therefore, the correct answer is Choice (B).

13. **B.** If firefighters suspect that a backdraft could occur, they should not open doors or windows. Rather, they should vent gases from the highest point above the fire.

14. **A.** Although both Choice (C) and Choice (D) are mentioned in the passage, they simply represent details that support the main idea: avoiding backdraft situations. The correct answer is Choice (A).

15. **D.** The position with the largest increase — $27,000 — between starting and maximum salaries is firefighter. To answer this question, look only at the positions listed in the four answer choices; this cuts the number of calculations you have to do in half. The correct answer is Choice (D).

16. **A.** The assistant fire chief is ranked directly above the battalion chief. The starting salary for an assistant fire chief is more than for a battalion chief, but the battalion chief has the potential to earn a higher maximum salary. An easy way to answer this question is to remember that the starting salaries are in order from lowest to highest. Therefore, you only have to find a place where the maximum salary is lower than the one before it.

17. **B.** The table lists a maximum salary of $84,000 for a battalion chief.

18. **B.** Subtract to find the difference in maximum and starting salaries. A fire captain has the potential to increase his or her pay by $12,000. A fire lieutenant has the potential to increase his or her pay by only $11,000.

19. **B.** This is a drawing-conclusions question; the correct answer isn't stated directly in the passage, so you have to use context clues to figure out the answer. The passage states that woven-jacket hose requires more maintenance than rubber and hard-suction hoses. It has to be washed and dried thoroughly before it can be returned to the apparatus. This implies that rubber and hard-suction hoses do not require washing or drying like woven-jacket hoses do. Therefore, you can conclude that these hoses can be returned to the apparatus wet. The correct answer is Choice (B).

20. **D.** The root of *maintenance* is *maintain*, which means "to keep in an existing state" — for example, a state of repair. The suffix *-ance* means "instance of an action," which in this case means "an instance of maintaining."

Chapter 5

Mastering Verbal Expression

In This Chapter

▶ Understanding the verbal expression component of the written test

▶ Answering questions about spelling

▶ Developing skills to answer questions about vocabulary

▶ Reviewing grammar rules

Have you ever tried to read a note that was sloppy and poorly written? Maybe words were misspelled, grammar was incorrect, or the wrong words were used to convey the author's meaning. Figuring out what the author was trying to say probably took you a while. Now think of a time when you had trouble understanding someone who was speaking. You probably had to ask the person to repeat the message.

Verbal expression refers to how you convey information or ideas to others. Firefighters must be able to express themselves well so they can pass along information to other firefighters, superiors, fire victims, police officers, witnesses, and even arson investigators. Firefighters need good verbal expression skills to perform their jobs efficiently.

The firefighter written exam may include a section on verbal expression. Although the phrase *verbal expression* includes both speech and writing, the test questions assess only your written skills. A verbal expression section on a firefighter exam will likely test you on vocabulary, spelling, and grammar.

In this chapter, we review the highlights of these topics that you may have forgotten since your high school days (or maybe you slept through them). Knowing some tricks for vocabulary and spelling, as well as the basic rules of grammar, can help you ace these questions when you encounter them on the firefighter exam.

Acing Vocabulary Questions

Do you have a large vocabulary? The only way to get a great vocabulary is to read often and look up the meanings of new words in a dictionary. Not a big reader? Don't panic. You can increase your vocabulary and correctly answer many vocabulary questions on the firefighter written test by knowing some common word parts — prefixes, roots, and suffixes. For example, if you know that the prefix *counter-* means *against,* you can figure out that the word *counterargument* means "an argument against something." Chapter 4 includes some prefixes, word roots, and suffixes for you to study. When you encounter an unfamiliar word, whether in daily life or on the firefighter exam, try to break it into familiar parts.

To improve your vocabulary, record new words in a notepad. Look up the definition of each word and record this, too. Then practice using each new word in speech and writing. In this section, we give you other tips for answering vocabulary questions.

Choosing the correct synonym

Some vocabulary questions ask you to choose a synonym for a word. *Synonyms* are words with almost the same meaning. Examples of simple synonyms are *rest/relax, student/pupil,* and *under/below.* Some more difficult synonyms include *magnanimous/charitable, repentance/regret,* and *arrange/catalog.*

If you use your knowledge of word parts — roots, prefixes, and suffixes — you can often eliminate incorrect answer options and choose the correct answer. Try this question: Choose the word that has nearly the same meaning as the underlined word.

A <u>belligerent</u> child

(A) kind-hearted

(B) argumentative

(C) cooperative

(D) forceful

The correct answer is Choice (B). The root word *bell,* which is also present in the word *rebellion,* means "war" or "bad." From this, you can eliminate Choices (A) and (C). The meaning of *argumentative* is closest to "war" or "bad," so this is the best answer.

Looking for context clues

Some vocabulary questions give you a few sentences with an underlined or italicized word. These questions ask you to choose the word with nearly the same meaning. You can often figure out the meaning of the underlined or italicized word by analyzing the *context clues,* or nearby words. Look carefully at the context clues in this question. Choose the word that has nearly the same meaning as the underlined word.

The <u>pretentious</u> woman wore a designer suit, carried an expensive purse, and had a diamond ring on each finger.

(A) beautiful

(B) modest

(C) noble

(D) flashy

The correct answer is Choice (D). Context clues in the sentence include the woman's designer suit, her expensive purse, and her diamond rings. The woman is showing off. Choice (A) is incorrect; although she may be beautiful, the context clues don't indicate this. She certainly isn't modest, or plain, so Choice (B) is also incorrect. She may be noble, but she's more likely *flashy.*

Acing Spelling Questions

The content of the written firefighter test can vary — but if it has a verbal expression section, you can bet that it has some spelling questions. Now, we know what you're thinking: "Why do I have to know how to spell words when I can just use a spell-checker to check my work?" Read this note:

> Too hour valued customer,
>
> We are sew sorry too here that you found a hare in your soup. Please except our sin sear Apollo-geez. To compensate four you're incontinence, we wood like to offer you a free diner.

Do you think a spell-checker would catch the errors in this note? Probably not. (Our spelling-and-grammar checker found only two mistakes, with the words *sew* and *hare!*) Being able to express yourself like a professional is important, which means you need to be able to spell common words in the English language. Although you can't memorize the dictionary before you take this test, you can study some spelling rules and figure out the correct spelling of some commonly misspelled words.

Remembering spelling rules

Spelling rules are not foolproof — you often see exceptions to a rule. However, applying spelling rules can help you eliminate incorrect answer options. Here are some spelling rules and example words:

✔ The letter *i* comes before *e*, except after *c* or when the sound is like *ay*.

> Examples: *Friend, thief, believe, receive, neighbor, sleigh*

Exceptions to this rule include *weird, protein,* and *foreign*.

✔ When the letter *c* follows a short vowel, it's usually doubled.

> Examples: *Tobacco, raccoon, stucco, occupy*

However, the letters *ck* are used instead of *cc* if the letter following the *c* sound is *e, i,* or *y*.

> Examples: *Frolicked, blackest, lucky*

✔ If the *j* sound follows a short vowel, it's usually spelled *dge*.

> Examples: *Dodge, judge, budget*

✔ The *ch* sound is usually spelled *tch* after a short vowel.

> Examples: *Witch, kitchen, catch, hatchet*

Exceptions to this rule include *rich, such,* and *much*.

✔ If a word has a short vowel sound, there must be two consonants between the vowel and an *-le* ending.

> Examples: *Tickle, little, bottle, angle*

✔ If a word has a silent *e*, drop the *e* before adding a *vowel suffix* (a word ending such as -*ed* or -*ing*).

> Examples: *Force/forcing, age/aging, ride/riding, convince/convincing*

Exceptions include words with soft *c* or *g* sounds, such as *manageable, courageous, noticeable,* and *enforceable.*

✔ When the *ee* sound comes before a vowel suffix, it's usually spelled with the letter *i.*

> Examples: *Ingredient, zodiac, material*

✔ The ending -*ist* is usually used to refer to someone who does something, and the ending -*est* is used to create superlative adjectives.

> People: *Machinist, druggist*

> Adjectives: *Strongest, longest*

✔ The ending -*cian* always refers to a person, whereas the endings -*tion* and -*sion* are not used to refer to people.

> People: *Musician, electrician*

> Objects/ideas: *Condition, expression*

Mastering commonly misspelled words

Unfortunately, not all words abide by spelling rules — there are a few troublemakers. The only way to deal with such words is to practice spelling them correctly. Table 5-1 lists some commonly misspelled words. Spend some time reviewing these words, just in case you encounter them on the written firefighter exam. For practice, you may want to have a friend read the words aloud, write down each word when you hear it, and use the table to check your spelling.

Table 5-1		Commonly Misspelled Words	
Word	*Hint*	*Word*	*Hint*
acceptable	not *acceptible*	intelligence	not *intelligance*
accommodate	double *c* and double *m*	jewelry	not *jewlry*
amateur	not *amature*	judgment	not *judgement*
apparent	not *apparant*	kernel	not *kernal*
argument	no *e* before *ment*	leisure	not *liesure*
calendar	not *calender*	license	*c* first, then *s*
category	not *catagory*	lightning (electricity)	not *lightening* (which means "making lighter")
cemetery	no *a* anywhere	maintenance	not *maintenence*
changeable	keep the *e* before *able*	millennium	double *l* and double *n*
committed	double *m* and double *t*	miniature	not *minature*
conscience	both *s* and *c*	misspell	double *s* and double *l*
discipline	both *s* and *c*	noticeable	*e* before -*able*
embarrass	double *r* and double *s*	occasionally	double *c*, single *s*, and double *l*
equipment	not *equiptment*	occurrence	double *c*, double *r*, and -*ence*
exceed	not *excede*	pastime	single *t*
existence	not *existance*	personnel	double *n* and single *l*

Word	Hint	Word	Hint
gauge	not *guage*	questionnaire	double *n*
grateful	not *greatful*	recommend	single *c* and double *m*
guarantee	not *guarranty*	referred	single *f* and double *r*
harass	single *r* and double *s*	relevant	not *relevent*
height	not *heighth*	rhythm	*rh* and then *th*
ignorance	not *ignorence*	separate	not *seperate*
independent	not *independant*	sergeant	not *sergant* or *sargeant*
indispensable	not *indispensible*	supersede	not *supercede*
inoculate	single *n* and single *c*	vacuum	double *u*

Acing Grammar Questions

Although grammatical slips are often acceptable in speech, they're more noticeable — and more inappropriate — in writing. Brush up on your grammar to ace the grammar questions on the verbal expression section of the firefighter test. You may see questions assessing your knowledge of the following:

✔ Verb tense

✔ Subject-verb agreement

✔ Pronouns

✔ Prepositions

✔ Comparative and superlative adjectives

We cover each of these topics in the following sections.

Choosing the correct verb tense

Verbs tell you what's going on (the action) or the state of being (an emotion or a condition). In addition, they tell you *when* the action or state is happening. The basic tenses are past, present, and future, and each tense has additional forms.

Some questions on the verbal expression section of the firefighter test may be about verb tense. These questions ask you to read a sentence with a blank in it. Then you have to choose the verb that best fits in the blank.

Before you tackle some sample questions, review the different verb tenses in Table 5-2. Study these tenses so you can easily identify a verb's tense. You don't need to know the names of the different tenses on the written firefighter exam, but you should be able to recognize the different forms and know when each one belongs in a sentence. Note that verbs in the progressive, perfect, perfect progressive, and future tenses use words in addition to the main verb, such as *am, are, is* (forms of the verb *to be*), *have, has, had* (forms of the verb *to have*), and *will*. These additional words are called *auxiliaries*.

To recognize different tenses, focus on the first word (or the only word if the verb stands alone) in the verb phrase. For all present tenses, the first word (either a basic verb or some form of *to be/to have*) is in the present tense. For all past tenses, the first word (either a basic verb or an auxiliary verb) is in the past tense. For all future tenses, the first word is always *will*.

Table 5-3		Present, Past, and Future Verb Tenses		
Tense	**Basic**	**Progressive**	**Perfect**	**Perfect Progressive**
Present	talk(s)	am/is/are talking	have/has talked	have/has been talking
Past	talked	was/were talking	had talked	had been talking
Future	will talk	will be talking	will have talked	will have been talking

Sometimes it's necessary to switch tenses. For example, it's okay to say, "I have been working with her on the project because she is the best." This sentence contains a verb in the present perfect progressive tense *(have been working)* and a verb in the present tense *(is)*. In this sentence, the change in tense is essential to the meaning.

When you answer questions about verb tense, look for clues in the sentence that indicate when the action took place.

Next summer, we _____ to the beach on vacation.

(A) had gone

(B) will go

(C) go

(D) had went

The words *next summer* are clues in this sentence. They tell you that this is something that hasn't yet happened, so you need the future tense. Choice (B) is the correct answer.

Choosing an agreeable answer: Subject-verb agreement

Some verbal expression questions on the firefighter written test ask you to choose a verb that agrees with the subject in a sentence. *Subject-verb agreement* means matching subjects and verbs based on the number of people or things performing the action. For instance, you use a singular verb with a singular subject *(the child sings)* and a plural verb with a plural subject *(the children sing)*. Study these rules to correctly answer these questions:

- Use a plural verb when two or more subjects are connected by *and*.

    Mary and Enrico play basketball after school.

- When subjects are joined by *or* or *nor,* the verb should agree with the part of the subject that is closest to the verb.

    The girl or *her friends are going* to help Mrs. Amesbury.

    Either James or *Sondra knows* the answer to that question.

- If a phrase comes between the subject and the verb, make sure the verb agrees with the subject and not the phrase.

    The people who live in that house *are* nice.

- Use a singular verb in sentences with *each, everyone, every one, someone, somebody, anyone,* and *anybody*.

    Each of the boys *shoots* the ball well.

✔ Use a singular verb with sums of money or periods of time.

> *Ten years is* a long time to wait.

> *Thirty dollars is* too much money for that coat.

✔ Use a singular verb with collective nouns such as *team* and *group.*

> *The team is* in the locker room.

> *The group knows* where to go.

✔ In sentences beginning with *there* or *here,* the subject of the sentence follows the verb. The verb should agree with that subject.

> There *are three girls* in that room.

Here is an example question:

There _____ many kinds of questions on this test.

(A) are

(B) is

(C) was

(D) had

The correct answer is Choice (A). The subject of this sentence is *kinds.* (The phrase *of questions* only modifies, or describes, *kinds,* so you can ignore it when deciding which verb to use.)

Choosing the correct pronoun (or pronoun-like adjective)

Read this paragraph:

> Ellen drove Ellen's car home from work this afternoon. Ellen put her keys on her desk, but when Ellen went to find Ellen's keys, they were gone! Ellen thinks Ellen's nephew may have taken Ellen's keys by mistake.

Do you see what's wrong with this paragraph? It doesn't use pronouns. A *noun* is a person, place, or thing, and a *pronoun* is a noun substitute. The noun that a pronoun refers to is called the *antecedent.* Pronouns make writing easier to read and less repetitive.

Some *adjectives* — words that describe nouns — resemble pronouns, because they refer to nouns and can be singular or plural. For instance, *Ellen's* here describes *keys* and *nephew,* and you can use an adjective, *her,* to stand in for *Ellen's.*

Some questions on the verbal expression section of the firefighter written test ask you to choose the correct pronoun or adjective in a sentence. You don't have to be able to tell the pronouns and adjectives apart, but you should know how to use them. In this section, we review some pronoun and pronoun-like-adjective basics so you can answer these questions correctly.

Subject and object pronouns

A pronoun may be either a subject pronoun or an object pronoun:

✔ **Subject pronouns:** *I, you, he, she, it, we, you, they, who*

✔ **Object pronouns:** *me, you, him, her, it, us, you, them, whom*

A *subject* pronoun may take the place of the subject in the sentence — whoever or whatever is doing the action. The same holds true for an object pronoun — it takes the place of the object in a sentence. The *object* is the person or thing that receives the action in a sentence. In most sentences, the subject of the sentence comes before the verb, and the object of the sentence comes after the verb. Read these sentences:

> *Juanita* received a good grade in math. [*Juanita* is the subject of the sentence.]
>
> *She* received a good grade in math. [The subject pronoun *she* is now the subject.]

Now read these sentences:

> Tyler crashed the *car*. [*Car* is the object of the sentence.]
>
> Tyler crashed *it*. [The object pronoun *it* is now the subject.]

Now that you know the difference between subject and object pronouns, review some rules about pronouns. Study each of these rules. They'll help you correctly answer questions about pronouns on the firefighter test.

- ✔ Use a subject pronoun when the pronoun is the subject of the sentence. This is also true when a compound subject contains a noun and a pronoun.

    DeShawn and I asked to speak to Mr. Miller.

- ✔ Use an object pronoun when the pronoun is the object of the sentence. Also use an object pronoun when a compound object contains a noun and a pronoun.

    Mr. Miller spoke *to DeShawn and me*.

- ✔ Use a subject pronoun to rename the subject (when the verb is a form of *to be: am, is, are, was, were, be, being,* or *been*).

    This is *she*.

    It is *I* who would like pizza for dinner.

- ✔ Use a subject pronoun after the words *than* or *as*.

    Renee runs faster *than I*. [It helps to complete this sentence mentally: Renee runs faster *than I do.*]

    She is as tall *as I*. [Same here: She is as tall *as I am.*]

- ✔ Use an object pronoun as the object of a prepositional phrase. **Note:** A preposition (such as *at, in, of, over, to, with*) shows the relationship between its object (a noun or pronoun that follows the preposition) and another word in the sentence.

    My brother tripped *over me*. [In this sentence, *over* is the preposition. It shows the relationship between the verb *tripped* and the object of the preposition *me*.]

Possessive pronouns and adjectives

Possessive pronouns and adjectives show ownership. The pronouns include *its, yours, his, hers, ours, theirs,* and *mine,* and the adjectives include *its, your, his, her, our, their,* and *my*. **Remember:** A possessive pronoun or adjective never needs an apostrophe.

> The baby bird flapped *its* [not *it's*] wings.
>
> The red scarf is *hers* [not *her's*].

Use possessive adjectives before nouns ending in *-ing*, such as *running, jumping, thinking,* and *reading*.

> *Your* [not *you*] calling me irresponsible is like the pot's calling the kettle black!
>
> *Their* [not *them*] coming to class late resulted in detention.

Some possessive pronouns and possessive adjectives sound like other words. For example, *its* sounds like the contraction *it's,* and *their* sounds like the contraction *they're* and the adverb *there.* On the written firefighter exam, expect to see questions that ask you to choose among these words to complete a sentence correctly. Consider these guidelines when you see them:

- ✔ **Its/it's:** *Its* is a possessive pronoun or possessive adjective.

   The dog flipped over *its* water bowl. [*Its* is a possessive adjective modifying the noun *water bowl.*]

   It's is a contraction meaning "it is."

   It's a pleasure to meet you.

- ✔ **Their/there/they're:** *Their* is a possessive adjective.

   The students left *their* jackets in the classroom. [*Their* is a possessive adjective modifying the noun *jackets.*]

   There is an adverb. It means "that location."

   Mrs. Jackson told us to put our jackets *there.*

   They're is a contraction meaning "they are."

   They're my best friends.

Here's an example question:

The firefighters wanted to give _____ fire chief an award for bravery.

(A) it's

(B) their

(C) there

(D) they're

The correct answer is Choice (B). *Firefighters* is plural, so you need a plural possessive adjective, *their,* to make the sentence complete.

Reflexive pronouns

Reflexive pronouns include *myself, yourself, yourselves,* and *ourselves.* Use reflexive pronouns only when they refer back to another word in the sentence.

   I fixed the door *myself.* [*Myself* refers back to *I.*]

   She told me about the crime *herself.* [*Herself* refers back to *she.*]

Indefinite pronouns

Indefinite pronouns don't refer to a specific person or thing. These pronouns can be singular or plural:

- ✔ **Singular indefinite pronouns:** *Another, anybody, anyone, anything, each, either, everybody, everything, everyone, nobody, no one, nothing, somebody, someone, something*
- ✔ **Plural indefinite pronouns:** *Both, few, many, others, several*

If a singular indefinite pronoun is used in a sentence with another pronoun or possessive adjective, the other pronoun or possessive adjective should also be singular.

   Each of the students in the play knew *his or her* [not *their*] lines well.

   Someone left *his or her* [not *their*] wallet on the desk.

Demonstrative pronouns

Demonstrative pronouns refer to nouns or pronouns that represent objects that are near or far away. *That, this, those,* and *these* are demonstrative pronouns.

> *This* is the best dip I've ever tasted! [*This* refers to *dip*.]

> *These* look like excellent books for beginning readers. [*These* refers to *books*.]

Looking at sentences using all sorts of pronouns

When you're taking the firefighter exam, the questions won't be grouped by pronoun type into nice little categories. You have to be able to read the sentence and figure out which word fits. Here are some example questions:

My sister Angeline is taller than _____.

(A) I

(B) me

(C) us

(D) all of them

The correct answer is Choice (A). Use a subject pronoun, *I,* after *than* or *as*. If you complete the sentence mentally, it reads, "My sister Angeline is taller than *I am*."

Each of the boys on the team needs to pay for _____ own t-shirt.

(A) their

(B) them

(C) its

(D) his

The correct answer is Choice (D). *Each* is singular, so a singular adjective is necessary to complete the sentence. Because the team is all male, *his* is the appropriate possessive adjective to modify *t-shirt*.

It is _____ who want their town's mayor to resign.

(A) they

(B) them

(C) he

(D) us

The correct answer is Choice (A). Use a subject pronoun, *they*, to rename the subject.

Navigating space and time: Prepositions

Prepositions are words that establish relationships between a noun (or pronoun) and another word in a sentence, and they typically revolve around space or time. Here are just a few examples of pronouns:

- ✔ **Space:** *Above, below, up, down, beside, around, near, within, to, toward, under, over*
- ✔ **Time:** *Before, during, after, since, until*

A preposition begins a *prepositional phrase,* which begins with a preposition and ends with an object (a noun or pronoun). For example, in the sentence "We drove *toward home,*" *toward* is the preposition and *home* is the object of the preposition.

Prepositional phrases may act as adjectives or adverbs:

✔ **Adjective:** An adjective is a word or phrase that modifies a noun. The following prepositional phrase acts as an adjective in the sentence:

> The children *on the bus* want a tour. [The prepositional phrase modifies the noun *children. On the bus* specifies which children you're talking about.]

✔ **Adverb:** An adverb is a word or phrase that modifies a verb, adjective, or another adverb. The following prepositional phrase acts as an adverb in the sentence:

> The raindrops fell *on the windshield.* [The prepositional phrase modifies the verb *fell. On the windshield* specifies where the falling occurred.]

Some verbal expression questions on the firefighter test may ask you to choose the right preposition to complete a sentence. Use common sense when answering these questions. Be sure to read the sentence carefully. Substitute each word in the answer choices to see which makes the most sense. This type of question may look like this:

The driver maneuvered _____ the curb.

(A) after

(B) toward

(C) until

(D) at

The correct answer is Choice (B). The sentence makes the most sense if you insert the preposition *toward.* The preposition *toward* establishes the relationship between the verb *maneuvered* and the object of the preposition *curb.*

Using the right adjective: Is it good, better, or best?

You may be asked a question or two about positive, comparative, and superlative adjectives on the firefighter test. Comparative and superlative adjectives compare two or more things. Follow these guidelines when choosing an answer:

✔ Use a positive adjective when the adjective stands alone. In other words, the sentence doesn't compare two or three things.

> Juan is a *smart* man. [The positive adjective is *smart.*]

✔ Use a comparative adjective to compare only two items, ideas, or people. Comparative adjectives usually end in *-er.*

> Juan is *smarter* than Bobby. [The comparative adjective is *smarter.*]

✔ Use a superlative adjective when comparing three or more items, ideas, or people. Superlative adjectives usually end in *-est.*

> Juan is the *smartest* guy in the class. [The superlative adjective is *smartest.*]

For some two-syllable adjectives, you may use -er and -est, more and most, or less and least to form the comparative and superlative. These words include clever, gentle, friendly, quiet, and simple.

> Juan is the *cleverest* guy in the class.
>
> Juan is the *most clever* guy in the class.
>
> Bobby is *less clever* than Juan.

For adjectives with three or more syllables, use *more* and *most* or *less* and *least* to form the comparative and the superlative.

> Juan is *more intelligent* than Bobby.
>
> Bobby is the *least intelligent* guy in the class.

Now check out an example question.

Firefighter Carlton is often asked to carry heavy hoses because he is the _____ of all the firefighters at the station.

(A) stronger

(B) most strongest

(C) strongest

(D) more stronger

The correct answer is Choice (C). This question compares Carlton to all the firefighters at the station — three or more people — so use the superlative form. Because the word *strong* is only one syllable, you don't need to use the word *most*.

Practice Verbal Expression Questions

The following questions are designed to help you master your verbal expression skills. Read the directions before each question set. Then carefully read each question. Choose the answer that *most correctly* answers the question.

Choose the word that has nearly the same meaning as the underlined word.

---

1. There was no name under the title of the poem because the author chose to remain <u>anonymous</u>.

   (A) ordinary

   (B) mainstream

   (C) predictable

   (D) unknown

2. The warm sun, chirping birds, and <u>tranquil</u> water were so relaxing that I fell asleep.

   (A) frenzied

   (B) turbulent

   (C) peaceful

   (D) comfortable

3. Monique is a <u>versatile</u> employee. She can work the front desk, cook in the kitchen, wait on tables, and help the bookkeeper.

   (A) adequate

   (B) resourceful

   (C) complete

   (D) intelligent

Choose the word that has nearly the same meaning as the italicized word.

4. A *notorious* criminal
   (A) infamous
   (B) skillful
   (C) inexperienced
   (D) misunderstood

5. A *chronic* cough
   (A) sudden
   (B) painful
   (C) severe
   (D) constant

Choose the word that is spelled correctly to complete the following sentences.

6. A _____ check should be made to most firefighting equipment once a year.
   (A) maintanance
   (B) maintenance
   (C) maintanence
   (D) manetanence

7. _____, a natural phenomenon that occurs during electrical storms, is a common cause of fires.
   (A) Lightining
   (B) Lightening
   (C) Lightning
   (D) Litening

8. It is important to use good _____ when making decisions regarding personal safety.
   (A) judgement
   (B) jugement
   (C) jugment
   (D) judgment

Choose the word that is spelled incorrectly.

9. Firefighters should work in pairs or teams when working in hazardus conditions or when at the scene of an emergency. A firefighter working alone may collapse from exhaustion.
   (A) hazardus
   (B) scene
   (C) collapse
   (D) exhaustion

10. A fire hose that is properly cared for can have a long lifespan. Firefighters should follow proper procederes for washing, drying, and storing fire hoses.
    (A) properly
    (B) proper
    (C) procederes
    (D) drying

Choose the correct word or words to fill in the blank.

11. Fire Chief Sanchez began _____ career 15 years ago.
    (A) their
    (B) there
    (C) his
    (D) he

12. By next year, the new firehouse _____.
    (A) is built
    (B) will have been built
    (C) was built
    (D) is being built

13. A news reporter wrote an article _____ two firefighters who rescued a group of boys who were lost in the woods.
    (A) about
    (B) by
    (C) for
    (D) to

14. Firefighter Rogers and _____ are on duty this week.

    (A) me

    (B) I

    (C) us

    (D) we

15. It would be _____ to become a firefighter if my town had its own training program and volunteer fire department.

    (A) more easier

    (B) the easiest

    (C) more easy

    (D) easier

Answers and Explanations

Use this answer key to score the practice verbal expression questions in this chapter. Remember, the more you practice vocabulary, spelling, and grammar, the more you'll improve these skills.

1. **D.** If the author's name is not included under the title of the poem, the author may be anonymous, or *not known*.

2. **C.** The sentence says the atmosphere was so relaxing that the author fell asleep. Therefore, *tranquil* means *peaceful*. Although Choice (D) also describes the scenario, water can't really be *comfortable*, so this isn't the best answer.

3. **B.** An employee who is *versatile* is resourceful and able to do many things. Although Monique may be *intelligent*, Choice (D), the context describes someone who can perform many different tasks.

4. **A.** A *notorious* criminal is an *infamous* criminal. Although a criminal may also be *skillful*, Choice (B) is not a synonym of *notorious*.

5. **D.** A *chronic* cough returns again and again. It is *constant*, Choice (D). Although the cough may be *painful*, Choice (B), or *severe*, Choice (C), only *constant* is a synonym of chronic.

6. **B.** The correct spelling is *maintenance*.

7. **C.** The correct spelling is *lightning*. *Lightening*, Choice (B), means "making lighter," as in "lightening the load."

8. **D.** The preferred spelling is *judgment*.

9. **A.** The correct spelling is *hazardous*.

10. **C.** The correct spelling is *procedures*.

11. **C.** The possessive adjective *his* is correct here. The adjective modifies *career*, but it refers back to *Fire Chief Sanchez*.

12. **B.** The sentence should read, "By next year, the new firehouse will have been built." The words *next year* tell you that this has not yet happened.

13. **A.** The article is *about* the firefighters and how they rescued a group of boys who were lost in the woods. Although Choices (C) and (D) also make sense in the sentence, a reporter probably wouldn't write the article *for* the firefighters or address the article *to* them. The article would be published in a newspaper.

14. **B.** The subject pronoun *I* is correct here, because it's part of the subject.

15. **D.** *Easier* is the only word that makes sense in this sentence.

Chapter 6

Testing Your Observation and Memory

. . . .

In This Chapter

▶ Identifying questions that test observation and memory

▶ Honing your observational skills

▶ Answering questions from memory

▶ Practicing your observational and memory skills

. . . .

*J*ust as you can hear a radio without actually listening to the song it's playing, you can see your surroundings without actually observing them. For example, you probably travel the same route to work or school each day. You drive or ride past the same homes and businesses, the same bus stops and street signs. Now consider how much of that route you can recall simply from memory. Can you list the businesses in the right order? How many homes did you pass? Which side streets are one-way streets? You travel this route every day, but it's difficult to remember every detail, isn't it?

The difference between seeing and observing is vast. To *see* something is to simply look at it. As you walk down the street, you may see a school. To *observe* something is to truly study it, absorbing as much information about it as you can. You may observe a two-story elementary school that's constructed of red brick and situated with the front of the building facing north on a one-way street. The main entrance, on the north-facing side of the building, includes three sets of glass doors and five concrete steps. Notice the difference between seeing and observing?

With each fire call, firefighters encounter new surroundings — they never know where the next emergency will take them. Firefighters must be able to absorb a lot of information as they observe, or *size up,* a scene, and they must be able to accurately recall this information later. The firefighter who observes and remembers a scene is better prepared to handle an emergency. That's why as part of the hiring process, firefighter candidates usually have to take a written exam, which may include questions that test their observation and memory skills.

You may think that being observant and having a good memory are innate skills — people are born with or without these abilities. It's possible, however, to improve. In this chapter, we offer advice to help you develop your observational skills and remember more of what you saw, and we also provide some practice exercises.

Watching Out for Observation and Memory Questions

The observation and memory portion of a firefighter candidate test typically includes diagrams or drawings followed by multiple-choice questions that ask you to recall information about the images. Some tests also include written material followed by questions that relate to the passage. The study material often appears in a separate booklet from the test questions (though some fire departments present the study material on computers, which means you may have to observe digital diagrams, pictures, or movies instead of paper booklets).

For these types of tests, you have a set amount of time — usually between 5 and 20 minutes — to study or read the material. In some places, you may have to attend a special study session in the morning and then answer questions about the material several hours later in the afternoon. During the study period, you aren't allowed to write anything down.

At the end of the study period, test administrators collect the booklets so you can't return to them while you answer the questions or view them in the hours between the study period and the actual test. When you receive permission to do so, you can start to answer the questions based on what you remember.

The time between the end of the study period and the time when you can start answering the observation and memory questions is critical. Try to stay focused on what you saw or read. In some cases, you may be permitted to take notes *after* the test administrator has collected the booklets, especially if you have several hours before the start of test. Use this time wisely to take notes, make outlines, and recall as much information as you can. If you're not allowed to take notes at this time, continue to review the information in your mind.

In this section, we give you an overview of the kind of information you may have to remember.

Observing diagrams and other images

The observation and memory portion of the written firefighter exam may include diagrams, photos, and drawings. Examples of these images include the floor plan of a home; a grid showing the layout of city streets; a labeled drawing or photograph of a piece of firefighting equipment; or an illustration of a fire, a motor vehicle accident, or some other emergency scene. These images include a number of details that you'll have to recall when you answer the questions.

The following are some important details that you should observe in diagrams and other images:

- ✔ **People:** Always look for signs of life. How many people do you see? How many of them are male, and how many are female? Are they adults or children? Where are they located in relation to potential hazards? Do they appear to be in distress? Which people are in the most danger? What is the fastest route to reach them?

- ✔ **Layout:** Consider the exterior layout. How is the building situated? Which direction does it face? Are any hydrants or other water sources available and easily accessible? What is the building's height? How many floors does it have? How close is it to other structures? Also consider the interior layout. If you can look at the floor plan of a building, what's the fastest route to the fire? Are any other rooms in jeopardy? How many doors and windows do you see?

- ✔ **Hazards:** Note potential problems. Do you see fire or smoke? Do you see other risks, such as leaking gasoline or downed electrical wires? Is traffic a problem? Are any other people or places located within or near the danger area? How might the fire spread?

- ✔ **Details:** Take notice of specifics. What time of day is it? What is the weather like? Does the building have smoke detectors or sprinklers? If so, how many and where are they located? Do you see any fire escapes? Do you see any obstacles? Does the building have its own water supply that firefighters can use? Do you see any signs, such as street signs or warning signs? Do you see any vehicles? If so, take note of visible license plate numbers. Such details are so small that you can easily overlook them, but many tests ask about them.

Observing and remembering all this information may seem difficult, and it can be if you're not prepared. Later in this chapter, however, we give you some strategies to make sure you don't miss a thing when you make your observations — see the section titled "Developing Great Observational Skills."

Reading the words accompanying an image

Many images include words that explain or further clarify information in the pictures. Here are a few examples of the types of words that may accompany an image:

- ✔ **Keys (legends):** Keys and legends include symbols that appear in the image along with words that explain what each symbol means. For example, in the floor plans for the ground level of a baseball stadium, you may see several tiny hamburger icons. The key for this diagram may explain that the tiny hamburgers represent concession stands.

- ✔ **Captions:** A caption is a word, phrase, or sentence located over, under, or beside an image. The caption usually explains what the image shows overall.

- ✔ **Labels:** Labels are words or phrases that identify a specific detail in a diagram, such as an individual piece of a machine. Often a line or arrow extends directly from the label to the part of the diagram it identifies.

- ✔ **Directional cues:** Many diagrams, maps, and other images contain directional cues, which indicate the orientation of buildings, streets, and so on. For example, maps often include a compass rose, which shows observers which direction they need to turn to face north, south, east, or west.

Words that accompany an image are just as important as the picture they describe. As you study an image during the observation and memory portion of the written test, pay attention to any and all words that appear with the image. A certain symbol, such as one used to represent sprinkler heads, may represent one sprinkler head or a hundred sprinkler heads. Knowing the difference has a large impact on how well you observe and remember the information in the image. In addition, you never know what the questions may ask you to recall. If a legend or key is part of a diagram, it's fair game for questions.

Reading and recalling written information

Images aren't the only type of material you may find on the observation and memory portion of the written firefighter exam. Some exams also require candidates to read passages and answer questions about them from memory. Reading passages are short blocks of text that may range from a paragraph or two to several pages in length. (To review reading passages in detail, see Chapter 4.)

Like the diagrams and images, the reading passages in this portion of the test are often in a separate booklet from the test questions, or you may have to read them on a computer. Departments will give you a set amount of time to read and study the passages. During this time, you're not allowed to take notes or otherwise record the information that you read. After the study session, you may have some time to take notes and recall as much as you can about what you read.

You can't review the questions before you read, so identifying the most important information in the passage is a bit more difficult. You can, however, ask yourself some important questions to help you recall the information later:

- ✔ **Who?** Identify the people (victims, rescuers, witnesses) and organizations (fire departments, ambulance units, and so on).

- ✔ **What?** Identify the event/effect (the result of a cause).

- ✔ **When?** Identify the time and date.

- ✔ **Where?** Identify the location.

- ✔ **Why/how?** Identify the cause (the reason the event/effect occurred).

Don't try to memorize the entire passage. Focus on the most important details and try to make connections between these details and your prior knowledge as you read. This strategy helps you remember the information when you start to answer the questions.

Another good idea is to figure out the main idea of the passage as you read. The *main idea* is what it's all about — it describes the central message of the passage. All the supporting details in passage relate to each other in some way to reveal the main idea.

As you read, try to summarize each paragraph into a few words. When you finish reading, think about the connections between your brief summaries; the common thread among them all is the main idea.

Developing Great Observational Skills

Some people are naturally observant. They notice everything from your new haircut to the loose thread on your shirt. Nothing gets by them. For others, good observational skills take some work. Improving these skills requires practice and discipline. If you were born with hawk eyes and an elephant's exceptional memory, congratulations! The observation and memory portion of the firefighter test will probably be a breeze for you. If not, read on for tips on how to become a better observer.

Covering space: How to observe using a pattern

If you've ever read a crime novel or watched a forensic investigation show, you've probably heard the characters talk about *walking the grid*. They square off a crime scene and methodically walk back and forth, moving from west to east, east to west, and back again until they've covered the whole square. Then they do the same thing again, this time moving north to south, south to north, and back again. Walking the grid allows them to catch every detail in every inch of the crime scene.

You can use a similar method when you look at diagrams or images on the observation and memory section of the firefighter exam. Develop a pattern that works for you, and use it the same way each and every time you observe an image. (Eventually, you can use the same technique when you become a firefighter. Each time you approach a new emergency, you'll have to conduct a *size-up* of the scene, which is a mental assessment of the situation. You'll only have a few seconds to do this, but it's an important step. Remember to look past the main event — the fire, the car accident — and take note of the sideshows — the building construction, the leaking fluids.)

Try the following steps when you study an image on the exam:

1. **See the big picture.**

   Look at the picture as a whole to determine what you're seeing. Is it a fire scene? A car accident? A chemical spill? Look for details that immediately jump out at you. Also notice whether the image has a key or legend that identifies any unfamiliar symbols.

2. **Choose a pattern.**

   Which pattern you use doesn't matter, as long as it works for you. Your pattern may move left to right, top to bottom, or in a spiral, from the outermost region to the innermost region.

3. Scan the picture.

Using your pattern, scan the entire image. For example, begin in the upper left corner of the diagram or image and scan left to right. When you reach the right side, adjust your gaze slightly lower on the diagram or image and scan back to the left. Repeat this process until you've scanned the entire image.

4. Catch the details.

As you complete your scan, look for important information: people, layout, hazards, and other specific details. (For info on these details, see the earlier section "Observing diagrams and other images.") Also remember to look for any words that may accompany the diagram or image, such as keys or legends, captions, directional cues, and labels (see "Reading the words accompanying an image").

5. Return to the big picture.

After you've absorbed all the minute details of the image, consider the picture as a whole once again. Think about how all the little details relate to the big picture.

Some diagrams may include lengthy lists of words or terms. Memorizing long lists in a short amount of time may seem like a daunting task. For this reason, you should study the list in a methodical fashion instead of jumping chaotically around the page. Not only does a systematic approach help you avoid missing important information, but it also helps you remember more information when it's time to answer questions. Remember that pattern you established for observing images? Continue to use it when studying lists that accompany diagrams.

For example, look at Figure 6-1, which shows a diagram of a self-contained breathing apparatus (also known as an SCBA or air pack). Each piece of the SCBA in the diagram is labeled with a number, which corresponds to the numbered list in the diagram. Consider studying the diagram by looking at each piece in numerical order. Another method is to study the diagram from left to right, matching each piece of the SCBA with its name in the list as you go.

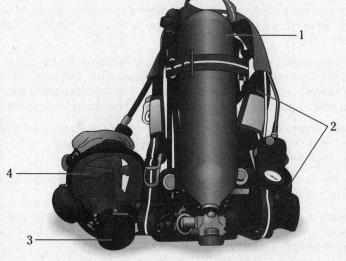

Figure 6-1:
A diagram of the parts of a self-contained breathing apparatus, or SCBA.

1. Air cylinder assembly

2. Backpack assembly

3. Regulator assembly

4. Facepiece assembly

Covering topics: How to observe using memory devices

Mnemonic devices are tricks that people use to remember things. If you recall your science classes from school, you may remember the sentence "King Philip came over for ginger snaps." This strange little sentence helps many people remember the order in which scientists classify living things: *k*ingdom, *p*hylum, *c*lass, *o*rder, *f*amily, *g*enus, *s*pecies. Notice how the first letter or letter combination in each word of the sentence matches the first letter or letter combination in each classification level. Science class isn't the only place where mnemonic devices come in handy, however; firefighters use them, too.

Take a look at this odd phrase:

COAL WAS WEALTH

This may not mean much to you now, but firefighters often use this mnemonic device to recall 13 important factors when they size up an emergency situation. Read the following list to see why they put so much stock in this phrase.

- **Construction:** Construction refers to the materials used to build a structure. Knowing the type of materials, such as wood or concrete, used in the construction of a building can help firefighters determine how and where a fire may spread and the best way to attack it.

- **Occupancy:** Occupancy refers to the intended use of the building. Is the building primarily commercial (related to business), residential (related to living), or mixed?

- **Area:** Area refers to the size of the fire scene. By determining the size of the structure or space involved, firefighters can determine how big the fire may grow.

- **Life:** Life refers to living beings who may be in danger. Though life is the fourth item on this list, it's usually firefighters' first thought when they approach an emergency situation. Protecting life is their primary concern.

- **Weather:** Weather, as you may have guessed, refers to weather conditions. On a hot, windy day, a structure fire has the potential to spread to nearby homes or businesses. On a cold day, water used to fight the fire could freeze on roadways and create slippery conditions for drivers.

- **Apparatus and equipment:** *Apparatus and equipment* refers to the emergency units that respond to the fire. Examples include fire engines, ladder trucks, tanker trucks, and so on. Also lumped in this category is manpower. Firefighters should know what equipment is on scene and available for their use and how many firefighters can assist.

- **Street conditions:** Street conditions are circumstances at the street level that firefighters must consider, such as the accessibility of fire hydrants, the placement of utility poles, the position of fire apparatus, traffic, and so on.

- **Water:** Water is the firefighters' water supply. Can they attach to a hydrant? Do they need a tanker truck or a portable water tank?

- **Exposures:** Exposures are anything the fire could endanger if it spreads. Some examples of exposures include nearby buildings or equipment and even separate rooms or floors within the same structure.

- **Auxiliary appliances:** Auxiliary appliances are devices that could assist firefighters in stopping a fire, such as a standpipe system (which is like a building's very own system of fire hydrants), a sprinkler system, or fire extinguishers.

- **Location:** Location is the position of the fire. Where is the fire? Firefighters need to know the fire's location so they can decide how to attack it. The fire's location also helps them determine whether and how the fire may spread.

✔ **Time:** Time is when the fire is occurring. Time is important when determining the potential threat to human lives. For example, during the day, the threat to human life during a fire in a department store is much greater than in the middle of the night.

✔ **Height:** Height refers to how tall the building stands. This is important when determining which fire apparatus is necessary. For example, a fire on an upper level of a tall apartment building may require a ladder truck. The height of the building is also important when determining how to rescue people from a burning building.

If you encounter an image of an emergency scene on the observation and memory portion of the written exam, consider using the COAL WAS WEALTH device during your observation (or if you want to rearrange the letters, you can try WALLACE WAS HOT). These 13 factors are important enough to consider during an actual fire, so you can expect to see a question or two about them on the test.

Shorter memory devices for firefighters include IDEAL (identify arriving units, describe what you see, explain what you intend to do, assume command, let incoming units know what you want them to do or where you want them to go); ENAMES (environment, number of patients, additional resources, mechanism of injury/illness [MOI], extrication, special consideration); and BELOW (building, extent, location, occupancy, water supply). As you can see, each one is slightly different, but COAL WAS WEALTH essentially captures everything you should notice.

Handling Questions Involving Recall

At some point on the observation and memory part of the written firefighter exam, you stop observing and concentrate on remembering. If you're allowed to take notes at end of the study period, jot down whatever you remember about what you saw or read. If you're not permitted to take notes, continue to think about the details of what you saw or read to maintain your focus. When you're given permission to do so, begin answering the questions based only on what you remember. In the following sections, we give you some advice for answering questions about both visual and written material.

Answering questions about visual material

Questions on the observation and memory section of the firefighter exam can — and will — ask about *anything* in the image. Of particular importance are people, hazardous conditions, layout or orientation, and special details such as obstacles or doors and windows. Also important are any words that accompany the image, such as a key or legend, directional cues, captions, or labels. In addition, remember the mnemonic device COAL WAS WEALTH to recall 13 critical factors that firefighters use to size up a fire (see the preceding section for info on what the letters stand for).

When answering questions about visual material, try to visualize the image — that is, map out the image in your mind. If you initially used a pattern to observe the image (see the section titled "Covering space: How to observe using a pattern"), use it again to recall the image and all its details. Work through the image in your mind — left to right, top to bottom, outer region to inner region — just as you did when you tried to absorb the details the first time. As soon as you have a clear picture in your head, read the questions and choose the best answers based on what you recall.

Carefully read the questions one at a time. Think about what each question asks. Then search your mental picture to find the answer.

Answering questions about written material

The observation and memory portion of the written firefighter exam may include reading passages or other written materials (for example, a sign with a lot of text). Questions about written material can — and will — ask about *anything* you read. When answering these questions, keep significant details such as people, events or effects (what actually happened), times, places, and causes (the reasons an event or effect occurred) in mind. Before you start answering questions about a reading passage or other written material, ask yourself these questions, and try to recall the answer to each one:

- ✔ Who?
- ✔ What?
- ✔ When?
- ✔ Where?
- ✔ Why/how?

The answers to these questions will point to key details in the passage and help you recall the main idea. After you make a mental note of the key details and the main idea, carefully read the questions one at a time. Think about what each question asks. Then search your mental notes to find the best possible answer.

Practice Observation and Memory Questions

The following practice exercises include images or written materials followed by question sets designed to help you practice your observation and memory skills. Here's how to use them:

- ✔ Give yourself 5 minutes to study the image or read the passage. To practice your observational skills, we suggest you scan images in a methodical fashion, following the same pattern for each one. For reading passages, ask yourself questions as you read and determine the main idea.

- ✔ At the end of 5 minutes, turn the page or cover up the image or passage and answer the questions about the image or passage. Read each question carefully and choose the best answer.

- ✔ DO NOT return to the image or passage when you're answering the questions. You must answer the questions based only on what you can recall.

For all questions, choose the answer that *most correctly* answers the question.

Practice exercise one

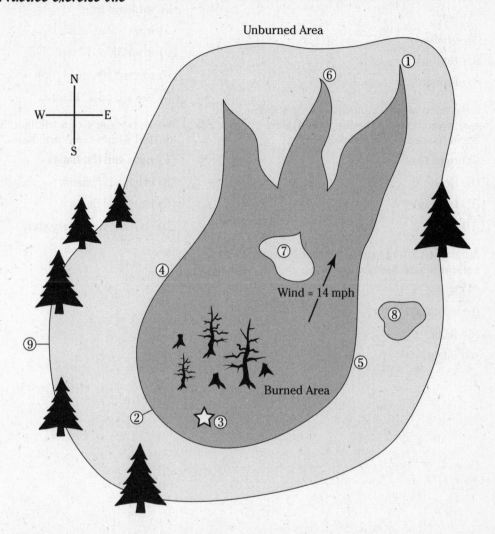

1. **Head:** The fastest-burning portion of a wildland fire that often causes the most destruction; wind usually determines the direction in which the head will burn

2. **Heel:** The typically slower-burning portion of a wildland fire opposite the head

3. **Origin:** The point at which a wildland fire began

4. **Left flank:** The left side of a wildland fire that runs about parallel to the head; it has the potential to turn into a new head if the wind changes direction

5. **Right flank:** The right side of a wildland fire that runs about parallel to the head; it has the potential to turn into a new head if the wind changes direction

6. **Finger:** A narrow strip of fire that extends from the main wildland fire; has the potential to turn into a new head if the wind changes direction

7. **Island:** An unburned area inside the already burned region of a wildland fire that has managed to avoid fire damage

8. **Spot fire:** A small fire caused by sparks or embers that land outside a wildland fire, with the potential to grow into a separate wildland fire

9. **Perimeter:** The boundary surrounding the outer edge of a wildland fire

1. The spot fire is located closest to the

    (A) heel.

    (B) origin.

    (C) right flank.

    (D) island.

2. If the wind began to blow from the south-east, which part of the fire would likely begin to spread more rapidly?

    (A) right flank

    (B) heel

    (C) left flank

    (D) head

3. A narrow strip of fire that extends from the main wildland fire is a(n)

    (A) island.

    (B) spot fire.

    (C) flank.

    (D) finger.

4. What are the wind direction and speed at the wildland fire?

    (A) from SW at 14 mph

    (B) from NE at 14 mph

    (C) toward NW at 14 mph

    (D) toward SE at 14 mph

5. Which two parts of a wildland fire are located within the burned area?

    (A) right and left flanks

    (B) origin and island

    (C) head and heel

    (D) spot fire and perimeter

Practice exercise two

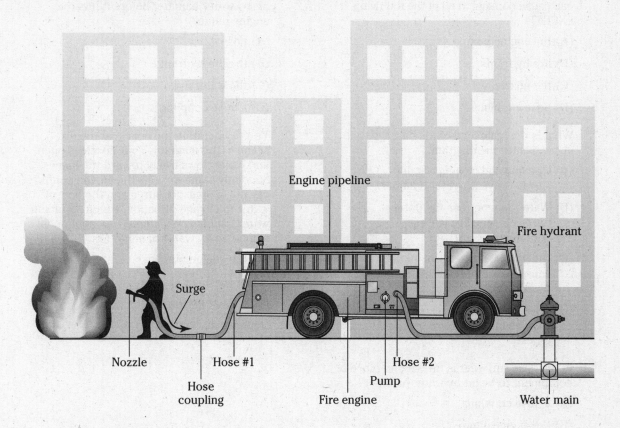

Water Hammer

Imagine you are at a fire scene. You stand at the nozzle, spraying water on a fire. Suddenly, a man approaches the scene with a sledgehammer and bashes the hose coupling between two lengths of hose. He strikes your hose, the pump on your fire engine, and even the hydrant that supplies your water. Fortunately, this is an unlikely scenario; however, water hammer, like the man and his sledgehammer, can cause a lot of damage to your firefighting equipment.

What is water hammer? Water hammer occurs when a flow of water through a pipeline system suddenly stops or changes direction. This can cause a pressure surge, or wave, within the pipes, which can result in serious damage. Water hammer can cause pipes to knock, vibrate, or even rupture.

On a fire scene, opening or closing a hose nozzle too quickly can result in water hammer. For example, if you abruptly close the hose nozzle, you'll create a pressure surge within the hose. This surge can travel backward through your water supply line. It can hammer on your hose couplings and hose, pound the pipes within your fire engine, wallop the fire engine's pump, and hit the hose that connects your engine to the hydrant. The surge will continue, eventually striking both the hydrant and the water main that feeds the hydrant. Therefore, you should always remember to open and close hose nozzles slowly to avoid water hammer.

6. According to the passage, water hammer can cause damage to all of the following EXCEPT

    (A) the engine pump.

    (B) fire hydrants.

    (C) the nozzle.

    (D) hose couplings.

7. What is the main idea of the passage that accompanies the diagram?

    (A) Opening and closing nozzles slowly prevents water hammer.

    (B) Water hammer has the potential to damage firefighting equipment.

    (C) Quickly closing a hose nozzle causes a pressure surge in the hose.

    (D) A water hammer is a special sledgehammer for use on pipes.

8. In the diagram, what is the second piece of equipment to be hit by water hammer?

    (A) a hose coupling

    (B) the engine pump

    (C) hose #1

    (D) the engine pipelines

9. In the diagram, which piece of equipment is hit by water hammer before it hits the engine pump?

    (A) hose #2

    (B) the fire hydrant

    (C) the water main

    (D) a hose coupling

10. You're operating the nozzle at the fire scene in the diagram. Your nozzle is open, and water flows freely toward the flames. Suddenly someone kills the engine pump, causing a pressure surge and the flow of water to change direction, which results in water hammer. Which piece of equipment will be hit by water hammer first?

    (A) the engine pipelines

    (B) hose #1

    (C) the fire hydrant

    (D) hose #2

Practice exercise three

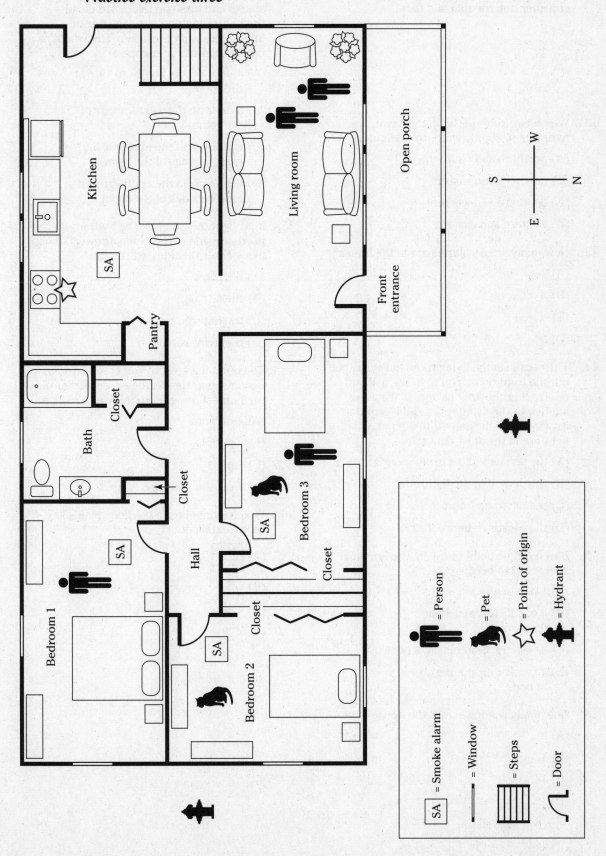

11. How many lives are in danger if you consider both people and pets?

    (A) 2

    (B) 4

    (C) 6

    (D) 7

12. Which two sides of the home have hydrants to supply water to firefighters?

    (A) northern and southern

    (B) northern and eastern

    (C) southern and western

    (D) western and eastern

13. How many smoke alarms are in the house?

    (A) 2

    (B) 3

    (C) 4

    (D) 6

14. The people in the living room have escaped out the front door. You're in the hall and realize that the fire has spread from the kitchen to the living room and is working its way down the hall. At this point, which lives are in the most danger?

    (A) the person and pet in bedroom 3

    (B) the person in the bathroom

    (C) the pet in bedroom 2

    (D) the person in bedroom 1

15. Based on the point of origin, the fire most likely started because

    (A) a pan of grease caught fire.

    (B) a candle torched some curtains.

    (C) an electric heater malfunctioned.

    (D) a smoker dropped a cigarette in bed.

16. How many windows does the house have?

    (A) 9

    (B) 12

    (C) 14

    (D) 15

17. To protect the woman in bedroom 1 from smoke and fire, you tell her to close the bedroom door, assuring her that firefighters will rescue her. The woman's remaining ways to escape are

    (A) a door on the southern side of the room.

    (B) a door on the western side of the room.

    (C) windows on the northern and eastern sides of the room.

    (D) windows on the southern and eastern sides of the room.

18. If firefighters attach to the hydrant on the northern side of the home, they will most likely enter the house through

    (A) bedroom 2.

    (B) the kitchen.

    (C) the bathroom.

    (D) the living room.

19. To conduct a search, you enter through a window near the northeastern corner of the home. From this room, you'll rescue

    (A) 1 person.

    (B) 2 people.

    (C) 1 pet.

    (D) 1 person and 1 pet.

20. Which symbol from the floor plan's key represents a door?

    (A)

    (B)

    (C) ———

    (D) ☆

Practice exercise four

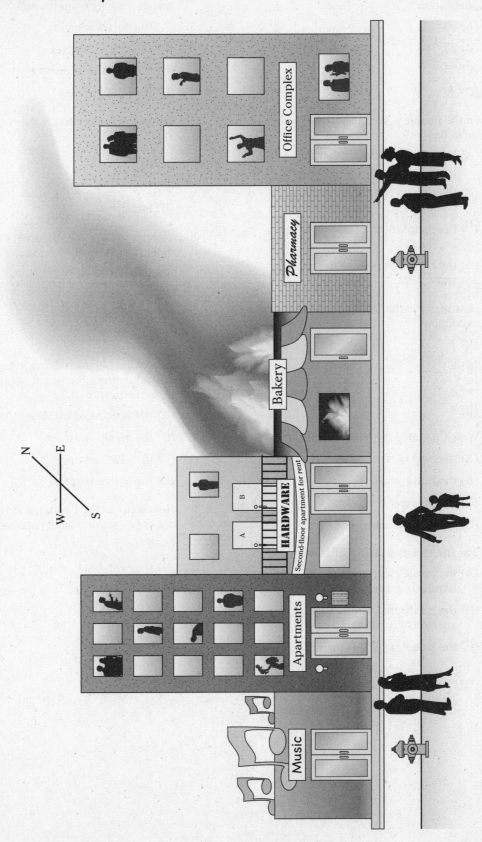

21. How many people are visible in the illustration?

    (A) 19

    (B) 23

    (C) 25

    (D) 30

22. Of the people you can see, who is in the most danger?

    (A) the person above the hardware store

    (B) the person entering the office complex

    (C) the people in the apartment building

    (D) the people in front of the hardware store

23. How many of the buildings are residential occupancy?

    (A) 1

    (B) 2

    (C) 3

    (D) 4

24. Which building is constructed of brick?

    (A) the bakery

    (B) the music store

    (C) the pharmacy

    (D) the office complex

25. The fire is in the building between

    (A) the music store and the hardware store.

    (B) the hardware store and the apartment building.

    (C) the bakery and the office complex.

    (D) the hardware store and the pharmacy.

26. Which building has a fire hydrant directly across from its front doors?

    (A) the hardware store

    (B) the office complex

    (C) the apartment complex

    (D) the music store

27. From which direction is the wind blowing?

    (A) west

    (B) east

    (C) south

    (D) north

28. Which building is in the least amount of danger from the fire?

    (A) the hardware store

    (B) the music store

    (C) the pharmacy

    (D) the office complex

29. If the wind begins to blow from the opposite direction, which building would be in the most danger?

    (A) the apartment building

    (B) the music store

    (C) the office complex

    (D) the hardware store

30. How many of the buildings in the picture are only commercial occupancy?

    (A) 2

    (B) 4

    (C) 5

    (D) 6

Answers and Explanations

Use this answer key to score the practice observation and memory questions in this chapter. The answer explanations give you a little more insight on how to find the right answers. Remember, the more you practice your observational and memory skills, the more you'll improve these skills.

1. **C.** The spot fire is located at the far right of the illustration, which is close to the right flank of the wildland fire, so Choice (C) is correct. The heel, origin, and island are all located to the left of the right flank.

2. **C.** The wind is currently blowing from the southwest to the northeast, which has caused the right flank to become the head of the fire. If the wind were to blow from the southeast to the northwest, it would likely cause the left flank of the fire to spread more rapidly. It could even cause the left flank to turn into a new head, so Choice (C) is correct.

3. **D.** The list that accompanies the diagram defines a finger as a narrow strip of fire that extends from the main wildland fire, so Choice (D) is correct.

4. **A.** The arrow indicates wind direction and speed, and the compass rose serves as a directional cue. The arrow extends from the southwest to the northeast and indicates a wind speed of 14 mph. From these details, you can tell that the wind is blowing from the southwest at 14 mph, so Choice (A) is correct.

5. **B.** Both the origin and the island are located within the region identified as the burned area, so the right answer is Choice (B). The left and right flanks create the edges of the burned area, so Choice (A) is incorrect. Choice (C) is incorrect because the head and heel create the rear and front edges of the burned area. The spot fire and the perimeter are outside the burned area, so Choice (D) is also incorrect.

6. **C.** The third paragraph states that water hammer can damage the engine pump, the fire hydrant, and the hose coupling. It mentions that opening or closing the nozzle too quickly can cause water hammer, but it doesn't say whether the nozzle is or isn't damaged, so Choice (C) is correct.

7. **B.** Short summaries of each paragraph can help you determine the main idea. The first paragraph compares water hammer to a sledgehammer's hitting equipment. The second describes water hammer and the damage it can cause. The third explains how water hammer affects firefighting equipment. These details suggest the main idea that water hammer causes damage to firefighting equipment, so Choice (B) is correct.

8. **C.** If you think about the diagram from left to right, you'll recall that the pressure surge begins behind the hose nozzle on the left side of the diagram. It then travels right, where water hammer first hits the hose coupling and then hits hose #1. Choice (C) is correct.

9. **D.** Visualize the diagram in a left-to-right pattern. The first piece of equipment hit by water hammer is the hose coupling, which means Choice (D) has to be correct. If you continue visualizing the image from left to right, you'll note that hose #2, the fire hydrant, and the water main all experience water hammer after the engine pump, not before it.

10. **D.** Visualize the diagram again, but consider the scenario in the question. In the scenario, the water starts out moving in the same direction that it was moving in the original diagram: left to right. However, the point of the surge — when the direction of the water changed — has moved from behind the hose nozzle to the engine pump. In this case, the first piece of equipment to experience water hammer will be hose #2, so Choice (D) is the correct answer.

11. **C.** The COAL WAS WEALTH memory device should remind you that life is a critical factor to observe at a fire scene. In this case, the lives at stake include both people and pets. The diagram shows four people and two pets, for a total of six lives, so Choice (C) is correct.

12. **B.** Remember to look for directional cues in diagrams. The compass rose below the floor plan shows north at the bottom of the page, south at the top, west on the right, and east on the left. Hydrants appear at the bottom and the left side of the floor plan, or the northern and eastern sides of the home, so Choice (B) is correct.

13. **C.** Remember to check diagrams for keys or legends. In this case, the key shows smoke alarms as a box surrounding the letters SA. Four of these symbols appear in the floor plan: one in the kitchen and one in each of the three bedrooms, so Choice (C) is correct.

14. **A.** Visualize the diagram from right to left. The fire began in the kitchen and has progressed into the hall, so it's moving right to left. The first room the fire will reach is the bathroom, which is empty, so Choice (B) is incorrect. The second room it will reach is bedroom 3. The person and pet in bedroom 3 are in the most danger, so Choice (A) is correct.

15. **A.** Recall the key from the diagram. The point of origin is represented by a star. The star appears on the stove in the kitchen. This suggests that the fire started on the stove. It seems likely, then, that a pan of grease caught fire, so Choice (A) is correct.

16. **B.** One of the details you should note during your observation of a fire scene is layout, which not includes only rooms but also windows and doors. Bedrooms 1 and 2 and the kitchen each have two windows; bedroom 3 and the bathroom each have one window; and the living room has four windows. That means the house has 12 windows, so Choice (B) is correct.

17. **D.** Visualize the floor plan of the home. Bedroom 1 is in the top left, or southeastern, corner of the home. It has one door. If the woman closes the door to this room, she has two other means of escape: a window on the eastern side of the home or a window on the southern side of the home. Choice (D) is correct.

18. **D.** The COAL WAS WEALTH memory device should remind you to look for a water supply during your observation. The hydrant on the northern side of the home is near the front entrance, which enters into the living room. This is likely the fastest route for firefighters to reach the fire, so Choice (D) is correct.

19. **C.** Visualizing the layout from left to right, you should recall that both the east-facing and north-facing windows are near the northeastern corner of the home and would allow access to bedroom 2. Bedroom 2 shows one pet symbol, so Choice (C) is correct.

20. **B.** If you remember the key that accompanies the diagram, you'll recall that the symbol for a door looks like a slanted line with a hook on it, which describes the image in Choice (B). Choice (A) shows the symbol for steps, Choice (C) shows the symbol for a window, and Choice (D) shows the symbol for the point of origin.

21. **B.** The COAL WAS WEALTH memory device should help you remember that life is one of 13 critical factors to consider during your observation of a fire scene. In the illustration, eight people are in the apartment building, one is above the hardware store, seven are in the office complex, and seven are outside, which makes 23 people. Choice (B) is correct.

22. **A.** COAL WAS WEALTH should help you recall that exposures are a critical factor in fire-scene observations. In this case, the pharmacy and the hardware store with the apartments above it are exposed to the fire at the bakery. This places the person in the apartment above the hardware store in a lot of danger, so Choice (A) is correct.

23. **B.** Occupancy is a factor that the COAL WAS WEALTH memory device can help you identify during your observation. The music store, bakery, pharmacy, and office complex are commercial. The apartment building is residential. The hardware store includes two upstairs apartments, so it is both commercial and residential and should be counted when determining residential occupancies. Two of the buildings are residential, so Choice (B) is correct.

24. **C.** If you use the COAL WAS WEALTH memory device, you'll recall that construction is one factor to consider during your fire-scene observation. Only the pharmacy appears to be constructed of brick. Choice (C) is correct.

25. **D.** Location is one of 13 factors to remember with the COAL WAS WEALTH memory device. Recall that the location of this fire is the bakery. Exposures are also a factor in this memory device. The exposure to left of the bakery is the hardware store. The exposure to the right is the pharmacy. Therefore, Choice (D) is correct.

26. **D.** Using COAL WAS WEALTH, you should recall that water is one of the critical factors. In your observation, you should've noted two fire hydrants: one in front of the music store and another in front of the pharmacy. Because the pharmacy is not an answer choice, the music store, Choice (D), is correct.

27. **A.** The COAL WAS WEALTH memory device should help you recall that weather is a critical factor in your observation. In the diagram, you should've noticed that the smoke and flames are being pushed toward the east, which suggests that the wind is blowing from the west. Therefore, Choice (A) is correct.

28. **B.** COAL WAS WEALTH comes in very handy here. Consider the location of the fire (the bakery); the exposures (the hardware store and the pharmacy), and the weather (wind from the west is pushing smoke and flames to the east, toward the office complex). The music store is three buildings away from the bakery, in the opposite direction of the smoke and flames, so Choice (B) is correct.

29. **D.** Using COAL WAS WEALTH, consider weather and exposures. If the wind were to blow in the opposite direction — that is, from the east — it would push the flames west, toward the hardware store. The hardware store is also an exposure, putting it in immediate danger, so Choice (D) is correct.

30. **B.** Again, using COAL WAS WEALTH, you should recall that occupancy is a critical factor. The buildings that are only commercial occupancy are the music store, pharmacy, office complex, and bakery, so Choice (B) is correct.

Chapter 7

Sizing Up Your Spatial Orientation Skills

....

....

During your lifetime, you've likely ridden with one of two types of drivers: those who have a natural ability to navigate from one place to another with ease (even in unfamiliar territories) and those who manage to get lost in their own driveways. It's simply a fact of life that some people are better at understanding spatial orientation than others. How would you classify yourself — natural navigator or mixed-up map reader?

Firefighters must have exceptional spatial orientation skills. In addition to finding the fastest route to an emergency, firefighters also must wind their way through unfamiliar structures — often with limited or no visibility — all while keeping in mind where they are, where they've been, where they're going, and most important, how to get out. For these reasons, the written exam that firefighters have to take as part of the hiring process often includes questions about spatial orientation.

In this chapter, we help you sharpen your spatial orientation skills and show you how to answer questions about spatial orientation on the written exam. We also provide sample maps, floor plans, and questions that you can use to practice these skills.

Getting from Place to Place with Spatial Orientation

We're the first to admit that global positioning system (GPS) devices can be lifesavers when you're driving to an unfamiliar place. These devices receive information about your exact location on Earth from satellites in space and use it to direct you where to go. Unfortunately, as a firefighter, you'll lack the luxury of a GPS device to help you navigate the hallways of apartment buildings or the corridors of hospitals. Instead, you need to develop excellent spatial orientation skills.

Having good spatial orientation skills means having the ability to take a two-dimensional image, such as the map of a city, and use it to create a three-dimensional image in your mind. In other words, after studying the map, you have to be able to picture yourself driving down Third Avenue. You have to see the hospital on your right and the parking garage on your left and know that the next intersection, Pine Street, is a one-way street to the right.

Spatial orientation skills are important to firefighters for several reasons:

> ✔ **Firefighters are constantly entering new surroundings and moving around in unfamiliar spaces.** Therefore, they need to keep track of where they came from, their present location, and their destination. Otherwise, they can get lost and end up in danger.

✔ **Firefighters often work in conditions with very low visibility.** Smoke and flames make it difficult for firefighters to see exactly where they are, which can make it impossible to know where to go next.

✔ **Firefighters are responsible for protecting life.** They need to figure out the fastest route to the fire, to victims in need of rescue, and to exits that will take everyone to safety.

Answering Questions about Maps and Floor Plans

Many firefighter exams include questions that test your spatial orientation skills. Questions about spatial orientation assess your ability to interpret images such as maps or floor plans and answer questions based on your interpretations. Sometimes they include text that further describes the scene and provides additional information that you can use when answering questions.

Spatial orientation questions test your natural ability to visualize yourself in a certain location or amid certain surroundings. For example, map questions may ask you to figure out the most direct route from one location to another, taking into consideration traffic laws (such as one-way streets) or obstacles (such as roadblocks). Other map questions may present sets of directions and ask where you'll end up or which direction you'll be moving if you follow them. Questions about floor plans may ask about doors, windows, rooms, and fire escapes or the locations of extinguishers, sprinklers, fire apparatus, victims, and the fire. You may have to determine the best location to perform a ladder rescue or the best way to exit a building if the fire creates an obstruction.

Unlike the observation and memory questions on the written exam (see Chapter 6), the spatial orientation questions typically do not require memorization. You'll likely be able to look at the images while you answer the questions and take notes or draw on the images, but you should check with test administrators to make sure.

In the following sections, we outline ways to improve your chances of correctly answering questions about spatial orientation.

Noting the details

When answering spatial orientation questions about a map or a floor plan, take a few minutes to study the image carefully and note the details. First and foremost, determine what the image is — for example, a map of a city, the floor plan of a business, or the layout of a town. Read any text in the image, because it may provide important information such as the names of streets or buildings. Also look for legends, directional cues, and specific floor plan details:

✔ **Legend:** When studying a map, a floor plan, or another image, look for a legend. A *legend* — sometimes called a *key* — includes symbols that appear in the map or floor plan along with words that define what each symbol means. For example, a legend may explain that the tiny stars on a map represent fire hydrant locations.

✔ **Direction:** Many maps and floor plans include directional cues. One directional cue is a compass rose, which helps you identify the north, south, east, and west directions in an image. Sometimes the compass rose is a single arrow pointing north.

Other directional cues to look for on maps are arrows indicating the legal directions of streets — that is, one-way streets, which allow travel in only one direction, and two-way streets, which allow travel in both directions.

Figure 7-1 shows an example of a map similar to the ones you may see on the spatial orientation portion of the written firefighter exam. Notice the compass rose that indicates north, south, east, and west, and the arrows that indicate the legal direction of streets.

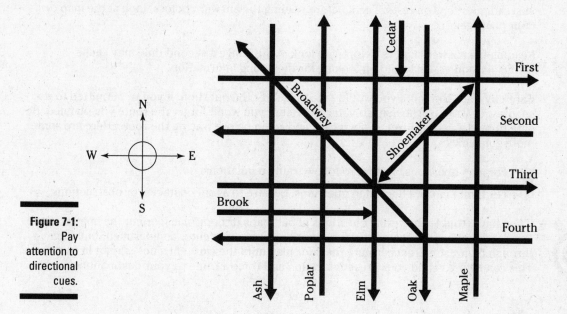

Figure 7-1:
Pay attention to directional cues.

✔ **Floor plan details:** Some details, such as the location of doors, windows, or rooms in a home or the number of stories in a hotel, are specific to floor plans. In addition, not all floor plans are the same; the symbol for a fire extinguisher in one floor plan may look nothing like the symbol for a fire extinguisher in another floor plan.

On the spatial orientation portion of the written exam, you may see a floor plan similar to the one in Figure 7-2. Notice in the legend for this floor plan that B stands for *booth,* T stands for *table,* and a door symbol represents an exit. Also notice the compass rose, a single arrow pointing north.

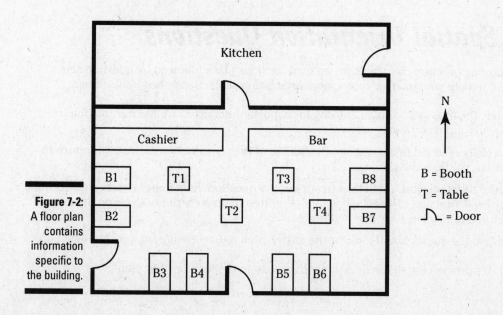

Figure 7-2:
A floor plan contains information specific to the building.

Reading the question and tracing the route

After studying the map or floor plan, carefully read each question and determine exactly what it asks. This may sound like common sense, but you'd be surprised how many people misread questions on tests. Then, before reading the answer choices, look at the map or floor plan again.

Reading the answer choices before you look at the image a second time may cause confusion, and you may end up looking for the wrong information.

Carefully trace the route you would take to answer the question. If you're permitted to do so, draw or write on the map so you can be sure you won't forget the route you planned. Be sure to mark one-way streets, obstacles, and so on before tracing the route. Here are some more guidelines:

- ✔ For map questions, be sure to follow traffic regulations.
- ✔ For both map and floor-plan questions, be sure to avoid obstacles or obstructions.

If you have trouble answering questions about maps or floor plans, orient the images in the correct direction. For example, if the question asks you to enter an apartment building through the west entrance, rotate the floor plan until the west entrance is right in front you. This can help you find your present location and trace a route to your destination.

Choosing the correct answer

After you've traced your route, read the question again and look at your planned route. Does it still make sense? If so, read the answer choices and find the one that matches the route you created. If you find a match, mark it; however, always check the remaining choices, just to make sure a better alternative doesn't exist. If none of the answer choices matches your planned route, review your work for unintentional mistakes, such as traveling the wrong direction on a one-way street or accidentally passing through an obstruction in a hallway. Repeat this process for each question.

Practice Spatial Orientation Questions

The following practice exercises include maps or floor plans followed by question sets designed to help you practice your spatial orientation skills. Here's how to use them:

- ✔ Study the map or floor plan, looking for important details as well as information from legends and directional cues.
- ✔ Carefully read the first question. DO NOT read the answer choices. Instead, return to the map or floor plan.
- ✔ Trace the route you would take to answer the question. Remember to take into account the legal direction of streets. If you're permitted to do so, write or draw on the map so you can remember your planned route.
- ✔ Reread the question and look for the answer that *most correctly* answers the question.

Repeat this process for all the questions that relate to the map or floor plan.

Practice map one

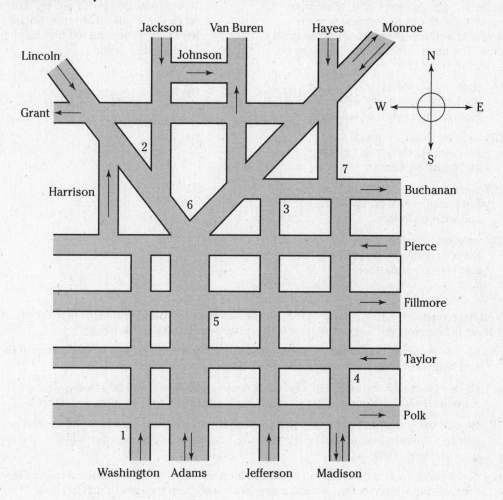

Arrows by street names indicate legal direction.

1. If you're located at point 1, the most direct route for you to take to get to point 2 is

    (A) north on Washington, west on Pierce, north on Harrison, and southeast on Lincoln.

    (B) east on Polk, north on Jefferson, west on Pierce, northeast on Monroe, west on Grant, and south on Jackson.

    (C) east on Polk, north on Adams, and northwest on Lincoln.

    (D) north on Washington, east on Fillmore, north on Adams, northeast on Monroe, west on Grant, and south on Jackson.

2. If you're located at point 3 and travel east one block, turn right and travel south three blocks, turn right and travel west two blocks, turn left and travel south one block, turn left and travel east one block, you'll be at the corner of

    (A) Polk and Madison.

    (B) Madison and Fillmore.

    (C) Adams and Taylor.

    (D) Jefferson and Polk.

3. You're driving the fire engine northeast on Monroe, approaching Grant, when you receive directions to respond to a car accident at the intersection of Adams and Polk. The most direct route for you to get to the accident is

   (A) south on Hayes, west on Buchanan, southwest on Monroe, and south on Adams.

   (B) west on Grant, south on Jackson, southeast on Lincoln, and south on Adams.

   (C) south on Hayes, east on Buchanan, south on Madison, and west on Polk.

   (D) west on Grant, south on Van Buren, southwest on Monroe, and south on Adams.

4. If you're located at point 4, facing west on Taylor, and you turn right on Madison, left on Pierce, right on Monroe, left on Grant, left on Jackson, and left on Lincoln, you'll be closest to point

   (A) 3.

   (B) 5.

   (C) 6.

   (D) 7.

5. You have responded to an alarm sent from the box at point 3, and you learn that the fire is at the corner of Harrison and Lincoln. Which is the best route to take to the scene?

   (A) Go less than one block east on Buchanan and turn north on Hayes. At the corner of Hayes and Monroe, travel southwest on Monroe. Then turn northwest on Lincoln.

   (B) Go one block east on Buchanan, one block south on Madison, and two blocks west on Pierce. Turn northeast on Monroe, then west on Grant, and finally turn southeast on Lincoln.

   (C) Go one block east on Buchanan, one block south on Madison, and two blocks west on Pierce. Continue west on Pierce through the Y intersection, go one more block, and then turn north on Harrison.

   (D) Go one block south on Jefferson and one block west on Pierce. Continue west on Pierce through the Y intersection, go one more block, and then turn north on Harrison.

Practice floor plan one

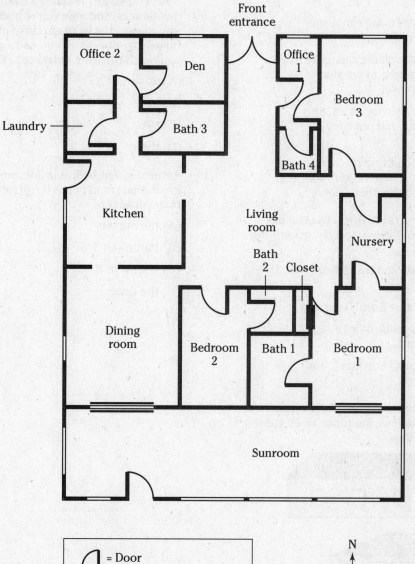

Front entrance

Office 2

Den

Laundry

Bath 3

Office 1

Bedroom 3

Bath 4

Kitchen

Living room

Nursery

Bath 2

Closet

Dining room

Bedroom 2

Bath 1

Bedroom 1

Sunroom

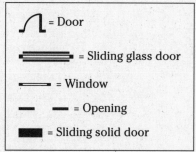

= Door

= Sliding glass door

= Window

= Opening

= Sliding solid door

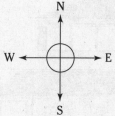

N

W ← → E

S

6. In the event of an electrical fire in office 1, the best way to evacuate the occupant of bedroom 2 is

   (A) through the living room and out the front door.

   (B) through the dining room, into the sunroom, and out the southern door.

   (C) through the living room, into bedroom 3, and out the window.

   (D) through the living room, into bedroom 1, into the sunroom, and out the southern door.

7. In the case of a dryer fire in the laundry room, those in the greatest danger are the occupants of

   (A) the kitchen and the dining room.

   (B) the den, office 2, and bathroom 3.

   (C) the living room, office 1, and bathroom 4.

   (D) the nursery, bedroom 1, and bathroom 1.

8. The illustration that most likely represents what this residence looks like when viewed from the north is

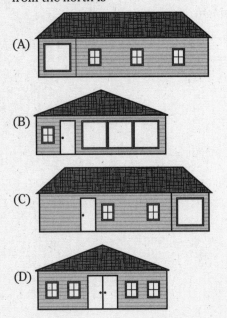

(A)

(B)

(C)

(D)

9. A fire in the kitchen has generated so much smoke that visibility in the home is near zero. You've just rescued a child and exited the nursery, and now you're making your way toward the front entrance of the home. How many doors will you encounter before you reach the front entrance?

   (A) none

   (B) one

   (C) two

   (D) three

10. Assuming that bedroom 3 is unoccupied, a fire in that room poses the greatest threat to occupants of

   (A) the nursery.

   (B) bathroom 3.

   (C) bedroom 1.

   (D) the den.

Practice map two

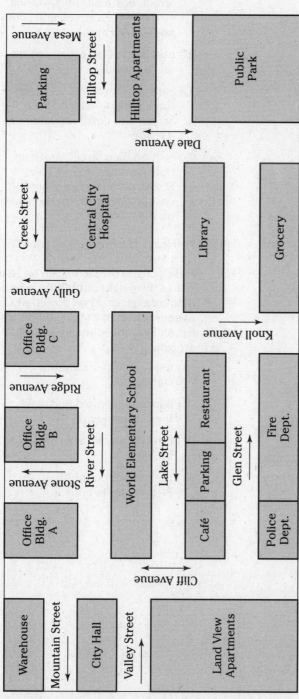

11. The fire department has been dispatched to a fire at the office building on the corner of River Street and Gully Avenue. What is the shortest legal route the engine driver can take to get there?

    (A) east on Glen Street, north on Dale Avenue, west on Lake Street, and north on Gully Avenue

    (B) east on Glen Street, north on Knoll Avenue, east on Lake Street, and north on Gully Avenue

    (C) west on Glen Street, north on Cliff Avenue, and east on River Street

    (D) east on Glen Street, north on Knoll Avenue, west on Lake Street, north on Cliff Avenue, and east on River Street

12. You meet an officer at the police station and together will patrol for illegal burning. From the police station, you drive east two blocks, north one block, west one block, north one block, west three blocks, and come to a stop facing west. What building is directly in front of you?

    (A) World Elementary School

    (B) Land View Apartments

    (C) City Hall

    (D) Central City Hospital

13. You're driving south on Ridge Avenue. You turn right on River Street, left on Cliff Avenue, left on Lake Street, and right on Knoll Avenue. Which direction are you now traveling?

    (A) north

    (B) south

    (C) east

    (D) west

14. The fire department is dispatched to a car fire in the parking garage on the corner of Dale Avenue and Hilltop Street, but road crews have the intersection at Dale Avenue and Hilltop Street blocked. What is the best route to get to the parking garage?

    (A) west on Glen Street, north on Cliff Avenue, east on Lake Street, north on Gully Avenue, east on Creek Street, and south on Dale Avenue

    (B) east on Glen Street and north on Dale Avenue

    (C) east on Glen Street, north on Knoll Avenue, east on Lake Street, and north on Dale Avenue

    (D) east on Glen Street, north on Dale Avenue, west on Lake Street, north on Gully Avenue, east on Creek Street, and south on Dale Avenue

15. You leave the fire station, traveling east on Glen Street. At Dale Avenue, you turn left, and then you turn left again on Lake Street. You make a right onto Gully Avenue, and then turn left on River Street. At Cliff Avenue you turn right, and then you turn left on Mountain Street and stop. Where are you?

    (A) between City Hall and a warehouse

    (B) between City Hall and Land View Apartments

    (C) directly across from an office building

    (D) parked in front of World Elementary School

Practice floor plan two

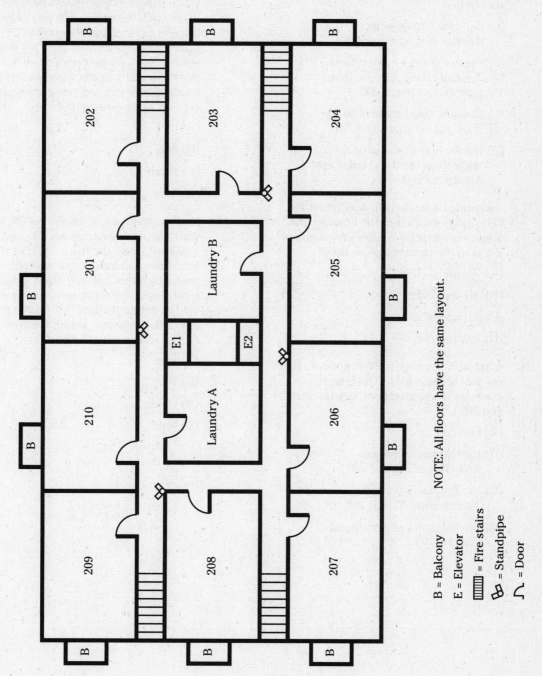

NOTE: All floors have the same layout.

B = Balcony

E = Elevator

▦ = Fire stairs

⚸ = Standpipe

⌓ = Door

16. In the case of a fire in Laundry A, firefighters should take

    (A) Elevator 1 and connect to the standpipe at Apartment 201.

    (B) the fire stairs by Apartment 209 and connect to the standpipe at Apartment 208.

    (C) Elevator 2 and connect to the standpipe at apartment 201.

    (D) the fire stairs by Apartment 207 and connect to the standpipe at Apartment 206.

17. Assuming the tenants in Apartment 202 have safely evacuated the building, the greatest danger from a fire in Apartment 202 is to the tenants in Apartments

    (A) 102 and 302.

    (B) 201 and 203.

    (C) 201 and 302.

    (D) 203 and 204.

18. A fire in Apartment 206 has spread across the hall to Laundry A. The best way to evacuate the residents of Apartments 204 and 205 is

    (A) Elevator 2.

    (B) the fire stairs between Apartments 207 and 208.

    (C) the fire stairs between Apartments 203 and 204.

    (D) the balconies of Apartments 204 and 205.

19. You arrive on the second floor via the fire stairs between Apartments 203 and 204. Visibility is near zero, but you know that there is a standpipe connection by Apartment 206. Putting your left hand against the wall, you start down the corridor. How many doors will your left hand touch before you reach the standpipe connection by Apartment 206?

    (A) one

    (B) two

    (C) three

    (D) four

20. You enter the second floor via the fire stairs between Apartments 202 and 203. You walk down the hall and make the first left. Then you make the next right. You walk down that hall and make another right. Then you make another left and exit via the fire stairs between Apartments 208 and 209. How many standpipe connections did you pass on your route?

    (A) one

    (B) two

    (C) three

    (D) four

Answers and Explanations

Use this answer key to score the practice questions in this chapter. The answer explanations give you a little more insight on how to find the right answers. How did you do? We hope these questions have given you some good practice for the spatial orientation component of the written firefighter exam.

1. **A.** Point 1 is at the corner of Washington and Polk. Point 2 is at the corner of Lincoln and Jackson. Lincoln is one-way to the southeast and Jackson is one-way to the south, so the shortest legal route to get there is to travel north on Washington to Pierce, west on Pierce to Harrison, north on Harrison to Lincoln, and southeast on Lincoln to Jackson. Choice (A) is correct.

2. **D.** Point 3 is at the corner of Jefferson and Buchanan. If you travel east one block, you'll be at the corner of Buchanan and Madison. Turning right and traveling south three blocks will put you at the corner of Madison and Taylor. Turning right and traveling west two blocks will put you at the corner of Taylor and Adams. Turning left and traveling south one block brings you to the corner of Adams and Polk. Turning left and traveling east one block puts you at the corner of Jefferson and Polk.

3. **B.** The most direct route to the car accident is to travel west on Grant, south on Jackson, southeast on Lincoln, and south on Adams. All the other answer choices would require you to travel the wrong way on one-way streets, in violation of traffic rules.

4. **C.** If you trace the route for these directions, you should arrive at the corner where Lincoln, Monroe, and Adams meet. This is point 6 on the map, located in the corner created by the Y intersection, so Choice (C) is correct. Note that the last street in this set of directions is Lincoln, and the two points closest to Lincoln are 2 and 6. Since 2 isn't an answer choice, point 6 is the best choice.

5. **C.** Choices (A) and (D) require you to break traffic laws by driving the wrong way on one-way streets. Both Choices (B) and (C) will get you to your destination, but Choice (B) is a more roundabout way of arriving there. It requires many more turns. Choice (C) is correct.

6. **B.** The most direct route to escape from the house and avoid the fire is for the occupant of bedroom 2 to go through the dining room, into the sunroom, and out the southern door. Choice (A) would require passing the fire. Choice (C) is a more difficult escape, and it requires getting closer to the fire. Choice (D) is an indirect route to the southern door.

7. **B.** The den, office 2, and bathroom 3 are very close to the location of the fire in the laundry room, so Choice (B) is correct. Occupants of the other rooms in the house all have other ways to escape without passing the fire or exiting through a window.

8. **D.** From the north, you see the front of the house. The easiest way to answer this question is to notice the number and locations of doors and windows on each side of the house. The front of the house has one set of double doors centered between four windows. Choice (D) shows the front entrance of the house.

9. **C.** If you've already exited the nursery, you'll encounter two doors before you reach the front entrance — the door to bedroom 3 and the door to office 1 — so Choice (C) is correct.

10. **A.** A fire in bedroom 3 poses the greatest threat to bathroom 4 and office 1, because they're connected to bedroom 3. However, these are not choices. Therefore, the best answer is the nursery, which is directly across the hall from bedroom 3. Choice (A) is correct.

11. **A.** Because Choices (B), (C), and (D) would require the engine driver to break traffic laws, the best route to reach the fire is to go east on Glen, north on Dale, west on Lake, and north on Gully.

12. **C.** If you trace the route for these directions, from the police station you go east two blocks to Dale. Then you go north one block to Lake and west one block to Gully. From there, you go north one block to River and west three blocks to the corner of River and Cliff. Facing west, City Hall is directly in front of you, so Choice (C) is correct.

13. **B.** If you focus on the last part of the directions, you see that the route ends on Knoll, a one-way street going south. Assuming you break no traffic laws, you should always end up going south on Knoll, regardless of how you got there. Choice (B) is correct.

14. **D.** Choices (A) and (C) would require you to travel the wrong direction on one-way streets. Choice (B) would take you through the roadblock. Choice (D) is the best answer.

15. **A.** This question includes a lot of directions, but if you look at the map carefully, you see that Mountain Street is a one-way street that connects to Cliff Avenue. No matter which route you take to get to Mountain Street, as soon as you turn onto it, you're between City Hall and a warehouse, so Choice (A) is correct.

16. **B.** Both Elevator 1 and Elevator 2 are in danger from the fire in Laundry A, so firefighters should avoid them. (In general, it's recommended that people avoid elevators during fires, because they could stop working.) This eliminates Choices (A) and (C). Both Choices (B) and (D) are safe options, but the most direct route is to take the fire stairs by Apartment 209 and connect to the standpipe by Apartment 208, which is very close to Laundry A and the location of the fire.

17. **C.** Apartment 201 is connected to Apartment 202, so it's in danger. Apartment 203 is across the hall from 202. It's in danger, too, but not as much as Apartment 201. From information in the floor plan, you know that all floors in the apartment building have the same layout. This means that Apartment 302 is directly above Apartment 202, so the fire is directly below Apartment 302. Therefore, Apartments 201 and 302 are in the most danger. Choice (C) is correct.

18. **C.** By taking the fire stairs between Apartments 203 and 204, the occupants of Apartments 204 and 205 will move away from the location of the fire and quickly escape. A rescue from the balconies is possible, but it would be more dangerous and time-consuming than exiting via the fire stairs. The other options would take the occupants closer to the fire. Choice (C) is correct.

19. **B.** Working your way down the hall, your left hand will first touch the door of Apartment 204. Next, it will touch the door of Apartment 205. Before you reach the next door, you'll find the standpipe connection by Apartment 206. You'll touch two doors, so Choice (B) is correct.

20. **C.** If you trace this route, you see that you'll first pass the standpipe at the corner of Apartment 203. Next, you'll pass the standpipe by Apartment 206. Then you'll pass the standpipe at the corner of Apartment 208. You won't pass another standpipe as you exit the fire stairs between Apartments 208 and 209, which means that you've passed three standpipe connections.

Chapter 8

Making Decisions Based on Reasoning and Judgment

....

In This Chapter

▶ Applying reason in firefighting operations and procedures

▶ Sharpening your judgment skills for interpersonal and public relations

▶ Understanding how to recognize patterns and use logic

....

Suppose an elderly woman from the neighborhood enters the firehouse and asks whether you could cut down the tree in her backyard. She says it loses too many leaves in the fall — her husband just can't keep up with them at his age. She tells you that her son volunteered to cut down the tree, but it's right next to a utility line, and she doesn't want her son to be blamed if the tree happens to fall and break the line. She pulls out her checkbook and offers to pay the fire department for this service. What should you do?

You can respond to the woman's request in a number of ways. You can tell her no; after all, it's not the fire department's responsibility to cut down unwanted trees. You can suggest that her son rake the leaves to ease the burden on her husband. You can go to her house with a fire department ax and chop down the tree immediately. Another option is to suggest that she call the utility company, which would likely send a crew to safely and efficiently take down the tree.

Any of these answers could solve the woman's problem, but from a firefighting perspective, only one option is correct. In this type of situation, it's best to be polite and use common sense. If the tree endangers a utility line, the woman should ask the utility company for help.

As a firefighter, you'll have to use sound reasoning and good judgment on a daily basis to make decisions in situations like this. You'll often have to make these decisions quickly and in potentially hazardous or stressful conditions. Making reasonable decisions and showing good judgment requires a combination of information you already know, common sense, and ethics.

Questions about reasoning and judgment appear on written firefighter exams because they test your ability to make sound decisions in complicated situations. In this chapter, we tell you how to identify and correctly answer judgment and reasoning questions related to firefighter operations, interpersonal relations, public relations, and following procedures, and we explain how to use logical reasoning.

Applying Reasoning and Judgment to Firefighting

Firefighters need to be able to think on their feet. They have to weigh pros and cons in mere seconds and immediately take action. Many times, lives depend on their ability to think quickly and keep a level head. You must try to put personal opinions aside, get a clear picture of the problem, and figure out the best solution. You may have a variety of options from which to choose, and you may need to think ahead and visualize the results of each option. You'll likely worry about positive and negative consequences for both yourself and others. The slightest misstep or misunderstanding of directions or procedures could have devastating consequences.

As a firefighter, you always have to consider the safety of those around you, whether you're working with the public, with your superiors, or on your own. You need to keep a clear head and stay calm, even in stressful situations. You need to stay true to your superiors and your fellow firefighters, but you also need to follow directions and protocol.

Reasoning and judgment questions on written firefighter exams vary greatly. We discuss different types of questions later, but it's important to know some general rules first:

- Always read the question or scenario carefully. Make sure you understand exactly what it asks before you attempt to answer. Be sure that you can identify the problem.

- Read every answer choice available to you. Don't stop when you *think* you have the right answer; read each one thoroughly. Find ones that may be possible solutions and eliminate those you know are incorrect.

- If you're stuck between two possible answers, choose the one you think could apply to any situation rather than the one that is correct in only a few instances.

- Make your decision only when you think you've figured out the best solution.

- Reread the question and apply the answer choice you think is best. Be sure that your answer satisfies every part of the question.

Pay close attention to the wording of each question. Look for capitalized, italicized, underlined, and bold words. Focus on words such as *all, always, every, never, except,* and *not,* because these words can help you eliminate incorrect answer choices.

Regardless of the situation, the best answer should not only solve the problem quickly but also keep everyone involved safe. When property is involved, the best solution should cost either the property owner or the city (town, county, and so on) the least amount of money.

Now it's time to look at the types of questions that test your reasoning and judgment about firefighting operations, interpersonal relationships, following procedures, public relations, and logical reasoning.

Answering questions about firefighting operations

You encounter judgment and reasoning questions about firefighting operations on just about any written firefighter exam you take. Such questions have both technical and emotional aspects because they often ask you to imagine yourself performing specific behaviors at emergency scenes. They test your ability to follow directions and act appropriately, despite any emotions you experience that may tempt you to stray from your orders.

Whether you're at the scene of a traffic accident, a hazardous spill, or a house fire, your priorities should always remain the same:

1. **Save lives.**

2. **Reduce property damage.**

3. **Stop or prevent fire.**

Questions about firefighting operations often describe short scenarios involving emergency situations. They then ask you to pick the most appropriate behavior for the situation. Using common sense and good judgment, you'll most likely be able to eliminate incorrect answers within a few seconds.

The following firefighting operations question is similar to ones you may see on a written exam:

You respond to a motor vehicle accident involving a single car in a residential area. When you arrive on scene, you see that a sport utility vehicle (SUV) has struck a tree. The tree has snapped and is leaning toward the nearest house. If it falls, it may crush the home's porch. The SUV isn't on fire, but a passenger is trapped inside. A crowd has formed around the scene. What should you do first?

(A) Find a way to prop up the tree so it doesn't crush the house.

(B) Get your hoses and gear ready in case a fire starts in the SUV.

(C) Remove the passenger from the SUV without causing further injury.

(D) Create a barrier around the emergency scene with caution tape.

All of these options may seem correct, but only one is the right answer because you can perform only one of these tasks *first*. Recall that your first priority is to save lives. Because the passenger is trapped in the SUV, it would be wise to rescue him and then tend to the other tasks. Therefore, Choice (C) is correct. As soon as the passenger is safe, you can create a barrier with caution tape, Choice (D), to protect those who have gathered around the scene. After everyone on the scene is safe, you can look for a way to stop the tree from damaging the house in question, Choice (A), because protecting property is your next priority. Finally, you should prepare to fight a fire, which is Choice (B). Saving lives and property should always be your first two concerns, however.

Did you notice the wording of the question in the sample passage? It doesn't simply ask you what you should do; it asks you what you should do *first*. This word makes Choice (C) correct. Watch for words such as *first*, *next*, and *last*, because they may help you eliminate incorrect choices.

Try one more question about firefighting operations. Remember to look for key words and keep your priorities straight!

A company responds to a water rescue at a river. A man had been fishing when his boat began to leak and started to sink. The temperature of the water is 40°F, and the man is clinging to a large rock in the middle of the river to stay afloat. He is wearing a bag on his back. To ensure the safety of the firefighter who will perform the rescue and also the safety of the victim, what is the first step the company should take?

(A) Swim out to the man to rescue him.

(B) Ensure that all firefighters' gear is on properly.

(C) Ask the victim to throw his bag ashore.

(D) Wait for instructions from the company superior.

This question also includes a key word — *first* — that makes the question easier to answer. What is the *first* step the company should take? It's obvious that the firefighters should perform all of the actions, but only one can happen first, and it should happen for a specific reason. Firefighters' first priority is to save lives — of both victims and fellow emergency personnel. The man in the river must be rescued, and a firefighter will have to swim out to get him. Before the firefighters take action and risk hurting a firefighter or the victim, however, all members of the company should wait for instructions from a superior. Choice (D) is correct. It's important to ensure that all firefighters' gear is working and on properly, Choice (B), and it's also critical to rescue the victim, Choice (A). These actions should not be performed, however, until firefighters on the scene receive orders to do so.

Answering questions about interpersonal relations

Interpersonal relations is a just a fancy way of describing your interactions with others. The bonds that form between firefighters are crucial — how can you feel comfortable putting your life in someone else's hands if you don't trust him or her? As a firefighter, you'll see that the men and women in your department or company become as close to you as family. All members respect each other and do what they can to keep everyone safe.

Judgment and reasoning questions about interpersonal relations ask you to keep your commitment to your department in mind. Such questions ask you to consider situations in which others depend on you or in which you depend on others. Although you should always take responsibility for your own actions, you should also never be afraid to ask for help when you need it.

Many interpersonal relations questions ask you to think about teamwork, but some may assess your respect for authority. At emergency scenes, you should always follow your superiors' instructions, whether you agree with them or not. If you'd like to confront a superior with an issue, do it respectfully, politely, and privately. Wait until the emergency is under control or, preferably, until you return to the station to talk. Never throw a superior or a fellow firefighter under the bus.

Similar to firefighting operations questions, interpersonal relations questions often ask you to imagine yourself performing a certain task. You then have to choose the most appropriate answer. When answering these questions, remember that you should always be honest and show respect.

The following interpersonal relations question is similar to ones you may see on a written exam.

Although he is exhausted, Firefighter Walters must perform inspections on the department's SCBA (self-contained breathing apparatus) tanks before he can go to his bunk to rest. As he nears the end of his task, he finds that one SCBA cylinder's pressure is well under the required 90 percent. Firefighter Walters is tired, achy, and may even have a head cold — the last thing he wants to do is determine what is wrong with the tank. What should Walters do?

(A) Leave the tank out for someone else to fix.

(B) Put the tank to the side and check it in the morning.

(C) Attach a note on the tank warning others not to use it.

(D) Figure out what is wrong with the cylinder's pressure.

Firefighter Walters may not feel 100 percent, but that doesn't mean that he can slack in his duties. If he were to leave a faulty tank anywhere on the floor, someone could easily pick it up in the hustle and bustle of responding to an emergency. If something is wrong with the pressure, this could put another firefighter's life at risk. Common sense should tell you that Firefighter Walters shouldn't set the tank aside, so you can eliminate Choice (B). Because Walters is responsible for checking the tanks, he shouldn't leave the work for someone else;

Choice (A) is also incorrect. Walters could put a note on the tank to keep others from using it until he feels well enough to fix it, Choice (C), but this isn't the best choice. The note could fall off the tank in an emergency, and anyone could pick it up and try to use it. Choice (D) is the correct answer. Before going to sleep, Walters should find out what is wrong with the cylinder's pressure. A self-contained breathing apparatus serves as a firefighter's air supply when he or she enters a burning building. This piece of equipment is crucial to a firefighter's survival; it's important that it works properly.

Try another question. Remember to read the question carefully so you understand exactly what to look for in the answer choices.

A firefighter has been ordered to construct a water chute in a building that is on fire. She's having difficulty seeing what she's doing because of all of the smoke, and the sides of the salvage tarp keep unrolling. What should she do?

(A) Open a window to vent out the smoke.

(B) Radio to request someone to help her with the chute.

(C) Leave the building until the smoke clears.

(D) Find something heavy to place on the tarp to hold it in place.

The firefighter's order is to construct a water chute. You may not know what a water chute is or what it does. You may not know that constructing a water chute usually requires at least two firefighters. However, you do know that a firefighter should always follow a superior officer's orders. Therefore you can eliminate both Choice (A) and Choice (C), because both would require the firefighter to ignore her orders. Choice (D) is a possibility, but the lone firefighter may have trouble lifting a heavy object on her own, so this isn't the best choice. Instead, she should radio for help. Choice (B) is correct.

Answering questions about following procedures

Judgment and reasoning questions about properly following procedures are easy to spot on written tests such as New York City's written exam; they often appear after a list of directions or instructions. Firefighters have to follow certain procedures in just about every setting, from behaving at a public event such as a parade to checking the water pressure on a fire hydrant.

Following-procedures questions test your ability to follow directions in every situation, regardless of whether it's an emergency or an everyday event. Typical questions present a passage or a set of directions about how to perform an action. Then one or two questions ask about specific steps in the process. These questions don't gauge your judgment skills as much as they assess your reasoning, comprehension, and understanding in regard to the procedure.

Watch for specific conditions and exceptions that you must meet before you can move to the next step in a list. To ensure that you understand what the question asks, look for key words such as *before*, *after*, *first*, *next*, and *last*.

Questions about following procedures that appear on written exams like the NYC test may appear similar to the following, with a passage and then a question or two that refers to parts of the passage.

Hoses can be heavy and difficult to maneuver, whether they are charged (flowing water) or uncharged (dry). At a fire scene, a firefighter may need to carry an uncharged hose to the site of a fire from the back of an engine. This process is called *working line drag*. Four steps make this process much easier for the firefighter tasked with carrying the hose. (NOTE: Be sure to face the direction in which you must carry the hose.)

1. Release a bit of the hose and stand alongside the first coupling or nozzle.

2. Lift the coupling or nozzle over your shoulder and hold it against your chest.

3. Move forward, holding the nozzle or coupling securely against your chest. The weight of the hose may require that you pull the hose with you as you walk or run.

4. If the distance to the fire is great enough that another coupling appears on the hose, call for an additional firefighter to aid in advancing the hose.

You have to carry a hose from the back of the engine to the site of the fire because the truck can't drive any closer to the building. What should you do first?

(A) Holding the nozzle close to your chest, move toward the fire.

(B) Lift the coupling or nozzle over your shoulder.

(C) Release some of the hose so that you can lift it easily.

(D) Face toward the direction of the fire, away from the truck.

Based on the passage and instructions, to correctly follow the procedures, you have to release some hose, Choice (C), before lifting the coupling or nozzle over your shoulder, Choice (B). After lifting the coupling or nozzle over your shoulder, you have to hold the nozzle close to your chest and move forward, which is Choice (A). Before you conduct any of these steps, however, the passage indicates that you must face the right direction. Therefore, Choice (D) is correct. Facing toward the fire, not the truck, makes the whole process of working line drag easier.

Always read the entire passage that accompanies a question about following procedures. The list of steps or directions isn't the only important part of the passage; the paragraph(s) before the list may contain valuable information that you need to answer the question correctly.

Answering questions about public relations

Whether at the scene of a fire or in the cereal aisle at the local grocery store, firefighters should always treat civilians with the utmost respect and courtesy. Firefighters' relationships to members of the public are critical; people need to know that they can depend on their town's fire department. All members of the public, including children, need to trust their local fire company. Children often look up to firefighters as role models; kids should understand that if they're ever in any trouble, they can turn to firefighters for help and protection.

As a firefighter, you may not always have the answer or solution to a civilian's problem, but you should still show respect when you respond — even if you can't fulfill the request. A fire company's relationship to the citizens of the town or city it serves is referred to as *public relations*.

Judgment and reasoning questions about public relations often appear on written firefighter exams. Such questions typically include a passage that describes a complicated situation involving a firefighter and a member of the public followed by a question. You then have to choose the answer that shows the most concern for the civilian's safety and feelings while simultaneously following all department rules and procedures.

Read every passage and answer choice carefully and completely, especially when dealing with public relations questions. Many answers may seem correct, but upon closer reading, you may notice that one shows a civilian more respect than another or clearly puts someone else in danger.

The following public relations question is similar to the ones you may see on a written firefighter exam.

On his day off, Firefighter McDonald is relaxing on his front porch when Anna, his 8-year-old neighbor, approaches him. Anna asks McDonald to confirm that he is a firefighter. When he does, she asks if he will rescue a doll she has just thrown into the tree in her backyard. What should McDonald do?

(A) Call an on-duty firefighter to rescue the doll.

(B) Tell Anna to ask her father to rescue the doll.

(C) Grab his ladder from the garage and rescue the doll.

(D) Pretend not to hear her and wait until she goes away.

Because a firefighter is always supposed to show respect to the people with whom he speaks, regardless of age, common sense suggests that you should immediately eliminate Choice (D). McDonald has no reason to be rude to his neighbor. Just because McDonald is off duty doesn't mean that he can't perform the duties of a firefighter. Therefore, he doesn't need to call an on-duty firefighter for help, so you can eliminate Choice (A). Although McDonald could tell Anna to ask her father to rescue the doll, Choice (B), he should recognize that Anna came to him for a reason. She asked whether he was a firefighter and then asked him for help. This shows that Anna knows that she should be able to depend on firefighters when she needs them. If McDonald chooses not to rescue Anna's doll, he could risk crushing the child's positive perception of the fire department. Choice (C) is the best answer. McDonald should rescue the doll, despite being off duty.

When answering questions about public relations, consider the effects of each answer choice. If you chose Choice (B), would it make anyone angry? Would it make the department look bad? Would anyone be injured? Eliminate choices that could have negative effects and closely consider those that appear to be positive.

Now try another question about public relations.

When Firefighter Ramirez and his team reach the scene of a two-car motor vehicle accident, they see that all the passengers have exited their cars without assistance. They have gathered on the sidewalk across the street from the crash and don't appear injured. They are arguing, however, so Ramirez approaches them. Before he can ask any questions, one of the drivers punches him in the face. Ramirez thinks he can smell alcohol on the man who hit him. What should Firefighter Ramirez do next?

(A) Accuse the man who hit him of drinking and driving.

(B) Push the man to the ground and hold him until police arrive.

(C) Return to the engine and ask another firefighter to handle it.

(D) Remove himself and his team from the scene and call the police.

The best thing Ramirez could do is remove himself from the situation and call the police to secure the scene. Although the man punched him, Ramirez shouldn't retaliate (no matter how much he may want to), so you can eliminate Choice (B). Without proof, Ramirez can't know for sure that the man was drinking and driving, so Choice (A) is also incorrect. Although Ramirez could return to the engine and ask another firefighter to handle the situation, Choice (C), the argument could escalate when he turns his back. Therefore, Ramirez's best option is to remove himself and his team from the situation and call the police for backup. Choice (D) is correct.

Answering questions about logical reasoning

Many judgment and reasoning questions on the written firefighter exam are situational, but others focus more on critical thinking and analysis. These questions may include items such as analogies, logic, and series and sequences.

Logical reasoning questions test your ability to detect patterns and form connections between two seemingly different ideas. These questions require you to use critical thinking skills, just like firefighters, who make difficult decisions each and every day — for example, deciding what to do next when rescuing a victim or considering how opening a door affects ventilation. Such questions can seem confusing, which makes them intimidating. Don't worry. If you really think about what the questions ask and how you should answer them, they're not that bad.

Analogies

Analogies appear on some written firefighter exams. Analogies test your ability to make connections and discover relationships between different ideas. These questions include two word pairs. One pair is complete; it's up to you to finish the other pair.

Try an analogy. Examine the statement. Then plug in each answer choice and pick the answer that seems most correct.

Pen is to writer as _____ is to firefighter.

(A) sirens

(B) helmet

(C) hose

(D) air

To answer this question, visualize the word pairs. You know that when people write, they use pens. Now consider this: When firefighters fight fires, what do they use? Firefighters may turn on sirens on the way to a fire, but they don't use the sirens to fight the fire, so Choice (A) is incorrect. Firefighters wear helmets when fighting fires, but again, they don't use helmets to attack the fire. Choice (B) is also incorrect. Firefighters use water, not air, when fighting fires, so you can eliminate Choice (D). Choice (C) is the best answer. A writer holds a pen in his or her hand when writing, just as a firefighter holds a hose in his or her hand when fighting fire.

Some analogies on the firefighter exam may relate to firefighting, but others may simply test your knowledge of word meanings and parts. Sometimes you have to envision parts of objects, such as leaves on trees or petals on flowers. The following is a list of analogy types commonly found on tests:

✔ Antonyms (words with opposite meanings)

✔ Synonyms (words with the same meaning)

✔ Part of the whole

✔ Function and purpose

✔ Cause and effect

✔ Descriptions of items

Analogies are only tricky when you overthink (or underestimate) them. Try to visualize each answer choice until you arrive at the correct answer. Use this technique as you work through the following analogy.

Respectful is to irreverent as _____ is to implausible.

(A) generic

(B) credible

(C) angry

(D) outstanding

This analogy involves antonyms, or opposites. *Irreverent*, which means "disrespectful," is an antonym of *respectful*. Therefore, to correctly complete the analogy, you need to find a word that means the opposite of *implausible*. *Implausible* means "hard to believe" or "unlikely," so the correct answer has to be a word that means "believable" or "probable." The word *credible* meets this criterion, so Choice (B) is correct.

Logic

Some questions on the written firefighter exam may require that you use logical thinking. Such questions provide just enough information for you to make a judgment or decision about a topic. Logic questions may involve listing the steps for completing a certain procedure in the correct order or even using the information to determine a true statement amidst the answer choices. In most cases, logic problems include a list of sentences or statements followed by a question. Read these sentences carefully. The items in this list may or may not be in order. If you miss a critical piece of information, you could jump to a false conclusion and end up choosing the wrong answer.

The following logic question is similar to the ones you may see on a written firefighter exam:

- ✔ Firefighters should always attempt to rescue all victims.
- ✔ Firefighters should worry about damage to property after everyone on the scene is safe.
- ✔ Firefighters should always show concern for the safety of the men and women in their company.
- ✔ Firefighters should attack the fire after everyone is out of harm's way.

According to the information provided, which of the following statements is most accurate?

(A) Firefighters' main priority is to save property.

(B) Firefighters' main priority is to save lives.

(C) Firefighters' main priority is their own safety.

(D) Firefighters' main priority is to fight fire.

Based on logic and the information in the list, you can probably detect a theme running throughout these statements. Consider what each statement has in common: (1) "rescue all victims"; (2) "after everyone on the scene is safe"; (3) "safety of the men and women in their company"; (4) "everyone is out of harm's way." All these sentences relate to protecting human life and safety. Therefore, you can logically conclude that firefighters' main priority is to save lives. Choice (B) is the best answer.

For logic questions that require you to think ahead or draw a conclusion about abstract information, consider drawing images or charts on scrap paper or the test booklet (if you're allowed to do so). Sometimes visualizing numbers and figures is easier than trying to make sense of a group of words with few concrete details.

Now try another logic question.

Use the following information to answer the question:

When a firefighter is alone in a room and discovers an unconscious victim, he or she has multiple options for moving the victim to safety. If the victim is small enough, the firefighter may be able to carry him or her to safety without assistance. To do so, the firefighter may employ the cradle-in-arms lift/carry. The following are tips for this specific lift, in no particular order:

1. Ensure that the victim's back is straight, and stand, using your knees to lift.

2. Put one arm underneath the victim's upper back.

3. Put the other arm underneath the victim's knees.

4. Move to safety.

5. Raise the victim to the height of your waist.

What is the logical order for performing a cradle-in-arms lift/carry?

(A) 1, 3, 4, 5, 2

(B) 2, 3, 1, 5, 4

(C) 3, 5, 2, 4, 1

(D) 4, 5, 1, 3, 2

Though you may have limited or no experience in performing the cradle-in-arms lift/carry, you can use logic to determine the correct order of the steps in the procedure. Visualize the different steps. The correct answer is Choice (B). First, you place *one arm* under the victim's back, and then you place the *other arm* under his or her knees. The phrases "one arm" and "other arm" are clues on how to perform these two steps. In addition, the firefighter would have to have the victim in his or her arms before he or she could lift the victim off the floor. Next, the firefighter should make sure the victim's back is straight and use his or her knees to lift the victim. The firefighter would raise the victim to waist height *after* lifting the victim off the floor. Finally, the firefighter would move the victim to safety.

Series and sequences

One type of logical reasoning question you may see on the written firefighter exam is a series or sequence question. These questions test your ability to reason without using words. They involve numbers, letters, and even shapes. In most cases, you have to detect a pattern and predict which number, letter, or image ends a sequence or which one is missing from a series.

Try a series/sequence question. Choose the letter-number combination that correctly completes the sequence.

x4, x6, o12, o14, x28, x30, _____.

(A) x32

(B) o32

(C) x60

(D) o60

This series includes both letters and numbers, so you have to figure out two patterns. Start with the letters. In the given information, the letter pattern appears to be *x, x, o, o, x, x*. From this, you can predict that the next letter is going to be an *o*. You can eliminate Choice (A) and Choice (C), because neither includes an *o*. Now look at the numbers. The pattern appears to alternate between increasing by 2 and then doubling. Because the last element in the given information is an increase by 2 (28 + 2 = 30), you can conclude that the next step is to double 30: 30 + 30 = 60. Therefore, answer Choice (D) is correct.

When examining sequences that involve numbers, determine the change that occurs from one number to the next. Do the numbers increase or decrease? By how much? Does anything reappear in the pattern? Pay close attention to all the details in the series or sequences.

Try one more. Don't be afraid to write or draw on scrap paper or in your test booklet if you're allowed to do so. Sometimes it's easier to work things out on paper than in your head.

Choose the image that correctly completes the sequence.

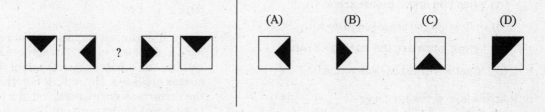

Can you identify the pattern in this series? As you move from left to right, the shaded triangle moves clockwise. It starts at the top and then moves to the right. If the series were to continue to follow this pattern, the shaded area would move to the bottom, then to the left, and then back to its original position at the top. The last square in the sequence does depict the shaded area in its original place, so the correct answer has to be Choice (C).

Practice Reasoning and Judgment Questions

The following passages and question sets are designed to help you practice your judgment and reasoning skills. For all questions, choose the answer that *most correctly* answers the question.

> *Use the following information to answer question 1.*

To salvage items in a burning home, firefighters may need to construct a water chute to collect water that threatens the home's foundation or the possessions inside. Firefighters may or may not use pike poles to make a water chute. The following are instructions to create a water chute without pike poles:

1. Lay the cover or tarp flat on the ground.

2. Roll two opposite edges of the cover or tarp toward the middle. Be sure to leave at least 3 feet between the rolled edges.

3. Lift the cover or tarp off the floor and turn the rolls toward the ground.

4. Lift one end of the chute to create a slope. Position the chute against an area that will help keep it elevated.

5. Position the opposite end of the chute through an opening such as a window or door.

1. You and your partner are constructing a water chute. You've just lifted the chute off the floor. What should you do next?

(A) Roll the edges of the cover toward the middle.

(B) Lift one end to create a slope.

(C) Push the chute through a window or doorway.

(D) Flip it over so the rolled edges face the ground.

2. Your department responds to a call for a water rescue. For water rescues, firefighters in your department are required to wear a thermal protective dry suit, flotation devices, and a water rescue helmet. Any firefighters who respond wearing their standard personal protective equipment will not be allowed near the ice or in the water. When should you put your dry suit on?

   (A) when you arrive on the scene

   (B) only when you are asked to do so

   (C) before you leave the station/en route

   (D) after the victim has been rescued

3. Arrow is to pressure gauge as _____ is to fire hose.

   (A) water

   (B) coupling

   (C) gloves

   (D) aim

4. While removing a Level 2 hazmat suit, Firefighter Owens accidentally creates a small tear in one of the sleeves. What should he do with the suit after he takes it off?

   (A) Throw the suit away.

   (B) Report the tear to his superior.

   (C) Hang the suit where it belongs.

   (D) Mend the tear with tape or stitching.

5. Firefighters from Station 51 participate in the local St. Patrick's Day parade every year. They typically walk beside their engine, honking the horn, waving, and throwing candy to the children who line the streets. After the parade this past year, a disgruntled man, who may have been consuming alcohol before the parade, approaches Firefighter Michelin and tells him that the firefighters shouldn't be wasting their time and the city's money with the parade. They should be saving lives, not marching down the street with candy. What should Michelin do?

   (A) Accuse the man of drinking in public.

   (B) Ignore the man and return to his company.

   (C) Ask the man to explain why he feels that way.

   (D) Tell the man about the company's involvement in the community.

> *For question 6, choose the numbers that correctly complete the sequence.*

6. 4, 4, 4, 1, 1, 1, 7, 7, 7, 4, 4, 4, _____,

   (A) 3, 3, 3

   (B) 7, 7, 7

   (C) 10, 10, 10

   (D) 12, 12, 12

7. While attacking an engine fire that resulted from a single-car crash, Firefighter Lee catches the driver of the car out of the corner of his eye. He noticed before that the driver was disoriented, but she refused to sit down on the curb until paramedics arrived. Suddenly, she faints. What should Lee do?

   (A) Ignore the woman and continue fighting the fire.

   (B) Wait to see whether anyone else notices that she fainted.

   (C) Stop attacking the fire and go to the driver's aid.

   (D) Ask a firefighter who is not fighting the fire for help.

8. Despite a recent injury to his shoulder, Firefighter Douglas insists on responding to calls. The chief tells Douglas that he can't respond to any emergencies until he sees a doctor and his shoulder properly heals. When the alarm sounds minutes after the end of their conversation, Douglas glances in the direction of his suit. He knows that he is healthy enough to go. What should he do?

   (A) Stay at the station while everyone else responds.

   (B) Put on his suit and respond with the rest of his team.

   (C) Beg the chief to allow him to respond to the emergency.

   (D) Transfer to another company that will let him work.

Use the following information to answer question 9.

Occasionally, a firefighter may need to raise a ladder more than 14 feet in length by him- or herself. Because the ladder is more than twice the size of the average firefighter, this may seem difficult at first. The following are four tips to raising a ladder of this height by oneself, in no particular order:

1. Pull the bottom end of the ladder far enough away from the building to constitute a safe and reasonable angle at which to climb.

2. Lay the ladder flat on the ground.

3. Push upward to raise the ladder vertically against the building.

4. Push the bottom end of the ladder against the building.

9. What is the logical order for raising a 14-foot ladder?

   (A) 4, 3, 1, 2

   (B) 2, 4, 3, 1

   (C) 2, 1, 4, 3

   (D) 1, 4, 3, 2

Use the following information to answer question 10.

If you must remove a victim from a building on your own and know you will encounter an incline along the way (stairway, ramp, etc.), you may choose to drag, rather than carry, the victim. This will allow you to see the incline as you descend and will prevent you from dropping the victim if you trip. The following are the steps to perform a successful incline drag:

1. Roll the victim onto his back and kneel near his head.

2. Supporting the victim's neck and back, push the victim upward into a seated position.

3. Place the victim's hands in his lap.

4. Reach underneath the victim's arms and grab his wrists, pulling his arms against his chest.

5. Stand and move toward the exit. The victim's heels should drag on the floor as you move backward.

10. You have just pulled the victim's arms against his chest and are preparing to move toward the exit. Which step did you complete directly *before* this?

   (A) dragged the victim's heels across the floor

   (B) supported the victim's neck and back

   (C) pushed the victim into a seated position

   (D) placed the victim's hands in his lap

Answers and Explanations

Use this answer key to score the practice reasoning and judgment questions.

1. **D.** This judgment and reasoning question focuses on firefighter procedures. Step 3 of this procedure requires the completion of two tasks. After you lift the cover off the floor, you have to turn it so the rolls face the ground.

2. **C.** This question focuses on firefighting operations. In the interest of time and to be prepared when you arrive on scene, you should put on your thermal protective dry suit before you leave the station or en route to the emergency. You should be ready to take action as soon as you leave the truck.

3. **B.** This question involves a "part of the whole" analogy. An arrow is part of a pressure gauge, and a coupling is part of a fire hose.

4. **B.** This question focuses on firefighting operations. You should always report all faulty equipment to your superior. Equipment that is not working correctly could injure a fellow firefighter in action. Choice (D) may seem like a plausible response, but keep in mind that the firefighter has torn a "hazmat" suit, which is worn around "hazardous materials." A flaw could allow hazardous materials to enter the suit, thereby compromising its effectiveness. A superior officer can decide whether to completely discard the suit or fix it.

5. **C.** This involves public relations. The best way for Firefighter Michelin to handle the disgruntled civilian is to first ask him to explain his feelings. This will help Firefighter Michelin better understand the man's perspective and form an appropriate response. Firefighter Michelin may decide to explain that the parade is just one of the many ways that the fire department contributes to community, Choice (D), and explain why the department thinks it's necessary to participate in the parade. However, understanding the man's point of view should come first.

6. **C.** This question involves a sequence. In the sequence, the pattern repeats, increases, and decreases. After three 4s, you subtract 3 and then repeat 1s three times. Then you add 6 and repeat 7 three times. After another subtraction of 3 and repetition of three 4s, you would add 6 (4 + 6 = 10). Therefore, the next numbers would be 10, 10, 10.

7. **D.** This question focuses on firefighting operations. The health and safety of the victim is always a firefighter's main priority, but Firefighter Lee can't stop fighting the fire to tend to the victim. Instead, he needs to rely on the other women and men in his company. He can take action, however, by calling attention to the situation.

8. **A.** This focuses on interpersonal relations. It's important for firefighters always to obey authority. Because Firefighter Douglas's superior told him that he cannot respond until his injury heals, he should stay behind while the others go on the call.

9. **B.** This question requires logical reasoning. Before raising a ladder, you should lay the ladder flat on the ground. Then you need to push the bottom of the ladder against the building. After pushing the ladder upward so that it's standing vertically against the building, you should pull the bottom away from the building to create a comfortable climbing angle.

10. **D.** This question focuses on firefighting procedures. According to the set of instructions, before you pull the victim's arms and hands against his chest, you first have to place his hands in his lap.

Chapter 9

Performing Mathematical Calculations

● ●

In This Chapter

▶ Reviewing basic math principles and operations

▶ Solving math problems using fractions, decimals, and ratios

▶ Using algebraic formulas to determine area, distance, and volume

▶ Solving equations and word problems

● ●

Suppose you respond to a fire at an office building. The building is eight stories high, and each story is 16 feet tall. You have ladders to raise, hoses to couple and drag, and victims to rescue. You also have questions: What percentage of the building is on fire? How many gallons of water per minute may be needed to extinguish the fire? How many feet of hose do you need? How high do you have to aim the water stream? How tall should the ladder be? Should you establish a collapse zone, and if so, how far from the building should that area extend? Questions like these require almost immediate answers, especially when lives are at stake.

In such situations, firefighters have to perform calculations commonly taught in basic math, algebra, and geometry courses. At times, they need to quickly determine averages and percentages. Every day, firefighters work with numbers to determine the length of hoses they need, the total number of miles they have to travel to an emergency, or the ratio of firefighters to victims who need assistance at the scene. It's important that they be confident in their math skills.

Familiarizing yourself with commonly used equations, formulas, rules, and operations will not only help you pass the written firefighter exam but also further prepare you for field experience. You'll undoubtedly have to perform math in this line of work, and lives depend on your ability to think quickly and accurately and to act immediately.

The National Firefighter Selection Inventory Test and other written firefighter exams include questions that require math. You don't have to feel intimidated by these questions, even if you haven't taken a math course in years. In this chapter, we explain how to recognize, solve, and correctly answer math questions.

Laying Out Basic Rules and Reminders

You find tips, notes, and reminders throughout this chapter, but some rules are important enough that they warrant a refresher right up front. These are the basics; the rules you may have *thought* you'd never forget but may have lost along the way:

✔ **Following the order of operations:** Use the sentence "Please excuse my dear Aunt Sally" to remember the order in which you should perform operations:

1. Parentheses

2. Exponents

3. Multiplication, division

4. Addition, subtraction

In other words, you should work with information inside parentheses first. Then use *exponents*, which are superscript numbers that represent the number of times a number has been multiplied by itself — for example, $5^2 = 5 \times 5 = 25$. (For details on exponents, see the later section "You got the power! Properties of exponents.") Multiplication and division are interchangeable, as are addition and subtraction, but multiplying and dividing must always be completed *before* adding and subtracting (unless parentheses tell you otherwise).

For example, in the problem $4 + 2(2 + 3)^2$, you first find the value inside parentheses, $(2 + 3) = 5$. The problem becomes $4 + 2(5)^2$. Then use the exponent, turning $(5)^2$ into $5 \times 5 = 25$; the problem now looks like this: $4 + 2(25)$. Next, multiply $2(25) = 50$, which makes the problem $4 + 50$. Finally, you can add: $4 + 50 = 54$.

✔ **Rounding:** To make things easier on you, questions on the written firefighter exam may ask you to "round to the nearest whole number" or provide an estimated or approximate value. When rounding, first determine how many decimal places you need in your answer. For example, one number after the decimal point is in the tenths place; two numbers, in the hundredths place; three numbers, in the thousandths place; and so on. (If you have no decimal point, you may be rounding to the nearest whole number, the tens place, the hundreds place, and so on.) Next, look at the digit to the immediate right of the place you want to round to. If that number is a 5 or higher, round up. If it's less than 5, round down.

Don't forget to review addition, subtraction, multiplication, and division. It's obvious that you'll need them. If you find the problems in this chapter to be extra challenging, consider borrowing or purchasing a mathematics textbook or even finding a math tutor to work with you.

Working with Units of Measurement

Many math problems on the firefighter exam involve units of measurement. A *unit of measurement* defines terms of distance, time, weight, and so on. The number 7 is just a number, but 7 miles describes a specific distance, 7 minutes describes a specific time, and 7 pounds describes a specific weight.

Be familiar with the differences between measurements using the traditional (United States) and metric systems. Table 9-1 features traditional-to-metric conversions for various units of measurement, and Table 9-2 shows metric-to-traditional conversions. To use the tables, all you have to do is multiply. For example, if a distance is equal to 2 miles, multiply by 1.6 to determine that distance in kilometers: $2 \times 1.6 = 3.2$, so 2 miles is equal to about 3.2 kilometers. If a mass (or weight) is given as 2 kilograms, multiply by 2.2 to find the same weight in pounds: $2 \times 2.2 = 4.4$, so 2 kilograms is equal to about 4.4 pounds.

Table 9-1	Traditional to Metric
Traditional	*Metric*
1 mile	1.6 kilometers
1 quart	946 milliliters or 0.946 liters
1 inch	2.54 centimeters
1 pound	454 grams
1 yard	0.9144 meters

Table 9-2	Metric to Traditional
Metric	*Traditional*
1 kilometer	0.62 miles
1 centimeter	0.394 inches
1 liter	1.06 quarts
1 gram	0.035 ounces
1 kilogram	2.2 pounds

For temperatures, be familiar with the equation

$$F = \frac{9}{5}C + 32$$

where C is the temperature in Celsius and F is the temperature in Fahrenheit. This will help you convert temperatures measured in degrees Celsius (°C) to degrees Fahrenheit (°F).

For conversions within the traditional system, review the number of inches in a foot, the number of feet in a mile, and so on. These measurements will come in handy when responding to questions about hose lengths and distances. You'll be expected to know these measurements; they most likely won't be given to you on the exam. Table 9-3 shows some of the most common measurements you'll encounter.

Table 9-3	Common Traditional Equivalents		
Length	*Weight*	*Volume*	*Time*
1 foot = 12 inches	1 pound = 16 ounces	1 pint = 2 cups	1 minute = 60 seconds
1 yard = 3 feet	1 ton = 2,000 pounds	1 quart = 4 cups	1 hour = 60 minutes
1 mile = 5,280 feet		1 gallon = 4 quarts	1 day = 24 hours

Parts of the Whole: Breaking Down Common Math Concepts

Other chapters in this book cover reading (Chapter 4) and writing (Chapter 5). Are you ready for some arithmetic? In the following sections, you find math principles and problems similar to the ones you'll likely encounter on the written firefighter exam. Because you may not be allowed to use a calculator on the test, you should familiarize yourself with the problem-solving methods in this chapter. Pay close attention to the formulas and how they're used, because they may or may not be provided for you on the exam. In this section, we focus on parts of the whole: fractions, decimals, and percentages.

You'll most likely be allowed to use scrap paper. Use it! Don't try to do everything in your head; sometimes even the most basic math can be confusing if you don't write it down and work through it. Feel free to erase or scratch out mistakes, use the front and back of the paper, and draw boxes or images. Do whatever you think is necessary to answer the question.

Piecing together fractions

Yes, fractions can seem intimidating — but you're preparing for a career in which you'll frequently *run into burning buildings*. Fractions, by comparison, are a piece of cake. You need to know how to work with fractions so you can find percentages, solve algebraic equations, and determine answers to geometry questions. In the following sections, we break down what you need to know about converting fractions and how to do math with them.

Converting fractions

The following are the three types of fractions:

✔ **Proper fraction:** A fraction with a smaller number in the *numerator* (the top number) and a larger number in the *denominator* (the bottom number), such as $\frac{1}{4}$

✔ **Improper fraction:** A fraction with a larger number in the numerator and a smaller number in the denominator, such as $\frac{15}{4}$

✔ **Mixed number:** A fraction that includes a whole number and a proper fraction, such as $3\frac{1}{4}$

On the written exam, you may have to convert mixed numbers to improper fractions and vice versa. To convert a mixed number to an improper fraction, multiply the whole number by the denominator (bottom number) of the fraction. The result of a multiplication problem is called a *product*. Then add the numerator (top number) to the product and make the result the new numerator of your improper fraction. The denominator stays the same.

Here's an example. Check your multiplication and division before you select the correct answer.

Convert $8\frac{5}{6}$ to an improper fraction.

(A) $\frac{46}{6}$

(B) $\frac{48}{5}$

(C) $\frac{53}{6}$

(D) $\frac{53}{5}$

To solve this problem, first multiply the whole number by the denominator: $8 \times 6 = 48$. Then add the numerator of the fraction to the product: $48 + 5 = 53$. The denominator stays the same, so the correct answer is Choice (C), $\frac{53}{6}$.

To convert an improper fraction to a mixed number, use long division. Divide the numerator (top number) by the denominator (bottom number). The number of times the denominator evenly divides into the numerator becomes the whole-number part of the mixed fraction. If a remainder exists, place it in the numerator's spot in the fraction. The denominator stays the same. Here's an example.

Convert $\frac{19}{5}$ to a mixed number.

(A) $5\frac{3}{4}$

(B) $3\frac{4}{5}$

(C) $4\frac{3}{5}$

(D) $3\frac{3}{5}$

To answer this problem, first divide the numerator by the denominator: $19 \div 5 = 3$ with a remainder of 4. Next, place the remainder over the denominator, making the mixed number $3\frac{4}{5}$. Your work may look like this:

$$\frac{19}{5}$$

$$5)\overline{19} \quad \begin{array}{r} 3 \\ \hline \end{array}$$
$$\underline{-15}$$
$$4$$

$$3\frac{4}{5}$$

Equal fractions: Reducing fractions and increasing terms

The *terms* of a fraction are the numbers that appear in the top and bottom of the fraction. Two fractions can be equal to each other but have different terms. For instance, $\frac{1}{2}$ is equal to $\frac{3}{6}$. In math problems, sometimes it's necessary to *reduce* a fraction (put it in lowest terms) or to increase its terms so you can do calculations.

If you multiply or divide a fraction by another fraction that equals 1, then you can change the terms (numbers) in the fraction without changing the fraction's value. To understand how this works, think of a fraction bar (the line that separates the numerator from the denominator) as a division sign. If the numerator and denominator match, a fraction equals 1: $\frac{4}{4}$ means $4 \div 4 = 1$, $\frac{3}{3}$ means $3 \div 3 = 1$, and so on. So to *increase the terms* of a fraction, multiply the numerator and denominator by the same number — you multiply by a fraction that equals 1. Here's an example:

$$\frac{1}{3} = \frac{1 \times 3}{3 \times 3} = \frac{3}{9}$$

To *reduce* a fraction, divide the numerator and denominator by the same number — you divide by a fraction that equals 1. Here's an example:

$$\frac{6}{8} = \frac{6 \div 2}{8 \div 2} = \frac{3}{4}$$

Always remember to reduce your answer. If your math results in an improper fraction, convert it to a mixed number. If you have a fraction such as $\frac{6}{12}$ and you know it can reduce to $\frac{1}{2}$, reduce it. The answer choices most likely will have the reduced form of the fraction in them.

Multiplying and dividing fractions

To multiply fractions, all you have to do is multiply across the numerators and then multiply across the denominators. If necessary, reduce to lowest terms, and that's it! If you're dealing with a mixed number, convert it to an improper fraction before you multiply. If your result is an improper fraction, convert it to a mixed number before you select the right answer. (See the earlier section "Converting fractions" for more on mixed numbers and improper fractions.)

$\frac{3}{8} \times 2\frac{3}{4} =$

(A) $2\frac{3}{16}$

(B) $1\frac{1}{32}$

(C) $\frac{12}{144}$

(D) $\frac{18}{96}$

To solve this equation, first convert the mixed number to an improper fraction. Then multiply across and reduce:

$$\frac{3}{8} \times 2\frac{3}{4} = \frac{3}{8} \times \frac{11}{4} = \frac{3 \times 11}{8 \times 4} = \frac{33}{32} = 1\frac{1}{32}$$

Before you multiply fractions, consider canceling out common factors (if possible). If a number in the numerator and a number in the denominator are both divisible by the same number, they have a *common factor*. To cancel, divide the numbers by their common factor. Then multiply as usual.

Cancelation can make multiplying fractions a lot easier, and it saves you the trouble of reducing the fraction at the end. Take a look at fraction multiplication problem without canceling:

$$\frac{5}{8} \times \frac{4}{5} = \frac{20}{40} = \frac{20 \div 20}{40 \div 20} = \frac{1}{2}$$

However, in this example, 5 and 5 are both divisible by 5, and 4 and 8 are both divisible by 4. You can save work by canceling out a 5 and a 2 before multiplying:

$$\frac{^1\cancel{5} \times {}^1\cancel{4}}{_2\cancel{8} \times {}_1\cancel{5}} = \frac{1 \times 1}{2 \times 1} = \frac{1}{2}$$

Dividing fractions is almost as easy as multiplying fractions — in fact, it's basically the same thing. The only difference is that you have to invert the second fraction, which means you need to flip it. The numerator becomes the denominator and vice versa. The inverse of a fraction is called its *reciprocal*. Then just multiply across. If the result is an improper fraction, convert it to a mixed number. If you begin with a mixed number, convert it to an improper fraction before inverting and multiplying.

$$\frac{4}{5} \div \frac{3}{4} =$$

(A) $\frac{4}{3}$

(B) $\frac{3}{5}$

(C) $\frac{7}{9}$

(D) $1\frac{1}{15}$

To solve this problem, first invert the second fraction. Then multiply across and write the answer as a mixed number:

$$\frac{4}{5} \div \frac{3}{4} = \frac{4}{5} \times \frac{4}{3} = \frac{16}{15} = 1\frac{1}{15}$$

Adding and subtracting fractions

Before you can add or subtract fractions, you have to make sure that their denominators (bottom numbers) match. The most difficult part of adding and subtracting fractions is finding a common denominator when all the original denominators differ. After you find the common denominator, however, it's as easy as $2 + 2$ — literally!

To add or subtract a group of fractions that have different denominators, first look for a *common multiple* of all denominators involved. For example, to add $\frac{1}{2}$, $\frac{1}{3}$, and $\frac{1}{4}$, first find some multiples of each denominator. Some multiples of 2 are 2, 4, 6, 8, 10, and 12. Some multiples of 3 are 3, 6, 9, and 12. Some multiples of 4 are 4, 8, and 12. Notice that 12 is a multiple for all three numbers. Therefore, you can use 12 as the common denominator.

After you know the common denominator you want, multiply the numerator and denominator of each fraction by a number that will allow you to obtain that denominator. (See the earlier section "Equal fractions: Reducing fractions and increasing terms" for info on changing the numbers in a fraction without changing its value.) Go back to $\frac{1}{2}$, $\frac{1}{3}$, and $\frac{1}{4}$. To make the denominator 12 in each of these equations, you have to multiply the numerator and the denominator of $\frac{1}{2}$ by 6, of $\frac{1}{3}$ by 4, and of $\frac{1}{4}$ by 3:

$$\frac{1}{2} \times \frac{6}{6} = \frac{6}{12} \qquad \frac{1}{3} \times \frac{4}{4} = \frac{4}{12} \qquad \frac{1}{4} \times \frac{3}{3} = \frac{3}{12}$$

This creates the new fractions $\frac{6}{12}$, $\frac{4}{12}$, and $\frac{3}{12}$.

Now you can easily add or subtract these fractions. Simply carry out the operations with the numbers in the numerators, keeping the denominator the same:

$$\frac{6}{12} + \frac{4}{12} + \frac{3}{12} = \frac{6+4+3}{12} = \frac{13}{12} = 1\frac{1}{12}$$

Try adding and subtracting a few fractions. Try to find the *lowest* common denominator for all the fractions in the problem to make adding them much easier.

$3\frac{1}{2} + 7\frac{2}{3} + 5\frac{1}{9} =$

(A) $1\frac{5}{18}$

(B) $15\frac{6}{17}$

(C) $16\frac{5}{18}$

(D) $26\frac{4}{108}$

First find a common denominator for the fractions. The lowest common denominator here is 18, because you can evenly divide 18 by 2, 3, and 9. Next, convert each fraction to a fraction with 18 in the denominator:

$$3\frac{1}{2} + 7\frac{2}{3} + 5\frac{1}{9} = 3\frac{9}{18} + 7\frac{12}{18} + 5\frac{2}{18}$$

Now that all your denominators are the same, just add across: $3\frac{9}{18} + 7\frac{12}{18} + 5\frac{2}{18} = 15\frac{23}{18}$. You're not done, because the fractional part is an improper fraction. Convert the improper fraction to a mixed number:

$$\frac{23}{18}$$

$$18\overline{)23} \\ \quad \underline{-18} \\ \quad \;\; 5$$

$$1\frac{5}{18}$$

Finally, add the mixed number to the whole number to get your answer: $15 + 1\frac{5}{18} = 16\frac{5}{18}$.

To subtract fractions, follow the same rules that you use to add them. Find a common denominator and make the same conversions, but then subtract instead of add.

Gimme tenths! Working with decimals

A decimal is similar to a fraction in that it represents part of a whole. Decimals can be added, subtracted, multiplied, divided, and even converted into fractions. A decimal, naturally, has a decimal point. The decimal point may fall before, after, or between numbers. The position of the decimal point determines the name of the decimal and the value of the number.

Each time a decimal point moves one place to the left, the value of the number decreases and the name of the decimal point changes. For example,

$$0.1 = \text{one-tenth} = \frac{1}{10}$$

$$0.01 = \text{one-hundredth} = \frac{1}{100}$$

$$0.001 = \text{one-thousandth} = \frac{1}{1,000}$$

Each time a decimal point moves one place to the right, the value of the number increases. Think of it this way:

$$0.01 = \text{one-hundredth} = \frac{1}{100}$$

$$0.1 = \text{one-tenth} = \frac{1}{10}$$

$$1.0 = \text{one} = 1$$

Converting decimals to and from fractions

Occasionally on the written firefighter exam, it's necessary to convert decimals to fractions or fractions to decimals. Or sometimes a question may present information in fraction form, but it's simply easier to work with a decimal. The conversions for either transformation aren't all that difficult.

 To convert a fraction to a decimal, simply divide the numerator (top number) by the denominator (bottom number). If it helps, you can add a decimal point and a zero to the end of the numerator so the decimal point is present throughout your math; then add additional zeroes as needed. The result is your decimal. Your work may look like this:

$$\frac{6}{8} =$$

$$\begin{array}{r} .75 \\ 8)\overline{6.00} \\ -56 \\ \hline 40 \\ -40 \\ \hline 0 \end{array}$$

To convert a decimal to a fraction, the numerals to the right of the decimal point become the numerator. To find the denominator, count the number of numerals after the decimal point. The first numeral to the right of the decimal point is in the tenths place, the second numeral to the right is in the hundredths place, and so on. Write a one and include a zero for each numeral that appears after the decimal point. For example, if you want to make 0.24 into a fraction, you'd place 24 in the numerator. Then, because 0.24 extends to the hundredths place, the denominator becomes 100. Therefore, 0.24 is the same as $\frac{24}{100}$. Reduced, this fraction becomes $\frac{6}{25}$, because 24 and 100 are both divisible by 4.

Adding and subtracting decimals

Unlike when adding fractions, you don't have to find a common link between two decimals to add or subtract them. Just be sure to align the decimal points when you set up your addition or subtraction. If you need to add a zero to the end of a number to make the decimal points line up, feel free to do so, because adding zeros to the *end* of a decimal doesn't alter its value. Try a quick addition problem using decimals.

0.46 + 82 + 2.45 =

(A) 3.730

(B) 8.491

(C) 37.30

(D) 84.91

The right answer is Choice (D). To solve this problem, first line up the decimal points. Then add the numbers together. The decimal point in your total should be in the same location as the decimal points in your other numbers:

$$
\begin{array}{r}
0.46 \\
82.00 \\
+\ 2.45 \\
\hline
84.91
\end{array}
$$

Multiplying and dividing decimals

Multiplying decimals is a little trickier than adding them. The best way to multiply decimals is to take the decimal points out of the equation entirely. After the math is complete, put them back in.

For example, instead of multiplying 8.2 by 0.55, multiply 82 by 55: $82 \times 55 = 4{,}510$. To put the decimals back in, count the total number of digits after the decimal point in both of the numbers you multiplied. In 8.2, the 2 is the only digit after the decimal. In 0.55, two 5s fall after the decimal. Therefore, three digits fall after the decimal points, so the answer should have three digits behind the decimal point. The correct answer is 4.510.

Work through another problem and read through the answer explanation.

$6.8 \times 0.87 =$

(A) 0.767

(B) 5.916

(C) 7.670

(D) 59.16

To solve this problem, first take away the decimal points and multiply: $68 \times 87 = 5{,}916$. Because the first number has one digit after the decimal point and the second number has two digits after the decimal point, move the decimal in the product (answer) three places to the left. Therefore, 5,916 becomes 5.916. Choice (B) is correct.

Dividing decimals, like multiplying them, is complicated only by the movement of the decimal point. After you've moved the decimal points around, however, dividing is pretty easy. In division problems that include decimals, first move the decimal point in the divisor (the number by which you're dividing) to the right until it becomes a whole number. Then move the decimal point in the dividend (the number you're dividing) the same number of places to the right. When the decimal points are in their correct places, place a decimal point in the space for the quotient (the answer) directly above the decimal point in the dividend. Then divide as you normally would — don't touch those decimal points again!

Look at an example. To divide 8.226 by 0.06, you first move the decimal point in the divisor two places to the right to get a whole number; therefore, 0.06 becomes 6. Because you moved the decimal point two places to the right in the divisor, move it two places to the right in the dividend. Therefore, 8.226 becomes 822.6. Your work for this equation may look like this:

$$.06\overline{)8.226} \to 6\overline{)822.6} \to 6\overline{)822.6}^{137.1}$$

Try another problem.

$6.572 \div 0.53 =$

(A) 0.12

(B) 1.11

(C) 11.1

(D) 12.4

Choice (D) is correct. After shifting the decimal points two places to the right, you divide 657.2 by 53. Your work should look similar to this:

$$0.53\overline{)6.572} \to 53\overline{)657.2} \to 53\overline{)657.2}^{12.4}$$

Out of 100: Using percentages

Consider this: The word *century* means 100 years, because *cent* means *hundred*. A quick glance at the word *percent* may lead you to believe that percentages involve the number 100, and you'd be right. Percentages represent fractions that always have a denominator of 100. The word *percent* is defined as "per 100 parts."

You can represent percentages in three different ways:

- ✔ As a percentage: 40%
- ✔ As a fraction: $\frac{40}{100}$
- ✔ As a decimal: 0.4

You often can't work with percentages directly, so you usually have to convert to fractions or decimals before you can do calculations. When working with percentages, sometimes it's easier to use decimals and multiplication, and other times it's easier to use fractions. Occasionally, you also need to add, subtract, or divide. Note that in percentage problems, you can usually translate the word *of* as a multiplication sign.

Cross-multiplication: Using fractions to solve percent problems

Finding percentages isn't difficult. One option is to change a percentage into a fraction and then set up a proportion. In a *proportion,* you set two fractions equal to each other (see the later section "Comparing things with fractions: Ratios and proportions" for details).

Recall that a percentage stands for a fraction. One fraction in your proportion will always represent your percentage — a number in the numerator with 100 in the denominator. The other fraction represents a part of given number. Use x as a variable to stand in for the unknown number.

Suppose you have to find 10% of 60. You already know that 10% is $\frac{10}{100}$. This is your first fraction. The other will be $\frac{x}{60}$. Then solve for x. Start by writing your proportion:

$$\frac{10}{100} = \frac{x}{60}$$

To find the answer, cross-multiply. When *cross-multiplying,* you multiply the numerator of each fraction by the denominator of the other: $10 \times 60 = 600$, and $100 \times x = 100x$. Your new equation is

$$600 = 100x$$

To solve for x, divide both sides by 100:

$$\frac{\cancel{100}x}{\cancel{100}} = \frac{600}{100}$$
$$x = 6$$

If $x = 6$, then 10% of 60 is 6.

Converting percentages to decimals to solve percent problems

You can change a percentage to a decimal. To change a percentage to a decimal, simply take the number from the percentage and move the decimal point two places to the left; then drop the percent sign. For example, 10% becomes 0.10.

If you want to find 10% of 60 using decimals, you can do so easily. You already know that 10% is 0.10. Therefore, you simply have to multiply 60 by 0.10 to find your answer: $60 \times 0.10 = 6.0$.

Now try a question similar to those you may see on the written exam.

What is 60% of 25?

(A) 5

(B) 10

(C) 15

(D) 20

To solve this problem, you could use cross-multiplication or multiplication of decimals to find the answer. In this question, you can view 60% as 0.60 or as $\frac{60}{100}$:

✔ To find the answer using decimals, multiply 25 by 0.60: $25 \times 0.60 = 15.0$.

✔ To use a proportion, set up your equation and cross-multiply. Then divide by 100 to solve for x. Your work should looked like this:

$$\frac{60}{100} = \frac{x}{25}$$
$$1,500 = 100x$$
$$\frac{1,500}{100} = \frac{\cancel{100}x}{\cancel{100}}$$
$$15 = x$$

Whether you solve with a proportion or multiplication of decimals, Choice (C) is correct.

Solving Algebraic Equations

Algebra. The word has the ability to strike fear in the hearts of warriors. Algebraic equations supply some information, which you have to use to determine unknown information. The unknown is called a *variable,* which is represented by a letter such as x or y. You solve the equation by figuring out what the variable is equal to; that is, you get the variable by itself on one side of the equal sign.

Algebraic equations aren't as difficult as they may seem. To solve them, you have to use basic math skills such as addition, subtraction, multiplication, and division to solve for a variable while keeping both sides equal. To move information from one side of the equal sign to the other, you have to use *inverse* operations. For example, if a term on one side of the equation uses addition, you have to use subtraction to cancel out that information.

Here are some ways you can manipulate an algebra problem without upsetting the balance:

- ✔ Divide both sides of an equation by the same number.

- ✔ Multiply both sides of an equation by the same number.

- ✔ Add the same number to both sides of an equation.

- ✔ Subtract the same number from both sides of an equation.

- ✔ Take the square root of both sides of the equation.

Think of an equation as a scale: For it to balance, both sides must be equal. And to keep that balance, whatever is done to one side of the equation must be done to the other. For example, if you subtract 2 from one side, you must subtract 2 from the other side.

Many types of algebraic equations exist, and they may contain different components, but all are solved using the sample principles. On the firefighter exam, you may need to set up basic algebraic equations to solve problems, and you'll probably have to figure them out without a calculator.

Keeping the balance: Basic algebraic equations

Some algebra problems may be basic equations for which you have to plug in numbers for the known variables and then solve for the unknown variable. Here are some examples.

$x + y = z$. If $x = 7$ and $z = 15$, what does y equal?

In the original equation, plug in 7 for x and 15 for z. Because this equation uses addition, subtract 7 from each side. Here's what the calculations look like:

$$7 + y = 15$$
$$7 + y - 7 = 15 - 7$$
$$y = 8$$

Here's another problem:

$xy = z$. Solve for y if $x = 5$ and $z = 45$.

Plug in the values of x and z:

$$5y = 45$$

Because this equation uses multiplication, divide each side by 5.

$$\frac{\cancel{5}y}{\cancel{5}} = \frac{45}{5}$$
$$y = 9$$

Now try another one:

Solve the following equation: $4x + 2 = 3(2 + 4)$

(A) 4

(B) 4.5

(C) 9

(D) 18

First, use addition and multiplication to find the value of the right side of the equation: $3(2 + 4) = 3(6) = 18$. Now you know that the left side of the equation must equal 18, so $4x + 2 = 18$. Because the equation uses addition, subtract 2 from each side: $4x + 2 - 2 = 18 - 2$. Therefore, $4x = 16$. Now divide each side by 4, because the equation uses multiplication: $x = 4$. Choice (A) is the correct answer. Your work should look something like this:

$$4x + 2 = 3(2 + 4)$$
$$4x + 2 = 3(6)$$
$$4x + 2 = 18$$
$$4x + 2 - 2 = 18 - 2$$
$$4x = 16$$
$$\frac{\cancel{4}x}{\cancel{4}} = \frac{16}{4}$$
$$x = 4$$

You've got the power! Properties of exponents

A *power,* such as 2^3, represents a number multiplied by itself. For example, $2^3 = (2)(2)(2)$. The *exponent,* 3, stands for the number of times the *base,* 2, is multiplied by itself. This process is also called *raising to the power.* Solving equations that involve exponents is no more difficult than solving any other type of problem on the firefighter exam.

Use the following guidelines when working with exponents:

- Any number raised to the power of zero equals one: $x^0 = 1$

- Any number raised to the power of one equals itself: $x^1 = x$

- To multiply powers with the same base, add the exponents: $x^3(x^4) = x^{3+4} = x^7$

- To divide powers with the same base, subtract the exponents: $x^6 \div x^4 = x^{6-4} = x^2$

- When a product has an exponent, each factor is raised to that power: $(xy)^2 = x^2y^2$

- When a power is raised to a power, multiply the exponents: $(x^2)^4 = x^{2(4)} = x^8$

- A power with a negative exponent equals the base's reciprocal with a positive exponent (a *reciprocal* is the inverse of a fraction; in other words, the denominator becomes the numerator and the numerator becomes the denominator): $2^{-3} = \frac{1}{2^3} = \frac{1}{(2)(2)(2)} = \frac{1}{8}$

You can't simplify an expression if the powers have different bases. For instance, x^2y^3 can't be simplified any further because the bases, x and y, are not the same.

Here are some examples of problems with powers:

What is the value of x^y if $x = 5$ and $y = -3$?

Plugging in the numbers gives you 5^{-3}. Use the reciprocal to get

$$5^{-3} = \frac{1}{5^3} = \frac{1}{(5)(5)(5)} = \frac{1}{125}$$

Simplify the following: $x^9 \div x^3$

(A) x^3

(B) x^6

(C) x^{12}

(D) x^{27}

When dividing powers with the same base, subtract the exponents. In this problem, $9 - 3 = 6$, so answer Choice (B) is correct. Your work should look something like this: $x^9 \div x^3 = x^{9-3} = x^6$.

Coming to terms with FOIL: Multiplying binomials

On the written firefighter exam, you may have to multiply two binomials by each other. A *binomial* is an expression that has two terms. A *term* is a number, variable, or number-variable combination that's separated from the rest of the problem by a plus or minus sign. For example, in the binomial $3x + 5$, the two terms are $3x$ and 5. In the binomial $x - 2$, the terms are x and -2. Notice that a negative sign is part of the term.

The two binomials you need to multiply are usually wrapped in parentheses, so a problem may look like this: $(3x + 5)(x - 2)$. The answer is usually a *trinomial,* which has three terms. For example, the answer $3x^2 - x - 10$ is a trinomial, and its terms are $3x^2$, $-x$, and -10.

You use the FOIL method to multiply two binomials to create a trinomial. *FOIL* is a *mnemonic device,* or memory device, that helps you remember to multiply each term in the first set of parentheses by each term in the second set. Here's how it works:

- **First:** Multiply the first terms in each set of parentheses
- **Outer:** Multiply the outer terms in each set of parentheses
- **Inner:** Multiply the inner terms in each set of parentheses
- **Last:** Multiply the last terms in each set of parentheses

Then add the results and simplify.

To solve these types of questions, you need to use multiplication, addition, and subtraction. The following is an example:

$$(3x + 5)(2x + 4)$$

Now use FOIL:

- **First:** $(3x)(2x) = 6x^2$
- **Outer:** $(3x)(4) = 12x$
- **Inner:** $(5)(2x) = 10x$
- **Last:** $(5)(4) = 20$

Altogether, you have $6x^2 + 12x + 10x + 20$. Then simplify by adding the like terms. *Like terms* are terms with the same variable parts, such as $12x$ and $10x$. When the variable parts of a term match, you can add or subtract their numerical parts (called the *coefficients*), so $12x + 10x = 22x$. Therefore, the answer is $6x^2 + 22x + 20$.

When multiplying binomials, be mindful of your signs and remember that a negative number multiplied by another negative number results in a positive number. A positive number multiplied by a negative number results in a negative number.

Try a sample question:

$(-2x + 6)(7x - 5)$

(A) $-14x^2 - 32x + 30$

(B) $14x^2 + 52x + 30$

(C) $14x^2 - 32x - 30$

(D) $-14x^2 + 52x - 30$

Use FOIL to solve this question. First, multiply the *first* term from each set of parentheses: $(-2x)(7x) = -14x^2$. Next, multiply the *outer* term from each set of parentheses: $(-2x)(-5) = 10x$. Then multiply the *inner* term from each set of parentheses: $(6)(7x) = 42x$. Then multiply the *last* term from each set of parentheses: $(6)(-5) = -30$. Finally, put it all together and combine like terms: $-14x^2 + 42x + 10x - 30 = -14x^2 + 52x - 30$. Choice (D) is correct.

Comparing things with fractions: Ratios and proportions

As a firefighter, you'll need to be able to solve ratio and proportion problems. Firefighters use ratios and proportions to compare things, such as the number of firefighters to the number of victims, the number of fire hydrants to the number of homes in a neighborhood, and so on. A *ratio* is a comparison of two numbers. A ratio can be written as a ratio notation (1:2) or as a fraction $\left(\frac{1}{2}\right)$.

For example, suppose Alpha Fire Department has 15 firefighters and Bravo Fire Department has 20 firefighters. The ratio of Alpha firefighters to Bravo firefighters is 15:20. The ratio can also be expressed as a fraction: $\frac{15}{20}$.

A *proportion* is an equation with an equal ratio on each side:

$$15{:}20 :: 3{:}4 \text{ or } \frac{15}{20} = \frac{3}{4}$$

Ratio questions on the firefighter exam may test your ability to solve proportions. You'll use given information to solve for an unknown variable. Consider the following problem:

If Lieutenant Franco can run 2 miles in 12 minutes, how far can he run in 20 minutes?

Let x represent the number of miles traveled in 20 minutes and write a proportion in which the ratios compare miles to minutes:

$$\frac{2 \text{ miles}}{12 \text{ minutes}} = \frac{x \text{ miles}}{20 \text{ minutes}}$$

You have two fractions set equal to each other, so cross-multiply (see the earlier section "Cross-multiplication: Using fractions to solve percent problems" for details on cross-multiplication):

$$\frac{2}{12} = \frac{x}{20}$$
$$40 = 12x$$

Next, divide each side by 12:

$$\frac{40}{12} = \frac{12x}{12}$$
$$x = \frac{40}{12} = 3\frac{4}{12} = 3\frac{1}{3}$$

Lieutenant Franco can run $3\frac{1}{3}$ miles in 20 minutes.

Here's another example.

If you can complete 6 training exercises in 3 days, how many training exercises can you complete in 9 days?

(A) 3

(B) 9

(C) 18

(D) 24

First, plug the given information into an equation, letting x represent the unknown information (in this case, the number of training exercises you can complete in 9 days):

$$\frac{6 \text{ training exercises}}{3 \text{ days}} = \frac{x \text{ training exercises}}{9 \text{ days}}$$
$$3x = 54$$

Because this equation uses multiplication, you' need to divide each side of the equation by 3 to solve for x:

$$\frac{3x}{3} = \frac{54}{3}$$
$$x = \frac{54}{3} = 18$$

You can complete 18 training exercises in 9 days. Choice (C) is correct. See, that wasn't so hard. You use basic division and multiplication skills to solve for an unknown.

Shaping Up Your Geometry Skills

Firefighters use geometry more than you may think. For example, they may need to determine the volume of a rectangular drop tank (a rectangular prism, or box) so they can figure out how much water it can hold. Just as when working with algebraic equations, the key is to plug in the known information and then solve for the unknown variable.

Table 9-4 includes some commonly used geometric formulas for flat shapes. Perimeter and circumference measure the distance around shapes. *Circumference* is the distance around a circle, and *perimeter* refers to the distance around other shapes, such as a triangle or a rectangle, and it's equal to total length of all of that shape's sides.

Note: For the triangle perimeter formula, *a, b,* and *c* represent the lengths of the sides of a triangle; in the triangle area formula, *b* is a triangle's base, and *h* is its height. For rectangles, *l* is a rectangle's length and *w* is its width. For circles, *r* is the *radius* (the distance from the center of the circle to a point on the circle) and *d* is the *diameter* (the distance across the circle), which equals $2 \times r$.

A number of circle formulas use π, which is a Greek letter known as *pi*. Pi is a mathematical constant (number) with a value equivalent to any circle's circumference divided by its diameter. Its value, rounded to eight decimal places, is 3.14159265. In most cases on the firefighter exam, you can safely round π to 3.14.

Table 9-4	Formulas for Flat Shapes	
Shape	*Perimeter or Circumference*	*Area*
Triangle	$P = a + b + c$	$A = \frac{1}{2}bh$
Rectangle	$P = l + w + l + w$ $= 2l + 2w$	$A = l \times w$
Circle	$C = 2\pi r$ $= \pi d$	$A = \pi r^2$

Table 9-5 provides some volume formulas for 3-dimensional objects. If you take a flat shape and give it height, you get a *prism.* Examples of prisms include a triangular prism (a triangular box with rectangular sides), a building block (a rectangular prism or box), and a soup can (a cylinder).

Note: In the volume formulas, *h* represents the object's height, and *l* is the length between two triangular bases.

Table 9-5	Volume Formulas for 3-D Solids
Solid	*Volume*
Triangular prism	$V = \frac{1}{2}bhl$
Rectangular prism (box)	$V = l \times w \times h$
Cylinder	$V = \pi r^2 h$

As long as you familiarize yourself with the formulas in these two tables, you should be able to solve geometry problems on the written firefighter exam. The following is an example of the types of geometry problems you may see there:

Find the perimeter of the triangle shown below.

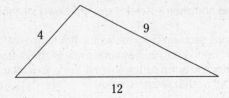

(A) 72

(B) 50

(C) 25

(D) 12.5

To find the perimeter of a triangle, add all three sides of the triangle together using the formula $P = a + b + c$. Plug the known numbers into the equation: $P = 4 + 12 + 9 = 25$. The perimeter of the triangle is 25 units long, so Choice (C) is correct.

Here's another one:

If the length of a rectangular room is 5 feet and the width is 7 feet, what is its area?

To find the area of rectangle, use the formula $A = l \times w$. Plug in the values you know (length and width) and then do the math:

$A = l \times w$

$A = 5 \text{ ft.} \times 7 \text{ ft.}$

$A = 35 \text{ ft.}^2$, or 35 square feet

When an area or volume problem includes units of measurement, be careful if the answer is given in a different unit of measurement (see the earlier section "Working with Units of Measurement" for info on conversions). Length conversions aren't quite the same as area and volume conversions. Consider this example for the area of a rectangle:

$A = l \times w$

$A = 12 \text{ inches} \times 18 \text{ inches}$

$A = 216 \text{ inches}^2$

Suppose the question asks for the answer in square feet. Although 1 foot equals 12 inches, 1 square foot equals 144 inches (because $A = 12 \text{ inches} \times 12 \text{ inches} = 144$ square inches). Therefore, to convert 216 square inches to square feet, you have to divide by 144, not 12: $216 \div 144 = 1.5$ square feet. You can avoid some of this math by converting the units *before* finding the area. For instance, 12 inches = 1 foot, and 18 inches = 1.5 feet. Therefore, the problem becomes $A = 1 \text{ foot} \times 1.5 \text{ feet} = 1.5$ square feet.

Look at another geometry problem.

A tanker trunk has a cylindrical tank with a radius of 5 feet and a height of 10 feet. If 1 cubic foot can hold about 7.5 gallons of water, how many gallons of water can the tank hold?

First, find the volume of the tank using the formula $V = \pi r^2 h$. Your work may look something like this (the $\approx$ sign means *approximately equal to;* you use it because when you round π to 3.14, your answer isn't exact):

$$V = \pi r^2 h$$
$$V = \pi (5^2)(10)$$
$$V = \pi (25)(10)$$
$$V = 250\pi$$
$$V \approx 250 \times 3.14$$
$$V \approx 785$$

Therefore, the volume of the tank is about 785 cubic feet. Now multiply 785 (the total cubic footage of the tank) by 7.5 (the number of gallons that fit into 1 cubic foot): $785 \times 7.5 = 5{,}887.5$. The tank can hold about 5,887.5 gallons of water.

Making Sense of Word Problems

Many of the math questions on the written firefighter exam appear as word problems. A word problem is a short passage that contains information that you must plug into an equation to solve the problem. Word problems can range in size from a single sentence to a few paragraphs. Don't let the size of a word problem intimidate you.

Sometimes word problems contain irrelevant information that's just there to confuse you. Use the following steps to figure out what's important in word problems:

1. **Read the entire problem.**

2. **List the information provided in the word problem.**

   For example, if a sentence states the number of miles traveled, write down this information.

3. **Determine which information you need to solve the problem.**

   After you determine what you need, ignore irrelevant information. If you're allowed to write in the test booklet, draw a line through anything that you don't need.

Some word problems contain key words that help determine how you'll solve a problem. When working with word problems, look for the following key words in passages and questions to determine which operation you should use:

- ✔ **Addition:** *Sum, more, greater, total, altogether*
- ✔ **Subtraction:** *Difference, less, fewer, remain, left over*
- ✔ **Multiplication:** *Of, product, times*
- ✔ **Division:** *Each, per*

We have one more formula for you. Many word problems on the written firefighter exam require you to determine distance (such as the number of miles traveled), rate (the speed of travel), and time (the amount of time it takes to travel a certain distance). Therefore, you need to know the following formula:

$$d = r \times t$$

In this formula, d = distance, r = rate of speed, and t = time.

Try an example word problem.

In the past seven days, Alpha Fire Department responded to 9 house fires, 3 car accidents, and 14 emergency situations. How many total incidents did the fire department respond to in the past week?

(A) 26

(B) 25

(C) 12

(D) 9

After reading the word problem, you can determine you need to use addition because of the word *total* in the question. You can also determine that the information *seven days* is irrelevant to solving the problem and disregard it. To solve this problem, add together the number of house fires (9), the number of car accidents (3), and the number of emergency situations (14): 9 + 3 + 14 = 26.

Check out one more example of a word problem.

You're responding to the scene of a car accident 5 miles from the station. If you travel at an average speed of 30 miles per hour, how long will it take for you to arrive at the scene?

(A) 5 minutes

(B) 7 minutes

(C) 10 minutes

(D) 14 minutes

To solve this problem, use the formula $d = r \times t$. The distance (d) is equal to 5 miles, and the rate (r) is equal to 30 miles per hour. Therefore, you have to solve for time (t). Your work may look something like this:

$$d = r \times t$$

$$5 \text{ miles} = (30 \text{ miles per hour})(t)$$

$$\frac{5 \cancel{\text{ miles}}}{30 \cancel{\text{ miles}} \text{ per hour}} = \frac{(\cancel{30 \text{ miles per hour}})(t)}{\cancel{30 \text{ miles per hour}}}$$

$$\frac{1}{6} \text{ hour} = t$$

Notice that dividing by 30 miles per hour on the right side, you cancel out all terms except t, which is your variable for time. You can cancel out words that represent units of measurement just as you can cancel out numbers. On the left side, 5 miles and 30 miles are both multiples of 5 miles. When you simplify, the *miles* cancel each other out, the numerator reduces to 1, the denominator reduces to 6, and only the time unit, *hours,* remains on the left side. Because the result is in hours and the answer choices are in minutes, you have to multiply by 60 (the number of minutes in 1 hour) to convert the answer from hours to minutes. Your work may look something like this: $\frac{1}{6} \times 60 = \frac{1}{6} \times \frac{60}{1} = \frac{60}{6} = 10$ minutes. Choice (C) is the right answer.

Practice Mathematics Problems

The following problems are designed to help you practice your math skills. Read each question carefully. Do not use a calculator. If necessary, use scrap paper to perform your calculations. Then choose the correct answer.

1. $\frac{1}{4} \times 0.34 + \frac{6}{8} - \frac{4}{25}$

    (A) 0.675

    (B) 1.584

    (C) 9.090

    (D) 85.89

2. $(-5x + 4)(-2x + 7)$

    (A) $10x^2 - 27x - 28$

    (B) $7x^2 - 7x + 11$

    (C) $10x^2 - 43x + 28$

    (D) $6x^2 - 3x - 28$

3. What is 68% of 420?

    (A) 0.285

    (B) 2.856

    (C) 28.56

    (D) 285.6

4. $(3x^{12})(x^{13})$

    (A) $3x^{-1}$

    (B) $3x^{25}$

    (C) $3x^1$

    (D) $3x^{156}$

5. $3\frac{2}{5} \div \frac{6}{14} + \frac{38}{15} \times 2 =$

    (A) 3.8

    (B) 7

    (C) 13

    (D) 20.14

6. On your last 24-hour shift, you spent 5 hours fighting fires, 2 hours at the scene of a car accident, and your remaining hours at the station. What percentage of your shift was spent at the station? Round to the nearest whole number.

    (A) 29%

    (B) 46%

    (C) 71%

    (D) 83%

7. $\frac{30x}{6} = 45$

    (A) 9

    (B) 12

    (C) 18

    (D) 27

8. $0.083 + 0.46 - 0.004 + 0.62 \div 0.02 =$

    (A) 0.5700

    (B) 26.411

    (C) 31.539

    (D) 57.950

9. \$382.57 − \$99.97 × \$0.53 + \$4.57. Round to the nearest hundredth.

    (A) \$127.28

    (B) \$154.35

    (C) \$279.48

    (D) \$334.16

10. Your fire department is hosting a chicken dinner, and you're in charge of breading the chicken. If it takes 2 cups of bread crumbs to coat 24 pieces of chicken, how many pieces of chicken can you coat with 5 cups of bread crumbs?

    (A) 24

    (B) 48

    (C) 60

    (D) 120

11. If the area of a rectangular room is 120 ft.^{2} and the width of one side is 10 ft., what is the length of the room?

    (A) 10 ft.

    (B) 12 ft.

    (C) 24 ft.

    (D) 44 ft.

12. You respond to a fire about 15 miles from the station. You predict that $\frac{1}{3}$ of the drive will be at the city speed limit of 35 miles per hour. About $\frac{1}{6}$ of the drive will be at 5 to 10 miles per hour as you wait for drivers ahead of you to pull to the side of the road. The rest of the drive will be at a safe speed but over the speed limit. What percentage of the drive will you spend over the speed limit?

    (A) 16.7%

    (B) 33%

    (C) 50%

    (D) 88.7%

13. $\frac{4x+2}{2} = 42$

    (A) 20.5

    (B) 18

    (C) 16.5

    (D) 12

14. $\frac{18}{6} + \frac{21}{2} - \frac{14}{8} + \frac{7}{12} - \frac{5}{4} = ?$ Round to the nearest hundredth.

    (A) 3.38

    (B) 6.75

    (C) 11.08

    (D) 22.16

15. If Truck 14 can travel 7 miles in 10 minutes, how far can it travel in 14 minutes? Round to the nearest whole number.

    (A) 10 miles

    (B) 14 miles

    (C) 16 miles

    (D) 24 miles

16. If a rectangular drop tank has a length of 14 feet, a height of 5 feet, and a width 9 feet, how many cubic feet of water can it hold?

    (A) 400 ft.³

    (B) 630 ft.³

    (C) 950 ft.³

    (D) 1400 ft.³

17. The fire engine responds to an activated fire alarm at a school that is 8 miles from the station. If the truck arrives at the school in 12 minutes, what was the average speed the engine traveled on the way to the school?

    (A) 30 miles per hour

    (B) 35 miles per hour

    (C) 40 miles per hour

    (D) 45 miles per hour

18. What is the radius of a circle with a diameter of 30 inches?

    (A) 6 inches

    (B) 10 inches

    (C) 15 inches

    (D) 30 inches

19. On your summer vacation, you travel abroad with two fellow firefighters. You've been told that the average summer temperature in the country you're visiting is 38.5°C. What is the temperature in degrees Fahrenheit (°F)?

    (A) 37.3°F

    (B) 69.3°F

    (C) 101.3°F

    (D) 104.3°F

20. $(6x + 5)(7x + 4)$

    (A) $42x^2 + 59x + 20$

    (B) $13x2 + 22x + 9$

    (C) $42x2 + 11x - 9$

    (D) $13x^2 + 59x - 20$

21. $7\frac{1}{4} + 3\frac{1}{2} - \frac{5}{12} =$

    (A) $10\frac{1}{3}$

    (B) $11\frac{1}{2}$

    (C) $10\frac{1}{6}$

    (D) $10\frac{1}{12}$

22. Find the circumference of the circle shown below, using π ≈ 3.14. Round your answer to the nearest whole number.

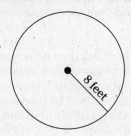

8 feet

(A) 24 ft.

(B) 50 ft.

(C) 64 ft.

(D) 128 ft.

23. You walk to and from work each day to stay in shape, save gas money, and lessen your impact on the environment. Your house and the fire station are approximately 3 miles apart. If you made five trips to and from work this week, how many total miles did you travel?

(A) 15 miles

(B) 20 miles

(C) 30 miles

(D) 40 miles

24. You worked the following shifts in the past 8 days: 12 hours, 8 hours, 7 hours, 10 hours, 11 hours, 5 hours, 9 hours, and 8 hours. What is the average length of your shifts?

(A) 5 hours

(B) 8 hours, 45 minutes

(C) 9 hours, 15 minutes

(D) 12 hours

25. Simplify the following: $\frac{1}{2^{-3}}$

(A) $-\frac{1}{2}$

(B) $\frac{1}{8}$

(C) -8

(D) 8

Answers and Explanations

Use this answer key to score the practice mathematics questions in this chapter. How did you do? We hope these questions have given you some good practice for answering math questions on the firefighter written exam.

1. **A.** In this problem, converting the fractions to decimals is easier than converting the decimal to a fraction. Otherwise, you'd have to find a common denominator before adding and subtracting. Also, the answer choices are decimals, so you want your answer in decimal form. To convert to decimals, divide each numerator (top number) by its denominator (bottom number). After converting all fractions to decimals, multiply first, and then add and subtract: $0.25 \times 0.34 + 0.75 - 0.16 = 0.085 + 0.75 - 0.16 = 0.835 - 0.16 = 0.675$.

2. **C.** This question can be answered using the FOIL method. Remember to watch your signs. First = $(-5x)(-2x) = 10x^2$; Outer = $(-5x)(7) = -35x$; Inner = $(4)(-2x) = -8x$; Last = $(4)(7) = 28$. After combining like terms $(-35x - 8x = -43x)$, the correct answer is $10x^2 - 43x + 28$.

3. **D.** To answer this question, use a proportion and cross-multiplication or multiplication of decimals. To use multiplication of decimals, note that $68\% = 0.68$. To find 420×0.68, move the decimal point two places to the right and multiply to make the equation $420 \times 68 = 28,560$. Then put the decimal point back in by moving it two places to the left: 285.60.

4. **B.** When multiplying powers that have the same base, add the exponents. Your work should look like this:

    $(3x^{12})(x^{13})$

    $= 3x^{12+13}$

    $= 3x^{25}$

5. **C.** Stick with fractions throughout this question. Convert mixed numbers to improper fractions. Remember your order of operations and divide and multiply first. Then add it all together. After reducing the fraction, the result is 13. Your work should look something like this:

$$\left(3\frac{2}{5} \div \frac{6}{14}\right) + \left(\frac{38}{15} \times 2\right) = \frac{17}{5} \times \frac{14}{6} + \frac{76}{15}$$

$$= \frac{238}{30} + \frac{76}{15}$$

$$= \frac{238 \div 2}{30 \div 2} + \frac{76}{15}$$

$$= \frac{119}{15} + \frac{76}{15}$$

$$= \frac{195}{15} = 13$$

6. **C.** This question asks you to find the percentage of hours you spent at the station. Twenty-four hours total minus the 7 hours you spent on calls leaves 17 hours that you spent at the station. The fraction $\frac{17}{24}$ represents the number of hours out of the total you were at the station. However, you need the answer as a percentage, so you have to divide to covert the fraction to a decimal. Then you move the decimal point to get a percentage. Therefore, $17 \div 24 = 0.708333\ldots$ Rounded to the nearest whole percentage, this equals 0.71 or 71%.

7. **A.** To solve this equation, multiply each side by 6, which creates the following equation: $30x = 270$. Then divide each side by 30. Therefore, $x = 9$. Choice (A) is correct.

8. **C.** To solve this equation, remember your order of operations and divide before you add or subtract: $0.62 \div 0.02 = 31$. Then add: $0.083 + 0.46 - 0.004 + 31 = 0.543 - 0.004 + 31 = 0.539 + 31 = 31.539$.

9. **D.** You start with $382.57 − $99.97 × $0.53 + $4.57. To solve this equation, multiply before you add or subtract: $99.97 × $0.53 = $52.9841. Then subtract and add: $382.57 − $52.9841 + $4.57 = $329.5859 + $4.57 = $334.1559. Rounded to the nearest hundredth, the answer is $334.16. Choice (D) is correct.

10. **C.** To solve this problem, set up a proportion; the two ratios represent the number of chicken pieces to the cups of bread crumbs. Use cross-multiplication and division to solve for *x;* you get 60. Your work should look something like this:

$$\frac{24}{2} = \frac{x}{5}$$
$$2x = 120$$
$$\frac{2x}{2} = \frac{120}{2}$$
$$x = 60$$

11. **B.** To solve this problem, use the formula $A = l \times w$ and solve for length: 120 = 10*l*. After dividing both sides by 10, the result is *l* = 12. Therefore, the length of the room is 12 feet.

12. **C.** First determine how much of the route you spend at or under the speed limit by adding the fractions: $\frac{1}{3} + \frac{1}{6} = \frac{2}{6} + \frac{1}{6} = \frac{3}{6} = \frac{1}{2}$. Half the route is 50%. You spend the rest of the drive over the speed limit, and 100% − 50% = 50%, so the right answer is Choice (C).

13. **A.** To solve this equation, first multiply each side by 2. Then subtract 2 from each side. Finally, divide each side by 4. The result is 20.5. Your work should look something like this:

$$\frac{4x+2}{2} = 42$$
$$(2)\frac{4x+2}{2} = 42(2)$$
$$4x + 2 = 84$$
$$4x + 2 - 2 = 84 - 2$$
$$4x = 82$$
$$\frac{4x}{4} = \frac{82}{4}$$
$$x = 20.5$$

14. **C.** The common denominator for this problem is 24. After multiplying each fraction to achieve a common denominator, you just have to add and subtract. The result should be $\frac{72}{24} + \frac{252}{24} - \frac{42}{24} + \frac{14}{24} - \frac{30}{24} = \frac{266}{24}$, which equals 11.08333... Rounded to the nearest hundredth, the result is 11.08.

15. **A.** Set up a proportion in which the fractions represent miles to minutes. To solve for *x*, first cross-multiply and then divide to get 9.8, which rounds up to 10. Your work should look something like this:

$$\frac{x}{7} = \frac{14}{10}$$
$$10x = 98$$
$$\frac{10x}{10} = \frac{98}{10}$$
$$x = 9.8$$
$$x \approx 10$$

16. **B.** To find the volume of a 3-D rectangular object, such as a portable water tank, use the formula $V = l \times w \times h$: $V = 14$ ft. $\times 9$ ft. $\times 5$ ft. $= 630$ ft.³

17. **C.** To answer this question, use the formula $d = r \times t$ and solve for r. Your work may look like this:

$$d = r \times t$$
$$8 \text{ miles} = r \times 12 \text{ minutes}$$
$$\frac{8 \text{ miles}}{12 \text{ minutes}} = \frac{(12 \text{ minutes})r}{12 \text{ minutes}}$$
$$\frac{2 \text{ miles}}{3 \text{ minutes}} = r$$

The result is $\frac{2}{3}$ of a mile per minute, but the answer choices are in miles per hour. You know that an hour is 60 minutes long, so you have to multiply the answer by 60 to determine the number of miles you could travel in 60 minutes:

$$\frac{2 \text{ miles}}{3 \text{ minutes}} \times \frac{60 \text{ minutes}}{1 \text{ hour}} = \frac{120 \text{ miles}}{3 \text{ hours}} = 40 \text{ miles/hour}$$

Therefore, the engine traveled at an average speed of 40 miles per hour to reach the school.

18. **C.** The radius of a circle is half the diameter, so to find the radius of a circle with a diameter of 30 inches, simply divide 30 by 2: $30 \div 2 = 15$. Therefore, the radius is 15 inches.

19. **C.** Using the formula $F = \frac{9}{5}C + 32$, plug in 38.5 for C, multiply, and then add: $69.3 + 32 = 101.3°F$.

20. **A.** This question can be answered using the FOIL method. First = $42x^2$; Outer = $24x$; Inner = $35x$; and Last = $20x$. After combining like terms ($24x + 35x = 59x$), the result is $42x^2 + 59x + 20$.

21. **A.** To solve this problem, first find a common denominator for 2, 4, and 12. In this case, the common denominator is 12. Then convert each fraction to a fraction with 12 as the denominator. Next, add and subtract before reducing the fraction. Your work may look like this:

$$7\frac{1}{4} + 3\frac{1}{2} - \frac{5}{12} = 7\frac{3}{12} + 3\frac{6}{12} - \frac{5}{12}$$
$$= 10\frac{9}{12} - \frac{5}{12}$$
$$= 10\frac{4}{12} = 10\frac{1}{3}$$

22. **B.** To find the circumference of a circle, use the formula: $C = 2\pi r$. Now plug in the numbers and multiply: $C \approx 2(3.14)(8 \text{ ft.}) \approx 50.24$, which rounds down to 50 feet.

23. **C.** You live 3 miles from the fire station, so a trip to and from the station is $3 + 3 = 6$ miles long. You made 5 trips, so multiply the number of miles per trip by 5: $6 \times 5 = 30$. The correct answer is 30 miles.

24. **B.** To solve this problem, find the total number of hours worked in the past 8 days by adding the number of hours you worked each day: $12 + 8 + 7 + 10 + 11 + 5 + 9 + 8 = 70$. Then divide that number by the number of shifts worked (8): $70 \div 8 = 8.75$ hours.

25. **D.** To solve this problem, change $\frac{1}{2^{-3}}$ to its reciprocal with a positive exponent: $\frac{2^3}{1} = 2^3$. Now solve: $2^3 = (2)(2)(2) = 8$. Choice (D) is correct.

Chapter 10

Mechanical Aptitude: Knowing the Nuts and Bolts of Machines

In This Chapter

▶ Recognizing common firefighting tools and their uses

▶ Applying mechanical and physical principles

▶ Understanding simple machines and other mechanical devices

Have you ever fixed a flat tire or assembled a bookshelf? If you answered yes, then you've used your mechanical aptitude to help with these tasks. You may not realize that you apply mechanical aptitude to everyday situations such as these. If you answered no, don't worry! The questions on the written exam touch on only the most basic principles, and we help you give your mechanical aptitude a tune-up.

The written exam that firefighters have to take as part of the hiring process often includes questions designed to test your mechanical skills. *Mechanical aptitude* is a person's ability to work with tools and machines and understand mechanical and physical principles. As a firefighter, you'll have to work with tools every day and rely on your mechanical aptitude in certain situations. For example, if a wall collapses on a fellow firefighter, you'll have to not only figure out the best way to rescue him or her but also determine which tools to use to get the job done. It's important that you're familiar with these tools and how they work.

In this chapter, we describe common firefighting tools and explain how to apply your mechanical aptitude to everyday situations. We also discuss some simple mechanical devices such as pulleys and levers. We even provide some practice exercises to help you prepare for the mechanical aptitude portion of the written firefighter exam. So get those gears turning!

Tinkering with Tools

Many written firefighter exams include questions about tools. Some questions may present a picture or a scenario and ask you to identify the best tool to use based on the information. Others may provide a picture of a tool and ask you to identify its purpose. A few tests ask test-takers to look at a picture and choose the correct name for the tool, but most avoid such questions.

Though you don't need to be a tool expert to pass the mechanical aptitude portion of the written exam, being able to recognize the most common firefighting tools is helpful. We break them into two general categories: common handheld tools (those found in most garages and tool boxes) and forcible entry tools (those that are more specific to firefighting). In this section, we explain the various types of tools and their purposes.

You don't have to be a tool expert to answer the mechanical aptitude questions on the written firefighter exam. In addition, it would be nearly impossible for us to name and describe each and every tool you may encounter or use during your firefighting career. By familiarizing yourself with some of the most common tools that firefighters use, however, you greatly improve your chances of answering questions about tools correctly.

Common handheld tools

Handheld tools are the most common types of tools, and they require nothing but human power to operate. If you've ever fixed anything around the house, you're probably familiar with most of these tools. They're everyday-use tools such as shovels, hammers, and screwdrivers — the tools that almost everyone has in the garage. The following are just a few commonly used handheld tools (check out Figure 10-1 to see what these tools look like):

- **Clamp:** A fastening device used to hold two or more objects together tightly

- **Cutters:** A tool used — depending on size, shape, and design — to cut through materials such as wire, tree limbs, or metal

- **Hammer:** A tool with a short handle and a metal head used to drive and remove nails or break up materials

- **Handsaws (carpenter's, keyhole saw, hacksaw, or coping saw):** Handheld tools with a variety of blade types, handles, and shapes used to cut through wood or metal

- **Pliers:** A handheld tool with two handles and a set of pincers used for gripping objects and for bending and cutting wire

- **Rake:** A common gardening tool with a long handle and several prongs used to break up or smooth out soil or to gather materials such as leaves or pieces of small debris into a pile

- **Rope:** A long cord of twisted or braided fibers or other material used to hoist, secure, or lower objects or persons

- **Screwdriver:** A tool used to tighten and loosen screws

- **Shovel:** A long-handled tool with a scoop on one end used to dig holes or to carry or move materials such as soil, gravel, or small debris

- **Utility knife:** A cutting tool used to cut through light materials such as paper or cardboard

- **Wrench (nonadjustable, adjustable, and special-use wrenches):** A handheld tool used to tighten or loosen bolts, nuts, pipes, and so on

As a firefighter, you'll probably use handheld tools every day. For example, during salvage and overhaul operations for a structure fire, you may have to rake up burned debris and use a shovel to haul it outside. At the scene of a car fire, your chief may order you to use a wrench to tighten the couplings of a hose. You may use rope to hoist a length of hose to the third story of a burning structure. Ordinary handheld tools come in handy for many firefighting-related tasks.

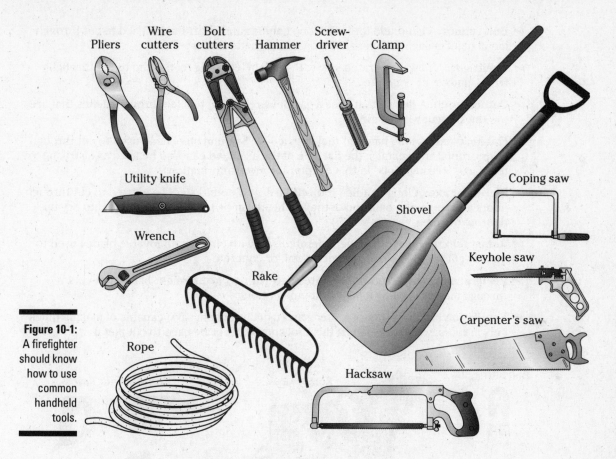

Figure 10-1:
A firefighter should know how to use common handheld tools.

Forcible entry tools

Firefighters can use ordinary handheld tools to complete many jobs, but they rely on special *forcible entry* tools to breach an otherwise inaccessible area. For example, firefighters may use a saw to cut a hole in the roof of a structure to vent out heat and smoke. A *Halligan bar,* a short bar with a claw at one end and a combination pick/blade at the other end, is excellent for prying open locked doors. Firefighters may use a *pike pole,* a long pole with a metal head that includes both a point and a hook, to push through and pull down a ceiling while checking for fire in a structure. They may opt to strike a wall with a sledgehammer to create an opening.

Each of these tools falls into one of the four categories of forcible entry tools — cutting, prying, pushing/pulling, and striking — which we discuss in further detail in this section.

Cutting tools

Have you ever tried to cut through a piece of metal with a pair of scissors? It didn't work very well, did it? Scissors, like all tools, are designed for a specific purpose, and cutting through metal is not one of them. To complete a task quickly and efficiently, you need to use the correct tool for the job. As a firefighter, you'll likely have to cut through many different materials — wood, metal, drywall — as part of your forcible entry operations. Therefore, you need to know how and when to use a variety of cutting tools. The following are some commonly used cutting tools (Figure 10-2 shows you what these tools look like):

- ✔ **Bolt cutters:** A handheld tool with long handles and short blades used to cut through metal objects such as chains, iron bars, and metal fences

- ✔ **Chain saw:** A power-operated saw with a chain featuring teeth used to cut through trees, lumber, or concrete

- ✔ **Cutting torch:** A device that uses a gas-powered flame to slice through metals that are too thick to cut with a saw

- ✔ **Flat-head axe:** A long-handled tool with a 6- or 8-pound steel head used to cut through floors, roofs, and ceilings; the flat side of the axe head can also be used as a striking tool (see "Striking tools" in this chapter for more information)

- ✔ **Pick-head axe:** A long-handled tool with a 6- or 8-pound steel head used to cut through floors and roofs; the pick end of the axe head can be used as a prying tool to pry up floorboards (see "Prying tools")

- ✔ **Rotary (circular) saw:** A power-operated saw with circular removable blades used to quickly cut through wood, plastic, metal, or concrete

- ✔ **Reciprocating saw:** A power-operated saw with a short straight blade that cuts through materials using a push-and-pull motion

- ✔ **Ventilation saw:** A power-operated saw (usually a chain saw) capable of making quick cuts in roofs, walls, or ceilings; this tool should never be used to cut metal

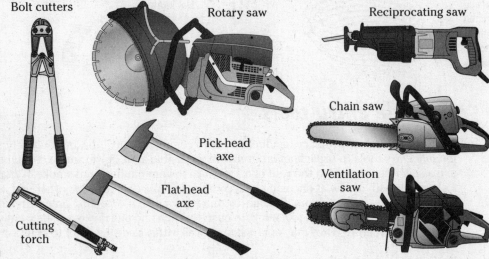

Figure 10-2: Firefighters use a variety of cutting tools at emergency scenes.

The situations that require the use of cutting tools vary greatly. For example, after a tornado rips through an area, causing trees to fall and block roadways, you may need a chain saw to cut the trees into smaller pieces so you can move them off the road. During a shed fire, you may need bolt cutters to cut through a padlock on the door so you can reach the fire.

Prying tools

Locked doors and windows can be troublesome for firefighters who need to get inside a building to put out a fire or open a window to create ventilation. For such situations, firefighters use prying tools, which can force open doors, windows, or locks. Prying tools can also be used as levers (see "Looking at levers" later in this chapter) to move heavy objects. The following are some examples of prying tools (check out Figure 10-3 to see images of these tools):

✔ **Claw tool:** A heavy-duty prying tool with a hook on one end and a fork on the other end used to pull up floorboards, baseboards, window casements, and door frames

✔ **Crowbar:** A metal bar used as a lever to force objects apart; one end is inclined for prying, and the other end is curved to remove nails or staples

✔ **Flat bar:** A flat metal bar with a curved fork on one end and a flat, slightly inclined fork on the other end used for prying

✔ **Halligan bar:** A short bar with a claw at one end and a combination pick/blade at the other end used to pry open locked doors

✔ **Hux bar:** A wrench with a spur on one end and two receptacles on the other end used to turn hydrants on or off

✔ **Hydraulic door opener (or rabbit tool):** A tool, operated by a hand pump, that uses hydraulic pressure to open doors

✔ **Hydraulic spreader:** A power-operated tool that uses hydraulic pressure to push apart metal using two arms; it's often used to help remove trapped car accident victims

✔ **Kelly tool:** A straight steel bar used for both prying and striking; one end is a chisel, and the other end is an *adz,* a tool with a with a thin, arched blade

✔ **Pry axe:** A long-handled tool that has a wooden shaft with an axe on one end and a pick on the other end

✔ **Pry or pinch bar:** A straight bar used to gain leverage to open doors, remove boards, or even remove concrete blocks

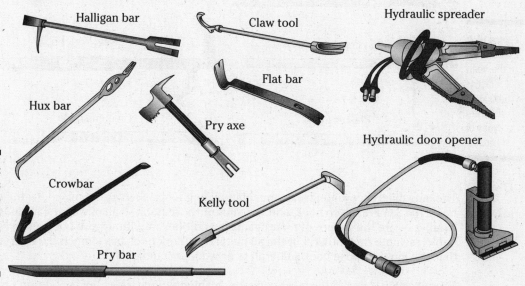

Figure 10-3: Firefighters need to familiarize themselves with these prying tools.

As a firefighter, you'll use prying tools for many tasks. For example, to lift a floorboard or baseboard, you may use a claw tool to pry the board loose. You may use a hydraulic spreader, such as the Jaws of Life, to pry open a car to rescue an accident victim trapped inside the vehicle.

Pushing/pulling tools

During a fire, breaching walls or ceilings to check for fire is often necessary. As a firefighter, you'll use pushing/pulling tools, such as the ones that follow, to complete these tasks (see what they look like in Figure 10-4):

- ✔ **Clemens hook:** A long-handled tool used to remove plaster or siding and to ventilate ceilings

- ✔ **Drywall hook:** A long-handled pole used to remove drywall, wood, plaster, or sheet metal on walls or ceilings

- ✔ **Multipurpose hook:** A long pole used during fires to remove walls, ceiling, or roofs

- ✔ **Pike pole:** A pole with a long, slender body and a metal head that includes both a point and a hook; the point is perfect for pushing into a ceiling to create a hole, and the hook is just right for pulling down the ceiling to check for flames

- ✔ **Plaster hook:** A pole with retractable blades that, when opened, pull through walls and ceilings, similar to the drywall hook

- ✔ **New York hook:** A metal hook used for heavy-duty prying and pulling; it's the only pushing/pulling tool that can be used for leverage

- ✔ **San Francisco hook:** A long pole with a built-in gas shut-off and directional slot used for ventilation

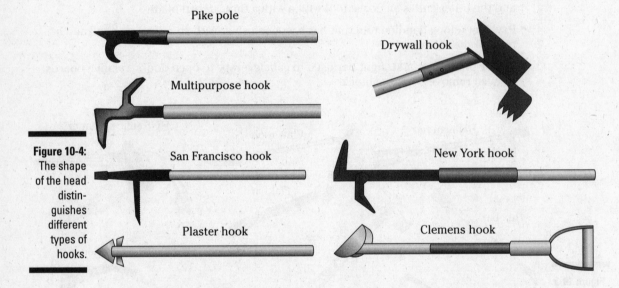

Figure 10-4:
The shape of the head distinguishes different types of hooks.

Pike pole

Drywall hook

Multipurpose hook

San Francisco hook

New York hook

Plaster hook

Clemens hook

The only difference among many pushing/pulling tools, such as the pike pole, the drywall hook, the San Francisco hook, and the multipurpose hook — all of which have long handles — are the shapes of their heads. In addition, a multipurpose hook and a New York hook resemble each other, but the all-metal New York hook has a much stronger handle than the multipurpose hook's fiberglass or wooden handle.

The pike pole is one of the most common pushing/pulling tools, but that doesn't mean that you won't need the other tools. For example, if you arrive at the scene of a fire, you may need to use the San Francisco hook to turn off a gas line.

Striking tools

We hope you're ready to hit something, because the final category of forcible entry tools is striking tools. Striking tools typically have a weighted head attached to a handle. As a firefighter, you'll use striking tools to hit, break, or crush materials. Striking tools are an important part of forcible entry operations. The following list includes some examples of striking tools (Figure 10-5 shows these tools):

✔ **Battering ram:** A heavy metal bar with handles used to break down objects such as locked doors

✔ **Chisel:** A metal tool with a sharp edge that, when used in combination with a striking tool such as a hammer, can cut through wood, metal, or stone

✔ **Mallet:** A handheld tool with a barrel-shaped head used to deliver a soft blow

✔ **Maul:** A long, hammer-like tool with a dual-sided head used to split wood along the grain; one side of its head resembles an axe, and the other side can be used as a sledgehammer

✔ **Pick:** A heavy-duty tool with a long handle and a metal head with one or two points used to break up earth or stone

✔ **Punch or window punch:** A spring-loaded tool used to shatter windows safely during emergency rescues

✔ **Sledgehammer:** A long-handled tool with a large metal head used for heavy-duty pounding or breaking

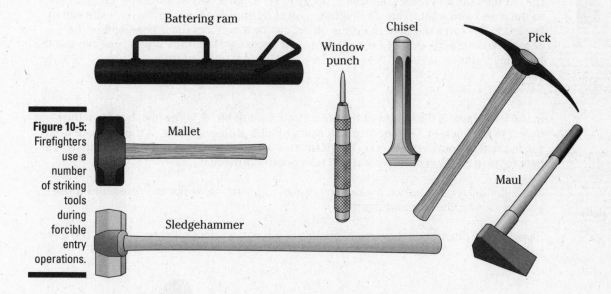

Figure 10-5: Firefighters use a number of striking tools during forcible entry operations.

As a firefighter, you may find yourself in a variety of situations in which striking tools will come in handy. For example, to rescue a fellow firefighter who's stuck behind a wall in a burning building, you may use a sledgehammer to break through the wall. To gain access to a locked apartment, you may have to rely on a battering ram to break down the door.

Mechanical Devices

The mechanical aptitude portion of the written firefighter exam usually includes some questions about mechanical devices. The mechanical devices you encounter on the exam are typically simple machines that give you a *mechanical advantage* by reducing the amount of effort you must exert to complete a task. In other words, they make everyday tasks easier. For example, you can lift an object with your arms, but the amount of weight you can lift has limits. A lever is a simple mechanical device that enables you to lift a heavy object without straining yourself. Some other examples of simple mechanical devices are inclined planes, wheels and axles, pulleys, gears, springs, screws, and fasteners.

Questions about mechanical devices on the firefighter exam may test your knowledge of how these devices work. For example, they may ask you to identify the purpose of a lever or an inclined plane. In addition, these questions may require you to apply what you know about mechanical devices to predict the outcome of certain situations.

Looking at levers

Believe it or not, one of the best places to find out more about levers is at the playground. Consider this: A *lever* uses a metal or wooden bar that pivots on a fixed point — a *fulcrum* — to lift heavy objects. Sound familiar? A seesaw is a type of lever. One person sits on one end of the bar, and his or her weight causes the person on the other side of the bar to lift into the air. The fixed point on which the seesaw pivots is the fulcrum. You can apply your personal seesawing experiences to your understanding of levers.

To lift heavy objects using minimal force, position one end of a lever under the heavy object and make sure the lever itself is positioned over a fulcrum. The closer the heavy object is to the fulcrum, the less force you have to apply to lift it. If necessary, move the fulcrum closer to the object you want to lift. Then lift the object by applying force to the opposite end of the lever. The force required to lift the object can be much less than the weight of the object. To determine exactly how much force is necessary to lift the object, you can use the following formula:

$$w \times d_1 = f \times d_2$$

In the formula, w is the weight of the object you want to lift, d_1 is the distance from the object to the fulcrum, f is the force necessary to lift the object, and d_2 is the distance from the fulcrum to you. Depending on the exam, this formula may or may not be provided. It's best to learn it just in case the test you take doesn't provide it.

The following lever question demonstrates how this formula works and resembles those you may see on the written exam:

Based on the illustration, how many pounds of force must the firefighter apply to the lever to lift the box?

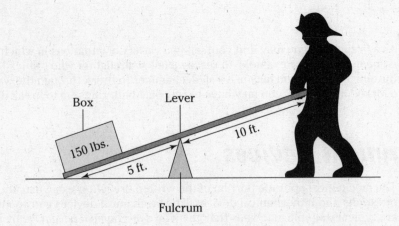

(A) 50

(B) 75

(C) 100

(D) 125

To answer this question, plug the information you know into the equation. The weight of the object is 150 pounds, so $w = 150$. The distance from the object to the fulcrum is 5 feet, so $d_1 = 5$. The distance from the firefighter to the fulcrum is 10 feet, so $d_2 = 10$. You must solve for force, f:

$$w \times d_1 = f \times d_2$$
$$150 \times 5 = f \times 10$$
$$\frac{750}{10} = \frac{\cancel{10}f}{\cancel{10}}$$
$$75 = f$$

Therefore, the correct answer is (B). The firefighter has to exert 75 pounds of force to lift the 150-pound box.

Ramping up your effort with inclined planes

A playground slide is an example of an inclined plane. Like a slide, an *inclined plane* is a flat, slanted surface that is higher on one end. It moves objects from the top to the bottom. Unlike a slide, however, you can also use an inclined plane to move objects from the bottom to the top. Some other examples of inclined planes include ramps and hills.

The mechanical advantage in using an inclined plane is to increase the distance an object must travel to reduce the amount of force required to move it. In other words, lifting an object straight up requires a lot of force applied over a short distance; however, using an inclined plane requires a little force over a longer distance.

As the angle of an inclined plane increases — that is, the incline gets steeper — the speed of the object moving down the incline also increases. As the angle of the inclined plane decreases, the speed of the object moving down the incline slows down.

To answer questions about inclined planes on the written firefighter exam, you must use what you know about decreasing and increasing inclined planes and consider the size and weight of the object moving up or down the incline, because forces such as gravity and friction affect the movement of objects on inclined planes. Use the following tips when answering questions about inclined planes:

✔ When you apply force to push something up an incline, it moves upward. When you apply force to move something down an incline, it moves downward.

✔ Objects moving down an inclined plane move more slowly than objects traveling straight down.

✔ Because gravity pulls down on an object moving up an incline, you need to exert more effort (force) to move an object up an incline than down it.

✔ Friction occurs at the point where the surface of the object meets the surface of the incline. Objects with a larger surface-to-surface contact area move up and down the incline more slowly than objects with a smaller surface-to-surface contact area.

Take a look at the following inclined plane question, which is similar to those you might see on the written firefighter exam:

Box 1 and Box 2 are made of the same material and have the same weight. Based on the illustration, which box will require more effort to slide up the ramp?

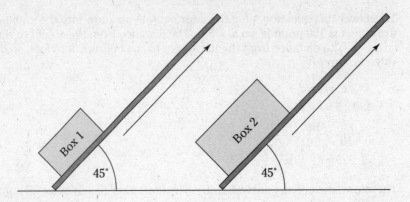

(A) Box 1 will require more effort to slide up the ramp.

(B) Box 2 will require more effort to slide up the ramp.

(C) The boxes will require an equal amount of effort to slide up the ramp.

(D) Neither box will require any effort to slide up the ramp.

Consider what you know. The boxes are made of the same material, weigh the same amount, and based on the illustration, you know that the ramps are positioned at the same angle. The only difference is that Box 1 is smaller than Box 2. This means more friction will exist between the surface of Box 2 and the ramp than will exist between the surface of Box 1 and the ramp. Therefore, Box 2 will require more effort to slide up the ramp. The correct answer is (B).

Turning to wheels and axles

If you've ever ridden a Ferris wheel, turned a doorknob, or turned on a faucet, then you have an idea of how wheels and axles work. A *wheel and axle* is a simple machine that consists of a large wheel that rotates around either a small shaft or another smaller wheel (the *axle*). When the axle turns, the wheel moves a greater distance than the axle in one full rotation. The wheel and axle acts as a lever rotating around a fulcrum. (See "Looking at levers" earlier in this chapter for details on how levers work.)

Turning an axle, like lifting a heavy object, requires a great amount of force. The wheel, like a lever, gives you a mechanical advantage, because it allows you to apply less force to make the axle turn.

To determine the mechanical advantage of a wheel and axle, you have to divide the radius of the wheel (the distance from the outer edge to the middle) by the radius of the axle. You can use the following formula:

$$\text{Mechanical Advantage } (MA) = \frac{\text{radius of wheel}}{\text{radius of axle}}$$

The following wheel and axle question is similar to those you may see in the mechanical aptitude portion of the written firefighter exam:

If the radius of a wheel is 12 inches and the radius of the wheel's axle is 2 inches, what is the mechanical advantage?

(A) 2

(B) 4

(C) 6

(D) 12

To answer the question, plug the information you know into the formula. The radius of the wheel is 12 inches, and the radius of the axle is 2 inches:

$$MA = \frac{r_{wheel}}{r_{axle}}$$
$$MA = \frac{12}{2}$$
$$MA = 6$$

Therefore, the mechanical advantage is 6. The correct answer is (C).

Perusing pulleys

You're probably familiar with the mini blinds that many people have hanging on their windows. If you've ever tugged on the string to raise the blinds, then you've operated a pulley. Like a lever, a pulley, which is a variation of a wheel and axle, is a simple machine that includes a wheel and a rope or belt. Pulleys do the following:

- **Change the direction of an applied force:** In other words, you pull down to lift something up. A single pulley, such as the one in window blinds, uses a wheel and a rope or belt to hoist objects. The wheel has a grooved rim that holds the rope or belt in place. To operate the pulley, you have to secure one end of the rope to the object you want to lift and run the rope over the wheel. As you pull down on the other end of the rope, the object lifts into the air. By changing the direction of the applied force, the pulley makes it easier to lift a heavy object.

- **Transmit rotational motion:** In a pulley system with two wheels connected by a belt, the rotation of one wheel results in the rotation of the belt, which in turn rotates the other wheel. *Belt-drive pulleys* consist of two or more wheels connected by a belted loop. The rotation of one wheel causes the belt to rotate, which it turn causes the other wheels in the belt-drive pulley system to rotate.

In a belt-drive pulley system, all the wheels rotate in the same direction. If the belt between two wheels is crossed, however, the wheels rotate in the opposite directions. In a belt-drive pulley system, smaller wheels spin faster and make more revolutions per minute than larger pulleys. A conveyor belt at the supermarket is an example of a belt-drive pulley.

The mechanical aptitude portion of the written firefighter exam often includes questions about pulleys. Take a look at the following pulley question, which is similar to those you may encounter:

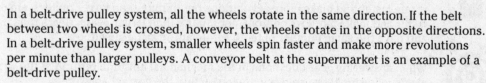

Based on the illustration, Pulley A

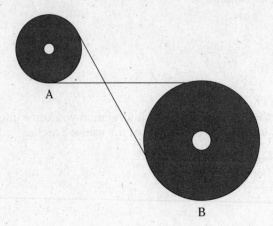

A

B

(A) spins counterclockwise.

(B) spins clockwise.

(C) spins faster than Pulley B.

(D) makes fewer revolutions per minute than Pulley B.

To answer this question, consider the information provided in the illustration. The illustration doesn't indicate which direction either pulley is moving, so you can eliminate both Choice (A) and Choice (B). In terms of size, Pulley A is smaller than Pulley B, which means that it must spin faster and make more revolutions per minute than Pulley B. Therefore, you can eliminate Choice (D). The correct answer is Choice (C).

Sinking your teeth into gears

Everyday items such as can openers, watches, clocks, and cars all have gears. Like a pulley, a gear is another version of a wheel and axle. A *gear* is a rotating wheel with teeth that usually fit together with the teeth of other gears.

When two gears touch and their teeth interlock with each other, they always rotate in opposite directions. However, when two gears are connected by a chain but do not touch each other, such as on a bicycle, they spin in the same direction. Just as smaller pulleys rotate faster and make more revolutions per minute than larger pulleys, smaller gears rotate faster and make more revolutions per minute than larger gears. Gears that are the same size and have the same number of teeth rotate at the same speed.

When answering gear questions in the mechanical aptitude portion of the written firefighter exam, following these steps can help you find the correct answer:

1. **Identify the gear for which the direction of rotation is provided.**

   This gear is called the *driver gear*. Follow the driver gear's movement and take note of where it makes contact with the other gears.

2. **Determine the rotational direction of the other gears by identifying how the driver gear will move the teeth of the other gears.**

3. **If the question asks you to determine the direction of a gear that is not in contact with the driver gear, figure out the direction of the gears that are in contact with the driver gear first.**

   Then base your answer on the rotational direction of the other gears.

Look at the following question about gears, which is similar to the questions you may see on the written exam:

Based on the illustration, if Gear A rotates in a counterclockwise direction, Gear B

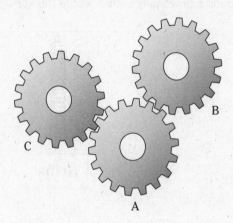

(A) rotates clockwise.

(B) rotates counterclockwise.

(C) does not rotate.

(D) rotates in the opposite direction of Gear C.

Based on the illustration, you can see that the teeth of Gear A and the teeth of Gear B interlock, which means they have to spin in opposite directions. If Gear A, which is the driver gear because you know the direction of its movement, rotates counterclockwise, then Gear B (and Gear C) must rotate clockwise, so Choice (A) is correct.

Stretching out with springs

If you ever played with a Slinky as a child, then you're familiar with how springs work. A *spring* is an elasticized coil that returns to its original shape after being compressed (pushed together) or extended (pulled apart). Look closely and you can find springs in everyday objects such as cars and retractable ink pens.

When answering questions about springs on the mechanical aptitude portion of the written firefighter exam, you can assume that all springs behave linearly, which means a spring that stretches 5 inches under a pull of 50 pounds will stretch 10 inches under a pull of 100 pounds. The written firefighter exam usually avoids questions about a spring's *elastic limit*, or the point at which a spring has been stretched so far that it can never return to its original shape. Remember that Slinky? If you extended it too far, you'd break its elastic limit, and its coils would bend and twist. After that, it'd never look the same.

Springs can be arranged in two patterns:

- **Series:** Springs in series hook together from end to end. In a series, the total pulling force passes through each spring. For example, if you have two springs of the same size and each spring stretches 1 inch under a pull of 10 pounds, when you hook them together in a series, each spring will still stretch 1 inch under a pull of 10 pounds.

- **Parallel:** Springs in parallel line up side by side. With parallel springs, the pulling force is divided equally among the springs. For example, if you have two springs of the same size and each spring stretches 1 inch under a pull of 10 pounds, when you line them up in parallel, each spring bears only half the weight, or 5 pounds, which means that each spring stretches half as much, or only 0.5 inch.

EXAMPLE EXAM

The following spring question is similar to the ones you may encounter on the written firefighter exam:

A spring bearing a 10-pound weight has stretched 0.5 inches. If you were to increase the weight to 15 pounds, how many inches would the spring stretch?

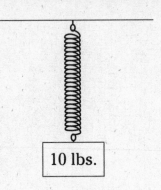

10 lbs.

(A) 0.75 inches

(B) 1 inch

(C) 1.5 inches

(D) 4 inches

You know that the spring moves 0.5 inches under a pull of 10 pounds. You also know that springs behave linearly. Therefore, if you add another 5 pounds, which is half of the 10-pound pull, the spring will stretch another 0.25 inches, which is half the distance it stretched under a pull of 10 pounds. Then you just have to add: 0.5 + 0.25 = 0.75. The spring would stretch 0.75 inches under a pull of 15 pounds. The correct answer is (A).

Sorting out screws

A *screw*, which is a type of threaded hardware, is formed by wrapping an inclined plane around a cylinder. The inclined plane creates ridges on the cylinder, which are the *thread* of the screw. You insert a screw into another object by rotating it, which causes the thread to cut into the object and hold the screw in place. If the object also has grooves, the screw's thread fits into the grooves to lock into place. Nuts and bolts are examples of threaded hardware.

REMEMBER

When answering questions about screws on the written firefighter exam, you should remember the following:

✔ To tighten a screw into an object, turn it clockwise. This creates a tight bond between the screw and the object. To loosen a screw, turn it counterclockwise. This creates a weak bond between the screw and the object. (When using most screws, the phrase "righty-tighty, lefty loosey" can help you remember which way to turn them to tighten or loosen.)

✔ For a reverse-threaded screw, turn the screw counterclockwise to tighten it and clockwise to loosen it.

✔ The slope of the inclined plane determines the distance between the threads. If the inclined plane is steep, the screw will have wider threads. Screws with wide threads are more difficult to turn than screws with narrow threads.

Based on the illustration of a standard threaded nut and bolt, what will most likely happen if you turn the nut counterclockwise?

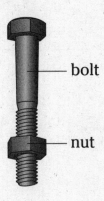

(A) It will move down the screw.

(B) It will move up the screw.

(C) It will lock into place.

(D) It will be difficult to turn.

To answer this question, consider what you know about screws. Most screws, when turned counterclockwise, will loosen. Like screws, nuts and bolts are types of threaded hardware, so the same is probably true of them. Therefore, turning the nut counterclockwise will likely loosen the nut from the bolt, which means that it will move down the screw. Therefore, the correct answer is (A).

Practice Mechanical Aptitude Questions

The following passages and question sets are designed to help you assess your mechanical aptitude. Read each question carefully. If a question includes an image, study it carefully to see how it relates to the question and what information it provides. Then select the answer choice that *most correctly* answers the question.

> *Use the following image to answer questions 1 and 2.*

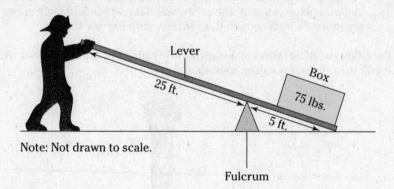

Lever

Box

25 ft.

75 lbs.

5 ft.

Note: Not drawn to scale.

Fulcrum

1. Based on the illustration, how many pounds of force must the firefighter apply to the lever to lift the box?

   (A) 5 pounds

   (B) 10 pounds

   (C) 15 pounds

   (D) 20 pounds

2. If the firefighter moved the fulcrum 5 feet farther from the box, how much force would he have to apply to lift the load at the opposite end of the lever?

   (A) 7 pounds

   (B) 12.5 pounds

   (C) 25 pounds

   (D) 37.5 pounds

> *Use the following image to answer question 3.*

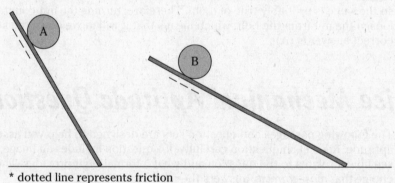

A

B

* dotted line represents friction

3. Ball A and Ball B are the same size and weight. Based on the illustration, what will most likely happen?

   (A) Ball A will reach the bottom before Ball B.

   (B) Ball B will reach the bottom before Ball A.

   (C) Ball A will roll, but Ball B will not move.

   (D) Ball A and Ball B will reach the bottom at the same time.

Use the following image to answer question 4.

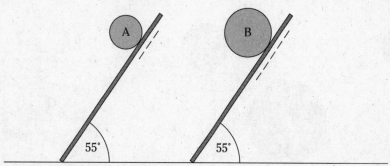

* dotted line represents friction

4. Ball A and Ball B are different sizes, but their weights and composition are the same. Each ball is positioned on an inclined plane set at the same angle and constructed of the same material. Based on the illustration, what will most likely happen if both balls begin to roll at the same time?

    (A) Ball A and Ball B will roll at the same speed.

    (B) Ball A will roll faster than Ball B.

    (C) Ball B will roll faster than Ball A.

    (D) Ball A will stop halfway down, but ball B will roll to the bottom.

5. In a wheel-and-axle setup, if the radius of a wheel is 144 inches and the radius of its axle is 12 inches, what is the mechanical advantage?

    (A) 12

    (B) 24

    (C) 48

    (D) 96

Use the following image to answer questions 6 and 7.

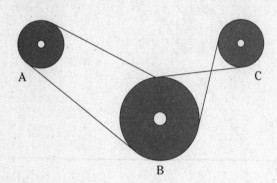

Use the following image to answer question 8.

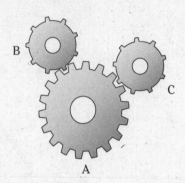

6. Wheel B is twice the size of Wheels A and C, and Wheels A and C are the same size. If Wheels A and C make 50 revolutions per minute, how many revolutions per minute does Wheel B make?

    (A) 5

    (B) 25

    (C) 50

    (D) 100

7. Based on the pulley setup in the image, which of the following statements is correct?

    (A) If Wheel B spins clockwise, Wheels A and C must spin counterclockwise.

    (B) If Wheel B spins counterclockwise, Wheels A and C must spin clockwise.

    (C) If Wheel B spins clockwise, Wheel A must spin clockwise and Wheel C must spin counterclockwise.

    (D) If Wheel B spins clockwise, Wheel A must spin counterclockwise and Wheel C must spin clockwise.

8. Based on the image, which of the following statements about the gears is true?

    (A) Gear B makes fewer revolutions per minute than Gears A and C.

    (B) Gear A makes more revolutions per minute than Gears B and C.

    (C) Gears B and C make the same number of revolutions per minute as Gear A.

    (D) Gears B and C make the same number of revolutions per minute.

Use the following image to answer question 9.

9. If Gear 2 turns clockwise, which of the following statements about the gears is true?

    (A) Gears 1 and 3 turn counterclockwise.

    (B) Gear 4 turns counterclockwise.

    (C) Gears 3 and 5 turn clockwise.

    (D) Gears 1 and 5 turn clockwise.

10. If a spring stretches 2 inches under a pull of 8 pounds, how many inches will the spring stretch under a pull of 64 pounds?

    (A) 4 inches

    (B) 8 inches

    (C) 16 inches

    (D) 24 inches

Use the following image to answer question 11.

Set A
Springs in parallel

Set B
Springs in a series

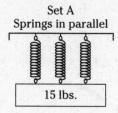

15 lbs.

Note: Not drawn to scale.

15 lbs.

---

11. The six springs in this illustration are the same size. In Set A, the stretch of each spring caused by the 15-pound weight is

    (A) three times as much as each spring in Set B.

    (B) four times as much as each spring in Set B.

    (C) one-third as much as each spring in Set B.

    (D) the same as each spring in Set B.

Use the following image to answer question 12.

A   B

---

12. Based on the illustration, which of the following statements is correct?

    (A) Screw A would require a counter-clockwise turn to tighten into place.

    (B) Screw B would require a counter-clockwise turn to tighten into place.

    (C) Screw A would be easier to insert into an object.

    (D) Screw B would be easier to insert into an object.

Use the following image to answer question 13.

---

13. Look at the tool shown above. This tool would most likely be used to

    (A) ram open a door.

    (B) chip away stone.

    (C) open a fire hydrant.

    (D) ventilate a ceiling.

14. What do a battering ram, a mallet, and a sledgehammer have in common?

    (A) They are used to cut through materials.

    (B) They are used to tighten bolts.

    (C) They are used to pry open locks.

    (D) They are used to break materials.

15. Which of these tools would a firefighter most likely use to open a fire hydrant?

    (A) a screwdriver

    (B) a Kelly tool

    (C) a wrench

    (D) pliers

> *Use the following image to answer question 16.*

16. Look at the tool above. This tool would most likely be used to

    (A) pry open a car door.

    (B) cut through light materials.

    (C) pry nails loose.

    (D) cut through metal.

17. Which of the following tools would a firefighter most likely use to free a car accident victim trapped in a vehicle?

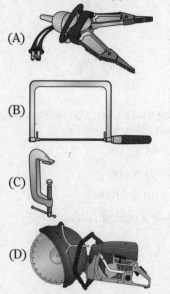

    (A)

    (B)

    (C)

    (D)

18. Which of these tools should never be used to cut through metal?

    (A) ventilation saw

    (B) cutting torch

    (C) handsaw

    (D) bolt cutters

19. During forcible entry operations, a pike pole would most likely be used for

    (A) prying.

    (B) cutting.

    (C) striking.

    (D) pushing/pulling.

20. Which of these tools is designed to be used as a lever?

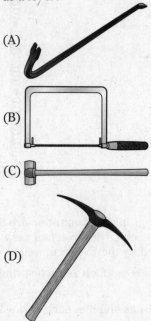

    (A)

    (B)

    (C)

    (D)

Answers and Explanations

Use this answer key to score the practice mechanical aptitude questions in this chapter. The answer explanations give you a little more insight on how to find the right answers. How did you do? Remember, the more you study tools and machines, the more you'll improve these skills.

1. **C.** To answer this question, use the equation $w \times d_1 = f \times d_2$:

$$w \times d_1 = f \times d_2$$
$$75 \times 5 = f \times 25$$
$$\frac{375}{25} = \frac{25f}{25}$$
$$15 = f$$

   Therefore, Choice (C) is the correct answer. The firefighter would have to use 15 pounds of force.

2. **D.** Again, use the equation $w \times d_1 = f \times d_2$. The fulcrum moves 5 feet to the left, so $d_1 = 10$ feet and $d_2 = 20$ feet:

$$w \times d_1 = f \times d_2$$
$$75 \times 10 = f \times 20$$
$$\frac{750}{20} = \frac{20f}{20}$$
$$37.5 = f$$

   Therefore, Choice (D) is the correct answer.

3. **A.** Recall that the steeper the incline, the faster an object will move down it. Because Ball A's incline is steeper, it will roll faster and, therefore, reach the bottom before Ball B. Choice (A) is correct.

4. **B.** Because Ball A is smaller than Ball B, Ball A has a smaller surface-to-surface friction area; therefore, it will roll down the incline faster (even though the balls have the same weight, are made of the same material, and sit on the same degree of incline), which means Choice (B) is correct.

5. **A.** To figure out the mechanical advantage of wheel and axle, divide the radius of the wheel (144) by the radius of the axle (12): $144 \div 12 = 12$. Choice (A) is correct.

6. **B.** Because Wheel B is twice the size of Wheels A and C, it spins half as fast. If Wheels A and C make 50 revolutions per minute, then Wheel B makes half as many revolutions. Therefore, Choice (B), 25, is the correct answer.

7. **C.** Wheel A and Wheel B are connected by an open belt, which means they must rotate in the same direction. Wheel B and Wheel C are connected by a crossed belt, which means they must rotate in opposite directions. Therefore Choice (C) is correct: If Wheel B spins clockwise, Wheel A must spin clockwise and Wheel C must spin counterclockwise.

8. **D.** Because Gears B and C are the same size and have the same number of teeth, they make the same number of revolutions per minute. Gear A is larger than Gears B and C, so it makes fewer revolutions per minute than Gears B and C.

9. **A.** If Gear 2 rotates clockwise, Gears 1 and 3 have to rotate counterclockwise. This means that Gear 4 will rotate clockwise and Gear 5 will spin counterclockwise. Therefore, only Choice (A) is true.

10. **C.** If a spring stretches 2 inches under a pull of 8 pounds, it'll stretch 16 inches under a pull of 64 pounds. If you divide 64 by 8, the answer is 8, which means that 64 pounds is 8 times heavier than 8 pounds; therefore, the spring will stretch 8 times as far under a pull of 64 pounds: $8 \times 2 = 16$. Choice (C) is the correct answer.

11. **C.** The springs in Set A distribute the 15 pounds of weight evenly, which means that each spring bears 5 pounds. Each spring in Set B bears the full 15 pounds of weight. Therefore, each spring in Set A bears one-third as much weight as the springs in Set B. Choice (C) is correct.

12. **C.** Based on the illustration, you can determine that Screw B has a wider thread than Screw A. Screws with a wider thread are more difficult to turn, which means that Screw A would be easier to insert into an object. Choice (C) is correct.

13. **B.** The tool in the picture is a striking tool called a *chisel,* which can be used to chip away stone. Choice (B) is correct.

14. **D.** A battering ram, a mallet, and a sledgehammer are striking tools, which are often used to break up materials. Choice (D) is correct.

15. **C.** A firefighter would most likely use a wrench to open a fire hydrant. Choice (C) is correct.

16. **B.** The tool in the picture is a utility knife, which is used to cut through light materials. Choice (B) is correct.

17. **A.** Firefighters would most likely need a prying tool to free someone trapped inside a vehicle. Only a hydraulic spreader is a prying tool, so Choice (A) is correct.

18. **A.** A cutting torch, a handsaw, and bolt cutters can all cut through metal. A ventilation saw, however, is used to make quick cuts in roofs, ceilings, or walls and shouldn't be used to cut through metal. Choice (A) is correct.

19. **D.** A pike pole is a pushing/pulling tool used to open burning walls or ceilings during fires. Choice (D) is correct.

20. **A.** A coping saw is a cutting tool, and a sledgehammer is a striking tool. A pick is also a striking tool, typically used to break up earth or stone. The pick shouldn't be confused with a pick-head axe, which is a cutting tool sometimes used to pry up floorboards. Only the crowbar, a prying tool, is designed to be used as a lever. Choice (A) is correct.

Chapter 11

Acing the National Firefighter Selection Inventory Test

....

....

Many fire departments require applicants to take and pass a written test, but they don't all give the same written test. Sound crazy? Well, it's not as bad as you may think. Written firefighter tests all have the same goal — to see whether applicants have what it takes to be a firefighter. These tests measure whether an applicant has the necessary skills and personality traits to succeed on the job. You don't need knowledge of firefighting to pass this type of written test.

How does a test do this? Think about the skills and personality traits firefighters need on the job. They must be able to make good decisions. To make these decisions, they must be able to remember important details, such as the location of exits in a building. They must be team players — a firefighter should not have an enormous ego and try to be a hero. Firefighters must be able to stay calm under pressure. They shouldn't panic and run out of the building if someone inside needs their help!

To make sure the firefighter exam asks the right questions, some fire departments give a test called the National Firefighter Selection Inventory (NFSI) test. We tell you what you need to know to do well on the NFSI in this chapter.

Checking Out What's on the NFSI

Instead of developing individualized written exams, many departments use the standardized NFSI, one of many standardized tests available, to test entry-level candidates. The word *standardized* means that the test follows the same rules, format, and so on, regardless of where you take it. The NFSI, unlike many written exams, doesn't contain questions about mechanical aptitude, spatial orientation, or observation and memory, but it still measures skills that firefighters use regularly. When creating the NFSI, a team of firefighting experts pinpointed a number of tasks that firefighters must do on the job. They correlated these tasks to 11 essential areas for testing, which they divided into two sections on the NFSI: a *cognitive*, or thinking, section and a *behavioral*, or personality, section.

Multiple-choice questions on the NFSI test your skills in the following cognitive areas:

- ✔ Verbal comprehension
- ✔ Verbal expression
- ✔ Problem sensitivity
- ✔ Deductive reasoning
- ✔ Inductive reasoning
- ✔ Information ordering
- ✔ Mathematical reasoning
- ✔ Number facility

Also expect to answer questions on the following personality traits:

- ✔ Stress tolerance
- ✔ Team orientation
- ✔ Motivation/attitude

The cognitive part of NFSI contains 105 multiple-choice questions. Most questions have five answer options — (A), (B), (C), (D), and (E) — but some questions have only four options. The behavioral part has 55 questions for which you must rate your responses on a scale of 1 (Strongly Agree) to 5 (Strongly Disagree).

You have 2.5 hours to complete this test. On the day of the test, you need to bring two sharpened number-two pencils, an eraser, and a watch.

Only correct answers count on the NFSI, so if you're unsure of an answer, take a good guess. Use the process of elimination to cross off answer options that you're certain are incorrect. It's better to try to guess the correct answer than to leave it blank and know it'll be marked wrong.

Assessing Your Cognitive Skills

The first part of the NFSI measures your ability to understand written material, your judgment and reasoning skills, and your aptitude for math and numbers. In this section, we explain what each part of the test measures, and we provide examples of the types of questions you encounter.

Testing your verbal comprehension

The NFSI has questions about *verbal comprehension,* which is your ability to understand words, phases, or sentences (see Chapter 4 for tips on verbal comprehension). Now, you know how to read, but do you always remember the details of what you've read? The verbal comprehension questions on the NFSI test your ability to remember or find details in passages.

Read this paragraph:

> Engine 2 was dispatched at 7:12 p.m. to put out a fire at the Murray Apartment Complex in Exeter. It arrived at the scene at 7:18 p.m. The building was fully engulfed but had no occupants at the time. Firefighters O'Hara and Reagan assisted many others in putting out the flames. After the fire was extinguished, Firefighter O'Hara spoke to Mrs. Langan, who lives near the complex. Mrs. Langan said she saw some teenagers smoking behind the complex before the fire. Engine 2 left the scene to return to the fire station at 9:15 p.m.

The passage on the test is longer than the one you just read, and when you take the actual test, you can reread to find what you need to know to answer the questions. But to practice recalling details, cover up this passage and see how many of the following questions you can answer correctly.

✔ What time did Engine 2 arrive at the scene?

✔ What was the name of the woman who lives near the complex?

✔ What time did Engine 2 arrive back at the fire station?

Read the following passage, which is the same length as one you may see on the test. As you answer the example questions, you may refer back to the passage as needed.

Engine 9 was dispatched at 6:16 p.m. to a home to put out a kitchen fire. The firefighters arrived at 658 Main Street at approximately 6:22 p.m. The front door of the house was open, and several older children were nervously waiting in the yard. A woman inside the smoke-filled home identified herself as Mrs. Milano. The woman said her husband was cooking when he left the room to answer the telephone. While he was out of the room, a pan caught on fire and a smoke alarm went off. Mr. Milano saw the fire and grabbed a fire extinguisher. He started to put out the fire, which had spread to two walls in the kitchen and the ceiling. At this time, Mrs. Milano came downstairs and called the fire department. She told the children to leave the house and wait outside.

Firefighter Rodriguez inspected the kitchen to make certain the fire was out. Firefighter Simonson took Mr. and Mrs. Milano outside. He then examined the burns on Mr. Milano's arms, right shoulder, and face. Firefighter Simonson decided that Mr. Milano should be transported to the hospital. He was given oxygen and helped into the ambulance, which was waiting by the curb. Mrs. Milano sent the children to a neighbor's house and accompanied Mr. Milano in the ambulance. She was also given oxygen. They arrived at the hospital at 7:31 p.m. Mr. Milano's burns were mostly first degree. Only a few burns were second degree. He was treated and released from the hospital two hours later. The Milanos are staying with a relative across town.

The children were in the yard because _____ told them to leave the house.

(A) Mr. Milano

(B) Firefighter Simonson

(C) a neighbor

(D) Mrs. Milano

(E) Firefighter O'Hara

If you look back at the passage, you see that Mrs. Milano told the children to leave the house, so Choice (D) is the correct answer.

Mr. Milano arrived at the hospital at _____.

(A) 8:02 p.m.

(B) 7:31 p.m.

(C) 6:31 p.m.

(D) 6:22 p.m.

(E) 6:16 p.m.

According to the passage, Mr. Milano arrived at the hospital at 7:31 p.m., so Choice (B) is correct.

Examining your verbal expression skills

Firefighters have to communicate with many people on the job, including fire victims, witnesses, other firefighters, emergency personnel, and supervisors. The verbal expression questions on the NFSI measure your ability to use language to communicate effectively with others. It tests your knowledge of vocabulary, distinctions among words, grammar, and the way in which words are ordered. Turn back to Chapter 5 to find out more about verbal expression.

Questions on verbal expression may look like these:

Please choose the appropriate word or phrase to complete the sentence.

As soon as they arrived at the scene, the firefighters saw that the building _____ in flames.

(A) is engulfed

(B) was engulfed

(C) had engulfed

(D) has engulfed

(E) did engulf

To answer this question correctly, you need to pay attention to the tense of the sentence. The word *arrived* in the introductory clause lets you know that the sentence is past tense. Also, the flames, not the building, were doing the engulfing, so (C), (D), and (E) are wrong. Therefore, Choice (B) is correct. Firefighters saw that the building was engulfed in flames. Try one more:

Firefighter O'Brian said the parade _____ at 10:00 a.m. next Saturday morning.

(A) began

(B) had begun

(C) will begin

(D) beginning

(E) has begun

The words "next Saturday" tell you that the parade will take place in the future. Therefore, the correct answer is Choice (C), "will begin." Don't be confused by the past tense verb "said" in the main clause. Firefighter O'Brian made the statement about the parade in the past, but his statement refers to an upcoming event, which requires a future tense verb.

Identify which one of the underlined words is spelled incorrectly.

Firefighters must be in <u>excellent</u> <u>physicle</u> condition to perform their jobs <u>effectively</u>. Carrying heavy <u>equipment</u> takes great <u>muscle</u> strength.

(A) excellent

(B) physicle

(C) effectively

(D) equipment

(E) muscle

Choice (B) is the correct answer. The correct spelling of the word is *physical*.

Not all fire extinguishers are <u>identical</u>. They are <u>designed</u> to fight <u>different</u> types of fires. For example, a Class C fire extinguisher should be used to put out fires <u>involving</u> <u>electrikal</u> equipment.

(A) identical

(B) designed

(C) different

(D) involving

(E) electrikal

Choice (E) is correct. The correct spelling of the word is *electrical*.

Appreciating problem sensitivity questions

Some questions on the NFSI ask you to identify a problem. Don't panic! You don't have to solve the problem. You just have to indicate that a problem exists and choose an answer choice stating what kind of problem it is. This section of the NFSI is called "Problem Sensitivity." Problem sensitivity questions are similar to the judgment and reasoning questions you may encounter on other firefighter exams. (For more info, review Chapter 8.)

Read this paragraph:

> Firefighter Martino has been observing the behavior of Firefighter Davis, who has worked at the fire department for more than 30 years. Firefighter Davis used to be very efficient, but over the past few months, he has been forgetting appointments and losing personal items such as his glasses and keys. He recently forgot to attend an important training meeting. When Firefighter Martino asked him why he wasn't at the meeting, he looked confused. Sometimes Firefighter Davis asks the same questions over and over again and has trouble completing routine tasks.

Based on the information given in the paragraph, if Davis were having a problem, it would most likely be _____.

(A) financial

(B) drugs

(C) job stress

(D) marital

(E) health related

Firefighter Davis's behavior seems health related, so Choice (E) is the correct answer. He shows signs of dementia or possibly Alzheimer's disease, which often appear later in life, and the paragraph specifically states that he was an efficient firefighter for more than 30 years and only recently started exhibiting memory problems. Some drugs cause memory problems, but drugs also cause physical symptoms — red, watery eyes, sleeplessness, and weight loss, to name just a few — which the paragraph doesn't discuss. Therefore, you can rule out Choice (B).

Read this paragraph:

> Firefighter Kelly has been observing the behavior of Firefighter Lombardo, who has worked for the department for several years. Firefighter Lombardo's appearance has become disheveled, and her hands often shake. Firefighter Kelly has noticed that Firefighter Lombardo is restless and often perspires even when it is not warm outside.

He knows that she takes medication for back pain, but lately he has seen her take it more often than she used to. Last week, she was late for her shift because she and her husband had an argument. Firefighter Kelly heard her tell a friend that she has been having trouble sleeping.

Based on the information given in the paragraph, if Firefighter Lombardo were having a problem, it would most likely be _____.

(A) drugs

(B) domestic violence

(C) marital

(D) job stress

(E) financial

Firefighter Lombardo's behavior seems to be related to drugs, which is Choice (A). She may be addicted to the medication she is taking for her back. Although the paragraph says that she had an argument with her husband, the argument likely occurred because of her problem.

Applying deductive reasoning

To answer some questions on the NFSI, you have to use deductive reasoning. When you use *deductive reasoning*, you read general information and then apply this information to a specific situation and draw a conclusion. The deductive reasoning questions on the NFSI are similar to the judgment and reasoning questions you may encounter on other written firefighter exams.

Consider this statement: All birds have feathers. Your friend Burt has a parakeet named Squeaky. A parakeet is a kind of bird. You can use deductive reasoning to draw this conclusion: Squeaky has feathers. See how it works? You moved from the general (all birds) to the specific (Squeaky).

Now read this passage.

Physicians use the following guidelines to classify burns by severity:

- ✔ **First-degree burn:** Also called a *superficial burn,* this type of burn is the least severe. The skin reddens but does not blister. A first-degree burn may be a sunburn or a burn from hot liquid. First-degree burns usually heal on their own with no scarring.

- ✔ **Second-degree burn:** Also called a *partial thickness burn,* a second-degree burn causes blistering and damage to the top layers of the skin. This type of burn may result in scarring. Second-degree burns can result from flames and scalding liquids.

- ✔ **Third-degree burn:** Also called a *full thickness burn,* a third-degree burn damages all layers of the skin. Third-degree burns almost always require surgery and rehabilitation. This type of burn may result from prolonged exposure to flames or chemicals or electrical injuries.

- ✔ **Fourth-degree burn:** Fourth-degree burns destroy all layers of the skin and damage tendons and muscles. With a fourth-degree burn, there is no sensation in the burn area. A fourth-degree burn may result from prolonged exposure to flames or a high-voltage electrical injury.

- ✔ **Inhalation burn:** This type of burn results from the inhalation of hot air, which damages the upper airways. It may be caused by inhaling smoke or toxic chemicals.

According to the burn guidelines, if a person has a burn that blisters but damages only the top layers of the skin, what type of burn does the person have?

(A) first degree

(B) second degree

(C) third degree

(D) fourth degree

(E) inhalation

To answer this question, you have to use the general burn guidelines and apply them to a specific situation. According to the passage, a burn that blisters but damages only the top layers of the skin is a second-degree burn, so the answer is Choice (B).

During a house fire, a firefighter suffers a burn on his arm that has damaged all layers of his skin but not his muscles and tendons. The firefighter has suffered a _____ burn.

(A) first-degree

(B) second-degree

(C) third-degree

(D) fourth-degree

(E) inhalation

According to the descriptions of the burn classifications, a burn that damages all layers of the skin but not the muscles and tendons is a third-degree burn. Therefore, the firefighter in this situation has suffered a third-degree burn. Choice (C) is the answer.

Drawing conclusions with inductive reasoning

Inductive reasoning is the opposite of deductive reasoning. With *inductive reasoning*, instead of applying general information to a specific situation, you assess specific details and try to draw a general conclusion, develop a general rule, or figure out how several events relate to each other. Inductive reasoning questions sometimes require using a bit of prior knowledge — things you already know — in addition to reading the passage. Inductive reasoning questions on the NFSI are similar to the judgment and reasoning questions you may encounter on other written firefighter exams.

Suppose your coworker has a red, stuffy nose. Her eyes are watery, and she is coughing. She tells you that her muscles ache. Using inductive reasoning, you assess your co-worker's specific symptoms and draw the general conclusion that she has a cold.

Now read this passage:

> A driver of a pickup truck falls asleep while driving on Kennedy Boulevard, crosses the divider, and hits a minivan head on. It is late at night, but two people who witnessed the accident call 911. The area dispatch center alerts police, emergency medical service, and fire rescue units simultaneously.
>
> Firefighters arrive on the scene and proceed to assess the situation. They examine the scene, the vehicles, and their drivers. The driver of the pickup truck is holding his left arm and is in pain. He is conscious and says he cannot move his fingers. He has a cut on his hand, which is oozing blood. The driver of the minivan is alive, but she is unconscious and is not wearing a seatbelt. The windshield is cracked, and blood oozes

from her forehead. A firefighter determines that she has a head injury. The woman must be removed from the minivan immediately.

After the woman is safely extricated from the minivan, she is transported to the local trauma center for further assessment and treatment of her injuries.

The driver of the pickup truck also receives attention. Other firefighters assess his injuries and general physical condition. Other than the wounded arm, he has no apparent injuries. He is transported to the trauma center.

What symptom of the pickup truck driver most likely indicates a broken arm?

(A) He has a cut on his hand.

(B) His hand is bleeding.

(C) He cannot move his fingers.

(D) He is holding his arm.

(E) He is in pain.

You have to use some prior knowledge and pay attention to key words to answer this inductive reasoning question. All of these answer choices could be symptoms of a broken arm, but the question asks which symptom *most likely* indicates a broken arm. The fact that the pickup driver cannot move his fingers indicates that he may have broken his arm, so Choice (C) is correct. You can — and probably have — experienced all of the symptoms in Choices (A), (B), (D), and (E) without having a broken arm.

An appropriate title for this passage is

(A) "Assessing Victims at the Scene of an Accident."

(B) "The Consequences of Falling Asleep While Driving."

(C) "How to Help a Person with a Head Injury."

(D) "Vehicle Rescue Procedures."

(E) "Head-on Vehicle Accidents."

You may wonder why this type of question falls within the inductive reasoning portion of the NFSI when it resembles the reading comprehension questions in Chapter 4. The truth is, this question requires the use of both reading comprehension and inductive reasoning skills. Consider this: To choose the best title, which encompasses the general focus (main idea) of the entire passage, you must assess the specific details. In other words, you work from the details of a specific situation to create a general rule to fit the situation. The best title for the passage is "Assessing Victims at the Scene of the Accident," because this is what most of the passage is about. Choice (A) is correct.

Making sense of information ordering

Firefighters need to be able to follow directions in the correct order. Some questions on the NFSI are about information ordering. These questions are based on a passage that gives the order in which firefighters should do something or a list of steps that you must arrange in the correct order. These questions are similar to the judgment and reasoning questions you may encounter on other written firefighter exams.

Read this passage about the cradle-in-arms lift/carry:

> Firefighters often have to rescue fire victims who may or may not be conscious. Using the correct lift can protect both the victim and the firefighter from injury. The cradle-in-arms lift/carry should be used to lift children or small adults, as long as the victim is conscious. An unconscious victim presents challenges in terms of weight and the relaxed condition of the body, so a different lift/carry should be used. To perform the cradle-in-arms lift/carry, place one arm under the victim's arms and across the victim's back. Place the other arm under the victim's knees. Keep your back straight as you prepare to lift the victim. Lift the victim to about waist height. Carry the victim to safety.

Of the steps listed below, which would be the one that should be performed *last?*

(A) Place an arm under the victim's knees.

(B) Lift the victim to about waist height.

(C) Place one arm under the victim's arms.

(D) Make sure the victim is conscious.

(E) Keep your back straight as you prepare to lift.

Choice (B) is the correct answer. If you look back at the paragraph, you see that the last steps are to lift the victim and carry the victim to safety.

Determine the order in which you would perform the steps listed in the preceding question.

(A) A, D, E, B, C

(B) D, B, C, E, A

(C) B, A, E, D, B

(D) D, E, A, C, B

(E) D, C, A, E, B

Choice (E) is the correct answer. You should first make sure the victim is conscious and then place one arm under the victim's arms. Your second arm should then be placed under the victim's knees. Keep your back straight as you prepare to lift. Then lift the victim.

Measuring mathematical reasoning

Firefighters often have to "figure things out," such as what length of hose to use and how many firefighters are needed to carry it. The NFSI measures your ability to use mathematical reasoning to answer questions about real-life situations. You can't use a calculator to answer these questions, but you can practice your math skills in Chapter 9.

Consider this scenario:

> Happyville gives firefighters a 2 percent pay raise each year if they have fewer than 5 years of experience. Firefighters with 10 years of experience receive a 3 percent pay raise each year, and firefighters with 15 years of experience receive a 4 percent annual raise.

Now, based on this information, if the trend continues, what percentage raise would a firefighter with 20 years of experience receive? Did you say 5 percent? Good! You used mathematical reasoning to answer this question.

Now try to answer these questions:

Use the following table to determine which statement most accurately describes the relationship between the square footage of a building and the required number of fire extinguishers it must have.

Square Footage per Floor	Number of Fire Extinguishers Required
1,000	2
1,500	3
2,000	4
2,500	5
3,000	6

(A) As the square footage is increased by 500 feet, the number of fire extinguishers required is doubled.

(B) As the square footage is increased by 500 feet, the number of fire extinguishers required is tripled.

(C) As the square footage is increased by 500 feet, one additional fire extinguisher is required.

(D) As the square footage is increased by 500 feet, two additional fire extinguishers are needed.

(E) As the square footage is increased by 1,000 feet, one additional fire extinguisher is needed.

Analyze the information in the table before choosing a statement. In the square footage column, the numbers increase by 500 each time (1,000, 1,500, 2,000, and so on). In the number of fire extinguishers column, the numbers increase by one each time (2, 3, 4, and so on). This means that one fire extinguisher is needed for every 500 square feet. Therefore, Choice (C) is correct.

While training to be a firefighter, candidates are tested on their ability to do sit-ups. Using the following table, determine the statement that most accurately describes the relationship between the number of sit-ups and a firefighter's age.

Age	Number of Sit-Ups in One Minute
20–24 years	40
25–29 years	35
30–34 years	30
35–39 years	25
40+ years	20

(A) For every 10 years a firefighter's age increases, the number of sit-ups decreases by about 5.

(B) For every 10 years a firefighter's age increases, the number of sit-ups decreases by about 10.

(C) For every 5 years a firefighter's age increases, the number of sit-ups decreases by about 10.

(D) For every 5 years a firefighter's age increases, the number of sit-ups decreases by about 15.

(E) For every 15 years a firefighter's age increases, the number of sit-ups decreases by about 20.

This question may seem tricky because of the age ranges. If you look closely, however, you see that any age difference of 10 years results in a decrease of 10 sit-ups. For example, the difference in the number of sit-ups for a 20-year-old firefighter and a 30-year-old firefighter is 10 sit-ups (40 – 30 = 10). The difference in the number of sit-ups for a 25-year-old firefighter and a 35-year-old firefighter is also 10 sit-ups (35 – 25 = 10). For every 10 years a firefighter's age increases, the number of sit-ups decreases by 10. Choice (B) is the correct answer.

Navigating number facility questions

Firefighters must be able to add, subtract, multiply, and divide — and quickly. They may need to determine what size ladder is needed to reach the roof in a three-story building. They may need to quickly determine the area of a room. The NFSI has questions about "number facility," which test your basic math skills, and you can't use a calculator on the test. If you have trouble answering the questions in this chapter, brush up on your math skills by practicing (flip to Chapter 9 for a refresher).

Try this question:

Engine 1 is dispatched to the scene of an accident 10 miles from the fire station. The fire truck can travel to the scene at an average speed of 30 miles per hour (mph). How long will it take Engine 1 to reach the scene of the accident?

If Engine 1 can travel 30 miles per hour, it travels about half a mile a minute. If you divide 10 by 0.5, you get 20. It will take 20 minutes for Engine 1 to reach the scene of the accident. You can also use the formula distance = rate × time, or $d = r \times t$ (see Chapter 9). In that case, $10 = 30t$, so $t = \frac{1}{3}$ hour, or 20 minutes.

Now try these problems:

Firefighters respond to a fire in a garage. The garage is 25 feet long and 15 feet wide. What is the area of the garage?

(A) 37.5 square feet

(B) 40 square feet

(C) 80 square feet

(D) 375 square feet

(E) 400 square feet

To find the area, multiply the length by the width: 25 × 15 = 375. The answer is 375 square feet, so Choice (D) is correct.

During a training exercise, firefighters must carry a 50-pound dummy up six flights of stairs. Each flight of stairs has 20 steps. How many steps must each firefighter climb?

(A) 100

(B) 120

(C) 130

(D) 180

(E) 300

To answer this question, multiply 6, the number of flights, by 20, the number of steps in each flight: 6 × 20 = 120. Choice (B) is correct.

Showing Off Your Personality Attributes

The last section of the NFSI assesses your personality. The questions in this section look different from the other questions on the test. They contain a series of statements that you rate on this scale:

1 Strongly agree

2 Agree

3 Not sure

4 Disagree

5 Strongly disagree

Your answers in the behavioral section of the NFSI aren't scored as right or wrong. Your answers indicate your opinions and give the fire department an idea of your personality. The department compares your responses to the responses of successful firefighters. The closer your answers match, the higher your score will be.

Don't be afraid to use the full range of the scale for your responses. Many candidates tend to "hug the middle" of the scale, when in fact the highest points come from the ends of the scale. In addition, don't overanalyze the questions; just choose the first answer that comes to mind for better results.

The statements you must rate on a scale of 1 to 5 are about stress tolerance, team orientation, and motivation/attitude.

Evaluating your coping skills: Stress tolerance

Fighting fires is stressful work. Statements about stress tolerance on the Personality Attributes section of the NFSI measure your ability to perform your job under stressful conditions. Stress tolerance statements may look like these:

✔ I need to be in control of a situation to feel relaxed.

✔ When a deadline approaches, I often feel anxious.

Playing well with others: Team orientation

Do you work well with others? Firefighters must function as a team. Statements about team orientation let the fire department know how you feel about being part of a team. Team orientation statements may look like these:

✔ When I am part of a team, I tend to compete with my team members.

✔ When I am part of a team, I feel responsible for the team as well as myself.

Looking at what gets you going: Motivation/attitude

Your motivation is your desire to perform your duties well, and your attitude is how you feel about your duties. Statements about motivation/attitude give the fire department an idea about what motivates you and what your attitude will be about your work when you're on the job. The following are examples of statements about motivation/attitude:

- ✔ I prefer to do tasks that are enjoyable.
- ✔ I usually do what I am told without complaint.
- ✔ I sometimes give up on difficult tasks.

Practice NFSI Questions

The following questions are similar to those you may encounter on the cognitive section of the NFSI exam. Because the questions in the behavioral section have no right or wrong answers, we've omitted them from this practice. Be sure to read the directions that precede each passage or question. For all questions, choose the answer that *most correctly* answers the question.

> *Use the information in the following passage to answer questions 1 and 2.*

Engine 2 was dispatched at 3:10 a.m. to assist a man complaining of severe chest pain. The firefighters arrived at 278 Skytop Drive at approximately 3:14 a.m. Firefighters Brown and DiYanni exited the engine immediately and approached the house. When Brown knocked on the door, a woman greeted him. She identified herself as Mrs. Freeman, the man's wife. She led the firefighters into a bedroom where the man was lying on the bed. Mrs. Freeman told the firefighters that her husband had had a heart attack two years ago and underwent bypass surgery.

Firefighter DiYanni greeted Mr. Freeman and asked him specific questions concerning his chest pain. Mr. Freeman was suffering shortness of breath but was able to answer the questions clearly. He explained that he had severe pain in his chest and some pain in his arms and his back. He felt nauseous and was perspiring.

Firefighter DiYanni decided that Mr. Freeman should be transported to the hospital immediately. Paramedics had recently arrived on the scene. They gave Mr. Freeman oxygen and lifted him onto a gurney. They wheeled him out of the house and into an ambulance waiting in the driveway. The ambulance departed for the hospital at 3:52 a.m. and arrived at 4:03 a.m.

Mrs. Freeman accompanied her husband. The firefighters gathered their equipment and locked the front door to the house. Mr. Freeman's chest pains were diagnosed as a myocardial infarction. He was admitted to the hospital and later underwent surgery.

1. The room where Mr. Freeman was when the firefighters arrived was the _____.

   (A) kitchen

   (B) living room

   (C) bedroom

   (D) bathroom

   (E) entry hall

2. Mr. Freeman arrived at the hospital at _____.

   (A) 3:10 a.m.

   (B) 3:14 a.m.

   (C) 3:53 a.m.

   (D) 4:00 a.m.

   (E) 4:03 a.m.

Choose the words that best complete the sentence for questions 3 and 4.

3. The room Mrs. Martin was in _____ with smoke when firefighters arrived.

   (A) will fill

   (B) filled

   (C) has filled

   (D) was filled

   (E) is filling

4. Firefighter Cali is bringing those photographs with him to the meeting tonight _____ council members aware of the problem at the park.

   (A) to make

   (B) made

   (C) has making

   (D) will make

   (E) had made

For question 5, identify which one of the underlined words is spelled incorrectly.

5. A self-contained breathing apparates should be inspected before and after each use to ensure that it is working properly.

   (A) breathing

   (B) apparates

   (C) inspected

   (D) ensure

   (E) properly

Use the information in the following passage to answer question 6.

Firefighter Walker has been observing the behavior and attitude of Firefighter Yang, who was recently assigned to the company. Walker has noticed that Yang is usually cheerful and polite but on occasion seems withdrawn and worried. Yang frequently complains about having to pay a high child support payment each month. Yang also refrains from ordering takeout at the station and complains that his salary is not high enough. When a bill collector called looking for Yang, Walker asked if everything was okay in his personal life. Yang said it was job stress and burnout and not to worry about it, that things would get better in time. Walker was not convinced.

6. Based on the information given in the paragraph, if Yang were having a problem, it would most likely be _____.

   (A) health related

   (B) marital

   (C) job stress

   (D) financial

   (E) related to his children

> *Use the information in the following passage to answer questions 7 and 8.*

A fracture is a crack or break in the bone. The following are terms related to types of fractures:

- ✔ **Closed fracture:** A broken bone without an open skin wound

- ✔ **Comminuted fracture:** A bone that is broken in several places

- ✔ **Greenstick fracture:** A fracture where only one side of the bone is broken; common in children

- ✔ **Oblique fracture:** A fracture in which the break is curved

- ✔ **Open fracture:** A fracture that has a laceration in the skin or a piece of bone sticking through the skin

- ✔ **Transverse fracture:** A fracture at a right angle to the bone's axis

7. According to the fractures described here, a person who has broken her arm in several places most likely has _____ fracture.

   (A) a transverse

   (B) a greenstick

   (C) a closed

   (D) an oblique

   (E) a comminuted

8. A child falls in a park and has a piece of bone sticking through his skin. At the hospital, the doctor says it is _____ fracture.

   (A) an oblique

   (B) an open

   (C) a greenstick

   (D) a transverse

   (E) a closed

> *Use the information in the following passage to answer questions 9 and 10.*

A group of teenagers is fishing in a small boat on a river when a 17-year-old girl falls overboard. She is not wearing a life jacket. The current quickly takes her away from the boat. One of the teenagers on the boat calls 911. The area dispatch center alerts police, emergency medical service, and fire-rescue units simultaneously.

Firefighters arrive on the scene and assess the situation. They see that the group of teenagers and the boat are not on the shore. They spot the girl in the water. She is holding onto the lower branch of a tree. She is still in the water from the waist down. Firefighter Torres walks a few feet into the water and extends a pole. He tells the girl, who is conscious, to grab the pole. She does, and he carefully pulls her to the shore. She has a large cut on her forehead that is bleeding. She has several scrapes on her arms and one of her wrists is red and swollen. Her speech is slurred and she is shivering. Firefighter Torres suspects that she has hypothermia. He covers her with a blanket. She is immediately placed on a gurney and transported to the trauma center.

9. Most likely, which injury indicates hypothermia?

   (A) red skin on wrist

   (B) cut on the forehead

   (C) shivering

   (D) scrapes on arms

   (E) swollen wrist

10. An appropriate title for this passage is

    (A) "Safety While Boating"

    (B) "How to Save a Drowning Victim"

    (C) "Assessing a Victim Who Was in Water"

    (D) "The Consequences of Horseplay"

    (E) "Water Rescue Procedures"

Use the information in the following passage to answer questions 11 and 12.

Firefighters are trained to fight fire, but they are also trained to help people involved in medical emergencies. It is important that they know how to perform abdominal thrusts (formerly called the Heimlich maneuver) on choking victims. Following are the steps for performing abdominal thrusts on choking victims, in no particular order.

1. Press your fist into the victim's upper abdomen using a quick, upward thrust.

2. Repeat these thrusts until the object is expelled from the victim's mouth.

3. Make a fist, placing the thumb side of your fist against the victim's abdomen, right below the ribcage and above the naval, and grab your fist with your other hand.

4. Ask the victim to stand (if he or she is not already standing) and explain that you're going to help by performing abdominal thrusts.

5. From behind, place your arms around the victim's waist.

11. What is the logical order of the steps given in the passage.

(A) 3, 5, 1, 2, 4

(B) 5, 3, 4, 1, 2

(C) 5, 4, 3, 2, 1

(D) 4, 2, 3, 1, 5

(E) 4, 5, 3, 1, 2

12. According to the above statements, what should you do after explaining that you're going to help?

(A) Ask the victim to stand up (if he or she is not already standing).

(B) From behind, place your arms around the victim's waist.

(C) Press your fist into the victim's upper abdomen using a quick, upward thrust.

(D) Make a fist, placing the thumb side of your fist against the victim's abdomen.

(E) Repeat these thrusts until the object is expelled from the victim's mouth.

13. Use the following table to determine which statement most accurately describes the relationship between the number of years of work and the amount of paid time off a firefighter in a certain department receives.

Years of Service	Paid Time Off
1	5 days
2–4	12 days
5–9	19 days
10–14	26 days
15+	33 days

(A) As the years of service increases by 5 years, the days of paid time off increases by 5 days.

(B) After 1 year of service, as the years of service increases by 5 years, the days of paid time off increases by 7 days.

(C) After 1 year of service, as the years of service increases by 5 years, the days of paid time off doubles.

(D) After 1 year of service, as the years of service increases by 5 years, the days of paid time off increases by 8 days.

(E) After 1 year of service, as the years of service increases by 4 years, the days of paid time off increases by 8 days.

Choose the correct answer for questions 14 and 15.

---

14. If you need 12 feet of ladder to safely reach each story of a building, what size ladder is necessary to safely climb to the top of a five-story apartment building?

(A) 17 feet

(B) 36 feet

(C) 48 feet

(D) 60 feet

(E) 72 feet

15. Your fire engine has 5 hoses that are 125 feet long, 3 hoses that are 75 feet long, and 1 hose that is 150 feet long. If you attach all these hoses together, what would be the total length of the hose?

(A) 350 feet

(B) 850 feet

(C) 857 feet

(D) 1,000 feet

(E) 1,150 feet

Answers and Explanations

Use this answer key to score the practice questions in this chapter. How did you do?

1. **C.** This question tests verbal comprehension. The first paragraph of the passage says that Mrs. Freeman led the firefighters into a bedroom where Mr. Freeman was lying on the bed.

2. **E.** This question tests verbal comprehension. The third paragraph says that Mr. Freeman arrived at the hospital at 4:03 a.m.

3. **D.** This question tests verbal expression. This sentence is past tense. The correct answer is "was filled." Don't be fooled by Choice (B), "filled," which is also past tense. The sentence "The room Mrs. Martin was in filled with smoke when firefighters arrived" doesn't make much sense even though it's grammatically correct. The firefighters' arrival likely wasn't connected to the room's filling with smoke.

4. **A.** This question tests verbal expression. "To make" is the only answer choice that makes sense in this sentence: "Firefighter Cali is bringing those photographs with him to the meeting tonight to make council members aware of the problem at the park."

5. **B.** This question tests verbal expression. The correct spelling of the word is *apparatus*.

6. **D.** This question tests problem sensitivity. Most of the details in the passage support the idea that Yang is having financial problems: He complains about having to pay child support; he doesn't order takeout; he complains that his salary is not high enough; and a bill collector calls looking for him.

7. **E.** This question tests deductive reasoning. The passage gives you general information about a variety of fractures, which you must apply to a specific situation. A bone that is broken in several places is a comminuted fracture.

8. **B.** This question tests deductive reasoning. The passage gives you general information about a variety of fractures, which you must apply to a specific situation. Bone that has broken through the skin is an open fracture.

9. **C.** This question tests inductive reasoning. You have to take specific details in the passage, combine them with some prior knowledge, and draw a general conclusion. You probably know that hypothermia can result from being in cold water for a long time. The girl is shivering, which means she is cold. Slurring words is another sign of hypothermia.

10. **C.** This question tests inductive reasoning. You have to take specific details in the passage to determine the general message (main idea) the passage conveys. Most of the passage discusses how Firefighter Torres assesses the victim, so this is the main idea of the passage. The title of the passage should reflect the main idea.

11. **E.** This question tests information ordering. The correct order of steps is (4) Ask the victim to stand and explain that you're going to help; (5) From behind, place your arms around the victim's waist; (3) Make a fist, placing the thumb side of your fist against the victim's abdomen, right below the ribcage and above the navel, and grab your fist with your other hand; (1) Press your fist into the victim's upper abdomen using a quick, upward thrust; (2) Repeat these thrusts until the object is expelled from the victim's mouth.

12. **B.** This question tests information ordering. Based on the list, you should ask the victim to stand before you explain how you're going to help, so you can eliminate Choice (A). Then, from behind, you should place your arms around the victim's waist, Choice (B). This is the correct answer. Then you can make a fist and place it against the victim's abdomen, Choice (C), press your fist into the victim's abdomen using a quick upward thrust, Choice (D), and repeat the process until the object is expelled from the victim's mouth, Choice (E).

13. **C.** This question tests mathematical reasoning. After 1 year of service, the number of days of paid time off increases by 7 days every 5 years.

14. **D.** This question tests number facility. To solve this problem, multiply 12 feet by 5 stories. The answer is 60 feet.

15. **D.** This question tests number facility. To answer this question, multiply 5 by 125 feet, which is 625 feet. Multiply 3 by 75 feet, which is 225 feet. Then add 625 feet, 225 feet, and 150 feet. The answer is 1,000 feet.

Part III

Demonstrating Physical, Mental, and Emotional Fitness with Interactive Tests

The 5th Wave   By Rich Tennant

"It's not that kind of pole, Sean."

In this part . . .

Firefighting involves exhausting work under hazardous conditions. It probably comes as no surprise that to become a firefighter, you must prove that you're physically, mentally, and psychologically fit. If you hope to make firefighting a career, you have to pass a physical ability test, endure a formal job interview, and eventually receive clearance from medical and psychological professionals — just to enter a training academy. Overwhelmed? Don't worry — we're here for you.

Part III prepares you for all the tests that come *after* the written examination. It introduces the exercises you may encounter during the physical ability test. Part III also supplies interview tips and discusses why medical and psychological exams are necessary. If you have your heart set on becoming a firefighter, continue reading.

Chapter 12

Show Them What You Can Do: Passing the Physical Exam

In This Chapter
▶ Understanding the importance of physical fitness testing
▶ Breaking down the events of a standardized PAT

Reading books and watching videos about firefighting are excellent ways to mentally prepare yourself for your future career. All the books and all the videos in the world, however, won't prepare you for the physical demands of the job. Firefighting is strenuous work. Firefighters wear bulky, heavy protective clothing; at the same time, they're expected to move quickly and efficiently. After all, the fire's not going to wait; it's going to spread, doubling in size almost every minute.

In this chapter, we review the physical exam portion of the firefighter hiring process. Departments across the nation use these tests to see how well candidates handle the physical aspects of a firefighter's job. The elements of the physical exams may seem overwhelming at first. Keep in mind, however, that if you practice these tasks, you'll gain confidence and perform better when the time comes to participate in a physical exam. If you don't succeed in your first attempt to practice the physical exam events, keep trying until you master them.

The bottom line is that if you want to become a firefighter, you'll probably have to complete a physical exam to receive consideration for the job. So what are you waiting for? Read on.

Let's Get Physical: The Whys and Wherefores of Physical Exams

The physical exam is a fitness test or a physical ability test, and it typically follows the initial application and the written exam in the selection process. Under normal circumstances, only those candidates who have passed the written exam can continue to the next stage and participate in the physical test. Some departments may conduct an oral interview before the physical, in which case only those who pass the interview stage can participate in the physical exam. Candidates who pass the physical exam can continue to the next stage of testing.

Physical exams vary among cities and towns throughout the United States, but most departments require candidates to pass a physical exam to be considered for employment.

Why you have to take a physical exam

The purpose of physical testing is to make sure that you're physically capable to begin training to become a firefighter. Consider this: Firefighting involves exhausting work, often under hazardous conditions. You need the physical ability to keep yourself safe. In addition, firefighters must rely on each other and work as a team to get the job done. Would you want to trust your life to a team member who isn't physically prepared to help you? Probably not. And guess what? Your other team members feel the same way about you.

A physical exam gives those in charge of hiring new firefighters a chance to see you in action. During the physical exam, the *proctors* (those giving the test) watch you perform several tasks. These tasks measure your speed, strength, endurance, and flexibility as well as your ability to follow directions to safely and efficiently accomplish any assignments you receive. In addition, the physical exam narrows down the competition; those who don't pass the test don't get to continue to the next stage of the hiring process.

Successfully completing a department's physical exam simply means that you're physically capable to begin firefighter training. To actually become a firefighter, you have to pass all the other exams and receive additional instruction at an academy or another training program.

How a physical exam works

Before taking any physical exam, many departments require that you watch a video to see the events in action. Some require participation in a training program prior to the test to help you prepare. In many cases, you must present a medical release from your doctor, stating that you're healthy enough to participate. You also may have to sign a liability waiver, which relieves the hiring department of any responsibility if you get hurt during the test.

Each physical exam — depending on its events — has different requirements in regard to equipment, clothing, and protective gear, but we recommend workout clothes and sneakers for all of them so you can move freely and feel comfortable. Also, you should avoid wearing watches or other jewelry that could catch on tools or protective gear and hinder your movements. Check with the department before the day of the test to see whether you need to bring your own gear or whether gear will be provided for you.

Some tests are pass/fail, and others are scored on a particular scale. For the physical exam, departments may require you to take a physical ability test (PAT), a fitness test, or a combination of both. The following sections explain the differences.

To ensure success for whichever PAT or fitness test you have to take to become a firefighter, you should prepare by getting in shape before the day of the test (see Chapter 3 for details). Working out in preparation for the physical exam will boost your strength, stamina, flexibility, and endurance. As you prepare, be sure to eat plenty of fruits, vegetables, and lean proteins, which help you build muscle and trim fat.

Physical ability tests

Physical ability tests, or *PATs,* focus on firefighting-related tasks — the meat and potatoes of the job — such as carrying equipment, raising ladders, and performing rescues. For these tests, all candidates — young or old, male or female, short or tall — must complete the same tasks in the same amount of time while adhering to the same requirements.

A number of organizations have developed *standardized* PATs, which means that many departments use the test and that it's nearly identical in all locations. Keep in mind, however, that each organization's standardized test has its own events, time limits, and requirements. For example, in the mid-1990s, California-based Fire & Police Selection, Inc. (FPSI; formerly Biddle & Associates) designed an 11-event, continuously timed PAT for entry-level firefighters. (See the section "Acing the Physical Exam: A Closer Look at a Standardized PAT" in this chapter for more details.)

Another popular standardized test is the Candidate Physical Ability Test (CPAT). This test, copyrighted by the International Associations of Firefighters (IAFF) and used by many fire departments nationwide, adheres to strict rules and requires testing sites to obtain a special license before conducting testing. (For more info about the CPAT, visit the IAFF's Web site at www.iaff.org.)

Because the events in a PAT simulate firefighting tasks, you may have to carry tools or maneuver through confined spaces. Therefore, you usually have to wear work gloves and a helmet to protect your hands and head from injury. Some PATs require wearing a vest that simulates the weight of a *self-contained breathing apparatus* (also called an SCBA or air pack) and full turnout gear (protective clothing), which amounts to about 50 pounds. Others require wearing actual turnout gear and an air pack (see Figure 12-1).

Helmet

Air mask

Nomex hood

Air tank

Turnout coat

Structural firefighting gloves

Turnout pants

Steel-toed rubber boots

Figure 12-1: The protective gear typically worn by a firefighter.

Fitness and combination tests

Some fire departments rely on fitness tests to assess candidates. Fitness tests are often timed and have minimum requirements for various exercises. For example, you may have to complete a 1.5-mile run within a certain amount of time; bench press your own body weight for one repetition or lift a lighter weight multiple times; and complete a certain number of push-ups or sit-ups in one minute. Unlike PATs, which require all candidates to perform the same events in the same manner according to the same rules, fitness test requirements often take into account factors such as anatomical differences between the sexes, age, height, and weight.

Some departments create their own physical exams that include a combination of fitness and physical ability events. For example, candidates may have to not only drag hoses and climb stairs but also complete a timed run and do sit-ups and push-ups.

Getting the lowdown on the local test

To prepare for the physical exam, find out exactly what requirements you have to meet to begin a firefighter training program in your region. If you still have questions after reading the job announcement or visiting the department's Web site, contact your local government's HR department or local fire stations to determine the exact requirements of the physical exam in your region.

If you decide to call, be prepared to ask the following questions:

- Is a physical training program available? If so, when and where will it take place, and how can I sign up?
- Do I have to pay a fee? If so, how much does it cost to enroll?
- If a training program is unavailable, does the department have recommendations for preparing for the test, such as a special workout program?
- Does the fire department use a standardized PAT or its own test?
- Will the exam mainly test fitness, physical abilities, or both?
- Does the test require special attire or protective equipment? (Some departments may require wearing full turnout gear during the test. Others may allow you to wear sneakers and sweats.)
- How is the test graded?
- Is the test timed? If so, how long do I have to complete the test?
- How many events make up the test? What are the events?

Before you place the call, organize your questions about the physical exam, and get a pen and paper ready to record essential info about the test. Knowing this information early gives you time to prepare for the test — physically and mentally — and improves your chances of success. Keep in mind that fire departments and HR staffs are quite busy, so avoid being too pushy or persistent, which can result in your being labled as a "difficult" candidate.

Acing the Physical Exam: A Closer Look at a Standardized PAT

Not all departments use the same PAT to test candidates on their physical abilities. Although each PAT is different, many include similar events and requirements. For this reason, we provide a detailed look at each event in FPSI's PAT to give you an example of what you may encounter. FPSI's physical exam is considered a "work-sample" test, because it gives candidates a preview of the physical abilities they'll have to perform on the job while remaining as technique-free as possible — you don't need prior firefighting experience to successfully complete it. (To see FPSI's PAT in action, visit `fpsi.com/fire_pat.html` and view video clips of the events.)

The spirit of FPSI's PAT is fairly universal, but the specifics are modified to best fit the needs of each department. For example, a ladder's height or a sledgehammer's weight may change, but the event itself stays the same. In addition, you can expect FPSI's PAT to be continuously timed — from the start of the first event to the end of the eleventh event — with a maximum time limit to complete the test of 8½ to 9½ minutes. (**Note:** The distances between and within the events in this chapter are specific to the test used by 41 departments in Southern California, which were involved in the original validation study of FPSI's PAT. When adapted for other departments, however, these distances may vary.)

Before the test

Prior to taking FPSI's PAT, you have to sign a liability waiver. Some departments that use FPSI's test may require a medical release from your doctor, too. Before the test begins, proctors explain the content of the test. They walk you through each event, demonstrating how to complete it, including various techniques you can use. You also have to watch a video demonstration of the test.

Proctors check all equipment to make sure it's safe and working properly. They also try to provide as many sizes of protective gear as possible and preadjust it to ensure a good fit for all candidates. The following pieces of protective gear must be worn during the test:

- ✔ Gloves
- ✔ Helmet
- ✔ Turnout coat
- ✔ Self-contained breathing apparatus (SCBA)

If you can't find protective gear that fits, you must notify the proctors before the test begins.

It is your responsibility to put on all mandatory protective gear during the test. If you do not wear this gear, you have to repeat the test or accept a failing score.

During the test

FPSI's PAT consists of 11 events. Depending on the department, you have about 8½ to 9½ minutes to complete the entire test. Your time starts at the beginning of the first event and ends when you finish the eleventh event. To promote fairness and accuracy in scoring, FPSI recommends that all candidates complete the events in the same order with the same instructions and that at least two scorers track candidates' times with stopwatches.

You're not allowed to run between test events. Walking allows your breathing to slow and your heart rate to return to normal before you begin the next event. You may run — at a safe speed — within each event. You may not leave an event until you've completed it correctly, unless you want to stop the event and accept a disqualification from the test.

After you successfully complete an event, proctors direct you to the next one. This section provides a detailed look at the 11 events that make up FPSI's PAT.

Event 1: Dry Hose Deployment

The first event is the Dry Hose Deployment. To complete this event, you must advance a dry (without flowing water) length of hose for 150 feet. Keep in mind that this isn't your grandma's garden hose. You must pull 150 feet of heavy-duty (and just plain heavy!) 1¾-inch fire hose with a standard nozzle attached to the end around multiple turns or obstacles. Here's how to complete the event:

1. **Pick up the nozzle end of the hose.**

   Place the nozzle over your shoulder and onto your chest and keep one hand on the nozzle at all times.

2. **Lean your weight forward and, at a rapid pace, advance the hose line 50 feet toward the first corner or obstacle.**

   Overshoot (run past) the first obstacle or corner and touch a designated area on the course before making the turn. This helps reduce friction between the hose and the obstacle as you make the turn.

3. **Advance the hose another 50 feet around a second obstacle.**

   Again, overshoot the obstacle and touch the designated area on the course before making the turn.

4. **Advance the hose another 50 feet to the finish line.**

5. **Gently place the hose nozzle inside the designated boundary (a circle 2 feet in diameter) to signify completion of the event.**

During the Dry Hose Deployment, remember the following rules:

- ✔ Keep one hand on the nozzle at all times. If you take your hand off the nozzle, you receive a warning. If you continue to let go of the nozzle, you have to restart the event from the beginning.

- ✔ Remember to place the hose nozzle within the designated boundary at the completion of the event. You're not allowed to continue until you do this.

- ✔ Don't throw or drop the nozzle. Gently place it inside the boundary.

After successfully completing the Dry Hose Deployment, walk (don't run!) 5 feet to the second event.

Event 2: Charged Hose Deployment

The second event is the Charged Hose Deployment. To complete this event, you must advance a charged (flowing water) 100-foot length of 1¾-inch hose for 70 feet through two simulated doorways. The water pressure from the hydrant supplying water to your hose is about 80 pounds per square inch (psi) or less. Here's how this event works:

1. **Pick up the nozzle end of the hose.**

   Place the nozzle over your shoulder and onto your chest. Be sure keep one hand on the nozzle at all times.

2. **Lean your weight forward and, at a safe but rapid pace, advance the hose line 32 feet through a simulated doorway.**

   Face forward (toward the finish line) as you advance the hose line. At the end of 32 feet, you'll encounter a second doorway.

3. **Proceed through the second doorway, stooping progressively lower or crawling as you deploy the hose line another 38 feet.**

   The stooping/crawling motion simulates how you would advance a hose line in a hot, smoky environment. Continue facing forward as you move toward the finish line.

4. **Gently place the nozzle of the hose inside the designated boundary area (a circle 2 feet in diameter) to signify completion of the event.**

During the Charged Hose Deployment, remember the following rules:

- ✔ Keep one hand on the nozzle at all times. Removing your hand from the nozzle results in a warning. If you repeat this behavior, you have to restart the event from the beginning.

- ✔ If you turn your back toward the finish line during the event, you receive a warning. If you ignore the warning, you have to restart the event from the point at which you turned backward.

- ✔ You're not allowed to continue to the next event until you've placed the hose nozzle within the designated boundary at the end of the event.

- ✔ Don't throw or drop the nozzle. Gently place it inside the boundary.

After successfully completing the Charged Hose Deployment, walk 68 feet to the third event.

Event 3: Halyard Raise

The third event is the Halyard Raise. During the Halyard Raise event, you work with an extension ladder. Extension ladders are available in a range of heights and materials, but most contain the following parts (see Figure 12-2):

- **Side rails:** The outer beams of an extension ladder.

- **Anti-slip heel, foot, or shoe:** Grips attached to the bottom of each of the side rails; safety plates or spurs on the heel hold the ladder in place and protect the rails.

- **Rungs:** Horizontal bars between the side rails of the ladder (the steps).

- **Base or bed:** The bottom section of an extension ladder, where you would begin climbing.

- **Fly:** The portion of the ladder that you can raise to extend its overall height; it's attached to the bed.

- **Rope halyard and pulleys:** System used to raise and lower the fly section. (As you pull the rope halyard down, it engages the pulleys and raises the fly section up.)

- **Dogs and pawls:** Hooking mechanisms that lock into place and prevent the fly section from sliding down until they are disengaged.

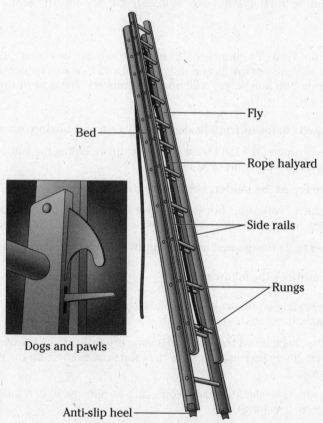

Bed

Fly

Rope halyard

Side rails

Rungs

Dogs and pawls

Anti-slip heel

Figure 12-2:
Parts of an
extension
ladder.

To complete the Halyard Raise, you must raise the fly section of a 35-foot aluminum extension ladder. The ladder has two sections and two pulleys, and the resistance for each pull is about 45 pounds. You don't have to erect the ladder yourself; it'll be in an upright position when you start the event.

1. **Foot the ladder.**

   To *foot* the ladder, place one foot at the base of the ladder. This prevents it from moving as you pull on the halyard.

2. **In a relatively straight standing position, grasp the halyard with both hands.**

   Place one hand higher than the other on the rope.

3. **Pull the halyard to raise the fly section.**

   You may use both hands to start the pull, but then you must switch to a hand-over-hand motion as you continue. You may use a thumbs-up or thumbs-down hand-over-hand motion, which instructors demonstrate before the test begins. The event ends when you've successfully raised the fly section.

During the Halyard Raise, remember the following rules:

- ✔ Keep one hand on the halyard at all times.

- ✔ Stand as straight as possible with both feet on the ground as you complete the raise. You may not jump to grasp the halyard or crouch down as you pull the halyard.

- ✔ Don't let the halyard slip. If the halyard slips out of your hands during the raise, you must restart the event from the beginning. If the halyard slips out a second time, you are disqualified from the test.

After successfully completing the Halyard Raise, walk 20 feet to the fourth event.

Event 4: Roof Walk

The fourth event is the Roof Walk. To complete this event, you must ascend and descend an 11-foot distance by either walking or crawling on the rungs of a 12-foot roof ladder positioned against a simulated rooftop. You must carry a 20-pound simulated chainsaw during the event.

1. **Retrieve the simulated chainsaw from its designated area and begin your ascent.**

   You must touch every rung of the ladder on your way up, including the rung near the top, which will be marked with paint or tape.

2. **When you reach the top of the ladder, begin your descent.**

   You don't have to touch every rung, but you do have to face the ladder as you back down. You may carry or slide the simulated chainsaw along the roof as you descend.

3. **Return the chainsaw to its designated area to signify completion of the event.**

During the Roof Walk, remember the following rules:

- ✔ You must touch every rung on the way up. If you skip rungs, you have to restart the event from the beginning.

- ✔ After reaching the top, back down the ladder. Turning around and walking down the ladder isn't permitted. If you do this, you have to restart the event from the point at which you turned around.

- ✔ Return the chainsaw to its designated area. You won't be allowed to continue until you put the chainsaw where it belongs.

After successfully completing the Roof Walk, walk 24 feet to the fifth event.

Event 5: Attic Crawl

The fifth event is the Attic Crawl. To complete this event, you must crawl across a simulated attic area while carrying a simulated flashlight (the simulated flashlight is a 12-inch long piece of wood with a diameter of about 2 inches). The attic area platform is 20 feet long and 4 feet wide and is constructed of 2-inch × 12-inch boards placed 16 inches apart. Four barriers standing about 4 feet high and placed 6½ feet apart ensure that you stay low as you cross the platform. Check out the Attic Crawl:

1. **Pick up the simulated flashlight from its designated area.**

2. **Proceed across the attic area.**

   Stay low (below the barriers) as you crawl across the boards.

3. **Return the simulated flashlight to its designated area to signify completion of the event.**

During the Attic Crawl, remember the following rules:

✔ Stay low to avoid knocking over the barriers. If you knock one over, a proctor will reset it and you'll have to restart the event from the beginning.

✔ Don't allow your hands or feet to slip through the spaces between the boards and touch the ground, or you'll have to start over from the beginning.

✔ Retrieve and replace the simulated flashlight from its designated area.

After successfully completing the Attic Crawl, walk 78 feet to the sixth event.

Event 6: Ventilation Exercise

The sixth event is the Ventilation Exercise. To complete this event, you must stand on a simulated rooftop and strike a designated area — a 2-foot × 2-foot area padded with old fire hoses, which absorb some of the force of each strike — 30 times with an 8-pound sledgehammer. This exercise is designed to simulate the force necessary to successfully create a ventilation opening for heat and smoke to escape through a rooftop.

1. **Pick up the sledgehammer from its designated area.**

2. **Proceed to the simulated rooftop and approach the strike area.**

   You may place your foot on the foot rest provided or move closer to the strike area, if necessary.

3. **Raise the sledgehammer over your helmet and strike the rooftop.**

   Repeat this motion 30 times, maintaining control of the sledgehammer with each strike. The proctor counts aloud as you strike the rooftop.

4. **Return the sledgehammer to its designated area to signify the end of the event.**

During the Roof Ventilation, remember the following rules:

✔ Raise the sledgehammer over your helmet for each strike. Failing to raise the sledgehammer over your helmet is an improper strike and won't be counted.

✔ Don't allow the sledgehammer to simply fall to the rooftop. This is an improper strike and won't be counted.

✔ You're not allowed to continue to the next event until you return the sledgehammer to its designated area.

After successfully completing the Roof Ventilation, walk 27 feet to the seventh event.

Event 7: Victim Removal

The seventh event is the Victim Removal. To complete this event, you must carry or carefully drag a 154-pound dummy a distance of 26 feet. The dummy's height may range from 5 to 6 feet, and you have to maneuver it around an obstacle.

1. **At the starting point, pick up the dummy.**

   You may grab the dummy under or on top of its arms, lifting its torso off the ground as you begin the drag. You may also drag the dummy by one or both of its arms. You may carry the dummy over one shoulder or cradle it in your arms. (We don't recommend carrying the dummy. It's more strenuous than dragging — and you still have four events to go!) Proctors demonstrate the various ways to carry or drag the dummy before the test begins.

2. **Drag the dummy 13 feet to a cone or other obstacle.**

   When you reach the obstacle, maneuver yourself and the dummy around the obstacle.

3. **Drag the dummy an additional 13 feet back to the starting point to signify completion of the event.**

During the Victim Removal, remember the following rules:

✔ Don't drag the dummy by its head, feet, or clothing.

✔ Drag or carry the dummy around the obstacle. If you don't do this, you'll have to go back and properly maneuver the dummy around the obstacle.

✔ Be sure to return the dummy to the starting point or you won't be allowed to continue to the next event.

✔ Avoid dropping the dummy. The dummy represents a person, so treat it like one during this event.

After successfully completing the Victim Removal, walk 77 feet to the eighth event.

Event 8: Ladder Removal/Carry

The eighth event is the Ladder Removal/Carry. To complete this event, you must remove a 24-foot aluminum extension ladder from mounted hooks, carry it around a 54-foot diamond-shaped course, and replace the ladder on the mounted hooks. The ladder will be positioned horizontally — on its side — so the ladder's side rails will be the top and bottom beams. The ladder weighs about 72 pounds, and the mounted hooks are positioned so the bottom beam of the ladder is 58 inches from the ground.

1. **Approach the balance point of the ladder and prepare to remove it from the hooks.**

   The balance point is near the ladder's middle rungs, which are marked.

2. **Remove the ladder from the hooks and carry it around the course.**

   You may carry the ladder in any of the following ways (which proctors demonstrate before the test):

   • **High shoulder carry:** The entire ladder sits on your shoulder (with the bottom beam touching your shoulder). You should bend your arm up to grasp the top beam (or near the top beam) to keep the ladder stable.

   • **Low shoulder carry:** The top beam of the ladder rests on the top of your shoulder. Your arm slides between two rungs of the ladder and you grasp a rung in your hand to maintain the ladder's stability.

   • **Suitcase carry:** The top beam of the ladder is held in one arm like a suitcase.

3. **At the end of the course, return the ladder to its original position on the mounted hooks.**

   The rungs that should be closest to the hooks will be painted to help you guide the ladder toward the correct position. When the ladder is back in its original position, the event is complete.

During the Ladder Removal/Carry, remember the following rules:

✔ Maintain control of the ladder during removal, carry, and replacement. You are allowed two penalties during this event. Penalties include the following:

   • **Dropping the ladder:** If you drop the ladder, you may pick it up (in any fashion) and continue the test.

   • **Losing control of the ladder:** If you lose control of the ladder — for example, by allowing either end to touch the ground — a proctor will intervene to help you regain control.

   • **Voluntarily setting the ladder down to regain control and stability:** If you feel like you're losing control, you may set the ladder down, and then pick it up (in any fashion) and continue the test.

   • **Allowing the ladder to fall over your neck:** If the ladder falls so that your head and neck end up between ladder rungs, the proctor will intervene to assist in removing the ladder so you can regain stability and begin again.

   A third penalty results in disqualification.

✔ Don't lean or brace the ladder against the wall during replacement. If you do this, you'll have to remove the ladder and replace it properly.

✔ Make sure you replace the ladder in its original position. Look for the painted rungs to guide you as you place the ladder on the mounted hooks. You won't be allowed to continue to the next event until you properly replace the ladder.

After successfully completing the Ladder Removal/Carry, walk 75 feet to the ninth event.

Event 9: Stair Climb with Hose

The ninth event is the Stair Climb with Hose. To complete this event, you must carry a hose bundle up four flights of stairs (63 steps, excluding the landings on each floor). The hose bundle includes 100 feet of synthetic 1¾-inch fire hose.

1. **Pick up the hose bundle.**

   You may carry the bundle over one of your shoulders or in your arms. (We recommend carrying it over your shoulder; it's more efficient.)

2. **Proceed up four flights of stairs.**

   You may skip steps on the way up.

3. **Place the hose bundle in the designated area on the fourth-floor landing to signify completion of the event.**

During the Stair Climb with Hose, remember the following rules:

✔ Place the hose bundle in the designated area. You won't be allowed to continue until you put the hose bundle in the correct spot.

✔ To avoid damaging the hose couplings, don't throw or drop the hose bundle. Gently place it inside the boundary.

After successfully completing the Stair Climb with Hose, you may move to the tenth event, which begins on the fourth-floor landing.

Event 10: Crawling Search

The tenth event is the Crawling Search. To complete this event, you must crawl 60 feet in a designated area on the fourth floor, which simulates searching for a victim. When you've completed your "search," you must pick up the hose bundle you used in Event 9, return to the ground floor, and place the bundle in the designated area.

1. **Get on your hands and knees to begin your search.**

2. **Crawl around the designated area, a distance of 60 feet.**

   The path you have to take is clearly marked with cones or other objects.

3. **Pick up the hose bundle.**

   You may carry the hose bundle over one of your shoulders or in your arms.

4. **Proceed down the steps.**

5. **Place the hose bundle in its designated area on the ground floor to signify the end of the event.**

During the Crawling Search, remember the following rules:

- Don't skip steps on your way to the ground floor. If you miss a step, you have to go back and touch that step with your foot before you can continue.

- Place the hose bundle within the designated area at the completion of the event or you won't be allowed to continue to the next event.

- Don't drop the hose, which could damage the couplings. Gently place it inside the boundary.

After successfully completing the Crawling Search, you immediately begin the final event.

Event 11: Stair Climb with Air Bottles and Hose Hoist

The eleventh — and final — event is the Stair Climb with Air Bottles and Hose Hoist. To complete this event, you must carry two air bottles over one shoulder as you ascend to the third floor of a building. The air bottles are connected by a 2-foot strap and weigh 29 pounds. On the third floor, you must set the bottles in a designated area and hoist a 100-foot section of 1¾-inch dry, extended hose line up and over the 4-foot-high railing of a balcony. Each 50-foot section weighs about 20 pounds. After placing the hose nozzle within the designated area, you must then pick up the air bottles, return to the ground floor, and cross the finish line. Here's how to complete this event:

1. **Pick up the air bottles.**

   Place the strap over one shoulder so you have one air bottle in front of your shoulder and one behind your shoulder.

2. **Proceed up the steps to the third-floor balcony.**

   You may skip steps on your way up.

3. **Place the air bottles in the designated area.**

4. **Pick up the rope and begin hoisting the hose line over the balcony's railing.**

   Try not to let the rope or hose touch the railing. You may stop hoisting when the second coupling of the hose comes over the railing.

5. **Drag the hose 8 feet and place the nozzle in the designated area, a circle with a diameter of 2 feet.**

   When you're dragging the hose, it's acceptable for the hose to rub against the balcony's railing.

6. **Pick up the air bottles and proceed down the stairs without skipping steps.**

7. **Cross the finish line with the air bottles.**

   This completes the entire PAT, and the scorers stop timing you.

During the Stair Climb with Air Bottles and Hose Hoist, remember the following rules:

- Don't drop the air bottles, which could damage them. Gently place them within the boundary on the third floor.

- Don't allow the rope or hose to rub against the balcony's railing as you hoist the hose. If the rope or hose touches the railing, you'll receive a warning. If either touches a second time, you'll be disqualified. If you drop the rope or hose, you may continue the event and try again.

- Don't drop the hose nozzle. Gently place the nozzle within the designated area.

- Remember to pick up the air bottles before you return to the ground floor.

- Don't skip any steps on your way down the stairs. If you do, you have to go back and touch the missed step with your foot before you can continue.

- Remember to cross the finish line *with* the air bottles.

After successfully completing the Stair Climb with Air Bottles and Hose Hoist, you are finished with the test.

After the test

At the end of the test, the scorers fill in a scoring form, which you have to initial. Though proctors do their best to make sure that all test results and necessary info are recorded on the scoring form, you should check everything before you initial it. Also, keep in mind that you may not be allowed to leave the testing site until you've recovered from the test. The test requires a lot of physical activity in a very short amount of time; it's more strenuous than you may think, and you'll need some time to cool down and let your heart rate and breathing return to normal.

Chapter 13

Acing Your Oral Interview

. . . .

In This Chapter

▶ Understanding the interview process

▶ Preparing for the interview

▶ Answering typical interview questions

▶ Following up after the interview

. . . .

We're the first to admit that the hiring process for firefighting jobs is a bit unconventional in comparison to other occupations, but you didn't think you'd get away without an interview, did you? If you want to become a firefighter, in addition to the written exam and the physical ability test, you have to endure an oral interview. Trust us — it's not as bad as it sounds, especially if you know what to expect. For example, consider the following:

> "Tell us why you want to become a firefighter."

The last thing interviewers want to hear after directing this statement toward a candidate is the sound of crickets. A well-prepared candidate — you! — will have a good, solid explanation ready. What will you say?

In this chapter, we explain everything you need to know about the oral interview, from the clothes you should wear to the questions you may have to answer (and how to answer them!). We even provide some tips you can use after the interview to show your appreciation for the interviewers. By the time we're done with you, you'll be looking forward to the opportunity to tell the hiring panel everything you know and more!

Preparing for the Interview

Many firefighter candidates spend months studying for the written exam. They spend weeks training for the physical ability test. And they spend just a few minutes prepping for the oral interview. You may think, "How can I prepare for an interview? I don't know what they're going to ask." This is true — you can't predict the future. But consider this: Many fire departments eliminate more candidates during the oral interview than during any other part of the hiring process.

The interview is your chance to shine — to truly leave a lasting impression in the minds of those who hold your future in their hands. For this reason, it's important that you spend an adequate amount of time preparing for the interview.

Try following this interview-preparation schedule:

✔ **In the weeks before the interview:** Spend some time reviewing common interview questions. Although you don't want your answers to sound rehearsed, it's beneficial to have an idea of what you want to say. Why do you want to become a firefighter? What are your strengths and weaknesses? Practice answering such questions out loud in front of a mirror so you'll feel more comfortable in front of the interviewers. See "Answering typical interview questions" later in this chapter for a list of example questions.

Consider spending some time with firefighters to get an idea of what fire departments look for in the candidates they select. Talk with firefighters who have been hired within the last few years to find out what their interviews were like. Also, review any information you supplied about your background, including your education, work history, or run-ins with the law. Make sure you can explain yourself and supply honest answers to any questions the interviewers may have.

✔ **In the days before the interview:** Double-check the date, time, and place of the interview. This may sound basic, but it'd be awful if you missed the interview because you thought it was on Wednesday and it was really on Tuesday. If necessary, rearrange your schedule to accommodate the interview. Many departments won't allow you to change the date. (Some departments have so many candidates that they actually count on some not showing up as part of the weeding-out process.) Consider doing a dry run to the interview site so you know how long it takes to get to there, where to park, and where the interview room is located.

✔ **On the day of the interview:** Make sure your appearance is neat and clean. Consider wearing a business suit or, at the very least, a dress shirt and dress pants for men or a blouse and dress pants or a skirt for women (don't forget to iron!). Men should shave the day of the interview because the Occupational Safety and Health Administration (OSHA) has strict grooming guidelines for firefighters, and you want to make a good impression.

Arrive 10 to 15 minutes before the time scheduled for your interview. And by all means, don't be late!

✔ **In the minutes before the interview:** Comb your hair, tuck in your shirt, and spit out your gum. Take a few deep breaths and recall what you want to say to leave a lasting impression. Then, good luck!

Putting Your Best Self Forward

One way to prove to others that you're the best candidate for a firefighting job is to tell them just that. During the oral interview, you have the opportunity to explain that you have the skills and motivation necessary to become a stellar firefighter. It's a time when you can share interesting facts about yourself, clear up any concerns the interviewers may have about your background, and answer any questions they may pose. As long as you remain honest and confident (but not arrogant!), you'll be fine.

Knowing what to expect during the interview

Interviews are always a little intimidating, but knowing what to expect when you enter the interview room should give you a little boost of confidence. For the firefighter hiring process, the interview is typically handled by a panel of interviewers that may include the following:

- ✔ A fire department higher-up, such as a captain or a chief
- ✔ Three or four firefighters from the department or surrounding departments
- ✔ A representative of the county/city/town human resources department
- ✔ Local professionals with hiring experience, such as business owners

The panel members typically sit at a table at the front of the room, facing the hot seat — a single chair in the middle of the room where you sit. It's important to leave the chair where it is — don't move it closer to the interviewers. They've placed it in the ideal location to observe your body language.

The panel members will likely be wearing their dress uniforms, and they won't appear very friendly. Most interviewers are instructed to keep their faces void of expression and emotion to maintain a neutral experience for all candidates. Don't expect them to smile at you (even if you smile at them) or to nod in agreement to your responses.

You can expect the panel to ask you questions during the interview. After all, the whole point of the interview is for the panel to get an overall impression of your attitude, goals, and communication skills. Questions will likely fall into one of the two following categories:

- ✔ **Unstructured:** In an unstructured interview, panel members typically ask open-ended questions. Such questions usually have no right or wrong answers. Rather, these questions give you an opportunity to express your thoughts and opinions and allow interviewers a chance to evaluate your ability to express yourself clearly.

- ✔ **Structured:** In a structured interview, panel members typically ask specific questions for which they have recorded appropriate responses. They ask the same questions in the same order for each candidate. Like the questions in the unstructured interview, these questions are usually open-ended. As you respond, panel members use rating sheets to evaluate your answer in comparison to the appropriate response.

The interview may be timed, so wear a watch. In many structured interviews, the panel members explain at the outset that you have a specific amount of time to answer a specific number of questions (for example, 20 minutes to answer 10 questions). It's up to you, however, to give yourself enough time to adequately answer each one.

The following subsections include tips on thinking through those questions, answering clearly, and using appropriate body language.

Paying attention to body language

During the interview, panel members observe you from the time you enter the room until the time you leave. Therefore, conducting yourself in a professional manner for the duration of the interview is important. This means beginning and ending the interview with a firm handshake and a friendly smile.

Remain aware of your body language. Interviewers interpret behavioral cues such as yawning or slouching as boredom and laziness — not the impression you want to leave at a job interview. Sit up straight, make eye contact, and remain alert to show interviewers that you're focused, interested, and confident.

Responding to questions

During the interview, listen carefully to what the question asks. Before answering, make sure you fully understand the question and give it thought and consideration. If you need the interviewers to clarify something, ask. It's better to ask for clarification than to misinterpret the question and provide an answer to a question that wasn't asked. Keep in mind, however, that during structured interviews, the interviewers probably won't be allowed to rephrase or reinterpret the question for you. At most, they may repeat the question.

Before answering, take a deep breath and think about what you want to say. By taking a few seconds to collect your thoughts, you'll avoid tripping over your words or rambling on and on. Interviewers will be impressed when you answer questions in an organized, well-spoken, deliberate way.

The most important thing to remember when answering interview questions is to be open and honest with the interviewers and to answer them with courtesy and respect. If you didn't pursue a college education because money was tight but you hope to one day enroll in some classes, tell them. If the six-month gap in your work history was because you had to care for your ailing father, explain the situation. If they question why you received three tickets for exceeding the speed limit, explain yourself — you know it's against the law and you're working on becoming more mindful of your speed. The interviewers will appreciate not only that you answered the question but also that you did so in a calm, self-assured manner.

Speak clearly during the interview, whether you're saying hello and introducing yourself or answering a tough question. It's common to feel a little bit nervous in an interview setting, which can cause you to talk faster than you normally would. When you speak too quickly, however, your words slur together, and the interviewers may have trouble understanding you. So slow down. After all, what's the use in giving an incredible answer (which we know you will!) if the panel members have no idea what you said?

Finally, pay attention and stay alert. The oral interview is not the time to let your mind wander. As a firefighter, you'll have to remain alert to changes in your environment every day, so the interviewers want to see that you can stay focused. When an interviewer speaks, listen to what he or she has to say and respond appropriately.

Never share information about the interview or interview questions with your friends or other candidates who will be in the interview process after you. Doing so could result in your elimination from the entire process for sharing confidential information about the test. The fire department may have to throw out the entire process if word gets out that the content has leaked and some candidates received an unfair advantage. In addition, your "friends" are competing for the same position you are, so by giving them a heads-up about what to expect, you're hurting your own chances.

Answering typical interview questions

Interview questions touch on a variety of areas, including your background, employment history, communication skills, personal goals, attitude, interests, and more. Some questions are personal in nature, whereas others are designed to assess your character or to determine how you would conduct yourself in difficult situations. The following sections provide sample questions that touch on all these areas.

Make a list of your own interview questions and then get a friend to interview you. Not only does this help you practice developing good, thorough answers to tough questions, but it also prepares you to speak in front of others.

Background and employment history questions

Questions about your background and employment history will likely arise from information you supplied to interviewers through your application or a background data collection form. Interviewers may asks questions similar to the following:

- ✔ Why did you decide to stop your college education after earning an associate's degree?
- ✔ Why do you want to leave your current job?
- ✔ What did you do in the six months between leaving Company A and starting to work for Company B?

✔ Describe the circumstances surrounding your departure from Company C/your brush with the law/your hospitalization record (you get the idea).

✔ What's the most important skill you learned while working for Company A?

Background questions vary greatly from one person to the next, but you should be prepared to explain anything and everything about your past, including any errors in judgment you may have committed. Answer questions honestly, and avoid becoming defensive.

The interviewers aren't trying to attack your life choices, but they do want to make sure that you've learned from your mistakes and that you have goals and aspirations for the future.

Character questions

The interview panel uses character questions to evaluate your attitude, values, and personality. Again, these questions vary greatly, but the following are some common character questions that you should be prepared to answer:

✔ Tell us why you want to become a firefighter.

✔ What are the benefits/drawbacks of teamwork?

✔ How would you define *honesty/integrity/pride/loyalty?*

✔ At this point, what do you consider your greatest accomplishment in life?

✔ Where do you see yourself in ten years?

✔ How have you prepared yourself for a career in the fire service?

✔ What are your hobbies/interests, and why do you enjoy them?

✔ How does your family feel about your decision to pursue a firefighting career?

✔ What are your greatest strengths/weaknesses?

✔ What will you do with your spare time while on duty?

If asked about your weaknesses during the interview, never say, "I have no weaknesses." Everyone has weaknesses, and by answering that you have none, you'll seem arrogant.

Situational questions

Situational interview questions are similar to the judgment and reasoning scenarios and questions we discuss in Chapter 8. For these questions, interviewers present scenarios, and you have to explain how you'd react to each situation. The following are some examples:

✔ At an accident scene, you're helping a victim with severe injuries and her husband questions everything you do. You know he's trying to "help," but he keeps getting in the way. What would you do and why?

✔ Your fire captain has told you to assist the search-and-rescue team at a structure fire. On your way to the team's location, you encounter a victim with bad burns who needs medical attention. What would do and why?

✔ You're a probationary firefighter, and you've noticed that the firefighters on the earlier shift rarely clean up after themselves or help with the daily station chores. They leave all the work for your shift. What would you do and why?

The scenarios presented in situational questions are endless, but you get the idea: The interviewers want to see how you'd handle yourself in uncomfortable situations. Like your responses to the character questions, your responses to the situation questions tell the interview panel a lot about your morals, values, attitude, personality, and overall nature.

When you answer situational questions, make sure your answer fits the guidelines. For example, consider this question: "You and your partner are in a structure fire rescuing an infant. Your partner goes unconscious. You can only remove the infant or your partner. Whom do you rescue and why?" Don't say you would rescue both people, because the scenario states that you can only rescue one. You might answer that you would take your partner because firefighter safety takes priority. Or you could answer that you would take the infant because you would have better success in exiting the building quickly and could call for help for your partner, whom you may not be able to move by yourself. These types of questions rarely have a definite right or wrong answer. The interviewers are more interested in your justification (or the why) for your answer.

Following Up After the Interview

At the conclusion of the interview, be sure to shake the interviewers' hands and thank them for taking the time to meet with you. When you get home, write a quick thank-you note to the interview panel and drop it in the mail. A thank-you note, although not required, is just a small gesture to show that you're truly interested in becoming a firefighter, and it shows the interview panel that you're a well-mannered, respectful, and considerate person. A handwritten note takes a bit more effort than firing off a quick e-mail and will likely land on a desk rather than in a spam or junk e-mail folder.

We know that playing the waiting game is no fun, but refrain from calling the interviewers to ask about the results of your interview. They have many candidates to interview — imagine if they all called! The interviewers will contact you (most likely by mail) after they make a decision, and you may not know your ranking in the process until after all phases have been completed. Besides, if you follow our advice, then you'll surely ace the interview. What are you worried about?

Chapter 14

Knowing What to Expect During Medical and Psychological Testing

• •

In This Chapter

▶ Recognizing why a medical exam is necessary

▶ Understanding what the medical exam entails

▶ Comprehending the need for a psychological evaluation

▶ Knowing what to expect during the psychological evaluation

• •

Firefighting is a physically exhausting and mentally demanding career. It takes a special person to lay his or her life on the line each day to help others in their time of need. And it's at those times that firefighters witness some of the most awful events in people's lives — motor vehicle accidents, fires, floods, and in unfortunate cases, even death. Because firefighting is so physically and mentally taxing, firefighters must be in top physical and mental health.

If you pass the other tests in the firefighter hiring process — the written exam, the physical ability test, and the oral interview — you may receive a conditional offer of employment from a fire department. The key word there is *conditional*. Many departments will offer you a firefighting job *on the condition* that you pass two more tests: a medical exam and a psychological evaluation.

Before departments hire you, they want to make sure that you don't suffer from any medical conditions or disabilities that may hinder your effectiveness as a firefighter. In addition, they want to make sure that you're mentally able to handle the stress of the job. The good news is that if you pass these last two exams, you're hired!

In this chapter, we provide information about the medical and psychological exams. You can't exactly prepare for the medical exam; after all, you have little control over things like your eyesight, hearing, and blood chemistry. In addition, you can't study for a psychological test that evaluates your personality. With our help, however, you discover why such tests are necessary and what to expect as doctors conduct them.

Understanding What Happens During the Medical Exam

The medical exam portion of the firefighting screening process is similar to other medical exams you've had. The doctor most likely will ask for a complete medical history, in which you provide details about your known health problems; past surgeries, immunizations, and vaccinations; daily medications; and allergies. The physician also may ask about your family's health history, your reproductive history, and even your occupational history. The physician uses all this information to determine whether you're at an increased risk for certain disorders or diseases.

Next, the physician records statistics such as your height, weight, temperature, and blood pressure. He or she may also check your eyes, ears, nose, and mouth for obvious signs of disease or infection and listen to your heart and lungs to identify any potential problems, such as an erratic heartbeat or difficulty breathing.

The purpose of the medical exam is to establish your Medical Base Line, which shows doctors what your body looks like and acts like when it's healthy. In the future, physicians can use your Medical Base Line to establish links between your health and injuries or conditions that have resulted from your career in firefighting.

Those are the basics of the medical exam, but fire departments may require physicians to conduct more in-depth exams. They don't want to eliminate you as a candidate, but they do want to make sure that all their employees are in tip-top physical condition. As a firefighter, your health directly affects the health and safety of the public.

Don't disqualify yourself from the running based on what you read here. It's important to receive an expert evaluation to determine whether you're healthy enough to begin training to become a firefighter. Each candidate is different, and physicians use a variety of diagnostic procedures to determine whether a condition should eliminate a candidate from the running. In most cases, the physician's determination depends on the severity of the condition in relation to the job of firefighting. Only a candidate who suffers from a disorder that could affect his or her performance of essential job tasks will be disqualified. Otherwise, doctors consider the candidates to meet the medical requirements of the job.

After your medical exam is complete, physicians analyze the results of all the tests and checks they performed to determine whether you're healthy enough to become a firefighter. If you come back with a clean bill of health, you move on to the final stage of the hiring process — the psychological exam.

The Americans with Disabilities Act makes it illegal for departments to conduct medical exams early in the hiring process. After a department has presented you with a conditional offer of employment, however, almost any disability can thwart your effort toward becoming a firefighter. For example, a higher-than-average blood pressure can be an indicator of hypertension (chronic high blood pressure), which is a symptom of heart disease, and it could eliminate you from the running. If a candidate has a disability or medical problem that prevents him or her from becoming a firefighter, he or she can sign an exclusion form. This allows the candidate to be hired on the condition that he or she can never collect a pension as a result of being medically retired for that specific disability or condition. In addition, the candidate may have the opportunity to show through medical records from his or her own physician that he or she can work as a firefighter.

The following sections name some other tests and checks that a physician may perform during the medical exam.

Putting your heart to the test

During routine doctor visits, your physician probably checks your pulse rate (how fast your heart beats). He or she may also use a stethoscope to listen to your heart to detect unusual rhythms. For the firefighter medical exam, your physician may send you for an electrocardiogram (ECG) or a cardiac stress test to determine your heart health.

An *ECG* is a test that records the electrical activity of your heart. During the test, you typically lie flat. The person performing the test attaches small electrodes to your skin in various locations, including your arms, legs, and chest. As your heart beats, the electrodes on your skin send information about the electrical activity of your heart to a recorder. The recorder generates wavy lines either on a screen or on paper, which the doctor interprets to diagnose a wide range of heart problems and learn about your overall heart health.

A *cardiac stress test* is another common test that physicians use to determine heart health. This test checks blood flow to the heart during exercise. A cardiac stress test is similar to an ECG in that you have electrodes attached to your skin to record information on an ECG machine. During this test, however, you walk on a treadmill, gradually increasing the intensity of your exercise. The physician periodically checks your pulse and blood pressure during the test. When the test is complete, you cool down for a while and then lie down until your heart rate and blood pressure return to normal. At this point, the electrodes are removed, and you're allowed to leave. Again, using the results of the cardiac stress test, doctors can diagnose heart problems that could put you at risk on the job.

Catching your breath: Lung tests

You probably don't think much about your breathing. During the firefighter medical exam, however, the physician tests your lung function through *spirometry,* or pulmonary function testing. The Occupational Safety and Health Administration (OSHA) requires that all employees who use respirators in their line of work undergo spirometry testing. Because firefighters rely on self-contained breathing apparatuses, or SCBAs, as their air supply during firefighting operations, firefighters must comply with this rule.

Spirometry uses a device called a *spirometer* to measure both the volume and the speed of air as you inhale and exhale. To complete the test, you inhale deeply and then exhale forcefully and for as long as you can into a sensor on the spirometer. You may also have to breathe normally into the sensor or rapidly inhale either before or after the forced exhalation.

The test measures your *forced vital capacity* (FVC), which is the volume of air that you can forcibly exhale after inhaling the maximum amount of air into your lungs. It also measures your *forced expiratory volume* in 1 second (FEV_1), which is the volume of air you exhale in the first second. Doctors use the FEV_1 and the FVC to determine your FEV_1/FVC ratio, which helps them determine your lung function. Healthy adults generally have an FEV_1/FVC ratio between 75 and 80 percent. Ratios below this mark are indicators of impaired lung function, and doctors may disqualify candidates based on these results.

Giving some fluids: Blood and urine tests

We hope you're not afraid of needles, because physicians may require you to have several lab tests. Your doctor will need to draw some blood, and he or she may ask you to provide a urine sample. Blood tests and urinalyses can help doctors learn a lot about your overall health. For example, blood tests may reveal a high cholesterol level, an indicator of heart disease. A urinalysis may reveal a high blood glucose (blood sugar) level, which can be a sign that you have *diabetes,* a condition caused by the body's inability to properly produce or use insulin.

Lab tests can help doctors detect other diseases and conditions, too, such as anemia, HIV/AIDS, hepatitis, or cancer. Physicians also may use these tests to screen for illicit drug use.

The presence of illicit drugs in a blood test or urinalysis will almost certainly result in the revocation of your conditional offer of employment. Illicit drugs alter both body and mind and can create serious risks for both firefighters and the public they work to protect.

Checking your organs

During the medical exam, the physician checks for hernias and genitourinary (genital/urinary) conditions.

Hernias

Hernias occur when the membrane, muscle, or tissue that surrounds an organ and holds it in place weakens or gets a hole in it, usually as a result of muscle strain, and a piece of the organ pushes through the opening. You may feel a lump or bulge in the location of the hernia. Hernias commonly occur in the abdomen and groin. Lifting something heavy, gaining weight quickly, being pregnant, and even coughing and sneezing for a long time can result in hernias.

The most common type of hernia is called an *inguinal hernia,* and it occurs when a part of the intestine pushes into the inguinal canal through a hole in the lower part of the abdomen. It differs for men and women:

- ✔ **Men:** In men, the *inguinal canal* is an opening between the abdomen and the scrotum. The spermatic cord passes through this opening and connects to the testicles.

   Men who have had physicals in the past are probably familiar with the old "turn your head and cough" routine, which is how doctors check for inguinal hernias. While men carry out these instructions, doctors press near the top of the scrotum to feel for any lumps or bumps that shouldn't be present.

- ✔ **Women:** In women, the *inguinal canal* is an opening through which the ligament that holds the uterus in place passes. Physicians check for hernias in women by pressing on their organs to feel for any bulges that could indicate hernias and by examining the surface of the body for similar lumps or bumps.

In most cases, hernias only temporarily disqualify you from becoming a firefighter because doctors can repair them through surgery. If a hernia is small, the doctor may simply recommend keeping an eye on it to make sure it doesn't grow larger or become more painful.

Reproductive and urinary problems

In addition to hernias, physicians may check for other *genitourinary conditions,* which are conditions of the reproductive organs and the urinary system. In men, physicians will likely check for the following conditions (as well as for other genital conditions that adversely affect the male reproductive system):

- ✔ **Testicular mass:** A lump, whether painless or painful, on the testes
- ✔ **Epididymal mass:** A lump on the *epididymis,* the coiled tube that connects the ducts at the rear of each testicle to its *vas deferens,* the tube that delivers sperm to the ejaculatory duct
- ✔ **Prostate gland problems:** Any problem (for example, enlargement) with the *prostate gland,* which is found near the base of a man's *urethra* (the tube that transports urine from the bladder and carries semen) and that contributes to the production of semen

In women, physicians will likely check for the following conditions (as well as for other gynecological conditions that adversely affect the female reproductive system):

- ✔ **Pregnancy:** Carrying a child
- ✔ **Ovarian cysts:** Fluid-filled sacs with thin walls found within ovaries
- ✔ **Endometriosis:** A painful condition in which *endometrial tissue* (the tissue that forms the lining of the uterus) grows outside the uterus and results in pelvic pain
- ✔ **Dysmenorrhea:** Severe pelvic pain and cramping during menstruation

Some conditions, such as pregnancy, are only temporarily disqualifying and disappear with the passage of time. Other conditions, such as masses or cysts, may not present significant problems or may be corrected through surgery or other curative measures. In each case, a physician makes a determination based on the severity of the condition in relation to its impact on firefighting.

In both men and women, physicians also check for problems with the urinary system — the kidneys, *ureters* (tubes that transport urine from the kidneys to the bladder), bladder, and *urethra* (which transports urine from the bladder and out of the body). Again, the severity of the condition plays a role in the physician's decision to disqualify a candidate.

Now see here: Examining eyes and ears

Firefighters must have good vision and hearing, because they need to be able to detect and respond to emergencies quickly. During the medical exam, physicians check both your eyes and ears for any problems. Physicians conduct a standard vision exam (you know — the chart with the big E at the top) that determines how well you see. Some departments have standards for how well you must be able to see with or without the aid of contacts or glasses. Physicians may also check your eyes for the following:

- **Color-blindness:** The inability to distinguish between certain colors
- **Eye diseases:** Any conditions that affect the health of the eye
- **Peripheral vision:** The ability to see from the outer part of the field of vision (what you can see from the corners of your eyes when you're staring straight ahead)

Certain eye conditions are only temporarily disqualifying, because they may be corrected. A physician will base his or her determination on the severity of the condition. Color-blindness, however, is usually permanently disqualifying because firefighters must be able to distinguish different colors when using imaging devices, such as thermal imaging cameras that can detect temperature variations (heat from fires) within walls.

When the physician looks into your ears, he or she checks for signs of infection. You'll likely know if you have an ear infection because it can cause an ache or pain in the ear. The physician also looks for signs of other conditions that may disqualify you from employment in the fire service, such as an ear injury that has resulted in permanent damage to your ear or an ear deformity.

In addition to checking for physical signs of infection and other ear conditions, the physician will likely conduct a hearing test. The physician uses an *audiometer* to measure how well you hear a series of tones. During the test, you wear headphones through which you hear various tones, ranging from very high-pitched sounds to very low-pitched sounds. You hold a feedback button in your hand that you press each time you hear a sound. Based on your feedback, the physician can tell how well you hear.

Walk this way: Monitoring muscular and skeletal disorders

During the medical exam, the physician looks for disorders of your muscular and skeletal systems (often called the *musculoskeletal system*), such as *arthritis* (inflammation of a joint that may cause pain, stiffness, or swelling), a *fracture* (a break in the bone), a *dislocation* (a bone that has become displaced, usually as the result of an injury), or a *muscle strain* (when overextended muscle fibers tear). In most cases, conditions such as broken bones or muscle strains, which heal over time, won't prevent you from being hired. Conditions such as arthritis, which can worsen over time, or a history of shoulder dislocations, however, could pose a threat to you on the job. In such cases, the doctor's determination depends largely on the severity of the condition.

Doctors may examine your back, neck, skull, spine, arms, hands, legs, and feet to check your range of motion and to look for any signs of deformity. They may have you move or stretch in certain ways to make sure that you have full range of motion along your spine and in your extremities. After all, firefighters sometimes find themselves crawling or duck-walking through tight spaces, climbing ladders, or carrying victims, so it's important that they can bend, stretch, and move without pain.

Getting a onceover for glandular and gastrointestinal disorders

Don't worry — just a few more things to check during the medical exam. As part of the exam, the physician will probably look for signs of glandular and gastrointestinal disorders. Many of your body's glands are part of the *endocrine system,* which is the body system responsible for regulating your body through the release of hormones. Many organs that are part of other body systems, such as the kidneys, liver, and pancreas, are part of the endocrine system, too. A physician may check your adrenal glands, pituitary gland, parathyroid glands, and thyroid gland for signs of diseases or disorders.

Because glands secrete hormones into the bloodstream, glandular disorders can present themselves in many ways. For example, a common symptom of a thyroid disorder (such as an overactive thyroid, called *hyperthyroidism,* or an underactive thyroid, called *hypothyroidism*) is the development of a *goiter,* which is a visible swelling of the neck caused by the swelling of the thyroid.

Some glandular disorders, such as diabetes, which results from the pancreas's inability to produce insulin and control blood sugar levels, are severe enough to permanently disqualify candidates from becoming firefighters. For example, if an insulin-dependent diabetic's blood sugar level drops too low, he or she can become disoriented and even lose consciousness. Other glandular disorders may disqualify candidates, but the doctor's determination depends on the severity of the condition.

After checking for glandular disorders, the physician looks for signs and symptoms of gastrointestinal disorders. These are disorders of the digestive system, which is responsible for breaking down food and absorbing nutrients into the body. The major organs of the gastrointestinal tract are the mouth, *esophagus* (the tube through which food passes from the mouth to the stomach), small intestine, large intestine, rectum, and anus.

Some common gastrointestinal conditions include the following:

- **Gastritis:** Inflammation of the lining of the stomach
- **Inflammatory bowel disease:** Inflammation of the colon (part of the large intestine) and small intestine
- **Ulcers:** Eroded or weakened areas along the acid-producing areas of the digestive tract
- **Intestinal (or bowel) obstruction:** An obstruction within the intestines that prevents the normal movement of digested food and waste materials through the intestines

In most cases, gastrointestinal disorders won't disqualify a candidate from taking the next step toward becoming a firefighter. It's up to the doctor, however, to determine whether gastrointestinal disorders are severe enough to disqualify a candidate.

Understanding What Happens During the Psychological Exam

We completely understand that undergoing a psychological evaluation may make you a little nervous. It's not every day that a psychologist or psychiatrist analyzes and interprets everything you say. Relax. Fire departments don't require a psychological exam because they think you need therapy. Rather, they want to make sure that you have the right personality for the job and the mental preparedness to handle the stressful conditions that often accompany it.

In some cases, the psychological exam is little more than a basic personality test. In others, the evaluation delves more deeply into your life and requires a session with a professional psychologist or psychiatrist. In this section, we outline what you can expect from the psychological exam.

Regardless of how detailed the psychological evaluation is, always remember one thing: Be honest. Don't try to hide your feelings or answer questions how you *think* the department wants you to answer; a professional will see right through your efforts.

Completing the personality questionnaire

Some fire departments may require candidates to complete a personality questionnaire, which is a list of questions designed to evaluate different aspects of your personality, such as your attitude, interests, and motivation for wanting to become a firefighter. Some of these tests can be rather lengthy — hundreds of questions — and it may take you several hours to answer all the questions. In most cases, the department or hiring agency responsible for administering the test lets you know how much time to allot for the personality test.

The questions on a personality test have no right or wrong answers. Rather, they often ask you to rank how strongly you feel about different topics or how you would respond to certain situations. Some contain multiple-choice or true-false questions, but in general, these questions are designed to measure your honest opinions.

You can't exactly study for a personality test, but we can try to calm your nerves by explaining what to expect. The following is a brief sampling of questions that you may see on a fire department's personality questionnaire:

- ✔ When I am unsure of how to complete a task, I ask for help.
- ✔ My judgment is better than it ever was.
- ✔ I am liked by most people who know me.

The questionnaire may ask for true-false responses to these questions, or they may ask you to rank your opinions of these statements on a scale such as the following:

1. Strongly Agree

2. Agree

3. Neither Agree nor Disagree

4. Disagree

5. Strongly Disagree

If you have to use the ranking system, don't be afraid to state how you truly feel. If you strongly agree or strongly disagree with a particular statement, select 1 or 5. For the sake of accuracy, it's best to go with your original "gut feeling" rather than analyze the question for a long time. The questions aren't designed to trick you. They're designed to compare your responses to the responses of other successful firefighters to see whether you have the right personality traits to become a firefighter. In addition, the same question may be asked in different ways to test for consistency in your answers.

Interviewing with a psychologist

Some departments take the psychological evaluation beyond a simple personality questionnaire and require candidates to meet with a professional psychologist or psychiatrist. You shouldn't feel nervous about this meeting. Its purpose is not getting you to open up about your deepest, darkest secrets or explain why that incident in gym class in sixth grade has scarred you for life. Rather, the psychologist likely will ask questions about your personal history, such as your past school and work experiences. He or she may ask about family relationships and friendships or your personal interests and hobbies.

In some cases, the psychologist may review your responses to the personality questionnaire and ask you to further expand upon your answers. For example, if you answered (4) Disagree to the statement, "When I am unsure of how to complete a task, I ask for help," the psychologist may question why you disagree with asking for assistance. Do you think asking for help is a sign of weakness? Do you prefer to do things your own way? Do you have trouble working with others? The way in which you respond to these questions helps the psychologist learn more about your personality and your ability to handle the stress that many firefighters experience on the job.

You can't study for an interview with the psychologist, because you have no idea what he or she may ask. The following tips, however, can help you during the evaluation:

- **Relax.** First and foremost, try to calm your nerves. If you act jittery and nervous during a simple interview, the psychologist may question your ability to handle a stressful emergency, which, as a firefighter, you'll encounter quite often.

- **Be honest.** Answer questions truthfully, and don't be afraid to say how you feel. If you have a strong opinion about something, voice it. Psychologists evaluate the way you answer a question as much as the answer you give.

- **Follow your first instinct.** Don't try to figure out the meaning behind the question or read too much into it. The questions are direct, so answer them directly.

- **Answer only the questions you're asked.** Think before you speak, and answer the question to the best of your ability. If you don't understand a question, ask the psychologist to clarify. Don't volunteer information, however, and don't get off track with a rambling response.

Finally, don't be surprised if the psychologist has few, if any, questions for you. If everything on the questionnaire matches up, the psychologist may send you on your way without asking any additional questions.

Part IV
Practice Firefighter Exams

The 5th Wave   By Rich Tennant

In this part . . .

You've heard it a thousand times: Practice makes perfect. What better way to prepare for a real written firefighter exam than to take some practice ones? The practice exams in Part IV can help you identify areas where you could use some extra study time, as well as areas where you're already proficient.

The first two practice exams in this part are similar to general firefighter exams used by departments across the nation. The third is based on New York City's written exam, and the fourth is based on the National Firefighter Selection Inventory (NFSI) test. Take one or take them all — each includes plenty of practice questions in a wide variety of subject areas and can help you get into the test-taking mindset.

Chapter 15

Practice Exam 1

. . . .

This sample test is similar to the written exams you may encounter during the firefighter hiring process. The test includes questions in the following areas: reading comprehension, verbal expression, observation and memory, spatial orientation, reasoning and judgment, mathematical calculation, and mechanical aptitude.

To get the most out of this practice test, take it like you'd take the real written exam:

- ✔ Allow yourself 3.5 hours to complete the exam, and take the whole exam at one time.
- ✔ Take the test in a quiet place, such as a library or a private office, to avoid interruption.
- ✔ Bring a timer, because you may need to time yourself during certain portions of the exam.
- ✔ Bring a pencil and some scratch paper.
- ✔ Use the answer sheet that's provided.

After you complete the practice exam, check your answers against the answer explanations in Chapter 16. The purpose of this practice exam is to help you identify your strengths and weaknesses on the written exam so you know where to focus your studies. For example, if you have trouble with the mechanical aptitude questions, you'll know that you need to brush up on those skills.

Answer Sheet for Practice Test 1

1 Ⓐ Ⓑ Ⓒ Ⓓ	41 Ⓐ Ⓑ Ⓒ Ⓓ	81 Ⓐ Ⓑ Ⓒ Ⓓ	121 Ⓐ Ⓑ Ⓒ Ⓓ
2 Ⓐ Ⓑ Ⓒ Ⓓ	42 Ⓐ Ⓑ Ⓒ Ⓓ	82 Ⓐ Ⓑ Ⓒ Ⓓ	122 Ⓐ Ⓑ Ⓒ Ⓓ
3 Ⓐ Ⓑ Ⓒ Ⓓ	43 Ⓐ Ⓑ Ⓒ Ⓓ	83 Ⓐ Ⓑ Ⓒ Ⓓ	123 Ⓐ Ⓑ Ⓒ Ⓓ
4 Ⓐ Ⓑ Ⓒ Ⓓ	44 Ⓐ Ⓑ Ⓒ Ⓓ	84 Ⓐ Ⓑ Ⓒ Ⓓ	124 Ⓐ Ⓑ Ⓒ Ⓓ
5 Ⓐ Ⓑ Ⓒ Ⓓ	45 Ⓐ Ⓑ Ⓒ Ⓓ	85 Ⓐ Ⓑ Ⓒ Ⓓ	125 Ⓐ Ⓑ Ⓒ Ⓓ
6 Ⓐ Ⓑ Ⓒ Ⓓ	46 Ⓐ Ⓑ Ⓒ Ⓓ	86 Ⓐ Ⓑ Ⓒ Ⓓ	126 Ⓐ Ⓑ Ⓒ Ⓓ
7 Ⓐ Ⓑ Ⓒ Ⓓ	47 Ⓐ Ⓑ Ⓒ Ⓓ	87 Ⓐ Ⓑ Ⓒ Ⓓ	127 Ⓐ Ⓑ Ⓒ Ⓓ
8 Ⓐ Ⓑ Ⓒ Ⓓ	48 Ⓐ Ⓑ Ⓒ Ⓓ	88 Ⓐ Ⓑ Ⓒ Ⓓ	128 Ⓐ Ⓑ Ⓒ Ⓓ
9 Ⓐ Ⓑ Ⓒ Ⓓ	49 Ⓐ Ⓑ Ⓒ Ⓓ	89 Ⓐ Ⓑ Ⓒ Ⓓ	129 Ⓐ Ⓑ Ⓒ Ⓓ
10 Ⓐ Ⓑ Ⓒ Ⓓ	50 Ⓐ Ⓑ Ⓒ Ⓓ	90 Ⓐ Ⓑ Ⓒ Ⓓ	130 Ⓐ Ⓑ Ⓒ Ⓓ
11 Ⓐ Ⓑ Ⓒ Ⓓ	51 Ⓐ Ⓑ Ⓒ Ⓓ	91 Ⓐ Ⓑ Ⓒ Ⓓ	131 Ⓐ Ⓑ Ⓒ Ⓓ
12 Ⓐ Ⓑ Ⓒ Ⓓ	52 Ⓐ Ⓑ Ⓒ Ⓓ	92 Ⓐ Ⓑ Ⓒ Ⓓ	132 Ⓐ Ⓑ Ⓒ Ⓓ
13 Ⓐ Ⓑ Ⓒ Ⓓ	53 Ⓐ Ⓑ Ⓒ Ⓓ	93 Ⓐ Ⓑ Ⓒ Ⓓ	133 Ⓐ Ⓑ Ⓒ Ⓓ
14 Ⓐ Ⓑ Ⓒ Ⓓ	54 Ⓐ Ⓑ Ⓒ Ⓓ	94 Ⓐ Ⓑ Ⓒ Ⓓ	134 Ⓐ Ⓑ Ⓒ Ⓓ
15 Ⓐ Ⓑ Ⓒ Ⓓ	55 Ⓐ Ⓑ Ⓒ Ⓓ	95 Ⓐ Ⓑ Ⓒ Ⓓ	135 Ⓐ Ⓑ Ⓒ Ⓓ
16 Ⓐ Ⓑ Ⓒ Ⓓ	56 Ⓐ Ⓑ Ⓒ Ⓓ	96 Ⓐ Ⓑ Ⓒ Ⓓ	136 Ⓐ Ⓑ Ⓒ Ⓓ
17 Ⓐ Ⓑ Ⓒ Ⓓ	57 Ⓐ Ⓑ Ⓒ Ⓓ	97 Ⓐ Ⓑ Ⓒ Ⓓ	137 Ⓐ Ⓑ Ⓒ Ⓓ
18 Ⓐ Ⓑ Ⓒ Ⓓ	58 Ⓐ Ⓑ Ⓒ Ⓓ	98 Ⓐ Ⓑ Ⓒ Ⓓ	138 Ⓐ Ⓑ Ⓒ Ⓓ
19 Ⓐ Ⓑ Ⓒ Ⓓ	59 Ⓐ Ⓑ Ⓒ Ⓓ	99 Ⓐ Ⓑ Ⓒ Ⓓ	139 Ⓐ Ⓑ Ⓒ Ⓓ
20 Ⓐ Ⓑ Ⓒ Ⓓ	60 Ⓐ Ⓑ Ⓒ Ⓓ	100 Ⓐ Ⓑ Ⓒ Ⓓ	140 Ⓐ Ⓑ Ⓒ Ⓓ
21 Ⓐ Ⓑ Ⓒ Ⓓ	61 Ⓐ Ⓑ Ⓒ Ⓓ	101 Ⓐ Ⓑ Ⓒ Ⓓ	141 Ⓐ Ⓑ Ⓒ Ⓓ
22 Ⓐ Ⓑ Ⓒ Ⓓ	62 Ⓐ Ⓑ Ⓒ Ⓓ	102 Ⓐ Ⓑ Ⓒ Ⓓ	142 Ⓐ Ⓑ Ⓒ Ⓓ
23 Ⓐ Ⓑ Ⓒ Ⓓ	63 Ⓐ Ⓑ Ⓒ Ⓓ	103 Ⓐ Ⓑ Ⓒ Ⓓ	143 Ⓐ Ⓑ Ⓒ Ⓓ
24 Ⓐ Ⓑ Ⓒ Ⓓ	64 Ⓐ Ⓑ Ⓒ Ⓓ	104 Ⓐ Ⓑ Ⓒ Ⓓ	144 Ⓐ Ⓑ Ⓒ Ⓓ
25 Ⓐ Ⓑ Ⓒ Ⓓ	65 Ⓐ Ⓑ Ⓒ Ⓓ	105 Ⓐ Ⓑ Ⓒ Ⓓ	145 Ⓐ Ⓑ Ⓒ Ⓓ
26 Ⓐ Ⓑ Ⓒ Ⓓ	66 Ⓐ Ⓑ Ⓒ Ⓓ	106 Ⓐ Ⓑ Ⓒ Ⓓ	146 Ⓐ Ⓑ Ⓒ Ⓓ
27 Ⓐ Ⓑ Ⓒ Ⓓ	67 Ⓐ Ⓑ Ⓒ Ⓓ	107 Ⓐ Ⓑ Ⓒ Ⓓ	147 Ⓐ Ⓑ Ⓒ Ⓓ
28 Ⓐ Ⓑ Ⓒ Ⓓ	68 Ⓐ Ⓑ Ⓒ Ⓓ	108 Ⓐ Ⓑ Ⓒ Ⓓ	148 Ⓐ Ⓑ Ⓒ Ⓓ
29 Ⓐ Ⓑ Ⓒ Ⓓ	69 Ⓐ Ⓑ Ⓒ Ⓓ	109 Ⓐ Ⓑ Ⓒ Ⓓ	149 Ⓐ Ⓑ Ⓒ Ⓓ
30 Ⓐ Ⓑ Ⓒ Ⓓ	70 Ⓐ Ⓑ Ⓒ Ⓓ	110 Ⓐ Ⓑ Ⓒ Ⓓ	150 Ⓐ Ⓑ Ⓒ Ⓓ
31 Ⓐ Ⓑ Ⓒ Ⓓ	71 Ⓐ Ⓑ Ⓒ Ⓓ	111 Ⓐ Ⓑ Ⓒ Ⓓ	
32 Ⓐ Ⓑ Ⓒ Ⓓ	72 Ⓐ Ⓑ Ⓒ Ⓓ	112 Ⓐ Ⓑ Ⓒ Ⓓ	
33 Ⓐ Ⓑ Ⓒ Ⓓ	73 Ⓐ Ⓑ Ⓒ Ⓓ	113 Ⓐ Ⓑ Ⓒ Ⓓ	
34 Ⓐ Ⓑ Ⓒ Ⓓ	74 Ⓐ Ⓑ Ⓒ Ⓓ	114 Ⓐ Ⓑ Ⓒ Ⓓ	
35 Ⓐ Ⓑ Ⓒ Ⓓ	75 Ⓐ Ⓑ Ⓒ Ⓓ	115 Ⓐ Ⓑ Ⓒ Ⓓ	
36 Ⓐ Ⓑ Ⓒ Ⓓ	76 Ⓐ Ⓑ Ⓒ Ⓓ	116 Ⓐ Ⓑ Ⓒ Ⓓ	
37 Ⓐ Ⓑ Ⓒ Ⓓ	77 Ⓐ Ⓑ Ⓒ Ⓓ	117 Ⓐ Ⓑ Ⓒ Ⓓ	
38 Ⓐ Ⓑ Ⓒ Ⓓ	78 Ⓐ Ⓑ Ⓒ Ⓓ	118 Ⓐ Ⓑ Ⓒ Ⓓ	
39 Ⓐ Ⓑ Ⓒ Ⓓ	79 Ⓐ Ⓑ Ⓒ Ⓓ	119 Ⓐ Ⓑ Ⓒ Ⓓ	
40 Ⓐ Ⓑ Ⓒ Ⓓ	80 Ⓐ Ⓑ Ⓒ Ⓓ	120 Ⓐ Ⓑ Ⓒ Ⓓ	

Part 1: Reading Comprehension

Directions: This section tests your reading comprehension skills. Read each passage and answer the questions that follow it. Choose the answer that *most correctly* answers each question. Mark the space on your answer sheet that corresponds to the question number and the letter indicating your choice.

Use the information in the following passage to answer questions 1–5.

Many rural fire departments lack the luxury of a hydrant on every street corner. For this reason, they have developed other means by which to generate a constant water supply at fire scenes. First, rural departments transport their water to fire scenes in large tanker trucks. They can usually extinguish a small fire with the tanker's onboard water supply. For bigger fires, however, rural departments rely on portable water tanks, which are collapsible temporary pools, to hold a generous supply of water. Oftentimes numerous tankers from the same department, and even tankers from other nearby departments, take turns delivering water to the portable tank and returning to a water source to refill. But how does the water get from a portable tank to a fire hose and, ultimately, to the fire?

When the fire department arrives on scene, firefighters set up the portable tank near the engine. A tanker truck empties its supply of water into the tank. Next, firefighters prepare large-diameter hard-suction hose for drafting, which is the use of suction to draw water into the engine's pump. Hard-suction hose is more rigid than other types of fire hose, because it's built to withstand the partial vacuum created by drafting. As a result, it cannot be wound or folded. Rather, lengths of hard-suction hose often are mounted to a fire apparatus. Firefighters attach one end of the hard-suction hose to the fire engine. They fit the other end with a strainer, which filters out debris that could damage the fire engine. After they submerge the strainer end of the hose into the portable water tank, firefighters engage the suction pump on the fire engine. The pump draws water from the portable tank through the hard-suction hose and into the engine. From there, the engine can pump the water wherever it needs to go.

An important thing to remember when using hard-suction hose is that the longer the distance the water has to travel, the harder the pump has to work. Therefore, firefighters typically position the portable water tank as close to the fire engine's suction pump as possible.

1. What is the purpose of a portable water tank?

 (A) to deliver water from a fire engine to a fire

 (B) to serve as a fill site for empty tanker trucks

 (C) to provide a temporary water source at a fire scene

 (D) to strain debris from water to prevent engine damage

2. According to the passage, all of the following are used in rural firefighting procedures EXCEPT

 (A) tanker trucks.

 (B) fire hydrants.

 (C) portable water tanks.

 (D) hard-suction hoses.

Go on to next page

3. Firefighters would likely use hard-suction hose for all of the following EXCEPT

   (A) drawing water from a pond to refill a tanker.

   (B) drafting water from a portable water tank to an engine.

   (C) sucking water from the basement of a flooded home.

   (D) spraying water on a fire to extinguish the flames.

4. The best title for this passage is

   (A) "Rural Firefighting Procedures"

   (B) "How to Set Up a Portable Water Tank"

   (C) "Drafting from Public Water Sources"

   (D) "Fire Hose Usage"

5. Based on the information in the passage, you can conclude that a fire engine's drafting water from a portable water tank is most similar to a person's

   (A) watering a garden with a hose.

   (B) drinking lemonade through a straw.

   (C) pouring liquid through a sieve.

   (D) filling a glass from a pitcher of iced tea.

Use the information in the following passage to answer questions 6–12.

A fire that occurs in a confined space, such as an enclosed room, is called a compartment fire. Compartment fires go through five main developmental stages. The first stage is ignition. Ignition occurs when heat, fuel, and oxygen combine to start the chemical chain reaction that creates and sustains fire. These four elements — heat, fuel, oxygen, and a chemical chain reaction — are the four sides of the fire tetrahedron, or pyramid, and are necessary for a fire to start and continue to burn.

Once the fire ignites, it enters the growth stage. At this point, a fire plume forms above the fuel source and begins to draw in air from the surrounding area. The fire plume gives off hot gases, which rise vertically and eventually spread horizontally when they reach the ceiling of the compartment. When the layer of hot gases reaches the walls of the compartment, it starts to thicken. If the compartment contains enough fuel, the growth stage will continue. The temperature of both the compartment and the gas layer will rise.

Flashover occurs between the growth stage and the fully developed stage of the fire. During the growth stage, the hot gas layer heats up all of the flammable materials within the compartment. The flashover occurs suddenly, when all of the combustible materials burst into flame at the same time.

Following flashover, the fire enters the fully developed stage. At this point, all fuel sources within the compartment are on fire. The fire continues to produce heat and fire gases until its fuel sources are depleted. Once the fire uses up its fuel sources, however, the flames die down, the fire produces less heat, and the temperature within the compartment begins to decline. This stage, known as decay, is the final stage in a compartment fire. Firefighters should note, however, that even the embers left in the decay stage can produce quite a bit of heat.

Go on to next page

6. All of the following are necessary for a fire to ignite EXCEPT

   (A) heat.

   (B) fuel.

   (C) fire gas.

   (D) oxygen.

7. During which stage of a compartment fire do all the combustible materials in the compartment simultaneously catch fire?

   (A) growth

   (B) ignition

   (C) decay

   (D) flashover

8. Which sentence from the passage best states its main idea?

   (A) Compartment fires go through five main developmental stages.

   (B) Once the fire ignites, it enters the growth stage.

   (C) The temperature of both the compartment and the gas layer will rise.

   (D) At this point, all fuel sources within the compartment are on fire.

9. Which of the following shows the stages of a compartment fire in the correct sequence?

   (A) growth → ignition → flashover → fully developed → decay

   (B) decay → growth → flashover → ignition → fully developed

   (C) ignition → growth → flashover → fully developed → decay

   (D) flashover → ignition → growth → fully developed → decay

10. During which stage of a compartment fire do the hot gases start to rise toward the ceiling and then move outward toward the walls?

    (A) growth

    (B) ignition

    (C) fully developed

    (D) flashover

11. According to the passage, which part of the fire tetrahedron disappears during the decay stage, causing the fire to stop burning?

    (A) heat

    (B) fuel

    (C) chemical chain reaction

    (D) oxygen

12. During which stage would a firefighter attempting to fight a compartment fire be at most risk?

    (A) ignition

    (B) growth

    (C) flashover

    (D) decay

Go on to next page

Use the information in the table to answer questions 13–15.

Total Body Surface Area (TBSA) for Measurement of Skin Burns

Age of Person	Head	Chest/ Abdomen	Back/ Buttocks	Arms	Legs	Genitalia/ Perineum
Adult	9%	18%	18%	18%	36%	1%
Child	17%	18%	18%	18%	26%	1%
Infant (< 22 lbs.)	20%	16%	16%	16%	32%	1%

13. A child accidentally pulls a pot of boiling water off the stove and suffers burns on his arms, chest, and abdomen. Approximately what percentage of the boy's skin surface has been burned?

    (A) 18%

    (B) 36%

    (C) 54%

    (D) 72%

14. In terms of total body surface area, which of these injuries would most likely lead to the greatest surface area of burned skin?

    (A) a baby touches the front of her right leg to a hot stove while trying to stand

    (B) a man burns his left arm while attempting to light a campfire

    (C) a child scalds the backs of both legs when he leans against a radiator

    (D) a woman involved in a car accident suffers burns on her head

15. All of the following account for the same percentage of total body surface area in both adults and children EXCEPT

    (A) head.

    (B) back/buttocks.

    (C) arms.

    (D) chest/abdomen.

Go on to next page

Use the information in the following passage to answer questions 16–20.

Firefighters are often required to deal with glass when entering structures or rescuing victims. Glass is most often an obstacle in dealing with automobile accidents. Removing automobile glass can be challenging and even dangerous. There are two major kinds of auto glass: safety (laminated) glass and tempered glass.

Safety glass is usually used for windshields and sometimes rear windows. It is a thick material made of sheets of glass laminated to a sheet of plastic. In impacts, the plastic laminate holds the glass. That way, the glass cracks and shatters but is still mostly held in place. Firefighters and other emergency personnel may have to chop through laminated glass. This may be a tough chore and require tools such as axes, saws, or air chisels. During the process, any immobilized victims must be covered with tarps or blankets to protect them from sharp fragments.

Tempered glass is most often used in automobile side windows. This kind of glass is designed to break into small pieces. This reduces the danger of large pieces of glass flying around during an accident, but small pieces of glass may be dangerous as well. Rescue personnel can shatter tempered glass by striking the lower corner of a window with a tool such as a spring-loaded punch.

16. Which of the following pieces of information is included in the passage?

    (A) how tempered glass is manufactured

    (B) what kind of glass is used in home windows

    (C) how laminated glass can be removed

    (D) when laminated glass was first used

17. Firefighters who need to break auto glass would likely use all of the following tools EXCEPT

    (A) winches.

    (B) saws.

    (C) spring-loaded punches.

    (D) air chisels.

18. The laminate material in safety glass is made of

    (A) metal.

    (B) springs.

    (C) broken glass.

    (D) plastic sheets.

19. In dealing with an immobilized victim in a crashed automobile, a firefighter should

    (A) remove the roof before removing windows.

    (B) provide protection from broken glass.

    (C) only attempt to break tempered glass.

    (D) refrain from attempting to remove windows.

20. What is the main idea of this passage?

    (A) Automobile glass has evolved and become safer and stronger in recent years.

    (B) Emergency workers use specialized tools to break windows.

    (C) Firefighters may need to deal with different kinds of glass at accident scenes.

    (D) Windshields are made of stronger glass than most other automobile windows.

Go on to next page

> *Use the information in the following passage to answer questions 21–24.*

Understanding how fire works is an important step in firefighting. A fire occurs when several factors take place at the same time. Firefighters used to focus on three factors in the combustion process, which they called the fire triangle. The three parts of the fire triangle were oxygen, heat, and fuel. To be more accurate, however, firefighters now refer to the combustion process as the fire tetrahedron. The tetrahedron, or pyramid, shape takes into account a fourth necessary element — a chain reaction — that unites the other three parts to cause fire.

Because fire is a product of a process, you can get rid of fire by limiting or stopping the process. The most well-known way to break the process is to reduce the heat element. This is often done with water. Water may be able to cool the fuel until it is unable to continue burning.

Firefighters may also attempt to remove oxygen or fuel from a fire. One way to remove oxygen is to cover or smother a fire, such as by covering a pot full of burning food. Oxygen can also be removed from the combustion process using foam or carbon dioxide extinguishing materials. Removing fuel might mean sopping up spilled oil or removing flammable shrubs or boxes from an area. Some chemicals, such as halons, can even stop the chemical chain reaction involved in combustion.

21. Which would be an example of removing oxygen from a fire?

    (A) Firefighters use controlled burns to remove brush near a forest fire.

    (B) A man uses a heavy blanket to smother a fire on his jacket sleeve.

    (C) Firefighters spray water on several homes alongside a house fire.

    (D) A woman breaks a window to save a child from a burning house.

22. Which element makes the fire tetrahedron more complete than the fire triangle?

    (A) chemical chain reaction

    (B) oxygen

    (C) fuel

    (D) heat

23. The word *combustion* most likely refers to

    (A) spreading.

    (B) reacting.

    (C) burning.

    (D) combining.

24. If you needed to extinguish a fire by chemically stopping the chain reaction, which of the following actions would you most likely take?

    (A) allowing the fire to consume fuel

    (B) applying carbon dioxide to the fire

    (C) dousing the fire with cool water

    (D) applying a halon agent to the fire

Go on to next page

Use the information in the following passage to answer questions 25–30.

There is no doubt that water is important in firefighting, but how the water is applied to a fire is also important. Firefighters must be aware of the pattern of the fire stream, the stream of water coming from the hose nozzle. The fire stream pattern can make a big difference in a dangerous situation.

There are three major kinds of fire stream pattern: solid stream, fog stream, and broken stream. Each pattern is suited to a particular kind of firefighting scenario. All of the patterns, however, are influenced by wind, gravity, heat, and friction with the surrounding air.

A solid stream of water is a compact stream. It is created by a fixed smoothbore (smooth on the inside) nozzle. The thin, rounded nozzle makes the stream strong, far-reaching, and fast. Firefighters often use solid streams to deliver water to hard-to-reach areas or areas that are far away.

Another common kind of stream pattern is the fog stream. A fog stream is made of fine water droplets that spray out of the hose. The droplets are useful for absorbing heat as well as dousing fires. Firefighters can use differently shaped fog tips on their hoses to produce straight, narrow-angle, or wide-angle fog streams.

A broken stream of water works on the same principle as the fog stream. A broken stream, however, produces larger drops of water that are able to absorb even more heat. Broken streams are most useful for fighting fires in confined spaces.

25. According to the passage, what is a fire stream?

(A) a tool through which water passes

(B) a flow of water from a hose nozzle

(C) a chemical process for putting out fire

(D) a flow of water broken into droplets

26. A firefighter who needs to send water across a far distance would most likely use a

(A) narrow-angle fog stream.

(B) broken stream.

(C) solid stream.

(D) wide-angle fog stream.

27. All of the following factors may influence stream patterns EXCEPT

(A) wind.

(B) light.

(C) gravity.

(D) heat.

28. In which location would a broken stream be most useful?

(A) a large building lobby

(B) a forest that has caught fire

(C) a street where a car is burning

(D) a small basement apartment

29. The main purpose of this passage is to

(A) explain the importance of water.

(B) teach how water extinguishes fire.

(C) show proper use of the fire hose.

(D) explain types of water streams.

30. According to the passage, a fog tip is used for

(A) adjusting fog stream angles.

(B) reducing air friction with water.

(C) making a smoothbore nozzle.

(D) creating a broken stream.

Go on to next page

Part 2: Verbal Expression

Directions: This section tests your verbal expression skills. Read each question and choose the answer that *most correctly* answers it. Mark the space on your answer sheet that corresponds to the question number and the letter indicating your choice.

For questions 31–33, choose the word that is spelled correctly to complete the following sentences.

31. For a fire to continue burning, it needs _____, heat, and fuel.

   (A) oxigen

   (B) oxigin

   (C) oxygen

   (D) oxygin

32. When entering a burning structure, look for an open door or window before resorting to _____ entry.

   (A) forcible

   (B) forcable

   (C) forsible

   (D) forsable

33. Overloading an _____ socket can result in a fire.

   (A) electricel

   (B) elektrical

   (C) elektricle

   (D) electrical

For questions 34–35, please identify which of the underlined words is spelled incorrectly.

34. By inserting wooden wedges into the loop of a sprinkler head <u>assembly</u>, firefighters can <u>impede</u> the <u>deluge</u> of water that occurs when a sprinkler system is <u>actavated</u> and prevent water damage.

   (A) assembly

   (B) impede

   (C) deluge

   (D) actavated

35. Vaporization is the <u>transformation</u> of a liquid to its <u>gasious</u> state. It occurs when <u>molecules</u> of the substance escape from the liquid's surface and rise into the <u>atmosphere</u>.

   (A) transformation

   (B) gasious

   (C) molecules

   (D) atmosphere

Choose the appropriate word or phrase to complete the following sentences.

36. Department 61 _____ fire code inspections at local businesses starting next week.

   (A) performs

   (B) will perform

   (C) performed

   (D) has performed

37. The firefighters from the local volunteer fire department hold a golf tournament each summer to raise money for _____ station.

   (A) there

   (B) their

   (C) they

   (D) they're

38. A tanker truck bearing two hazardous materials placards _____ in an accident on the interstate.

   (A) were involved

   (B) involved

   (C) was involved

   (D) had been involve

Go on to next page

39. The department made _____ decision regarding the equipment that needed to be replaced.

    (A) their

    (B) its

    (C) our

    (D) them

40. Chief Redding posted the new schedule _____ the bulletin board in the conference room.

    (A) to

    (B) from

    (C) at

    (D) for

For questions 41–44, choose the word has nearly the same meaning as the word in italics.

41. Any lapse in fire department safety standards might *jeopardize* firefighters on duty.

    (A) relieve

    (B) endanger

    (C) criticize

    (D) defend

42. The investigator began to *scrutinize* the burned building for any evidence of arson.

    (A) report

    (B) abandon

    (C) contest

    (D) examine

43. Concerned neighbors rushed to the house fire and tried to *interrogate* firefighters about what had happened.

    (A) question

    (B) assist

    (C) encourage

    (D) educate

44. Months of tough training were required to make the rookie firefighters *proficient* at their tasks.

    (A) alert

    (B) restricted

    (C) weary

    (D) skilled

For questions 45–47, choose the phrase that would best replace the underlined part of the sentence.

45. Using fire trucks in parades may help a community notice and to appreciate the presence of the local fire department.

    (A) community notice and to appreciate to the presence

    (B) community notice and appreciate the presence

    (C) community notice, and to appreciate, the presence

    (D) community, notice and appreciate, the presence

46. The most successful firefighters, they should have a basic knowledge of emergency medical care to help victims.

    (A) firefighters they should have

    (B) firefighters, should have

    (C) firefighters should have

    (D) firefighters that should have

47. Fire prevention inspections, and fire safety talks, are important ways for firefighters to help prevent future emergencies.

    (A) inspections and fire safety talks, are important ways

    (B) inspections and fire safety talks; are important ways

    (C) inspections and fire safety talks is an important way

    (D) inspections and fire safety talks are important ways

Go on to next page

For questions 48–50, choose the word that best completes the sentence.

48. Most fire departments judge firefighting candidates by a set list of _____ having to do with their abilities.

    (A) criteria

    (B) complaints

    (C) annotations

    (D) emergencies

49. Donations of time and money by local people were _____ in helping the small-town fire company operate.

    (A) residual

    (B) superficial

    (C) instrumental

    (D) controversial

50. The Springfield Fire Department recently _____ its new fire engine with a new rescue vehicle.

    (A) complicated

    (B) complemented

    (C) advanced

    (D) adjoined

Part 3: Observation and Memory

> **Directions:** This section tests your observation and memory skills. In this section, you'll need a timer and a partner. Follow the directions before each passage or image in this section.

Listening and memory

> **Directions for questions 51–60:** In this part, you'll be tested on your listening and memory skills, including your ability to hear, understand, and interpret information. Ask a partner to read aloud the passage in the appendix about water emergencies. DO NOT READ THE PASSAGE YOURSELF. DO NOT TAKE NOTES DURING THE READING. Immediately after your partner has finished reading, answer questions 51–60 based only on what you can remember from the reading. Choose the answer that *most correctly* answers each question. You may look at the passage only when checking your answers at the completion of Practice Exam 1.

51. What is firefighters' preferred order for the different water rescue methods?

    (A) go, row, throw, reach

    (B) throw, go, reach, row

    (C) reach, throw, row, go

    (D) row, go, reach, throw

52. Which of the following is a situation that requires firefighters to conduct a water recovery?

    (A) A fisherman discovers the remains of a drowning victim in a pond.

    (B) A child overturns a kayak in a lake and is struggling to swim to shore.

    (C) A flash flood washes a victim into a river, where she holds a tree branch to stay afloat.

    (D) An elderly man swimming in a lake begins to experience symptoms of a heart attack.

53. A firefighter swims to the middle of a lake to rescue a woman. What water rescue method is the firefighter using?

    (A) reach

    (B) throw

    (C) row

    (D) go

54. What is hypothermia?

    (A) a suit that protects the human body in water

    (B) a drop in body temperature

    (C) a flotation device

    (D) a method used to rescue victims from water

55. All of the following are appropriate for water rescue EXCEPT a

    (A) specially designed helmet.

    (B) personal flotation device.

    (C) standard set of PPE.

    (D) dry suit.

56. The purpose of a dry suit is to

    (A) warm up a victim suffering from hypothermia.

    (B) protect the body when working in the water.

    (C) serve as a flotation device for drowning victims.

    (D) protect standard PPE during water rescues.

57. Tossing a lifeguard's rescue can with an attached rope to a struggling swimmer is an example of the

    (A) reach method.

    (B) throw method.

    (C) row method.

    (D) go method.

58. The purpose of a PFD is to

    (A) keep a person in the water afloat.

    (B) prevent hypothermia in cold water.

    (C) protect the head during water rescues.

    (D) reach the victim of a water emergency.

59. If firefighters cannot extend a tool far enough to reach a victim in need of water rescue, their next step would most likely be to

    (A) ask a passing boater to help the victim.

    (B) swim to the victim's aid.

    (C) use a boat to reach the victim.

    (D) toss a life preserver to the victim.

60. What is the main risk associated with the go method?

    (A) The rescuer may end up with hypothermia.

    (B) The rescuer won't reach the victim in time.

    (C) The rescuer could easily become a victim.

    (D) The rescuer can't stay in the water very long.

Go on to next page

Visual Memory

Directions for questions 61–70: In this part, you'll be tested on your observational and memory skills, including your ability to see, understand, and interpret information. Study the Davis Street fire scene in the appendix for 5 minutes. DO NOT TAKE NOTES ABOUT THE IMAGE AS YOU STUDY IT. At the end of 5 minutes, answer questions 61–70 based only on what you can remember from the image. DO NOT LOOK AT THE IMAGE AS YOU ANSWER THE QUESTIONS. Choose the answer that *most correctly* answers each question. You may look at the image only when checking your answers at the completion of Practice Exam 1.

Set your timer for 5 minutes and begin studying the image.

61. Which building or buildings in the drawing are made of brick?

    (A) Midtown Movies only

    (B) Midtown Movies and Davis Street Apartments

    (C) Belle Maria Dance Studio only

    (D) Davis Street Apartments and Belle Maria Dance Studio

62. The greatest number of bystanders is located near

    (A) the trees.

    (B) the car.

    (C) Troy's Hardware.

    (D) Midtown Movies.

63. The fire appears to be concentrated in which part of Belle Maria Dance Studio?

    (A) the roof

    (B) the first floor

    (C) the northwest corner

    (D) the southeast corner

64. How many front windows does Belle Maria Dance Studio have?

    (A) 3

    (B) 4

    (C) 6

    (D) 8

65. The parked vehicle is facing

    (A) the viewer.

    (B) the fire.

    (C) Midtown Movies.

    (D) Troy's Hardware.

66. How many visible ground-level entrances does the Belle Maria Dance Studio have?

    (A) 0

    (B) 1

    (C) 2

    (D) 3

67. Flames are visible in how many windows of the Belle Maria Dance Studio?

    (A) 2

    (B) 3

    (C) 4

    (D) 5

68. Which building has the most visible windows?

    (A) Davis Street Apartments

    (B) Belle Maria Dance Studio

    (C) Troy's Hardware

    (D) Midtown Movies

69. How many people are standing by the car?

    (A) 0

    (B) 1

    (C) 2

    (D) 3

70. Which is the tallest building in the picture?

    (A) Davis Street Apartments

    (B) Belle Maria Dance Studio

    (C) Troy's Hardware

    (D) Midtown Movies

Go on to next page

Part 4: Spatial Orientation

Directions: This section tests your spatial orientation skills. Follow the directions before each map, floor plan, or image. Then read each question and choose the answer that *most correctly* answers it. Mark the space on your answer sheet that corresponds to the question number and the letter indicating your choice. You may look at the image as often as you'd like as you answer the questions.

Use the following town map to answer questions 71–75.

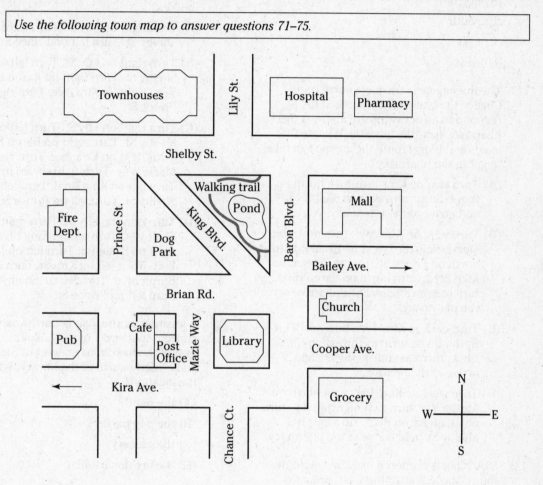

Go on to next page

71. A fire truck faces east when it leaves the fire department. The driver makes a right onto Prince St., a left onto Brian Rd., another left onto Baron Blvd., and a right onto Bailey Ave. From there, the driver makes a right into the parking lot of the church. What direction is the fire truck facing?

    (A) north

    (B) south

    (C) east

    (D) west

72. The fire engine is traveling north on Chance Ct. when it is dispatched to respond to an activated fire alarm at the pharmacy near the hospital. What is the most direct legal route the engine can take to get to the pharmacy?

    (A) Turn east on Kira Ave., turn north on Baron Blvd., turn east on Shelby St., and arrive at the pharmacy.

    (B) Turn west on Kira Ave., turn north on Mazie Way, turn west on Brian Rd., turn north on Prince St., turn southeast on King Blvd., turn north on Baron Blvd., turn east on Shelby St., and arrive at the pharmacy.

    (C) Turn east on Kira Ave., turn north on Baron Blvd., turn northwest on King Blvd., turn east on Shelby St., and arrive at the pharmacy.

    (D) Turn west on Kira Ave., turn north on Mazie Way, turn east on Brian Rd., turn north on Baron Blvd., turn east on Shelby St., and arrive at the pharmacy.

73. A building is bordered by Kira Ave. to the south, Mazie Way to the west, Brian Rd. to the north, and Baron Blvd. to the east. What is the building?

    (A) the post office

    (B) the café

    (C) the library

    (D) the dog park

74. The townhouses have a parking lot with one entrance/exit on the western side of Lily St. You live in the townhouses and work for the fire department as a firefighter. Today you have to stop at the post office on your way to work. If you leave from the parking lot of the townhouses, what is the most direct legal route you can take to go by the post office on your way to work?

    (A) Turn right on Lily St. Turn right on Shelby St. Turn left on Prince St.

    (B) Turn right on Lily St. Turn left on Shelby St. Turn right on Baron Blvd. Turn right on Kira Ave. Turn right on Prince St.

    (C) Turn right on Lily St. Turn left on Shelby St. Turn right on Baron Blvd. Turn right on Kira Ave. Turn right on Mazie Way. Turn right on Brian Rd. Turn left on King Blvd. Turn left on Shelby St. Turn left on Prince St.

    (D) Turn right on Lily St. Turn right on Shelby St. Turn left on King Blvd. Turn right on Brian Rd. Turn left on Mazie Way. Turn left on Kira St. Turn left on Baron Blvd. Turn left on Shelby St. Turn left on Prince St.

75. A location on the map is northwest of the church, southwest of the hospital, southeast of the townhouses, west of the mall, and directly north of the library. What is the location?

    (A) the pond

    (B) the dog park

    (C) the grocery

    (D) the fire department

Go on to next page

Use the following floor plan to answer questions 76–79.

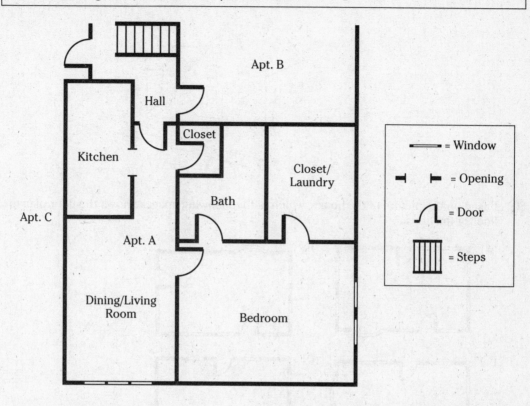

76. A dryer fire occurs in the closet/laundry area of apartment A. A firefighter approaches apartment A from the hall. How many doors must she walk through to reach the dryer?

   (A) 1

   (B) 2

   (C) 3

   (D) 4

77. How many windows does apartment A have?

   (A) 2

   (B) 3

   (C) 4

   (D) 5

78. A firefighter enters apartment A from the hall door. The kitchen opening is to his right and the closet is to his left. He walks to the next door on his left, enters a room, and then enters the first door on his left. Where is the firefighter?

   (A) the dining/living room

   (B) the bedroom

   (C) the bathroom

   (D) the closet/laundry

79. How many doors, excluding the opening into the kitchen, does apartment A have?

   (A) 3

   (B) 4

   (C) 5

   (D) 6

Go on to next page

Use the following image to answer question 80.

80. Based on the picture of the house, which of the following images shows the floor plan for the first floor of the house?

(A)

(B)

(C)

(D)

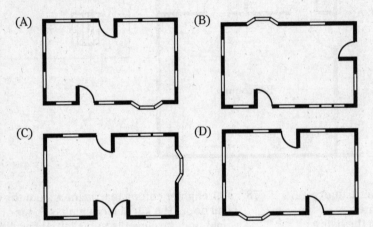

Use the following floor plan to answer questions 81–90.

N E S W (compass)

6

Storage

5

Hall 2

7 C

8

9

10

11

Hall 3

14

13

12

15

16

17

B

4

3

2

Office 1

Hall 1

Conference Room

Lavatory

Lounge

Cafeteria

A

Vending Machines

Lobby

Front Entrance

D

⌒ = Door

| = Window

⬥ = Standpipe

⊥ = Opening

Go on to next page

81. If a fire occurred in office 4, what would be the most direct route for the occupants of office 4 to exit the building?

    (A) Leave office 4, turn left into hall 1, pass through the lobby, and exit through the front entrance.

    (B) Leave office 4, turn left into hall 1, cut through the conference room, turn left into hall 3, pass through the cafeteria, and exit through the cafeteria entrance.

    (C) Leave office 4, go straight down hall 2, turn left into hall 3, pass through the cafeteria, and exit through the cafeteria doors.

    (D) Leave office 4, go straight down hall 2, turn left into hall 3, pass through the conference room, turn right in hall 1, pass through the lobby, and exit through the front entrance.

82. Which two standpipes would firefighters most likely use to put out a fire in the conference room?

    (A) A and B

    (B) A and C

    (C) C and D

    (D) A and D

83. If a firefighter walked down hall 1 from the lobby, how many doors would he or she pass before reaching standpipe B?

    (A) 4

    (B) 7

    (C) 8

    (D) 9

84. How many windows does the office building have?

    (A) 13

    (B) 18

    (C) 22

    (D) 25

85. You are fighting a fire in the office building, and visibility is near zero. You're standing by standpipe B and have to make your way toward the northern exit from the building. You place your right hand on the wall by standpipe B and proceed down hall 2, counting doors as you go. If you keep your right hand against the wall the whole time, how many doors should you count before you reach the northern exit?

    (A) 7

    (B) 8

    (C) 10

    (D) 11

86. A fire breaks out in the southwestern corner of the conference room. Which rooms are in the most immediate danger from the fire?

    (A) the cafeteria and the lobby

    (B) offices 12 and 17

    (C) the lavatory and office 11

    (D) the cafeteria and the lounge

87. Your fire department responds to a call for an activated fire alarm at the office building. You arrive on scene and you enter the building through the northern entrance, make a left, and proceed to the third door on your right. Where in the building are you?

    (A) the cafeteria

    (B) office 6

    (C) office 9

    (D) office 14

88. A fire in office 12 has spread into hall 3. What is the safest route to exit the building for the occupants of office 8?

    (A) Make a left into hall 3, a right into hall 2, a right into hall 1, pass through the conference room from hall 1 to hall 3, and go out the northern entrance.

    (B) Make a right into hall 3 and go out the northern entrance.

    (C) Make a left into hall 3, a right into hall 2, a right into hall 1, pass through the lobby, and go out the front entrance.

    (D) Make a right into hall 3, pass through the conference room from hall 3 to hall 1, make a right into the lobby, and go out the front entrance.

Go on to next page

89. Fire in hall 1 has blocked the door of office 16, trapping a firefighter. To escape, the firefighter will have to breach a wall with a sledgehammer. Which would be the best location for the firefighter to make the hole?

    (A) the middle of the wall between offices 16 and 17

    (B) the front corner of the wall where offices 15 and 16 meet

    (C) the middle of the wall between offices 13 and 16

    (D) the front corner of the wall where offices 16 and 17 meet

90. If a fire occurred near the vending machines, which of the following would be the safest exit for the occupants of all the offices in the building?

    (A) the front entrance

    (B) the cafeteria entrance

    (C) the window of office 5

    (D) the northern entrance

Go on to next page

Part 5: Reasoning and Judgment

Directions: This section tests your reasoning and judgment skills. Read each question and choose the answer that *most correctly* answers it. Mark the space on your answer sheet that corresponds to the question number and the letter indicating your choice.

Use the following information to answer questions 91–92.

The following are some common ladders used by fire personnel and their main purposes:

- **Wall (single) ladder:** A wall ladder, also called a *single ladder,* is a basic ladder that contains only one section. The length of a wall ladder cannot be adjusted. Its main purpose is to access windows or roofs of one- and two-story homes quickly.

- **Roof ladder:** A roof ladder is a single ladder with a set of folding hooks at the top. The ladder is designed to lie flat against the roof, and the hooks go over the peak of the roof and secure the ladder in place. Its main purpose is to help firefighters keep their footing while working on a roof.

- **Folding ladder:** A folding ladder is a type of single ladder, but its rungs have hinges that allow it to fold so that the two beams can rest against each other. Firefighters use folding ladders mainly when they have to travel through narrow corridors or tight spaces.

- **Extension ladder:** An extension ladder contains two or more sections, including a *bed section,* which sits on the ground, and one or more *fly sections,* which can be raised to extend the overall length of the ladder. Its purpose is to allow firefighters to reach windows and roofs beyond the reach of a wall ladder.

91. According to the information about ladders, if Firefighter Greene has been instructed to climb to the roof on a one-story home and cut a hole to vent out smoke and flames, which two ladders would he use?

(A) wall and folding

(B) extension and roof

(C) extension and folding

(D) wall and roof

92. While inspecting a home for fire, Firefighter Johnson must gain access to the attic through a small hole in the ceiling of a closet. To access the attic, Firefighter Johnson should use a(n)

(A) single ladder.

(B) folding ladder.

(C) roof ladder.

(D) extension ladder.

Go on to next page

Use the following information to answer questions 93–94.

You are the first responder at the scene of a motor vehicle accident. When you arrive, you see a red sedan, a blue pickup truck, and five victims. The red sedan appears to have swerved into the opposite lane and ended up in a head-on collision with the blue pickup. The following is a list of the victims:

1. **An elderly man:** He is in the driver seat of a red sedan. He is slumped over the steering wheel and is not moving.

2. **A 5-year-old girl:** She is buckled securely in a car seat in the backseat of the red sedan. She is sobbing uncontrollably but does not appear to have a mark on her.

3. **A middle-aged woman:** She is standing next to the blue pickup. She complains of pain in her right arm, which shows obvious deformity.

4. **A middle-aged man:** He is sitting in the driver's seat of the blue pickup. A cut on his forehead is oozing blood. He complains of pain in his right ankle.

5. **A 12-year-old boy:** He is sitting next to the man in the driver's seat of the blue pickup. He has a minor cut on his chin.

93. According to the information about the accident scene, which victim should you treat last?

(A) the 5-year-old girl

(B) the elderly man

(C) the middle-aged woman

(D) the middle-aged man

94. Determine the order in which you would help the victims of this motor vehicle accident.

(A) 1, 2, 3, 4, 5

(B) 1, 4, 3, 5, 2

(C) 2, 5, 3, 4, 1

(D) 4, 3, 5, 2, 1

Go on to next page

> *Use the following information to answer question 95.*

Firefighters must be able to don (put on) their bunker gear very quickly when an emergency arises. The following are tips for successfully donning bunker gear, in no particular order:

1. Ensure that your protective hood is around your neck, tuck the bottom of it under the collar of your coat, and zip your coat securely.

2. Pull your hood up, place your helmet on your head, and fasten the chin strap.

3. Remove the protective hood and gloves from your coat pocket and place them nearby for easy accessibility.

4. Check SCBA cylinder pressure, gauges, and alarms, and then put on SCBA unit over your bunker coat.

5. Once everything has been zipped, tightened, secured, and fastened, put on your gloves.

6. Put on bunker gear including trousers, boots, and coat, but leave the coat unzipped.

95. What is the logical order for putting on bunker gear?
    (A) 6, 5, 4, 3, 2, 1
    (B) 6, 3, 1, 4, 2, 5
    (C) 4, 3, 2, 1, 6, 5
    (D) 3, 2, 1, 4, 5, 6

> *Choose the word that correctly completes the following analogies.*

96. Glove is to hand as _____ is to foot.
    (A) ankle
    (B) leg
    (C) injury
    (D) boot

97. Chief is to fire station as principal is to _____.
    (A) student
    (B) teacher
    (C) school
    (D) friend

Go on to next page

Use the following information to answer question 98.

A Class A extinguisher can put out a fire involving ordinary combustibles. A Class B extinguisher can put out a fire involving flammable liquids. A Class C extinguisher can put out a fire involving energized electrical equipment. A Class D extinguisher can put out a fire involving combustible metals.

98. Based on this information, which of the following statements is true?
    (A) A Class ABC extinguisher can put any type of fire.
    (B) A Class B extinguisher can put out an electrical fire.
    (C) A Class ABC extinguisher can put out a wood fire.
    (D) A Class D extinguisher can put out a gas fire.

Choose the number that correctly completes each sequence.

99. 1, 2, 3, _____, 8, 13, 21, ...
    (A) 4
    (B) 5
    (C) 6
    (D) 7

100. 1, 3, 9, 27, _____, 243, 729, ...
    (A) 81
    (B) 108
    (C) 126
    (D) 189

Use the following information to answer question 101.

1. Sawdust requires more energy to ignite than sanding dust.
2. A log requires the most energy to ignite.
3. A piece of lumber requires more energy to ignite than sawdust.

101. Based on the information, which of the following is true?
    (A) A piece of lumber will catch fire faster than a log.
    (B) Sawdust will catch fire faster than sanding dust.
    (C) A piece of lumber will catch fire faster than sawdust.
    (D) A log will catch fire faster than sanding dust.

Go on to next page

> Use the following information to answer question 102.

A fire company is a group of fire personnel assigned to a particular type of apparatus. At minimum, a fire company consists of a company officer, a driver or an operator, and one or more firefighters. The following is a description of different types of fire companies:

- **Engine company:** An engine company has large hose lines that are used to attack fires.

- **Truck company:** A truck company is sometimes called a *ladder company.* This type of company provides access to the upper levels of a building. Firefighters working for this type of company also perform search and rescue, engage in forcible entry, and provide ventilation services.

- **Emergency medical company:** This type of company is called upon to care for persons injured in fires.

- **Hazardous materials company:** A hazardous materials company responds to fires and other incidents involving hazardous materials.

- **Rescue company:** This type of company rescues persons trapped in fires. Firefighters working for this type of company may also rescue animals trapped in fires.

- **Brush company:** A brush company is a fire company specializing in attacking wildfires. It aims to protect homes and buildings near brush fires.

102. Fire companies are dispatched to a fire. A tanker hauling gasoline has rolled over on the highway and caught fire. The driver of the tanker is badly burned and needs help. Which of the following companies will most likely respond to the fire?

(A) truck, rescue, and brush companies

(B) emergency medical, truck, and brush companies

(C) hazardous materials, engine, and emergency medical companies

(D) engine, truck, and emergency medical companies

> Choose the letter and/or number that correctly completes the sequence.

103. C5, F10, I15, _____, O25, ...

(A) K10

(B) M20

(C) L20

(D) P15

104. 21, 20, 18, 15, _____, 6, 0

(A) 11

(B) 12

(C) 8

(D) 3

Go on to next page

Choose the word that correctly completes the following analogies.

105. Bravery is to courage as intelligence is to
_____.

    (A) foolishness

    (B) daring

    (C) respect

    (D) aptitude

106. Electricity is to wire as water is to
_____.

    (A) wet

    (B) hose

    (C) extinguish

    (D) reservoir

Choose the image that correctly completes the sequence.

107.
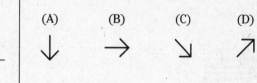

108.
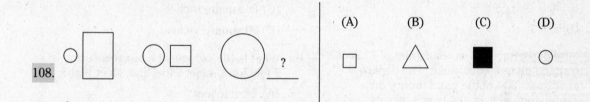

109.
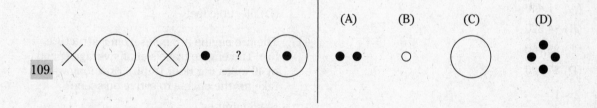

110.
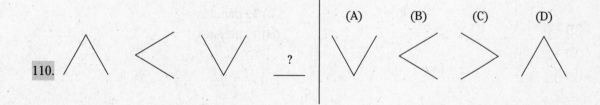

Go on to next page

Part 6: Performing Mathematical Calculations

Directions: This section tests your mathematical skills. Read each question and choose the answer that *most correctly* answers it. You may use scratch paper to figure out the answers, but you may NOT use a calculator. Mark the space on your answer sheet that corresponds to the question number and the letter indicating your choice.

111. Firefighter McDonald has one 50-foot hose, two 75-foot hoses, and three 100-foot hoses. What is the average length of Firefighter McDonald's hoses?

(A) 60 feet

(B) 83.3 feet

(C) 96.1 feet

(D) 100 feet

112. $\dfrac{15 + \sqrt{49} - 4}{3} =$

(A) 6

(B) 18

(C) 20

(D) 60

113. A fire department received a grant of $7,200 to spend on new equipment. The department spent 80% of the grant money on a combination of helmets, hoods, gloves, and boots. How much money did the department spend on this equipment?

(A) $1,440

(B) $4,320

(C) $5,760

(D) $7,120

114. $\dfrac{2}{3} \div \dfrac{1}{4} =$

(A) $\dfrac{1}{6}$

(B) $2\dfrac{2}{3}$

(C) 4

(D) 8

115. Find the area of the triangle shown below.

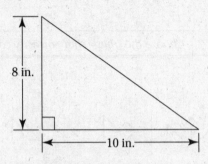

(A) 20 square inches

(B) 40 square inches

(C) 60 square inches

(D) 80 square inches

116. What is the volume of a box measuring 7 feet long, 4 feet wide, and 2 feet high?

(A) 7 cubic feet

(B) 14 cubic feet

(C) 28 cubic feet

(D) 56 cubic feet

117. The fire engine is 8 miles from a structure fire. The engine travels at an average speed of 40 miles per hour (mph). How long will it take for the engine to arrive on scene?

(A) 5 minutes

(B) 10 minutes

(C) 12 minutes

(D) 15 minutes

Go on to next page

118. A firefighter must use a salvage cover to protect the surface of a round table. If the table has a radius of 4 feet, approximately how big of an area does the salvage cover have to protect? (Round π to 3.14.)

    (A) 6.3 square feet

    (B) 19.7 square feet

    (C) 39.5 square feet

    (D) 50.2 square feet

119. What is $\frac{3}{8}$ written as a decimal?

    (A) 0.333

    (B) 0.350

    (C) 0.375

    (D) 0.380

120. Each story of an 8-story building is about 12 feet high. About how tall is the building?

    (A) 20 feet

    (B) 64 feet

    (C) 96 feet

    (D) 144 feet

121. Firefighter Paulson can run 1 mile in 8 minutes. How far can she run in 60 minutes at the same rate of speed?

    (A) 8 miles

    (B) 7.5 miles

    (C) 6 miles

    (D) 5.5 miles

122. Jorge needs to purchase 5 smoke detectors for his new home. He went shopping with $100 and returned home with $52.50. How much did each smoke detector cost?

    (A) $7.75

    (B) $8.25

    (C) $9.50

    (D) $10.15

123. Firefighter Jefferson weighs 165 pounds. When wearing all of his firefighting gear, he weighs 210 pounds. The self-contained breathing apparatus (SCBA) adds an additional 25 pounds. How much does Firefighter Jefferson weigh when wearing his firefighting gear and the SCBA?

    (A) 250 pounds

    (B) 245 pounds

    (C) 235 pounds

    (D) 220 pounds

124. There are 30 students in a firefighting class; 20 percent of the students are female. How many students are female?

    (A) 6

    (B) 10

    (C) 14

    (D) 20

125. $\frac{3}{5} - \frac{1}{6} =$

    (A) $\frac{1}{15}$

    (B) $\frac{13}{30}$

    (C) 14

    (D) 9

126. Firefighter Samuels needs to close off the perimeter of a rectangular building that has an area of 1,120 square feet. The front of the building measures 32 feet. How much caution tape will he need?

    (A) 112 feet

    (B) 142 feet

    (C) 134 feet

    (D) 167 feet

127. A wildland fire burns at a rate of $\frac{3}{4}$ of an acre per day. How many acres will burn in two weeks? (Change any improper fractions to mixed numbers.)

    (A) $10\frac{1}{2}$

    (B) 15

    (C) $12\frac{1}{4}$

    (D) 21

Go on to next page

128. A volunteer fire department collects donations at 5 locations around town. At the end of the day, the total amounts collected are $150, $225, $340, $310, and $295. What was the average amount collected?

    (A) $205

    (B) $240

    (C) $258

    (D) $264

129. Convert $\frac{27}{5}$ to a mixed number.

    (A) $4\frac{2}{3}$

    (B) $5\frac{2}{5}$

    (C) $6\frac{1}{3}$

    (D) $5\frac{1}{2}$

130. How many cubic feet of water will a cylindrical tank with a radius of 2 feet and a height of 7 feet hold? (Round π to 3.14.)

    (A) 98.23 cubic feet

    (B) 97.14 cubic feet

    (C) 87.92 cubic feet

    (D) 86.29 cubic feet

Go on to next page

Part 7: Mechanical Aptitude

Directions: This section tests your mechanical aptitude. Read each question and choose the answer that *most correctly* answers it. Mark the space on your answer sheet that corresponds to the question number and the letter indicating your choice.

131. Which tool would most likely be used to breach a wall during a fire?

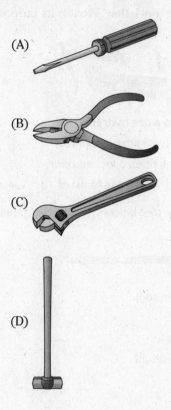

(A)

(B)

(C)

(D)

132. Which saw would a firefighter most likely use to cut up a large tree that has fallen across a roadway?

(A)

(B)

(C)

(D)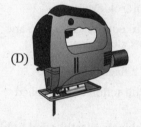

133. Which of the following tools would a firefighter use to pry open a door?

(A) a crowbar

(B) an axe

(C) a wrench

(D) a shovel

Go on to next page

Use the following image to answer questions 134–135.

134. If gear 3 turns clockwise, which other gear(s) also move(s) clockwise?

    (A) gear 1

    (B) gear 2

    (C) gears 1 and 4

    (D) gears 2 and 4

135. If gear 2 moves clockwise, which direction do gears 1 and 3 move?

    (A) Gears 1 and 3 move clockwise.

    (B) Gears 1 and 3 move counterclockwise.

    (C) Gear 1 moves clockwise and gear 3 moves counterclockwise.

    (D) Gear 1 moves counterclockwise and gear 3 moves clockwise.

136. The purpose of a fixed pulley is to

    (A) change the direction of an applied force.

    (B) fasten two objects together and hold them in place.

    (C) gain a mechanical advantage when lifting heavy objects.

    (D) spread work over a longer distance so it requires less force.

137. A firefighter has a lever with a fulcrum (or pivot point) 3 feet from the 75-pound box he wants to lift. The firefighter is standing at the other end of the lever, 6 feet from the fulcrum. How much force must the firefighter apply to the lever to lift the box?

    (A) 25 pounds

    (B) 37.5 pounds

    (C) 50 pounds

    (D) 61.5 pounds

138. If an extension spring stretches $\frac{1}{2}$ inch under a pull of 7 pounds, how many inches will the spring stretch under a pull of 49 pounds?

    (A) 3.5 inches

    (B) 7 inches

    (C) 10.5 inches

    (D) 14 inches

139. Look at the tool below. What is its purpose?

    (A) to open a fire hydrant

    (B) to tighten a screw in place

    (C) to break open a locked door

    (D) to hold something in place

140. Look at the tool below. What is the name of this tool?

    (A) Halligan tool

    (B) awl

    (C) pike pole

    (D) pick-head ax

Go on to next page

141. Which tool would most likely be used to pierce a hole through a roof to give a firefighter a good starting point for cutting?

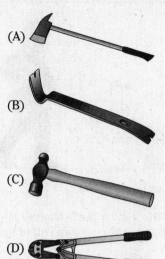

144. The lines below represent the angle of a ladder placed against the side of a building. Which line represents the ladder at the safest angle for climbing?

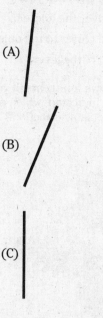

142. What do an axe, a reciprocating saw, and a set of bolt cutters have in common?

(A) They are all prying tools.

(B) They are all cutting tools.

(C) They are all pushing/pulling tools.

(D) They are all striking tools.

143. Which of the following tools would a firefighter most likely use to tighten a hose coupling?

(A) a chisel

(B) a maul

(C) a battering ram

(D) a spanner wrench

145. The extension spring in the image below stretches 1.5 inches under a pull of 10 pounds. If a second block weighing 5 pounds is added to this spring, how far will the extension spring stretch?

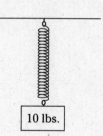

10 lbs.

(A) 2 inches

(B) 2.25 inches

(C) 2.50 inches

(D) 2.75 inches

Go on to next page

146. When using a lever to lift an object that is heavier than the force you want to apply, you should

    (A) move the fulcrum closer to you.

    (B) center the lever over the fulcrum.

    (C) move the fulcrum closer to the object.

    (D) extend the length of the lever.

147. The image below shows four gears. If gear 2 turns in the direction indicated, which other gear(s) will turn in the same direction?

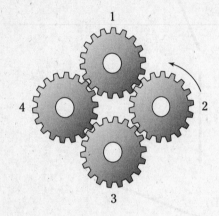

    (A) gears 1 and 3

    (B) gears 3 and 4

    (C) gears 1 and 4

    (D) gear 4 only

Use the following image to answer questions 148–149.

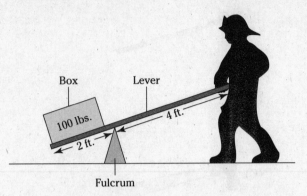

148. How much force must the firefighter apply to lift the load at the opposite end of the lever?

    (A) 35 pounds

    (B) 40 pounds

    (C) 50 pounds

    (D) 75 pounds

149. If the firefighter moves the fulcrum 1 foot closer to the box, how much force would he have to apply to lift the load at the opposite end of the lever?

    (A) 20 pounds

    (B) 25 pounds

    (C) 35 pounds

    (D) 40 pounds

150. Look at the tool below. What is the name of this tool?

    (A) coping saw

    (B) keyhole saw

    (C) chain saw

    (D) hacksaw

Chapter 16

Practice Exam 1: Answers and Explanations

• •

*I*f you've finished your first practice exam (see Chapter 15), you're probably curious to see how you did. Use the answers and explanations in this chapter to see how well you performed and to get info on answering any problems you missed. Remember, the practice exam can help you determine where you need to focus your studies for the real written fire-fighter exam. If you want to score your test quickly, flip to the end of the chapter, where the "Answer Key" gives only the letters of the correct answers.

Part 1: Reading Comprehension

1. **C.** The purpose of a portable water tank is to serve as a temporary water source at a fire scene. You can find the answer in the first paragraph, which describes portable water tanks as "collapsible temporary pools" that "hold a generous supply of water."

2. **B.** You can find the answer to this question in the first line of the passage, which states that "rural fire departments lack the luxury of a hydrant on every street corner."

3. **D.** The passage suggests, and the hose's name implies, that hard-suction hose is used only for suction. Choices (A), (B), and (C) all involve suction — drawing water, drafting water, and sucking water. Therefore, Choice (D) is the correct answer. Hard-suction hose would not likely be used to spray water on a fire.

4. **A.** The best title for the passage is "Rural Firefighting Procedures." The passage begins by explaining that rural fire departments rarely are able to hook to hydrants and that they transport their water to fires in a different way. It then explains how such departments create a large, continuous supply of water through the use of portable water tanks.

5. **B.** This passage requires you to make both a comparison and an inference. By combining your prior knowledge with information in the passage, you can infer that drafting water from a portable tank is like drinking lemonade through a straw. Both actions require suctioning liquid from one place to another. Therefore, Choice (B) is correct.

6. **C.** The first paragraph states that ignition will occur "when heat, fuel, and oxygen combine to start the chemical chain reaction that creates and sustains fire." After a fire starts, it produces fire gases. Therefore, Choice (C) is correct.

7. **D.** The third paragraph states that flashover occurs suddenly "when all of the combustible materials burst into flame at the same time." Choice (D) is correct.

8. **A.** The main idea of a passage is what the *entire* passage is about. This passage describes the stages of a compartment fire. The sentence "Compartment fires go through five main developmental stages" seems to represent the main idea very well. The other sentences from the passage are supporting details. Choice (A) is correct.

9. **C.** The five main stages of a compartment fire, in order, are ignition, growth, flashover, fully developed, and decay. If you review the passage, you'll see that the author presents these stages in this order, showing how each stage leads to the next. In addition, Choice (C) is the only answer option that has ignition first, so if you can remember that one fact, you'll get this question right.

10. **A.** The second paragraph explains that hot gases produced by the fire plume rise vertically to the ceiling and then spread horizontally toward the walls during the growth stage.

11. **B.** According to the first paragraph, heat, fuel, oxygen, and a chemical chain reaction make up the four parts of the fire tetrahedron. If one of these is missing, the fire cannot start or continue to burn; if one is removed, the fire stops burning. According to the last paragraph, the fire enters the decay stage when it runs out of fuel. Both Choice (C) and Choice (D) are technically correct. However, only Choice (B) is supported by the information in the passage.

12. **C.** According to the passage, flashover is the point at which all flammable materials in the compartment get hot enough to burst into flame at the same time. You can conclude that a firefighter in the compartment at this time would likely be in a lot of danger.

13. **B.** According to the table, arms account for 18 percent of a child's total body surface area (TBSA) and the chest and abdomen account for another 18 percent. By adding these two amounts together, you can determine that the child burned approximately 36 percent of the surface of his skin.

14. **C.** Legs make up 26 percent of a child's TBSA. By burning the backs of both legs (that is, only half of 26 percent), the child burns 13 percent of the surface of his skin. Both a man's left arm and a woman's head would account for only 9 percent each. The front of a baby's leg would account for only 8 percent. Choice (C) is correct.

15. **A.** Look at the first two rows of the chart and note where the numbers differ. The arms, the back/buttocks, and the chest/abdomen make up 18 percent each of the total body surface area of both adults and children. A child's head, however, accounts for 17 percent of the total body surface area; an adult's head accounts for 9 percent of the total body surface.

16. **C.** This passage includes information about how laminated glass can be removed. Firefighters may have to chop or saw out laminated glass to rescue people or enter structures.

17. **A.** Firefighters would not likely use winches to break auto glass. Winches are used for pulling or lifting. The author explains that many other tools, including saws, axes, air chisels, and spring-loaded punches, may be necessary for breaking glass.

18. **D.** The laminate material in safety glass is made of plastic sheets. If the glass breaks, the glass shatters but is mostly held in place by the plastic laminate.

19. **B.** Firefighters may have to break or cut windows, which may cause dangerous fragments of glass to be dislodged. The author explains that tarps or blankets should be used to keep victims safe from these glass fragments.

20. **C.** The main idea of this passage is that firefighters may have to deal with different kinds of glass (safety glass and tempered glass) at accident scenes.

21. **B.** An example of removing oxygen from a fire would be a man's using a heavy blanket to smother a fire on his jacket sleeve. A heavy blanket would keep oxygen from reaching the fire. Choice (B) is correct.

22. **A.** The fire triangle takes into account oxygen, heat, and fuel — all necessary factors in combustion. However, the fire tetrahedron also incorporates the chemical chain reaction that causes those factors to produce fire. Choice (A) is correct.

23. **C.** The word *combustion* most likely refers to burning. In this passage, the *combustion process* refers to the fire tetrahedron, the factors that come together to cause fire.

24. **D.** If you need to extinguish a fire by chemically stopping the chain reaction, you may try applying a halon agent to the fire. As the passage explains, halon is a kind of chemical that can break the chain reaction aspect of the fire tetrahedron. Choice (D) is correct.

25. **B.** According to the passage, a fire stream is the flow of water from a hose nozzle. The fire stream may take several different forms. Choice (B) is correct.

26. **C.** A firefighter who needs to send water across a far distance would most likely use a solid stream. This passage identifies the solid stream as a narrow, rounded, compact stream that is best used to cover large distances.

27. **B.** Many factors may influence stream patterns, but light isn't among them. Wind, gravity, and heat, however, may affect the flow of water from a hose. Choice (B) is correct.

28. **D.** A broken stream would be most useful in a small basement apartment. The passage explains that broken streams are effective in confined spaces. Streets, large lobbies, and forests are not confined, but a small underground apartment is. Choice (D) is correct.

29. **D.** This passage explains types of water streams. It gives many details, but all these details are based on the main idea of the streams of water used to fight fires. Choice (D) is correct.

30. **A.** According to the passage, a fog tip is used for adjusting fog stream angles. There are different fog stream angles, including straight, narrow angle, and wide angle. These can be created using different settings of fog tips. Choice (A) is correct.

Part 2: Verbal Expression

31. **C.** The correct spelling is *oxygen*.

32. **A.** The correct spelling is *forcible*.

33. **D.** The correct spelling is *electrical*.

34. **D.** The correct spelling is *activated*.

35. **B.** The correct spelling is *gaseous*.

36. **B.** The phrase "starting next week" is a clue that you're looking for a verb in the future tense, because the sentence is referring to something that hasn't happened yet.

37. **B.** This sentence needs a possessive adjective. The words *there, their,* and *they're* all sound the same, but only *their* is a possessive adjective, so Choice (B) is correct. *There* is an adverb used to point out location, *they're* is the contraction of *they are,* and *they* is a subject pronoun.

38. **C.** The verb form that correctly completes the sentence is *was involved.* The other choices do not fit within the context of the sentence. The subject is *tanker truck,* so the verb has to be singular; "bearing two hazardous materials placards" is a phrase that comes between the subject and the verb, so you can ignore it.

39. **B.** The noun *department* is singular, so the possessive adjective that refers back to it must also be singular. *Its* is a singular possessive adjective, so Choice (B) is correct.

40. **A.** The sentence has a missing *preposition,* which is a word that shows the relationship between its object (a noun that follows the preposition) and another word in the sentence. In this case, *the bulletin board* is the object, and the preposition that correctly completes the sentence is *to.*

41. **B.** *Jeopardize* means to *endanger.* Firefighters may be endangered if their department were to lower its safety standards. Choice (B) is correct.

42. **D.** *Scrutinize* means to *examine.* An investigator called to the site of a fire may examine the scene for evidence that arson took place there. Choice (D) is correct.

43. **A.** *Interrogate* means to *question.* A neighbor who attempts to interrogate a firefighter about a local house fire is trying to question that firefighter. Choice (A) is correct.

44. **D.** *Proficient* means *skilled.* Firefighters are called upon to be skilled in many tasks, and rookies must undergo a long process of training to reach that level of ability.

45. **B.** "Using fire trucks in parades may help a community notice and appreciate the presence of the local fire department." In the original sentence, the word *to* is unnecessary and out of place.

46. **C.** "The most successful firefighters should have a basic knowledge of emergency medical care to help victims." The original sentence is broken by a comma and the pronoun *they*, both of which are incorrect.

47. **D.** "Fire prevention inspections and fire safety talks are important ways for firefighters to help prevent future emergencies." In the original sentence, the phrase "and fire safety talks" is unnecessarily separated by commas.

48. **A.** *Criteria* best completes this sentence. Fire departments use *criteria,* or factors for judgment, when reviewing new candidates.

49. **C.** *Instrumental* best completes this sentence. *Instrumental* means very important. The citizens' donations were instrumental in keeping the fire company active.

50. **B.** *Complemented* is the best word choice. The Springfield Fire Department already had a new engine. When it got a new rescue vehicle as well, it *complemented* — or added to in an appropriate way — the engine.

Part 3: Observation and Memory

51. **C.** The preferred order is *reach, throw, row,* and *go.* The fifth paragraph states, "These methods (in order of preference) are as follows: *reach, throw, row,* and *go.*"

52. **A.** According to the third paragraph, firefighters perform recoveries when they "retrieve the remains of a person who has died as the result of a water emergency." Choice (A) is correct. The other choices involve live victims, which makes them water rescues.

53. **D.** Swimming to the aid of a victim is known as the go method. Firefighters use this method as the last alternative when other rescue methods won't work.

54. **B.** The last line of the fourth paragraph states, "Hypothermia is a significant drop in body temperature." Choice (B) is correct.

55. **C.** The fourth paragraph explains that standard PPE (*personal protective equipment,* also known as *bunker* or *turnout gear*) is much too bulky to wear in the water. The other answer choices all suggest appropriate water rescue attire. Choice (C) is correct.

56. **B.** The fourth paragraph states that "your department may require that you wear a thermal protective suit, called a dry suit, which protects your entire body except for your head and sometimes your feet when working in the water." The suit can prevent hypothermia in rescue workers, but it's not intended to warm victims who have hypothermia.

57. **B.** The throw method involves tossing a flotation device with an attached rope to a victim in need of rescue. The words *throw* and *toss* are big clues here. Choice (B) is correct.

58. **A.** PFD stands for *personal flotation device.* Therefore, the purpose of a PFD is to keep a person afloat in the water. Choice (A) is correct.

59. **D.** Firefighters try to use the rescue methods in the following order: reach, throw, row, and go. If firefighters cannot reach the victim with a tool, their next step will likely be to try to throw a life preserver to the victim. Choice (D) is correct.

60. **C.** The last sentence of the passage states, "Firefighters resort to the go method only when another method won't work, because it has the potential to result in two drowning victims: the original victim and the rescuer." Although all the answer choices have the potential to be correct, Choice (C) is the most correct answer based on the information from the passage.

61. **D.** Davis Street Apartments and Belle Maria Dance Studio both appear to be made of brick. The other buildings are made of other materials. Choice (D) is correct.

62. **D.** The greatest number of bystanders is near Midtown Movies. Three people are standing by the doorway of the movie theater. Choice (D) is correct.

63. **D.** The fire appears to be concentrated in the southeast corner of the Belle Maria Dance Studio. The smoke and flames appear from the windows in the near right corner. No smoke or flames are visible from other windows or areas of the building. Choice (D) is correct.

64. **A.** Belle Maria Dance Studio has three front windows. Another three windows appear on the side of the studio, but this question asks only about the front windows. Be careful to avoid counting the front door of the studio as a window. Choice (A) is correct.

65. **A.** The parked vehicle is facing the viewer on the east side of the block.

66. **B.** Belle Maria Dance Studio has a single front door at the center of the building.

67. **B.** Flames are visible in three windows of the Belle Maria Dance Studio. Smoke is coming from five windows, but the question asks only about flame. Choice (B) is correct.

68. **A.** Davis Street Apartments has the most visible windows. It has 11 visible windows in the front of the building. Choice (A) is correct.

69. **C.** Two people — a man in a suit and a woman in a dress — are standing by the vehicle.

70. **A.** Davis Street Apartments is the tallest building in the picture. It stands significantly higher than the other buildings on the block. Choice (A) is correct.

Part 4: Spatial Orientation

71. **B.** If you trace these directions, you see that the final right into the church parking lot points the driver south. In fact, because Bailey Ave. is a one-way street going east, turning right will always face him south, regardless of how he got to Bailey. Paying special attention to the end of a set of directions can you save you time when tracing the route.

72. **D.** Choices (A) and (C) are incorrect because they would require you to travel east on Kira Ave., which is a one-way street going west. Choice (B) would take you to the pharmacy, but the route requires many unnecessary turns. Choice (D) is the most direct route to the pharmacy.

73. **C.** The building bordered by Kira Ave. to the south, Mazie Way to the west, Brian Rd. to the north, and Baron Blvd. to the east is the library.

74. **B.** If you trace this route, you see that it takes you past the southern side of the post office and keeps you moving toward Prince St., where the fire station is located.

75. **A.** Using the compass rose for guidance, you see that the pond is northwest of the church, southwest of the hospital, southeast of the townhouses, west of the mall, and north of the library. Choice (A) is correct.

76. **C.** The firefighter must pass through three doors to reach the dryer. From the hall, she enters the apartment through one door. Then she enters the bedroom through a second door. She enters the closet/laundry area through a third door.

77. **D.** Apartment A has five windows. If you count the number of window symbols in the floor plan, you find five windows, three in the dining/living area and two in the bedroom.

78. **C.** Trace the route. Standing between the kitchen opening and the closet door, the firefighter walks to the next door and turns left into the bedroom. He then makes the first left, which puts him in the bathroom. Choice (C) is correct.

79. **C.** Apartment A has five doors. The legend shows what the symbol for a door looks like. You find one at the hall entrance, one at the closet right inside the hall entrance, one at the bedroom, one at the bathroom, and one at the closet/laundry area.

80. **A.** From left to right, the front of the house in the picture shows a window, a front door, another window, and then a picture window. You can also see that the left side of the house has two additional windows. Only the floor plan in Choice (A) matches all the features shown in the picture of the house.

81. **A.** The most direct route to exit the building from office 4 is to go left down hall 1, pass through the lobby, and exit through the front entrance. Choice (A) is correct.

82. **D.** In the floor plan, standpipe A is outside the southern entrance of the conference room. Standpipe D is very close to the northern entrance of the conference room.

83. **C.** From the lobby, the firefighter would pass the following doors on his or her way down hall 1 to standpipe B: the conference room, offices 1 and 17, offices 2 and 16, offices 3 and 15, and office 4. The firefighter would pass eight doors. Choice (C) is correct.

84. **B.** The office has 18 windows, each represented by the symbol in the legend. The building has 11 exterior offices, each with 1 window. The lavatory and the lounge also have 1 window each. The cafeteria has 5 windows.

85. **B.** From standpipe B, your right hand would come in contact with the following 8 doors (in order): office 5, the storage room, and offices 6, 7, 8, 9, 10, and 11. Choice (B) is correct.

86. **A.** Use the compass rose to locate the southwestern corner of the conference room. You see that this corner touches both the cafeteria and the lobby, which means that these two rooms are in immediate danger from the fire. Choice (A) is correct.

87. **D.** If you enter the northern entrance, the entrance opposite the front of the building, and turn left, you'll be in hall 3. As you walk down hall 3, the third door on your right will be office 14.

88. **C.** Choices (B) and (D) would take you through the fire, so neither of those options is correct. Choice (A) would take you around the fire, but it also would require you to pass by it again.

89. **C.** Because the fire is in hall 1, fire could also be blocking the doors to offices 15 and 17. Breaking into office 17, Choice (A), may leave the firefighter trapped. Breaking through either front corner, Choices (B) and (D), could lead the firefighter directly into the fire. Breaching the wall between offices 13 and 16 would allow the firefighter to move away from the fire.

90. **D.** Going out the front entrance would require everyone to pass the fire. The cafeteria entrance is farther away than the northern entrance. Getting everyone out the window of office 5 would take a lot of time. Therefore, everyone should exit through the northern entrance.

Part 5: Reasoning and Judgment

91. **D.** To answer this question, you must apply what you read about ladders to a specific situation. The passage states that firefighters use wall ladders to access windows or roofs of one- or two-story homes. They use roof ladders to keep their footing when working on roofs. Therefore, Firefighter Greene should use a wall ladder to reach the roof of the one-story home and a roof ladder to maintain his footing while he cuts the hole.

92. **B.** In the scenario presented in the question, Firefighter Johnson must access an attic through a hole in the ceiling of a closet, which is a tight space. Therefore, a folding ladder would be the best choice. Choice (B) is correct.

93. **A.** The 5-year-old girl in the car seat does not appear to have any injuries, and you know that she can breathe because she is crying uncontrollably. Until additional help can arrive, she is safe and secure in the car seat. Choice (A) is correct.

94. **B.** The correct order in which to help the victims would be 1, 4, 3, 5, 2. The elderly man appears to be unconscious, which means he may not be breathing, so he should be the first priority. The middle-aged man has a head wound, so he should be your next priority. The middle-aged woman likely has a broken arm, so she could come third. The 12-year-old boy has a minor cut, so you should help him fourth. Finally, you can try to comfort the 5-year-old girl.

95. **B.** Even if you've never donned bunker gear, you can use logic to determine the correct order in which to put on gear. The wording of step 5, "Once everything has been zipped, tightened, secured, and fastened, put on our gloves," suggests that this is the last step. Therefore, you can eliminate Choices (A) and (D). The first step in Choice (C) involves putting your SCBA on "over your bunker coat." To complete this step, however, you'd have to have already donned your bunker coat. Therefore, you can eliminate Choice (C).

96. **D.** Using logic, determine how these two sets of words are related. A glove goes over your hand to protect it. A boot goes over a foot to protect it.

97. **C.** Using logic, determine how these two sets of words are related. A chief is in charge of a fire station. A principal is in charge of a school.

98. **C.** Logic suggests that an ABC extinguisher can put out fires involving ordinary combustibles, flammable liquids, and energized electrical equipment. Wood is an ordinary combustible, so a Class ABC extinguisher will put out a wood fire. Choice (C) is correct.

99. **B.** To answer this question, use logic to determine the pattern. In this sequence, each number is the sum of the two numbers before it. For example, 1 + 2 is 3, 2 + 3 is 5 (the missing number), 3 + 5 is 8, 5 + 8 is 13, 8 + 13 is 21, and so on. Choice (B) is correct.

100. **A.** Use logic to determine the pattern. In this sequence, each number in the series has been multiplied by 3. The space between 27 and 243 should be 81, because $27 \times 3 = 81$ and $81 \times 3 = 243$.

101. **A.** According to the information, you can determine that sanding dust will ignite the fastest, followed by sawdust, a piece of lumber, and finally a log. Because a log requires the most energy, it's going to take longer to ignite than any other choice. Therefore, the true statement is "A piece of lumber will catch fire faster than a log."

102. **C.** A tanker truck hauling gasoline has rolled over and caught fire, which requires a hazardous materials company to clean up the spilled gasoline and an engine company to attack the fire. The driver has been badly burned and needs help, which requires an emergency medical company.

103. **C.** Determine the pattern. In this sequence, the first letter is the third letter of the alphabet, the second is the sixth letter, the third is the ninth letter, and the last is the fifteenth letter. This means that the twelfth letter, L, should appear in the blank, because each letter represents a count of three. Each number in the sequence is an increment of five. Because the number before the blank is 15 and the number after the blank is 25, you can logically guess that the number 20 should appear in the blank. Choice (C) is correct.

104. **A.** In this sequence, 1 is subtracted from the first number to get the second number, 2 is subtracted from the second number to get the third number, 3 is subtracted from the third number to get the fourth number, and so on. So if $21 - 1 = 20$, $20 - 2 = 18$, and $18 - 3 = 15$, then $15 - 4 = 11$, $11 - 5 = 6$, and $6 - 6 = 0$. Choice (A) is correct.

105. **D.** Determine how these two sets of words are related. *Bravery* and *courage* are synonyms; they share the same meaning. *Intelligence* and *aptitude* also share the same meaning.

106. **B.** Using logic, you can determine how these two sets of words are related. Electricity travels through a wire, just as water travels through a hose.

107. **C.** Each picture shows three arrows. The arrow in the middle is always pointing upward. The arrow on the far left always points to the left, and the arrow on the right always points to the right. In the first picture, the arrows are pointing upward at a diagonal. In the second picture, they are pointing straight out to the side. In the third picture, the arrow to the far left is pointing downward at a diagonal. The blank should contain an arrow pointing to the right at a downward diagonal.

108. **A.** Determine the pattern. The first image is a small circle, which is followed by a large square. The next two images represent a medium-sized circle and square. The fifth image is a large circle. To complete the pattern, which is created by alternating circles and squares in ascending and descending size order, you put a small white square in the blank.

109. **C.** The first image in the picture is an *X*, the second image is a circle, and the third image is an *X* inside of a circle. The fourth image is a dot, and the last image is a dot inside of a circle. The fifth image in the pattern should be an empty circle so that the sixth image represents the fourth image inside the fifth image. Choice (C) is correct.

110. **C.** The first image is an upside-down *V*, with the point at the top. In the second image, the point is on the left, as if the *V* has been turned 90° counterclockwise. The next image shows the *V* with its pointy end down, as if it's been turned counterclockwise again. If you rotate the image counterclockwise once more, its point will be on the right.

Part 6: Performing Mathematical Calculations

111. **B.** To find the average length, first find the sum of the lengths of all the hoses: 50 + 2(75) + 3(100) = 500 feet. Then divide by 6, the number of hoses: 500 divided by 6 equals about 83.3 feet.

112. **A.** The order of operations tells you to do what's in parentheses first, and the fraction bar acts as a grouping symbol, just like parentheses. Therefore, solve the top part of the fraction first. Start with the square root: The square root of 49 is 7, so the top part becomes 15 + 7 − 4 = 18. When you divide the top part, 18, by the bottom part, 3, the result is 6.

113. **C.** Taking 80% of $7,200 is the same as multiplying $7,200 by 0.80. Therefore, 80% of $7,200 is $5,760. Choice (C) is correct.

114. **B.** Dividing by a fraction is the same as multiplying by a fraction's reciprocal. In other words, ⅔ divided by ¼ is the same as ⅔ times 4, which equals 8/3. This is an improper fraction that, when converted to a mixed number, equals 2⅔.

115. **B.** The formula for the area of a triangle is $A = \frac{1}{2}bh$, where *b* is the base and *h* is the height. Therefore, $A = \frac{1}{2}(10)(8)$. The result is 40. The area of the triangle is 40 square inches.

116. **D.** The formula for volume is length times width times height, or $V = lwh$. In this case, $V = (7)(4)(2)$. Therefore, $V = 56$. The volume of the box is 56 cubic feet. Choice (D) is correct.

117. **C.** Use the formula $d = rt$, where *d* is the distance, *r* is the rate, and *t* is the time:

$$d = rt$$
$$8 = 40t$$
$$\frac{8}{40} = \frac{40t}{40}$$
$$\frac{1}{5} = t$$

The engine will take ⅕ of an hour, or 12 minutes (that is, 60 minutes ÷ 5), to reach the scene. Choice (C) is correct.

118. **D.** Use the formula for the area of circle:

$$A = \pi r^2$$
$$A = \pi(4)^2$$
$$A = 16\pi$$
$$A \approx 16(3.14)$$
$$A \approx 50.24$$

The firefighter needs a salvage cover big enough to protect an area that is about 50.2 square feet.

119. **C.** To convert a fraction to a decimal, divide the numerator (the top number) by the denominator (the bottom number). In this case, divide 3 by 8. The result is 0.375.

120. **C.** To find the height of the building, multiply the number of stories, 8, by the number of feet per story, 12: $8 \times 12 = 96$. The building is about 96 feet high.

121. **B.** Let x represent the number of miles run in 60 minutes. Set up a proportion and solve for x:

$$\frac{1 \text{ mile}}{8 \text{ min.}} = \frac{x \text{ miles}}{60 \text{ min.}}$$
$$8x = 60$$
$$x = \frac{60}{8}$$
$$x = 7.5$$

Firefighter Paulson can run 7.5 miles in 60 minutes. Choice (B) is correct.

122. **C.** First, find the cost of all five smoke detectors: Subtract the amount that Jorge returned home with from the amount he had when he went shopping: $100 – $52.50 = $47.50. Now divide this amount by the number of smoke detectors purchased: $47.50 ÷ 5 = $9.50.

123. **C.** Add the additional 25 pounds to Firefighter Jefferson's weight when he is wearing his firefighting equipment: 210 + 25 = 235 pounds. His weight without the firefighting gear, 165 pounds, isn't necessary information to solve this problem. Choice (C) is correct.

124. **A.** To solve this problem, multiply 30 by 0.20. There are 6 female students in the class.

125. **B.** To solve this problem, you must find the least common denominator, a number that divides evenly by both 5 and 6. The least common denominator for 5 and 6 is 30, so multiply each fraction by the number that will allow you to obtain that denominator. Multiply the numerator and denominator of ⅗ by 6, and multiply the numerator and denominator of ⅙ by 5. Then subtract:

$$\frac{3}{5} - \frac{1}{6} = \frac{18}{30} - \frac{5}{30} = \frac{13}{30}$$

126. **C.** The formula for area is the length multiplied by width. The area is 1,120 square feet, and the front of the building (the length) measures 32 feet. Divide 1,120 by 32 to find the width: 1,120 ÷ 32 = 35. From this, you can tell that the four sides measure 32, 35, 32, and 35 feet. Add these numbers together to find the perimeter: 32 + 35 + 32 + 35 = 134 feet. Choice (C) is correct.

127. **A.** Multiply ¾ by 14. Reduce where possible; 14 and 4 are both divisible by 2, so you can cancel out a 2 (divide both those numbers by 2) before multiplying:

$$\frac{3}{_2\cancel{4}} \times \frac{\cancel{14}^7}{1} = \frac{21}{2}$$

$$2)\overline{21} \quad \frac{10}{}$$
$$\underline{-2}$$
$$1$$

$$10\frac{1}{2}$$

128. **D.** To find the average, first add all the amounts collected at the five locations: $150 + $225 + $340 + $310 + $295 = $1,320. Then divide by the number of locations: $1,320 ÷ 5 = $264. The average amount collected is $264. Choice (D) is correct.

129. **B.** To convert to a mixed number, divide the numerator by the denominator:

$$5)\overline{27} \quad \frac{5}{}$$
$$\underline{-25}$$
$$2$$

Then place the remainder over the denominator: 5⅖. Choice (B) is correct.

130. **C.** Use formula for the volume of a cylinder:

$$V = \pi r^2 h$$
$$V = \pi (2)^2 7$$
$$V = \pi (4) 7$$
$$V = 28\pi$$
$$V \approx 28(3.14)$$
$$V \approx 87.92$$

Part 7: Mechanical Aptitude

131. **D.** Firefighters usually breach a wall, or bust through it, when they're searching for fire inside a wall. To do this, they need a heavy object that they can swing with a lot of force to punch through a wall. A sledgehammer is the ideal tool for this. Choice (D) is correct.

132. **C.** Jigsaws and circular saws are usually used to make precise cuts in wood, metal, or other materials, so neither of these is a good choice for cutting up a large tree. A firefighter may use a handsaw to cut a small tree, but cutting through a large tree would be nearly impossible with a handsaw. Therefore, a chain saw, Choice (C), is the best answer.

133. **A.** To pry open a door, a firefighter would need a prying tool. A crowbar is a prying tool, so Choice (A) is correct. An axe is a cutting tool, while wrenches are used to tighten pipes or nuts and bolts. A shovel is used for digging.

134. **A.** When two gears mesh together, one always turns in the opposite direction of the other. If gear 3 turns clockwise, then gears 2 and 4 would have to turn counterclockwise and gear 1 would have to turn clockwise. Therefore, Choice (A) is correct.

135. **B.** Because gear 2 meshes with both gears 1 and 3, those gears turn in the opposite direction of gear 2. Gear 2 moves clockwise, which means gears 1 and 3 move counterclockwise.

136. **A.** A fixed pulley changes the direction of the pulling force. A pulley allows you to pull down to make an object go up. Choice (A) is correct.

137. **B.** To figure out the force required to lift the box, you can use the simple formula $w \times d_1 = f \times d_2$. Solve for force (f) by multiplying the weight of the box $(w = 75)$ by the distance in feet from the box to the pivot point $(d_1 = 3)$ and dividing by the distance from the pivot point to the firefighter $(d_2 = 6)$. The force required to lift the box is 37.5 pounds.

138. **A.** The spring stretches ½ inch under a pull of 7 pounds. A pull of 49 pounds is 7 times greater than a pull of 7 pounds, so multiply 7 by ½; that's the same as dividing 7 by 2, which equals 3.5. Therefore, the spring would stretch 3.5 inches under a pull of 49 pounds.

139. **D.** The image shows a C-clamp, which is a device used to clamp, or hold, things in place.

140. **C.** The picture shows a *pike pole,* which is a pole with a point and a hook at one end. It's used for pushing and pulling. For instance, a firefighter may use a pike pole to push through and pull down a ceiling to check for fire. Choice (C) is correct.

141. **A.** A head of a pick-head axe has a pointed side for piercing and a sharp edge for cutting. Therefore, a pick-head axe would be a good choice for piercing a hole in the roof to create a good starting point for cutting. Choice (A) is correct.

142. **B.** Though an axe, a reciprocating saw, and bolt cutters look different, all can be used to cut through different materials. Therefore, Choice (B) is correct.

143. **D.** A spanner wrench is a special tool that fits against the rocker lugs on a hose coupling. You can use this wrench to tighten the hose coupling. Choice (D) is correct.

144. **B.** The angles of Choices (A) and (C) are too narrow. The angle in Choice (D) is too wide.

145. **B.** If the extension spring stretches 1.5 inches under a pull of 10 pounds, it would stretch half that amount, 0.75 inches, under a pull of 5 pounds. Therefore, under a pull of 15 pounds, the spring would stretch 1.5 inches + 0.75 inches, or 2.25 inches.

146. **C.** By moving the fulcrum, or pivot point, closer to the object, you reduce the amount of force you need to lift the object. Choice (C) is correct.

147. **D.** When two gears mesh together, one turns clockwise and the other turns counterclockwise. In the image, gear 2 is turning counterclockwise. It's touching gears 1 and 3, which means that those gears have to be turning clockwise. Because gears 1 and 3 both touch gear 4, gear 4 has to turn counterclockwise, just like gear 2.

148. **C.** To figure out the force required to lift the box, you can use the simple formula $w \times d_1 = f \times d_2$. Solve for force (f) by multiplying the weight of the box $(w = 100)$ by the distance in feet from the box to the fulcrum $(d_1 = 2)$ and dividing by the distance from the fulcrum to the firefighter $(d_2 = 4)$. The force required to lift the box is 50 pounds.

149. **A.** If the firefighter moves the fulcrum 1 foot closer to the box, it would change the distance from the box to the fulcrum to 1 foot and the distance from the fulcrum to the firefighter to 5 feet. To figure out the force required to lift the box, you can use the simple formula $w \times d_1 = f \times d_2$. Solve for force by multiplying the weight of the box $(w = 100)$ by the distance in feet from the box to the fulcrum $(d_1 = 1)$ and dividing by the distance from the fulcrum to the firefighter $(d_2 = 5)$. So the force required to lift the box is 20 pounds.

150. **D.** A hacksaw has a metal arch, a handle, a thin disposable blade, and pins that attach the blade to the arch. It's used for sawing through materials such as wood or metal.

Answer Key

Part 1: Reading Comprehension

1. C	7. D	13. B	19. B	25. B
2. B	8. A	14. C	20. C	26. C
3. D	9. C	15. A	21. B	27. B
4. A	10. A	16. C	22. A	28. D
5. B	11. B	17. A	23. C	29. D
6. C	12. C	18. D	24. D	30. A

Part 2: Verbal Expression

31. C	35. B	39. B	43. A	47. D
32. A	36. B	40. A	44. D	48. A
33. D	37. B	41. B	45. B	49. C
34. D	38. C	42. D	46. C	50. B

Part 3: Observation and Memory

51. C	55. C	59. D	63. D	67. B
52. A	56. B	60. C	64. A	68. A
53. D	57. B	61. D	65. A	69. C
54. B	58. A	62. D	66. B	70. A

Part 4: Spatial Orientation

71. B	75. A	79. C	83. C	87. D
72. D	76. C	80. A	84. B	88. C
73. C	77. D	81. A	85. B	89. C
74. B	78. C	82. D	86. A	90. D

Part 5: Reasoning and Judgment

91. D	95. B	99. B	103. C	107. C
92. B	96. D	100. A	104. A	108. A
93. A	97. C	101. A	105. D	109. C
94. B	98. C	102. C	106. B	110. C

Part 6: Performing Mathematical Calculations

111. B	115. B	119. C	123. C	127. A
112. A	116. D	120. C	124. A	128. D
113. C	117. C	121. B	125. B	129. B
114. B	118. D	122. C	126. C	130. C

Part 7: Mechanical Aptitude

131. D	135. B	139. D	143. D	147. D
132. C	136. A	140. C	144. B	148. C
133. A	137. B	141. A	145. B	149. A
134. A	138. A	142. B	146. C	150. D

Chapter 17
Practice Exam 2

• •

*T*his sample test is similar to the written exams you may encounter during the firefighter hiring process. The test includes questions in the following areas: reading comprehension, verbal expression, observation and memory, spatial orientation, reasoning and judgment, mathematical calculation, and mechanical aptitude.

To get the most out of this practice test, take it like you'd take the real written exam:

✔ Allow yourself 3.5 hours to complete the exam, and take the whole exam at one time. After you complete one section, you can move on to the next.

✔ Take the test in a quiet place, such as a library or a private office, to avoid interruption.

✔ Bring a timer, because you need to time yourself during certain portions of the exam.

✔ Bring a pencil and some scratch paper.

✔ Use the answer sheet that's provided.

After you complete the practice exam, check your answers against the answers and explanations in Chapter 18. The purpose of this practice exam is to help you identify your strengths and weaknesses on the written exam so you know where to focus your studies.

Answer Sheet for Practice Exam 1

1 Ⓐ Ⓑ Ⓒ Ⓓ	41 Ⓐ Ⓑ Ⓒ Ⓓ	81 Ⓐ Ⓑ Ⓒ Ⓓ	121 Ⓐ Ⓑ Ⓒ Ⓓ
2 Ⓐ Ⓑ Ⓒ Ⓓ	42 Ⓐ Ⓑ Ⓒ Ⓓ	82 Ⓐ Ⓑ Ⓒ Ⓓ	122 Ⓐ Ⓑ Ⓒ Ⓓ
3 Ⓐ Ⓑ Ⓒ Ⓓ	43 Ⓐ Ⓑ Ⓒ Ⓓ	83 Ⓐ Ⓑ Ⓒ Ⓓ	123 Ⓐ Ⓑ Ⓒ Ⓓ
4 Ⓐ Ⓑ Ⓒ Ⓓ	44 Ⓐ Ⓑ Ⓒ Ⓓ	84 Ⓐ Ⓑ Ⓒ Ⓓ	124 Ⓐ Ⓑ Ⓒ Ⓓ
5 Ⓐ Ⓑ Ⓒ Ⓓ	45 Ⓐ Ⓑ Ⓒ Ⓓ	85 Ⓐ Ⓑ Ⓒ Ⓓ	125 Ⓐ Ⓑ Ⓒ Ⓓ
6 Ⓐ Ⓑ Ⓒ Ⓓ	46 Ⓐ Ⓑ Ⓒ Ⓓ	86 Ⓐ Ⓑ Ⓒ Ⓓ	126 Ⓐ Ⓑ Ⓒ Ⓓ
7 Ⓐ Ⓑ Ⓒ Ⓓ	47 Ⓐ Ⓑ Ⓒ Ⓓ	87 Ⓐ Ⓑ Ⓒ Ⓓ	127 Ⓐ Ⓑ Ⓒ Ⓓ
8 Ⓐ Ⓑ Ⓒ Ⓓ	48 Ⓐ Ⓑ Ⓒ Ⓓ	88 Ⓐ Ⓑ Ⓒ Ⓓ	128 Ⓐ Ⓑ Ⓒ Ⓓ
9 Ⓐ Ⓑ Ⓒ Ⓓ	49 Ⓐ Ⓑ Ⓒ Ⓓ	89 Ⓐ Ⓑ Ⓒ Ⓓ	129 Ⓐ Ⓑ Ⓒ Ⓓ
10 Ⓐ Ⓑ Ⓒ Ⓓ	50 Ⓐ Ⓑ Ⓒ Ⓓ	90 Ⓐ Ⓑ Ⓒ Ⓓ	130 Ⓐ Ⓑ Ⓒ Ⓓ
11 Ⓐ Ⓑ Ⓒ Ⓓ	51 Ⓐ Ⓑ Ⓒ Ⓓ	91 Ⓐ Ⓑ Ⓒ Ⓓ	131 Ⓐ Ⓑ Ⓒ Ⓓ
12 Ⓐ Ⓑ Ⓒ Ⓓ	52 Ⓐ Ⓑ Ⓒ Ⓓ	92 Ⓐ Ⓑ Ⓒ Ⓓ	132 Ⓐ Ⓑ Ⓒ Ⓓ
13 Ⓐ Ⓑ Ⓒ Ⓓ	53 Ⓐ Ⓑ Ⓒ Ⓓ	93 Ⓐ Ⓑ Ⓒ Ⓓ	133 Ⓐ Ⓑ Ⓒ Ⓓ
14 Ⓐ Ⓑ Ⓒ Ⓓ	54 Ⓐ Ⓑ Ⓒ Ⓓ	94 Ⓐ Ⓑ Ⓒ Ⓓ	134 Ⓐ Ⓑ Ⓒ Ⓓ
15 Ⓐ Ⓑ Ⓒ Ⓓ	55 Ⓐ Ⓑ Ⓒ Ⓓ	95 Ⓐ Ⓑ Ⓒ Ⓓ	135 Ⓐ Ⓑ Ⓒ Ⓓ
16 Ⓐ Ⓑ Ⓒ Ⓓ	56 Ⓐ Ⓑ Ⓒ Ⓓ	96 Ⓐ Ⓑ Ⓒ Ⓓ	136 Ⓐ Ⓑ Ⓒ Ⓓ
17 Ⓐ Ⓑ Ⓒ Ⓓ	57 Ⓐ Ⓑ Ⓒ Ⓓ	97 Ⓐ Ⓑ Ⓒ Ⓓ	137 Ⓐ Ⓑ Ⓒ Ⓓ
18 Ⓐ Ⓑ Ⓒ Ⓓ	58 Ⓐ Ⓑ Ⓒ Ⓓ	98 Ⓐ Ⓑ Ⓒ Ⓓ	138 Ⓐ Ⓑ Ⓒ Ⓓ
19 Ⓐ Ⓑ Ⓒ Ⓓ	59 Ⓐ Ⓑ Ⓒ Ⓓ	99 Ⓐ Ⓑ Ⓒ Ⓓ	139 Ⓐ Ⓑ Ⓒ Ⓓ
20 Ⓐ Ⓑ Ⓒ Ⓓ	60 Ⓐ Ⓑ Ⓒ Ⓓ	100 Ⓐ Ⓑ Ⓒ Ⓓ	140 Ⓐ Ⓑ Ⓒ Ⓓ
21 Ⓐ Ⓑ Ⓒ Ⓓ	61 Ⓐ Ⓑ Ⓒ Ⓓ	101 Ⓐ Ⓑ Ⓒ Ⓓ	141 Ⓐ Ⓑ Ⓒ Ⓓ
22 Ⓐ Ⓑ Ⓒ Ⓓ	62 Ⓐ Ⓑ Ⓒ Ⓓ	102 Ⓐ Ⓑ Ⓒ Ⓓ	142 Ⓐ Ⓑ Ⓒ Ⓓ
23 Ⓐ Ⓑ Ⓒ Ⓓ	63 Ⓐ Ⓑ Ⓒ Ⓓ	103 Ⓐ Ⓑ Ⓒ Ⓓ	143 Ⓐ Ⓑ Ⓒ Ⓓ
24 Ⓐ Ⓑ Ⓒ Ⓓ	64 Ⓐ Ⓑ Ⓒ Ⓓ	104 Ⓐ Ⓑ Ⓒ Ⓓ	144 Ⓐ Ⓑ Ⓒ Ⓓ
25 Ⓐ Ⓑ Ⓒ Ⓓ	65 Ⓐ Ⓑ Ⓒ Ⓓ	105 Ⓐ Ⓑ Ⓒ Ⓓ	145 Ⓐ Ⓑ Ⓒ Ⓓ
26 Ⓐ Ⓑ Ⓒ Ⓓ	66 Ⓐ Ⓑ Ⓒ Ⓓ	106 Ⓐ Ⓑ Ⓒ Ⓓ	146 Ⓐ Ⓑ Ⓒ Ⓓ
27 Ⓐ Ⓑ Ⓒ Ⓓ	67 Ⓐ Ⓑ Ⓒ Ⓓ	107 Ⓐ Ⓑ Ⓒ Ⓓ	147 Ⓐ Ⓑ Ⓒ Ⓓ
28 Ⓐ Ⓑ Ⓒ Ⓓ	68 Ⓐ Ⓑ Ⓒ Ⓓ	108 Ⓐ Ⓑ Ⓒ Ⓓ	148 Ⓐ Ⓑ Ⓒ Ⓓ
29 Ⓐ Ⓑ Ⓒ Ⓓ	69 Ⓐ Ⓑ Ⓒ Ⓓ	109 Ⓐ Ⓑ Ⓒ Ⓓ	149 Ⓐ Ⓑ Ⓒ Ⓓ
30 Ⓐ Ⓑ Ⓒ Ⓓ	70 Ⓐ Ⓑ Ⓒ Ⓓ	110 Ⓐ Ⓑ Ⓒ Ⓓ	150 Ⓐ Ⓑ Ⓒ Ⓓ
31 Ⓐ Ⓑ Ⓒ Ⓓ	71 Ⓐ Ⓑ Ⓒ Ⓓ	111 Ⓐ Ⓑ Ⓒ Ⓓ	
32 Ⓐ Ⓑ Ⓒ Ⓓ	72 Ⓐ Ⓑ Ⓒ Ⓓ	112 Ⓐ Ⓑ Ⓒ Ⓓ	
33 Ⓐ Ⓑ Ⓒ Ⓓ	73 Ⓐ Ⓑ Ⓒ Ⓓ	113 Ⓐ Ⓑ Ⓒ Ⓓ	
34 Ⓐ Ⓑ Ⓒ Ⓓ	74 Ⓐ Ⓑ Ⓒ Ⓓ	114 Ⓐ Ⓑ Ⓒ Ⓓ	
35 Ⓐ Ⓑ Ⓒ Ⓓ	75 Ⓐ Ⓑ Ⓒ Ⓓ	115 Ⓐ Ⓑ Ⓒ Ⓓ	
36 Ⓐ Ⓑ Ⓒ Ⓓ	76 Ⓐ Ⓑ Ⓒ Ⓓ	116 Ⓐ Ⓑ Ⓒ Ⓓ	
37 Ⓐ Ⓑ Ⓒ Ⓓ	77 Ⓐ Ⓑ Ⓒ Ⓓ	117 Ⓐ Ⓑ Ⓒ Ⓓ	
38 Ⓐ Ⓑ Ⓒ Ⓓ	78 Ⓐ Ⓑ Ⓒ Ⓓ	118 Ⓐ Ⓑ Ⓒ Ⓓ	
39 Ⓐ Ⓑ Ⓒ Ⓓ	79 Ⓐ Ⓑ Ⓒ Ⓓ	119 Ⓐ Ⓑ Ⓒ Ⓓ	
40 Ⓐ Ⓑ Ⓒ Ⓓ	80 Ⓐ Ⓑ Ⓒ Ⓓ	120 Ⓐ Ⓑ Ⓒ Ⓓ	

Part 1: Reading Comprehension

Directions: This section tests your reading comprehension skills. Read each passage and answer the questions that follow it. Choose the answer that *most correctly* answers each question. Mark the space on your answer sheet that corresponds to the question number and the letter indicating your choice.

Use the information in the following passage to answer questions 1–4.

Firefighting is not your typical 9-to-5 job, and it creates a unique lifestyle for the men and women who choose this career. Many fire departments across the United States require firefighters to work 24-hour shifts. This may sound like a brutal schedule, but these firefighters usually get at least 24 hours to recover between shifts. Many firefighters embrace their days off to pursue hobbies, play sports, spend time with their families, or even take a second job in a different field.

When firefighters are on duty, they respond to all sorts of emergencies, but they spend the rest of their shift at the fire station, which becomes a sort of home away from home. Many rooms in fire stations resemble college dormitories. Firefighters share common areas such as the kitchen, restrooms, and lounge area. Some departments have separate rooms for firefighters to use as sleeping quarters, and others simply set up cubicles or partitions in one large room. Aside from being coworkers, these men and women are roommates and often grow as close as, if not closer than, family. They share everyday responsibilities, such as taking out the trash or doing the dishes. They learn to tolerate and accept different personalities, and over time, they build trust and learn to depend on each other. This trust is crucial, because firefighters must be able to rely on each other when they are out on calls, fighting fires and saving lives.

1. How many hours do firefighters usually get to rest between 24-hour shifts?

   (A) 0

   (B) 8

   (C) at least 24

   (D) no more than 48

2. The author compares firefighters who work at the same fire station to

   (A) students in a classroom.

   (B) colleagues at work.

   (C) members of a family.

   (D) close friends.

3. Based on the passage, you can conclude that the author values which of the following qualities in fellow firefighters?

   (A) determination

   (B) strength

   (C) optimism

   (D) trustworthiness

4. The best title for this passage is

   (A) "Firefighting: A Way of Life."

   (B) "Firefighter Employee Handbook."

   (C) "Fire Station Rules."

   (D) "Firefighting: A Dangerous Occupation."

Go on to next page

> *Use the information in the following passage to answer questions 5–11.*

For most emergency response calls, such as structure fires or motor vehicle accidents, firefighters wear turnout clothing, also known as bunker gear or personal protective equipment (PPE). Since 1971, all turnout clothing distributed by fire departments in the United States has required three essential layers: an outer shell, a moisture barrier, and a thermal barrier. Each of these components should be present in the trousers (typically overalls), boots, and jacket.

Although firefighters wear turnout clothing on most calls, certain events warrant the wearing of different types of suits. If firefighters respond to a chemical or aircraft fire, for example, they should wear a proximity suit. A proximity suit is similar to a normal turnout suit, but its outermost layer is made of a vacuum-deposited aluminized material that is metallic in color and is designed to reflect heat. A proximity suit protects firefighters who are exposed to extreme heat. The hood, jacket, pants, boots, and even gloves that comprise this suit are all made with this protective material.

Some emergencies may require firefighters to protect themselves from hazardous materials (hazmat). When faced with such scenarios, firefighters should wear hazmat suits. The United States has four levels of hazmat suits. For each level of danger, a different type of hazmat suit is required, with Level A and Level B suits offering the highest degree of protection. Both Level A and Level B hazmat suits are equipped with a breathing apparatus. Level A suits fit loosely. The breathing apparatus, along with a two-way radio, is inside the suit. Level A suits protect against gases, vapors, mists, and other particles. Level B suits, which fit snugly, are designed to protect against chemical splashes. The breathing apparatus is on the outside of the suit. Level C and Level D suits are not as involved as Level A and Level B suits, but the Level C suit does include a respirator that purifies the air.

Finally, if firefighters respond to the scene of a wildland fire, or forest fire, they are required to wear a lightweight uniform. This uniform is made of a flame-resistant material called Nomex and is accompanied by boots, a hard hat, and gloves. Boots should be made of leather rather than steel or rubber, due to the temperature of the fires.

5. Based on the passage, you can conclude that a firefighter dressed in what looks like silver bunker gear is most likely preparing to fight

(A) a structure fire.

(B) an aircraft fire.

(C) a wildland fire.

(D) a car fire.

6. All of the following hazmat suits include a type of breathing apparatus EXCEPT

(A) Level A.

(B) Level B.

(C) Level C.

(D) Level D.

7. Based on the passage, you can conclude that a firefighter called to respond to a chemical spill at a local industrial plant will most likely wear

(A) traditional bunker gear.

(B) a Level B hazmat suit.

(C) a proximity suit.

(D) a Level C hazmat suit.

Go on to next page

8. Which sentence from the passage best states its main idea?

   (A) Although firefighters wear turnout clothing on most calls, certain events warrant the wearing of different types of suits.

   (B) A proximity suit is similar to a normal turnout suit, but its outermost layer is made of a vacuum-deposited aluminized material that is metallic in color and is designed to reflect heat.

   (C) For each level of danger, a different type of hazmat suit is required, with Level A and Level B suits offering the highest degree of protection.

   (D) This uniform is made of a flame-resistant material called Nomex and is accompanied by boots, a hard hat, and gloves.

9. All of the following are worn to fight wildland fires EXCEPT

   (A) a Nomex uniform.

   (B) a hard hat.

   (C) a respirator.

   (D) boots.

10. Which of the following is NOT one of the three essential layers of turnout gear?

    (A) an outer shell

    (B) an aluminized barrier

    (C) a moisture barrier

    (D) a thermal barrier

11. A loose-fitting suit equipped with a two-way radio and an internal breathing apparatus is a

    (A) proximity suit.

    (B) wildland fire uniform.

    (C) Level A hazmat suit.

    (D) Level D hazmat suit.

Go on to next page

Use the information in the table to answer questions 12–15.

Fire Hose Construction

Type of Hose	Size Range (in inches)	Outer Covering	Lining	Reinforcement
Flexible non-collapsible intake hose	2.5 to 6	Rubber	Rubber	Fabric and plastic
Noncollapsible intake hose	2.5 to 6	Rubber	Rubber	Fabric and wire
Impregnated single-jacket hose	1.5 to 5	Polymer	Polymer	—
Woven-jacket hose	1 to 6	One or two woven-fabric jackets	Rubber	—
Booster hose	0.75 to 1	Rubber	Rubber	Fabric

12. All of the following hoses are reinforced EXCEPT

(A) a 3-inch noncollapsible intake hose.

(B) a 1-inch booster hose.

(C) a 2-inch woven-jacket hose.

(D) a 4-inch flexible noncollapsible intake hose.

13. A firefighter grabs a 1-inch, rubber-covered, rubber-lined, fabric-reinforced hose from the fire apparatus. What type of hose is the firefighter using?

(A) noncollapsible intake hose

(B) impregnated single-jacket hose

(C) woven-jacket hose

(D) booster hose

14. The lining of a woven-jacket hose is made of

(A) rubber.

(B) a woven-fabric jacket.

(C) a polymer.

(D) fabric and plastic.

15. The only difference between noncollapsible intake hose and flexible noncollapsible intake hose is their

(A) size.

(B) outer covering.

(C) lining.

(D) reinforcement.

Go on to next page

Use the information in the following passage to answer questions 16–20.

In the excitement and urgency of responding to an emergency, the last thing many teams want to experience is confusion about who is responsible for performing certain tasks. Although individuals may know which duties they must perform after they reach the incident, they may not know which tasks the men or women beside them are supposed to complete — especially when multiple departments or companies respond to the same emergency. If firefighters require immediate assistance with something, they need to be able to find someone who knows how to help them as quickly as possible. For this reason, many fire departments across the United States color-code their helmets.

Some color-coded systems are easy to understand. For example, the New York City Fire Department, or FDNY, uses colors on its helmets to show which individuals belong to each company and which functions they typically perform. The colored shields on the fronts of their black helmets represent this information. A strictly black helmet indicates a member of an engine company. The rest are as follows:

- Blue: Rescue company
- Red: Ladder company
- Yellow: Squad company
- Orange: Probationary firefighter
- Green: Hazardous materials and marine units

Unfortunately, not all departments use the same color-coding system to identify firefighter or company functions. A blue shield on a helmet in New York may have an entirely different meaning from a blue helmet worn by a firefighter in Los Angeles. In most departments, however, commanding officers wear white helmets to set them apart from the other firefighters.

16. Based on the passage, which of the following statements is true?

(A) An FDNY firefighter wearing a white helmet with a red shield is the commanding officer for a rescue company.

(B) An FDNY firefighter wearing an all black helmet is a probationary firefighter.

(C) An FDNY firefighter wearing a white helmet with an orange shield is the commanding officer for a ladder company.

(D) An FDNY firefighter wearing a black helmet with a green shield is prepared to handle a hazardous materials incident.

17. According to the passage, a drawback of using a color-coded helmet system is that

(A) it's difficult to see helmet colors during fires.

(B) different departments use different color codes.

(C) it creates competition among different companies.

(D) firefighters can show off only one of their specialties.

Go on to next page

18. If an FDNY firefighter wearing a black helmet with a yellow shield were to notice a person in the window of an upper-level apartment in a 15-story apartment building that is on fire, he would most likely look for a firefighter wearing a helmet with

    (A) an orange shield.

    (B) a green shield.

    (C) a red shield.

    (D) a white shield.

19. According to the passage, the main reason many departments color-code their helmets is so firefighters can

    (A) quickly find someone who can help them.

    (B) easily identify the officers in charge.

    (C) see each other when visibility is poor.

    (D) display their rank within the department.

20. You would expect FDNY firefighters involved in a river rescue to be wearing

    (A) black helmets with blue shields.

    (B) blue helmets with white shields.

    (C) black helmets with green shields.

    (D) blue helmets with green shields.

Use the information in the following passage to answer questions 21–25.

When a fire produces a lot of heat or smoke inside a room, firefighters must create an opening through which heat or smoke can escape. Creating such an opening is called ventilation. As the heat and smoke leave the room, firefighters can better see both the fire and their surrounding environment. Sometimes a window or door can serve as ventilation; however, if the smoke has gathered in an area without windows or doors, firefighters may have to create their own openings.

If a window or door is available, firefighters may open it to allow heat and smoke to escape. Sometimes they use water to improve ventilation. This process, called hydraulic ventilation, involves directing a hose stream toward an existing opening. As the pressure from the hose hits the smoke and heat, it forces those elements into the open space beyond the door, window, or skylight. Firefighters have found that this tactic is useful when trying to avoid property damage.

Unfortunately, windows and doors are not always available, and firefighters have to use other means to vent out heat and smoke. A common technique is cutting through the ceiling or roof with a saw to create a hole through which heat and smoke can escape. Firefighters always check for windows and doors before resorting to this method. The last thing they want to do is destroy more property than they save.

Go on to next page

Occasionally, a fire creates its own ventilation. A fire in an enclosed room may produce so much smoke, heat, and fire that the room can no longer contain it. In such cases, windows may shatter or the fire may burn a hole in the ceiling or the roof. When this phenomenon occurs, firefighters say that the building has either auto- or self-ventilated.

When using ventilation tactics, it's important to note that timing and location can greatly affect the outcome of the fire. A poorly placed or timed vent can feed oxygen into the fire, which will create larger flames, more smoke, and hotter temperatures.

21. The best title for this passage is

    (A) "Ventilation Tools."

    (B) "Ventilation Tactics."

    (C) "Ventilating Vertically."

    (D) "Ventilating Horizontally."

22. Using a hose stream to force smoke and heat through an opening is called

    (A) auto-ventilation.

    (B) forced ventilation.

    (C) hydraulic ventilation.

    (D) window ventilation.

23. The purpose of opening a window or door or cutting a hole in the ceiling of a room during a fire is to

    (A) reduce the amount of heat and smoke in the room.

    (B) allow fresh air into the room so firefighters can breathe.

    (C) establish an escape route for firefighters inside the room.

    (D) create an opening through which firefighters can insert a hose.

24. Which of the following is an example of self-ventilation?

    (A) Firefighters cut a hole in the roof above an attic fire.

    (B) Firefighters use a hose to force smoke out a window.

    (C) A vent feeds oxygen into a fire and causes flames to spread.

    (D) A fire produces so much heat and smoke that a window shatters.

25. Based on the passage, you can conclude that

    (A) auto-ventilation is less destructive than hydraulic ventilation.

    (B) cutting a ventilation hole in the ceiling is less destructive than self-ventilation.

    (C) hydraulic ventilation is less destructive than cutting a ventilation hole in the ceiling.

    (D) window or door ventilation is less effective than auto- or self-ventilation.

Go on to next page

Use the information in the following passage to answer questions 26–30.

Before, during, and after fires, firefighters who are not physically attacking the flames often work behind the scenes to salvage fire victims' property. Firefighters understand that some items are irreplaceable — photos of loved ones, keepsakes, money — and they work hard to ensure that property owners do not lose their most valued possessions. Salvage operations usually occur after a fire has been extinguished, but they may occur during the fire or even before firefighters start fighting the fire.

Firefighters use many tools in the salvaging process. These include salvage covers, floor runners, squeegees, water scoops, water vacuums, roofing supplies, and various power tools. It is important that this equipment be organized and stored in the correct areas of the fire apparatus so that firefighters waste no time locating what they need.

The majority of salvaging involves the movement of furniture. If the roof of a building is on fire, firefighters work to set up rooms in the basement and on the first floor so that if the fire were to spread through the walls, little would be lost. Firefighters move all furniture to the middle of the room, and they pile keepsakes and property displayed atop dressers and tables onto the furniture. Then they wrap the entire pile with large salvage tarps to protect the property from water damage. If a room is far from the flames, firefighters may completely remove objects such as furniture and personal items from the building to protect it.

Salvage operations create strong public relations between fire departments and their communities. Community members greatly appreciate that firefighters work hard to keep their property safe and minimize damage.

26. All the following are tools used during salvage operations EXCEPT

(A) squeegees.

(B) water vacuums.

(C) floor runners.

(D) hoses.

27. The purpose of salvage operations is to

(A) protect property owners' possessions from damage.

(B) help property owners rebuild after a fire.

(C) remove fire-damaged materials from a home.

(D) improve relations between firefighters and community members.

28. Why do firefighters wrap groups of furniture and other personal property with salvage tarps?

(A) to easily move a lot of furniture and personal property at one time

(B) to protect the furniture and personal property from water damage

(C) to indicate furniture and personal property that is damaged beyond repair

(D) to show furniture and personal property that should be removed from the structure

Go on to next page

29. Firefighters would most likely use roofing supplies during salvage operations to

    (A) create roofs that will protect furniture from water damage.

    (B) construct temporary shelters for victims of a fire.

    (C) completely replace the roof of a burned structure.

    (D) temporarily patch a hole in the roof caused by a fire.

30. During salvage operations, what is the purpose of moving furniture to the middle of a room?

    (A) It keeps the furniture away from walls through which fire can spread.

    (B) It makes it easier for firefighters to direct hose streams around furniture.

    (C) It allows firefighters to conduct faster search-and-rescue operations.

    (D) It prevents smoke from permeating the fabric of furniture.

Go on to next page

Part 2: Verbal Expression

> **Directions:** This section tests your verbal expression skills. Read each question and choose the answer that *most correctly* answers it. Mark the space on your answer sheet that corresponds to the question number and the letter indicating your choice.

For questions 31–33, please identify which of the underlined words is spelled incorrectly.

31. Each fire <u>apparatus</u> is designed to <u>ensure</u> that firefighters can quickly and easily <u>excess</u> all tools and <u>necessary</u> equipment in an emergency.

    (A) apparatus

    (B) ensure

    (C) excess

    (D) necessary

32. In Japan, first responders often ride motor-cycles <u>equipped</u> to fight fires; each of these <u>vehicles</u> carries a fire <u>extinguisher</u>, a fire blanket, a first aid kit, and an automated external <u>defibrillater</u>, or AED.

    (A) equipped

    (B) vehicles

    (C) extinguisher

    (D) defibrillater

33. When <u>launching</u> an <u>aeriel</u> attack on a wild-land fire, firefighters may use fixed-wing aircraft, <u>helicopters</u>, and smoke jumpers, who <u>parachute</u> to hard-to-reach locations.

    (A) launching

    (B) aeriel

    (C) helicopters

    (D) parachute

For questions 34–35, choose the word that is spelled correctly to complete the following sentences.

34. Firefighters use specially designed _____ vehicles to fight wildfires in heavily forested areas.

    (A) all-train

    (B) all-terain

    (C) all-terrain

    (D) all-terrane

35. Before firefighters can participate in a rescue service at an airport, they must run a statistical _____ of movements, meaning they have to evaluate the take-offs and landings scheduled for the landing strip they plan to use.

    (A) analysis

    (B) analisis

    (C) anylasis

    (D) analyses

Choose the appropriate word or phrase to complete the following sentences.

36. Firefighters McCoy and Miller must work together to operate a tiller, or hook-and-ladder, truck; McCoy operates the _____ wheel for the front wheels while Miller turns the back wheels from the rear of the extended truck.

    (A) stearing

    (B) steering

    (C) stering

    (D) steiring

Go on to next page

37. Firefighters called to an emergency that involves a liquid chemical spill may be required to wear _____ Level A or Level B hazmat suits.

    (A) there

    (B) their

    (C) they're

    (D) they

38. Next week, Station 32 _____ a local preschool to teach students how to stop, drop, and roll if they ever catch fire.

    (A) visits

    (B) will visit

    (C) visited

    (D) has visited

39. Two hours ago, firefighters used Station 51's new fireboat when they _____ to a boat fire approximately a mile off the coast.

    (A) responds

    (B) will respond

    (C) responded

    (D) had responded

40. The department's executive board announced _____ decision to postpone the purchase of new hoses for the fire engine.

    (A) our

    (B) them

    (C) their

    (D) its

For questions 41–43, choose the phrase that would best replace the underlined part of the sentence.

41. Sometimes firefighters are the first to encounter an injured victim at an emergency <u>scene and they are trained</u> as both EMTs and paramedics.

    (A) scene and they are trained

    (B) scene; therefore, they are trained

    (C) scene, while they are trained

    (D) scene and with training

42. When firefighters respond to an <u>emergency, firefighters typically use</u> active visual and audible warnings, such as lights and sirens, to warn other drivers.

    (A) emergency, firefighters typically use

    (B) emergency and they typically use

    (C) emergency; firefighters typically use

    (D) emergency, they typically use

43. If <u>fuel oil or gasoline or jet fuel</u> is on fire, firefighters should consider attacking the flames with foam rather than with water.

    (A) fuel oil or gasoline or jet fuel

    (B) fuel oil, or gasoline or jet fuel

    (C) fuel oil, gasoline, or jet fuel

    (D) fuel oil, or gasoline, or jet fuel

For questions 44–47, choose the word that has nearly the same meaning as the word in italics.

44. When Firefighter Jeffries performs an inspection of his self-contained breathing apparatus, he *carefully* opens the cylinder valve to make sure the alarm functions properly.

    (A) suspiciously

    (B) cautiously

    (C) awkwardly

    (D) courageously

Go on to next page

45. Firefighters who receive frequent reprimand for *obstinacy* typically find it difficult to take orders from others or view an issue from a different perspective.

    (A) stubbornness

    (B) laziness

    (C) compulsiveness

    (D) submissiveness

46. Chief Duncan is known for his *colloquial* interviews; members of the press often ask him for comments about arson investigations because he is easy to talk to and often provides them with the information they seek.

    (A) educated

    (B) lengthy

    (C) conversational

    (D) unintelligent

47. To ensure that rookie firefighters were awake and alert for any emergencies that occur before noon, Station 82 *incorporated* a mandatory breakfast hour into firefighters' schedules from 6:00 to 7:00 each morning.

    (A) required

    (B) cooked

    (C) changed

    (D) integrated

For questions 48–50, choose the word that best completes the sentence.

48. When firefighters enter a burning building, they should be _____ of weakened floors or ceilings that could give way at a moment's notice.

    (A) ashamed

    (B) distant

    (C) wary

    (D) curious

49. Firefighters often use helicopters during aerial firefighting because their aim is typically _____; the water or fire retardant they release almost always hits the burning area.

    (A) accurate

    (B) erroneous

    (C) difficult

    (D) widespread

50. Although many do not approve of the dangerous techniques that smoke jumpers use to fight wildfires, the positive results of their work usually _____ the risks they face.

    (A) alleviate

    (B) justify

    (C) expand

    (D) challenge

Part 3: Observation and Memory

Directions: This section tests your observation and memory skills. In this section, you'll need a timer and a partner.

Visual Memory

Directions for questions 51–60: In this part, you'll be tested on your observational and memory skills, including your ability to see, understand, and interpret information. Study the image of the crash scene in the appendix for 5 minutes. DO NOT TAKE NOTES ABOUT THE IMAGE AS YOU STUDY IT. At the end of 5 minutes, answer questions 51–60 based only on what you can remember from the image. DO NOT LOOK AT THE IMAGE AS YOU ANSWER THE QUESTIONS. Choose the answer that *most correctly* answers each question. You may look at the image only when checking your answers at the completion of Practice Exam 1.

Now, set your timer for 5 minutes and begin studying the image.

STOP DO NOT TURN THE PAGE UNTIL TOLD TO DO SO.

51. In the picture of the accident scene, how many vehicles can be seen?

    (A) 4

    (B) 5

    (C) 7

    (D) 8

52. How many cars are traveling west?

    (A) 0

    (B) 1

    (C) 2

    (D) 4

53. If all the victims of the car accident are still in their vehicles, how many victims are there?

    (A) 3

    (B) 4

    (C) 6

    (D) 7

54. In the picture of the accident scene, what is the weather like?

    (A) rainy and wet

    (B) sunny and dry

    (C) snowy and icy

    (D) cloudy and dry

55. How many people have gotten out of their cars to help the accident victims?

    (A) 0

    (B) 1

    (C) 2

    (D) 3

56. Where does First Street become a two-way street?

    (A) west of the road that runs north to south

    (B) south of the road that runs west to east

    (C) east of the road that runs north to south

    (D) north of the road that runs west to east

57. Which of the following hazards can be seen in the picture of the accident scene?

    (A) One of the cars is leaking fluid.

    (B) The southbound car has caught on fire.

    (C) The cars are near live electrical wires.

    (D) A third northbound car is sliding toward the cars.

58. What appears to have happened to one of the victims in the eastbound car?

    (A) He or she was ejected from the car and landed on the street.

    (B) He or she has gotten out of the car to check the damage.

    (C) He or she was thrown through the windshield of the car.

    (D) He or she is unconscious and slumped over the steering wheel.

59. Based on the picture, how did the motor vehicle accident most likely occur?

    (A) An eastbound car ran into the back of another eastbound car and pushed it through the stop sign into the intersection.

    (B) A southbound car swerved into the wrong lane and crashed into an oncoming car traveling north.

    (C) An eastbound car sped through an intersection without stopping and crashed into a car traveling south.

    (D) A southbound car slid through a stop sign, and a car traveling east on First Street crashed into the side of the southbound car.

60. The accident victim who appears to need the most help is

    (A) the passenger in the eastbound car.

    (B) the driver of the eastbound car.

    (C) the passenger in the southbound car.

    (D) the driver of the southbound car.

Go on to next page

Listening and memory

Directions for questions 61–70: In this part, you'll be tested on your listening and memory skills, including your ability to hear, understand, and interpret information. Ask a partner to read aloud the passage in the appendix about flammable liquids. DO NOT READ THE PASSAGE YOURSELF. DO NOT TAKE NOTES DURING THE READING. Immediately after your partner has finished reading, answer questions 61–70 based only on what you can remember from the reading. Choose the answer that *most correctly* answers each question. You may look at the passage only when checking your answers at the completion of the practice exam.

STOP DO NOT TURN THE PAGE UNTIL TOLD TO DO SO.

61. Why is it a bad idea to use water on a fire involving flammable liquids?

    (A) Water can cause the liquid to splatter, thereby causing the fire to spread.

    (B) Water can cause the liquid to burn hotter, resulting in an explosion.

    (C) Water adds a small amount of oxygen to the fire, which allows it to keep burning.

    (D) Water mixes with the liquid and changes into a new flammable liquid.

62. All of the following are examples of flammable liquids EXCEPT

    (A) crude oil.

    (B) jet fuel.

    (C) oxygen.

    (D) kerosene.

63. At the scene of a motor vehicle accident, a pool of gasoline near the curb has caught fire. Which method will firefighters most likely use to apply foam to the fire?

    (A) the rain-down method

    (B) the roll-on method

    (C) the bank-down method

    (D) the spray-in method

64. A firefighter attempts to extinguish a fire involving a small pool of flammable liquid using the roll-on method. Which of the following best describes this technique?

    (A) The firefighter aims the hose and expels the foam directly into the burning liquid.

    (B) The firefighter sprays the foam on an elevated area near the burning liquid, and eventually it spills over the side of the elevated area, gently covering the burning liquid.

    (C) The firefighter sprays the foam into the air, slowly sweeping the hose back and forth and allowing the foam to fall onto the burning liquid.

    (D) The firefighter places a stationary hose at the edge of the burning liquid and allows the foam to slowly push backward over the fire.

65. Which of the following is a polar solvent?

    (A) alcohol

    (B) benzene

    (C) gasoline

    (D) fuel oil

66. All of the following are required for a fire to ignite and continue to burn EXCEPT

    (A) fuel.

    (B) oxygen.

    (C) heat.

    (D) smoke.

67. The three methods for applying foam to a fire involving a burning liquid are

    (A) roll-on, pour-on, and bank-down.

    (B) bank-down, rain-down, and shoot-in.

    (C) roll-on, bank-down, and rain-down.

    (D) roll-on, cover-up, and rain-down.

68. As the foam applied to a fire dissipates, it leaves behind

    (A) alcohol.

    (B) acetone.

    (C) chemical residue.

    (D) water.

69. Firefighters are using foam to extinguish a fire involving a very large pool of flammable liquid. Which method will firefighters most likely use to apply foam to the fire?

    (A) the rain-down method

    (B) the roll-on method

    (C) the spread-over method

    (D) the bank-down method

70. When using foam to fight a liquid-fueled fire, firefighters should never

    (A) place the hose at the edge of the fire.

    (B) shoot foam directly into the fire.

    (C) allow the foam to gently fall on the fire.

    (D) move the hose from left to right.

Go on to next page

Part 4: Spatial Orientation

Directions: This section tests your spatial orientation skills. Follow the directions before each map, floor plan, or image. Then read each question and choose the answer that *most correctly* answers it. Mark the space on your answer sheet that corresponds to the question number and the letter indicating your choice. You may look at the image as often as you'd like as you answer the questions.

Use the following city map to answer questions 71–75.

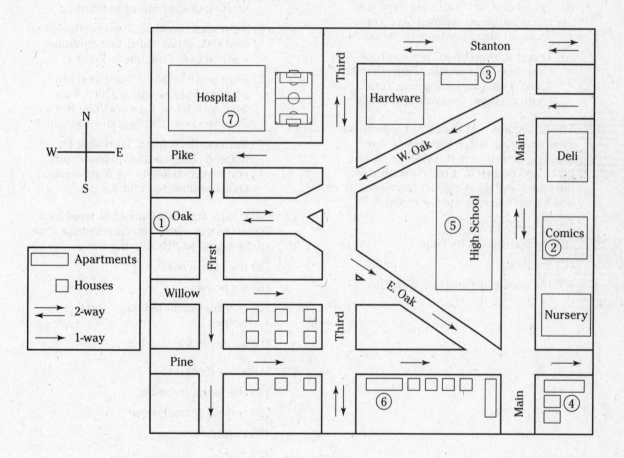

71. The fire engine is parked at Point 7 and must respond to an activated fire alarm at the deli. What is the most direct legal route the driver can take to get to the deli?

    (A) Travel east on Pike. Turn south on Third. Turn southeast on East Oak. Turn east on Pine. Turn north on Main. Continue to the deli.

    (B) Travel west on Pike. Turn south on First. Turn east on Pine. Turn north on Main. Continue to the deli.

    (C) Travel east on Pike. Cross third and travel northeast on West Oak. Turn south on Main. Continue to the deli.

    (D) Travel west on Pike. Turn south on First. Turn east on Oak. Turn north on Third. Turn east on Stanton. Turn south on Main. Continue to the deli.

72. The fire engine is at the corner of First and Pine, traveling east. It travels east two blocks and turns left. It travels north one block and turns left. It travels southwest one block and turns right. It travels north one block. Where is the fire engine?

    (A) the hardware store

    (B) the apartments by Point 3

    (C) the deli

    (D) the corner of Third and West Oak

73. From 7:00 a.m. to 8:30 a.m., Monday through Friday, West Oak between Third and Main is blocked to all traffic except school buses and parents dropping off students at the high school. The fire engine is near the deli on the corner of West Oak and Main at 7:43 a.m. on Wednesday and must respond to a car accident near Point 1. What is the fastest legal route the engine can take to get to Point 1?

    (A) Cross Main and travel southwest on West Oak. Cross Third, and continue west on Oak. Continue to Point 1.

    (B) Turn south on Main. Turn northwest on East Oak. Cross Third, and continue west on Oak. Continue to Point 1.

    (C) Turn north on Main. Turn west on Stanton. Turn south on Third. Turn west on Willow. Turn north on First. Turn west on Oak. Continue to Point 1.

    (D) Turn north on Main. Turn west on Stanton. Turn south on Third. Turn southwest on West Oak. Turn west on Oak. Continue to Point 1.

74. What is located in the area bordered by Willow to the north, Third to the east, Pine to the south, and First to the west?

    (A) the high school

    (B) six houses

    (C) two apartment buildings and five houses

    (D) an empty lot

75. Point 3 is closest to

    (A) the hardware store

    (B) the comic book store

    (C) Point 5

    (D) Point 7

Go on to next page

Use the following floor plan to answer questions 76–80.

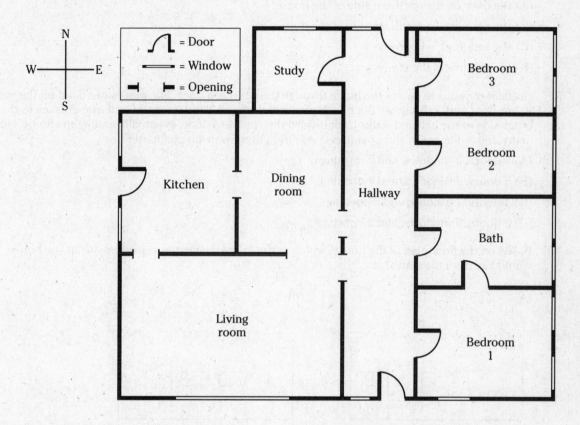

76. If a fire starts in the kitchen, what rooms are immediately exposed to the fire?

    (A) dining room, study, and hallway

    (B) living room and hallway

    (C) dining room and study

    (D) living room and dining room

77. A rapidly spreading fire has moved from the kitchen into the dining room. What is the safest route for the occupants of the living room to exit the house?

    (A) Enter the kitchen. Continue to the door on the western side of the house.

    (B) Enter the hall and make a right. Continue to the door on the southern side of the house.

    (C) Enter the corner of the dining room and quickly exit into the hall. Turn left and continue to the door on the northern side of the house.

    (D) Enter the kitchen and cross through it to the dining room. Cross through the dining room to the hall. Turn right and continue to the door on the southern side of the house.

78. Curtains caught fire in the study, and the fire has spread into the hallway. Which of the following is the safest way for the occupants of bedroom 3 to exit the house?

   (A) the door on the northern side of the house

   (B) the door on the southern side of the house

   (C) the windows in bedroom 3

   (D) the window of the study

79. Firefighter Swanson enters the home through the southern door. She places her hand on the wall to her right and walks down the hall. Never removing her hand from the wall, she crosses to the other side of the hall and walks back toward the southern door, eventually exiting the home. How many doors, windows, and openings does Firefighter Swanson encounter?

   (A) 6 doors, 2 windows, and 2 openings

   (B) 5 doors, 2 windows, and 1 opening

   (C) 4 doors, 1 window, and 2 openings

   (D) 2 doors, 6 windows, and 2 openings

80. Based on the floor plan of the house, which of the following images represents what the house would like from the south?

(A)
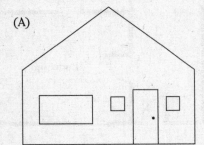

(B)
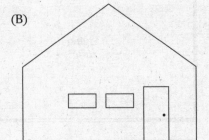

(C)
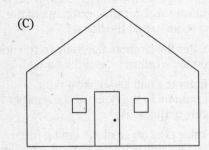

(D)
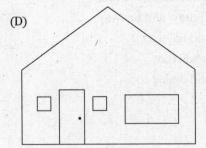

Go on to next page

Use the following city map to answer questions 81–90.

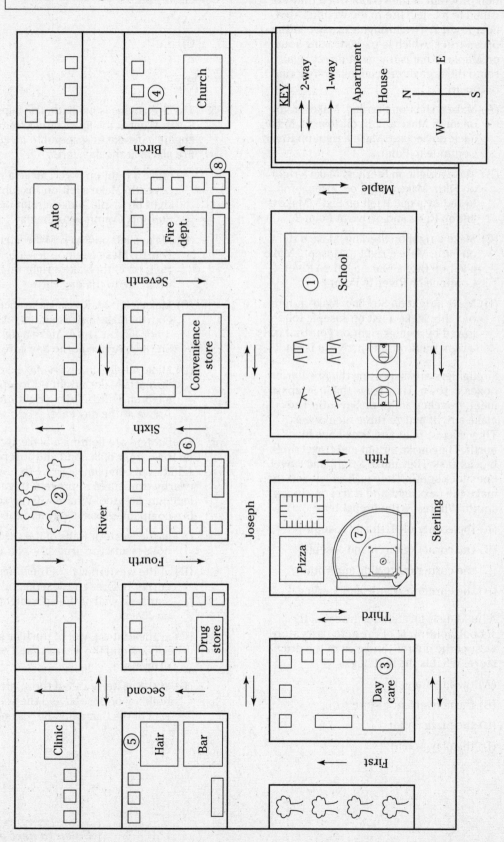

81. Firefighters are conducting a fire prevention program at the school when they are called to a brush fire in the wooded area near Point 2. Two firefighters leave in the brush truck, which is parked facing south on Maple. What is the most direct legal route the firefighters can take to respond to the fire?

    (A) Make a right on Sterling. Make a right on First. Make a right on Joseph. Make a left on Second. Make a right on River. Continue to Point 2.

    (B) Make a right on Sterling. Make a right on Fifth. Make a right on Joseph, followed by a quick left on Sixth. Make a left on River and arrive at Point 2.

    (C) Make a right on Sterling. Make a right on Fifth. Make a right on Joseph. Make a left on Birch. Make a left on River. Continue on River to Point 2.

    (D) Make a right on Sterling. Make a right on Fifth. Make a left on Joseph, followed by a quick right on Fourth. Make a right on River and arrive at Point 2.

82. Firefighters are inspecting the fire alarm boxes in town. They leave the fire department, traveling south on Seventh. They make a right and go three blocks west. They make a right and travel one block north. They make a right and travel three blocks east. They make a right and travel one block south. They make a left and then make the next right and travel one block south. Where are the firefighters?

    (A) the corner of Sixth and Joseph

    (B) the corner of Birch and Joseph

    (C) the corner of Sterling and Fifth

    (D) the corner of Maple and Sterling

83. A building is located northwest of the school, southwest of the auto parts store, west of the church, and east of the drug store. What is the building?

    (A) the fire station

    (B) the convenience store

    (C) the pizza parlor

    (D) the playground

84. How many apartment buildings are located on Joseph?

    (A) 3

    (B) 4

    (C) 5

    (D) 8

85. The fire engine is on Sixth, traveling toward River. What is the most direct route the engine can take to respond to an activated fire alarm at the day care?

    (A) Make a right on River. Make a right on Seventh. Make a left on Joseph. Make a right on Maple. Make a right on Sterling. Continue to the day care.

    (B) Make a left on River. Make a left on Fourth. Make a left on Joseph. Make a right on Fifth. Make a right on Sterling. Continue to the day care.

    (C) Make a left on River. Make a left on Fourth. Make a right on Joseph. Make a quick left on Third. Make a right on Sterling. Arrive at the day care.

    (D) Make a right on River. Make a right on Seventh. Make a right on Joseph. Make a left on Third. Make a right on Sterling. Arrive at the day care.

86. Firefighters are fighting a blaze at the bar on the corner of Second and Joseph. Additional companies arrive to hose down nearby exposures to prevent them from catching fire, too. Where will the additional fire companies most likely aim their hoses?

    (A) at the western walls of the three houses and the drug store on Second

    (B) at the western wall of the house on the corner of First and Joseph and the southern wall of the apartment building on Joseph

    (C) at the eastern wall of the hair salon on Second and the western wall of the drug store

    (D) at the eastern wall of the apartment building on Joseph and the southern wall of the hair salon on Second

Go on to next page

87. The fire engine leaves the station, traveling south on Seventh. The engine makes the first right and travels west for three blocks. The engine turns right and travels north for one block. The engine turns right and travels east for two blocks. The engine turns left and stops. Where is the engine?

    (A) to the east of a wooded area

    (B) to the east of three houses

    (C) to the west of the clinic

    (D) to the west of the convenience store

88. The fire engine travels south on Maple, west on Sterling, north on Fifth, east on Joseph, north on Sixth, east on River, and south on Seventh to return to the station. How many houses does the engine pass along this route?

    (A) 5

    (B) 6

    (C) 10

    (D) 13

89. A car accident blocks the intersection at Fourth and River. A driver on Sixth, about to turn left onto River to head to the clinic, asks a firefighter for the best alternate route he can take to reach the clinic. What will the firefighter most likely tell him?

    (A) Make a left and travel west two blocks. Make a right. The clinic will be on the left.

    (B) Make a right and travel east one block. Make a right and travel south one block. Make a right and travel west three blocks. Make a right and travel north one and a half blocks. The clinic will be on the left.

    (C) Make a right and travel east two blocks. Make a right and travel south one block. Make a right and travel west three blocks. Make a right and travel north one block. Make a left and travel west one block. Make a right. The clinic will be on the left.

    (D) Make a right and travel east one block. Make a right and travel south one block. Make a right and travel west two blocks. Make a right and travel north one block. Make a left and travel west one block. Make a right. The clinic will be on the left.

90. In which areas of the town would firefighters responding to a call have to be extra cautious due to a high concentration of children?

    (A) the northwestern and northeastern corners

    (B) the northwestern and southwestern corners

    (C) the southwestern and southeastern corners

    (D) the southwestern and northeastern corners

Go on to next page

Part 5: Reasoning and Judgment

> **Directions:** This section tests your reasoning and judgment skills. Read each question and choose the answer that *most correctly* answers it. Mark the space on your answer sheet that corresponds to the question number and the letter indicating your choice.

91. Firefighter Rigol is in the fire station's garage with the doors open when an elderly man stops to ask for help. The elderly man explains that he has locked his keys in the car, which is parked around the corner. He wants a firefighter to try to unlock his door for him so he's not late for a doctor's appointment. Firefighter Rigol should

    (A) explain that towing companies have the best tools to open the door without any damage and offer to call one for the man.

    (B) use a hammer and a chisel to break the man's car window so he can retrieve his keys and get to his appointment on time.

    (C) refuse to help the man and order him off the fire station's premises.

    (D) return to the car with the elderly man and try to get the door unlocked while causing as little damage as possible to the car.

> *Use the following information to answer questions 92–94.*

Firefighters use a variety of techniques to move victims to safety. If two firefighters are present when a victim is located, the seat lift/carry is a good technique to use. This carry is easy to perform and ensures the quick removal of a victim from potential harm. The following are steps for performing the seat lift/carry of an unconscious victim, in no particular order:

1. Each firefighter should place one arm across the victim's back.

2. Firefighters should carry the victim to safety.

3. Firefighters should stand at the same time, relying on their legs to lift the victim.

4. Each firefighter should place his or her free hand under the victim's legs.

5. Roll the victim onto his/her back and raise him/her into a seated position.

92. The seat lift/carry should be used only when

    (A) the victim is unconscious.

    (B) one or more firefighters are present.

    (C) at least two firefighters are present.

    (D) the victim is already in a seated position.

93. What is the first thing firefighters should do when conducting the seat lift/carry?

    (A) Each firefighter should place one arm across the victim's back.

    (B) Roll the victim onto his/her back and raise him/her into a seated position.

    (C) Firefighters should stand at the same time, relying on their legs to lift the victim.

    (D) Each firefighter should place his or her free hand under the victim's legs.

Go on to next page

94. Determine the correct order of the steps for performing the seat lift/carry of an unconscious victim.

    (A) 2, 3, 1, 4, 5

    (B) 5, 1, 4, 3, 2

    (C) 2, 4, 1, 3, 5

    (D) 5, 3, 2, 4, 1

95. While searching a house for victims, Firefighters Anderson and Michaels discover an unconscious, overweight male in a bed at the back of the house. Anderson has grabbed the victim's arms and started to drag him toward the front door when the two firefighters receive word that the roof is ready to collapse and they need to hurry. What should Firefighter Michaels do?

    (A) continue to search the house for additional victims

    (B) leave Anderson behind and head for the door

    (C) grab the victim's feet and help Anderson get him to safety

    (D) cover the furniture in the victim's room to prevent damage

For questions 96–99, choose the word that correctly completes the following analogies.

96. Flammable is to noncombustible as _____ is to destroy.

    (A) annihilate

    (B) consume

    (C) salvage

    (D) extend

97. Screwdriver is to screw as _____ is to nail.

    (A) hammer

    (B) board

    (C) roof

    (D) pound

98. Resolve is to determination as truthfulness is to

    (A) admiration.

    (B) generosity.

    (C) honesty.

    (D) corruption.

99. Extinguisher is to carbon dioxide as hydrant is to

    (A) street.

    (B) fire.

    (C) oxygen.

    (D) water.

100. Firefighters often perform inspections of buildings such as hospitals and schools. They are responsible for seeking out and reporting anything that defies fire safety regulations. While inspecting the first floor of a local hospital, firefighters discover a number of safety concerns. They are responsible for reporting all of the following EXCEPT

    (A) a fire extinguisher bearing an out-of-date inspection card.

    (B) a broken sprinkler head.

    (C) a mislabeled bag of medical waste.

    (D) an electrical wire protruding from an exposed outlet.

101. As Firefighter Jenkins secures the scene around a motor vehicle accident, she notices that Firefighter Lucas is struggling to pull a victim from the passenger side of a smashed car. The chief assigned Jenkins the duty of securing the scene, but she can tell that Lucas needs help and that the victim is in pain. What should she do?

    (A) She should help Lucas and then finish securing the scene.

    (B) She should finish securing the scene and ignore Lucas's predicament.

    (C) She should advise the chief that Lucas needs help and continue securing the scene.

    (D) She should finish securing the scene and then advise the chief that Lucas needs help.

Go on to next page

> *Use the following information to answer questions 102–103.*

According to the U.S. Department of Homeland Security, a hazmat suit is a "garment worn to protect people from hazardous materials or substances." Firefighters may have to don hazmat suits at incidents that involve chemical, nuclear, or biological agents or in the event that a fire reaches extreme temperatures that are too hot for typical turnout clothing. The United States classifies hazmat suits according to four levels, labeled A through D.

✔ **Level A:** This suit protects against gases, vapors, and mists. The suit covers every inch of the body. Inside the suit are a two-way radio and a breathing apparatus that feeds into an enclosed mask. Steel-toed boots and chemical-resistant gloves complete the suit.

✔ **Level B:** This suit protects against chemical spills and splashes. This suit fits more snugly than a Level A suit, especially around the wrists, ankles, neck, and waist to prevent chemicals from touching skin. A two-way radio and a breathing apparatus may be worn outside the suit. Steel-toed boots and chemical-resistant gloves complete the suit.

✔ **Level C:** This suit is similar to a Level B suit, but the breathing apparatus is much simpler. The respirator on this suit simply purifies the air the individual breathes. If a chemical has been identified and does not pose a respiratory risk, a Level C suit and respirator may be worn.

✔ **Level D:** This suit does not protect against chemicals, gases, or vapors.

102. Firefighters respond to a facility that produces industrial-grade cleaning agents. A machine malfunction has resulted in a chemical spill involving two agents that, when mixed together, produce a noxious vapor, which has caused a number of workers to feel ill. Which type of hazmat suit would you recommend for firefighters responding to this call?

 (A) a Level A suit

 (B) a Level B suit

 (C) a Level C suit

 (D) a Level D suit

103. Officials have confirmed that a white, powdery substance found at a postal facility is anthrax. The hazmat unit that responds to clean up the substance will most likely wear a

 (A) Level A suit.

 (B) Level B suit.

 (C) Level C suit.

 (D) Level D suit.

> *For questions 104–106, choose the number that correctly completes each sequence.*

104. 1, 4, 2, 8, 4, 16, _____, 32, 16, ...

 (A) 2

 (B) 4

 (C) 8

 (D) 12

105. 1, 1, 2, 6, 24, _____, 720, 5,040, ...

 (A) 72

 (B) 120

 (C) 320

 (D) 560

106. 0.00001, _____, 0.001, 0.01, 0.1, 1, 10, 100, ...

 (A) 0.00001

 (B) 0.0001

 (C) 0.001

 (D) 0.01

Go on to next page

Use the following information to answer question 107.

Firefighters may find it difficult to uncouple a hose, especially if one firefighter must complete the task on his or her own. He or she may need to use the knee-press method to uncouple the hose. This method requires strength, but it is quite simple to perform. The following steps will lead to the successful uncoupling of a fire hose:

1. Kneel by the hose coupling, and pick up the female part of the coupling.

2. Push the coupling forward so that the male end presses against the ground.

3. With knees spread apart for balance, press one knee where the hose meets the female coupling's shank.

4. In a counterclockwise direction, turn the swivel briskly while simultaneously applying body weight to loosen the connection.

107. Firefighter Rodriguez belongs to a small volunteer department. As a result, few volunteers responded to a small brush fire, and now Firefighter Rodriguez must uncouple a hose by himself. At this point, he has already pressed the male end of the coupling against the ground. What should he do next?

(A) Pick up the female part of the hose coupling.

(B) Turn the coupling in a counter-clockwise direction.

(C) Press one knee where the hose meets the female coupling's shank.

(D) Press one knee on either side of the hose coupling and pull the pieces apart.

108. Firefighters respond to a motor vehicle accident involving a single car. At the scene, they see that a small car has struck a fire hydrant. The fire hydrant is leaking heavily, filling the sidewalk, street, and a nearby lawn and driveway with rushing water. The driver of the car, who smells of alcohol, is seated across the street, where police officers are questioning him. What should the firefighters do first?

(A) They should secure the scene until a tow truck arrives.

(B) They should attempt to move the car.

(C) They should check on the driver of the car.

(D) They should attempt to divert the water and contact the water company.

Choose the image that correctly completes the sequence.

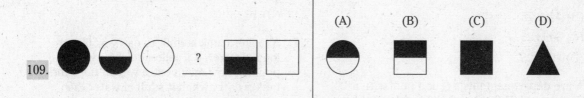

109.

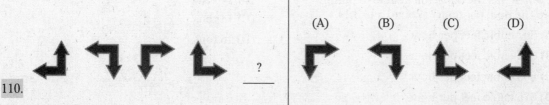

110.

Go on to next page

Part 6: Performing Mathematical Calculations

Directions: This section tests your mathematical skills. Read each question and choose the answer that *most correctly* answers it. You may use scratch paper to figure out the answers, but you may NOT use a calculator. Mark the space on your answer sheet that corresponds to the question number and the letter indicating your choice.

111. A rectangular portable water tank measures 6 feet long, 4 feet wide, and 5 feet deep. How many cubic feet of water will the tank hold if it's filled to capacity?

    (A) 4.8 cubic feet

    (B) 7.5 cubic feet

    (C) 24 cubic feet

    (D) 120 cubic feet

112. Convert the following fraction to a mixed number: $\frac{17}{5}$

    (A) $3\frac{2}{5}$

    (B) $2\frac{1}{3}$

    (C) $2\frac{1}{4}$

    (D) $4\frac{1}{5}$

113. A volunteer fire department sold foot-long hoagies for $5.00 a piece. The department sold a total of 387 hoagies, but a portion of their profits went toward purchasing the ingredients to make the hoagies. If the department earned $1,451.25 after expenses, how much did it spend on ingredients?

    (A) $387.75

    (B) $483.75

    (C) $493.25

    (D) $517.25

114. A fire department fills a round pool with a diameter of 24 feet to a height of 4 feet. It takes the department 3 hours to fill the pool. Approximately how many cubic feet of water was the department able to pump into the pool per hour? (Round π to 3.14.)

    (A) 507 cubic feet per hour

    (B) 567 cubic feet per hour

    (C) 603 cubic feet per hour

    (D) 675 cubic feet per hour

115. Firefighter Thomas places caution tape in a perfect square around an accident scene. If he uses 200 feet of tape, what is the total area of the accident scene?

    (A) 50 square feet

    (B) 100 square feet

    (C) 2,500 square feet

    (D) 10,000 square feet

116. $\frac{3}{4} - \frac{5}{8} =$

    (A) $\frac{1}{8}$

    (B) $\frac{8}{12}$

    (C) $\frac{2}{3}$

    (D) $\frac{1}{2}$

117. The ratio of males to females in the Lake City Fire Department is 4:1. If the department has 32 male members, how many female members does the department have?

    (A) 4

    (B) 8

    (C) 12

    (D) 16

118. A tanker trunk is built to carry 3,500 gallons of water. If 1 gallon of water weighs 8 pounds, how much extra weight does the tanker carry when it's full of water than when it's empty?

    (A) 10 tons

    (B) 12 tons

    (C) 14 tons

    (D) 16 tons

Go on to next page

119. What is $\frac{3}{5}$ written as a decimal?

    (A) 0.3

    (B) 0.6

    (C) 0.75

    (D) 0.8

120. A fire engine travels at an average speed of 35 miles per hour to a structure fire 7 miles away. How long will it take the fire engine to reach the fire?

    (A) 5 minutes

    (B) 7 minutes

    (C) 10 minutes

    (D) 12 minutes

121. An office building is 220 feet tall. Each story of the building is about 11 feet high. About how many stories does the building have?

    (A) 10

    (B) 11

    (C) 20

    (D) 22

122. Firefighter Gross is teaching a fire safety class and has fenced off a triangular area where children will learn to operate fire extinguishers. Using the image below, determine the size of the area Firefighter Gross has created for this exercise.

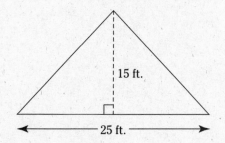

    (A) 40 square feet

    (B) 93.75 square feet

    (C) 187.5 square feet

    (D) 375 square feet

123. During its annual fund drive, the Leavenworth Volunteer Fire Department earned $15,000. Of this money, 75% was mailed to the fire department as part of a letter drive, 20% came from collection points in the city, and 5% came from contributions dropped off at the fire department. About how much money did the fire department earn just from collection points and contributions dropped off at the fire department?

    (A) $3,750

    (B) $4,125

    (C) $4,650

    (D) $5,175

124. Firefighter Shepard loaded 11 hoses of various lengths onto the fire apparatus. If he loaded a total of 975 feet of hose onto the apparatus, what was the average length of each hose?

    (A) 72.2 feet

    (B) 78.4 feet

    (C) 80.2 feet

    (D) 88.6 feet

125. Solve for the positive value of x in the following equation: $18 + 8x^2 = 50$.

    (A) $\frac{1}{2}$

    (B) $\frac{1}{4}$

    (C) 2

    (D) 4

126. When full, the tank on a tanker truck carries 1,500 gallons of water. If 1 cubic foot is equivalent to 7.5 gallons, what is the approximate volume of the tank in cubic feet?

    (A) 100 cubic feet

    (B) 200 cubic feet

    (C) 5,625 cubic feet

    (D) 11,250 cubic feet

Go on to next page

127. The equation used to calculate friction loss in a hose line is $FL = CQ^2L$. Given that the friction loss coefficient $(C) = 25$, the length of hose $(L) = 1.00$, and the total friction loss $(FL) = 1,500$, what is the approximate flow rate (Q)?

    (A) 6.3

    (B) 7.7

    (C) 8.3

    (D) 9.7

128. What is the volume of a cylindrical tank with a radius of 8 feet and a height of 15 feet? (Round π to 3.14.)

    (A) 201 cubic feet

    (B) 377 cubic feet

    (C) 3,014 cubic feet

    (D) 5,654 cubic feet

129. $\left(\dfrac{1}{2}\right)^2$

    (A) $\dfrac{1}{4}$

    (B) 1

    (C) $1\dfrac{1}{2}$

    (D) 2

130. A wildland firefighter is carrying a water tank, which he uses to put out small spot fires. The empty tank weighs about 2.5 pounds. It can carry 5 gallons of water. If 1 gallon of water weighs about 8 pounds, how much does the water tank weigh when it's full?

    (A) 40 pounds

    (B) 42.5 pounds

    (C) 44 pounds

    (D) 47.5 pounds

Go on to next page

Part 7: Mechanical Aptitude

Directions: This section tests your mechanical aptitude. Read each question and choose the answer that *most correctly* answers it. Mark the space on your answer sheet that corresponds to the question number and the letter indicating your choice.

Use the following image to answer questions 131–132.

131. If Gear 3 spins counterclockwise, which way do Gears 1 and 2 spin?

    (A) Gear 1 spins counterclockwise, and Gear 2 spins clockwise.

    (B) Gear 2 spins counterclockwise, and Gear 1 spins clockwise.

    (C) Both Gear 1 and Gear 2 spin counterclockwise.

    (D) Both Gear 1 and Gear 2 spin clockwise.

132. Which of the following statements about the gears is true?

    (A) Gear 1 makes more revolutions per minute than Gears 2 and 3.

    (B) Gear 2 makes more revolutions per minute than Gears 1 and 3.

    (C) Gear 3 makes more revolutions per minute than Gears 1 and 2.

    (D) Gears 1, 2, and 3 all make the same number of revolutions per minute.

133. A chain saw would most likely be used for

    (A) striking.

    (B) prying.

    (C) cutting.

    (D) turning.

134. An extension spring bearing a 10-pound weight has stretched 8 inches. Based on this information, how much would the extension spring stretch if it had a 15-pound weight attached to it instead?

    (A) 12 inches

    (B) 14 inches

    (C) 16 inches

    (D) 18 inches

Use the following image to answer question 135.

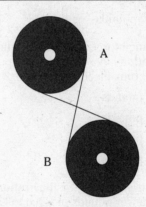

135. In the pulley setup shown in the illustration, Wheel A and Wheel B are connected by a crossed belt. If Wheel A spins clockwise, what does Wheel B do?

    (A) Wheel B spins clockwise.

    (B) Wheel B stops spinning.

    (C) Wheel B spins counterclockwise.

    (D) Wheel B spins half a revolution each way.

136. In a wheel-and-axle setup, when the axle turns, it moves

    (A) a greater distance than the wheel.

    (B) a lesser distance than the wheel.

    (C) the same distance as the wheel.

    (D) with less force than the wheel.

Go on to next page

Use the following image to answer questions 137–139.

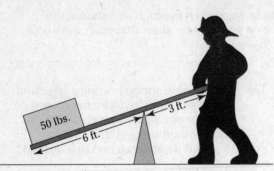

137. How much force must the firefighter in the illustration apply to the lever to lift the 50-pound box?

    (A) 25 pounds

    (B) 50 pounds

    (C) 75 pounds

    (D) 100 pounds

138. How much force would the firefighter in the illustration have to apply if he positioned the fulcrum 4 feet from the box?

    (A) 20 pounds

    (B) 30 pounds

    (C) 40 pounds

    (D) 50 pounds

139. If the firefighter in the illustration wants to apply fewer pounds of force to lift the 50-pound box, he should

    (A) increase the height of the fulcrum.

    (B) position the fulcrum at the center of the lever.

    (C) decrease the distance between the fulcrum and himself.

    (D) position the fulcrum closer to the box.

140. The main purpose of an inclined plane is to

    (A) spread work over a greater distance so it requires less force.

    (B) fasten two objects together and hold them in place.

    (C) gain a mechanical advantage when lifting heavy objects.

    (D) change the direction of an applied force.

Use the following image to answer question 141.

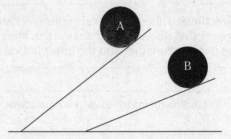

141. Ball A and Ball B are the same size and weight, and each is positioned on an inclined plane. Based on the illustration, what will most likely happen?

    (A) Ball A will roll faster than Ball B.

    (B) Ball B will roll faster than Ball A.

    (C) Ball A and Ball B will roll at the same speed.

    (D) Ball A will roll, but Ball B will not move.

Use the following image to answer questions 142–143.

142. In the pulley setup shown in the image, Wheel A is twice the size of Wheel B. If Wheel A makes 30 revolutions per minute, how many revolutions per minute does Wheel B make?

    (A) 10

    (B) 15

    (C) 40

    (D) 60

Go on to next page

143. Based on the pulley setup shown in the image, which of the following statements is correct?

    (A) Wheel A must spin clockwise, and Wheel B must spin counterclockwise.

    (B) Wheel A and Wheel B must spin in the same direction.

    (C) Wheel A must spin counterclockwise, and Wheel B must spin clockwise.

    (D) Wheel A must make more revolutions per minute than Wheel B.

144. Look at the tool shown below. This tool would most likely be used to

    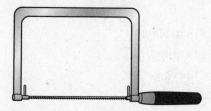

    (A) pull down a ceiling.

    (B) make precise cuts in wood.

    (C) pry open the door of a vehicle.

    (D) cut down a large tree.

145. Look at the tool shown below. This tool would most likely be used to

    (A) cut through a wire.

    (B) tighten a hose coupling.

    (C) split a log in half.

    (D) remove a nail.

146. Look at the tool shown below. What is the name of this tool?

    (A) an extinguisher

    (B) a drill

    (C) an oil can

    (D) a blowtorch

147. Which of the following tools would you use to cut through a wooden board?

    (A)

    (B)

    (C)

    (D)

Go on to next page

148. Which of the following tools would you use to cut through a heavy chain?

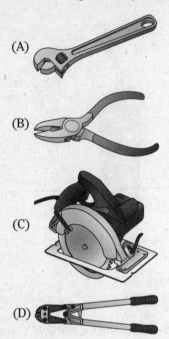

(A)

(B)

(C)

(D)

149. Look at the tool shown below. During forcible entry operations, this tool would most likely be used for

(A) striking.

(B) prying.

(C) pulling.

(D) cutting.

150. Look at the tool shown below. During forcible entry operations, this tool would most likely be used for

(A) pushing.

(B) cutting.

(C) prying.

(D) striking.

Chapter 18

Practice Exam 2: Answers and Explanations

• •

*I*f you've finished Practice Exam 2 (Chapter 17), you're probably curious to see how you did in comparison to your first practice exam. Use the answers and explanations in this chapter to see how well you performed and to get info on answering any problems you missed. Remember, the practice exam can help you determine where you need to focus your studies for the real written firefighter exam. If you want to score your test quickly, flip to the end of the chapter, where the "Answer Key" section gives only the letters of the correct answers.

Part 1: Reading Comprehension

1. **C.** The first paragraph states that firefighters get at least 24 hours between shifts.

2. **C.** In the second paragraph, the author states that the fire station becomes a home away from home for firefighters and that the men and women in a fire department are not only coworkers but also roommates, who "often grow as close as, if not closer than, family."

3. **D.** The last two sentences of the passage explain how firefighters build trust and explains that this trust is crucial because firefighters must depend on each other during emergencies. Therefore, you can conclude that the author values trustworthiness in fellow firefighters.

4. **A.** The best title for the passage is "Firefighting: A Way of Life." The passage begins by explaining the unique lifestyle created by the shifts that firefighters work and continues to describe the everyday lives of firefighters. The passage doesn't contain rules and regulations, so you can eliminate Choices (B) and (C). The passage doesn't discuss the dangers of firefighting, so you can cross off Choice (D), too. Choice (A) is correct.

5. **B.** This question asks you to draw a conclusion based on what you read. The passage states that proximity suits are similar to normal turnout, or bunker, gear and describes them as "metallic in color." The passage also states that proximity suits are used when fighting aircraft fires. Therefore, a firefighter wearing what looks like silver (metallic) bunker gear is likely preparing to fight an aircraft fire. Choice (B) is correct.

6. **D.** The passage states that a Level A hazmat suit has a breathing apparatus inside the suit. A Level B hazmat suit has a breathing apparatus outside the suit. A Level C suit includes a respirator that purifies the air. A Level D suit is the only one that doesn't include a type of breathing apparatus.

7. **B.** This question asks you to draw a conclusion based on what you read. The question describes a scenario that involves a chemical spill. According to the passage, a Level B hazmat suit protects against chemical splashes, so Choice (B) is correct. A proximity suit, Choice (C), might be worn if the chemicals were on fire, but the question doesn't say that the chemicals are burning.

8. **A.** The main idea of a passage is what the entire passage is about. This passage describes a variety of protective clothing that firefighters wear — traditional turnout gear, proximity suits, hazmat suits, and wildland firefighting gear. Therefore, the sentence "Although

firefighters wear turnout clothing on most calls, certain events warrant the wearing of different types of suits," best captures the main idea of the passage. Choice (A) is correct.

9. **C.** This is a simple details question. Three of these details are mentioned in the passage and one isn't. The last paragraph describes what's worn during a wildland fire: a fire-resistant Nomex uniform, boots, a hard hat, and gloves. A respirator isn't worn during a wildland fire.

10. **B.** The first paragraph describes the three essential layers of turnout gear: an outer shell, a moisture barrier, and a thermal barrier. Therefore, Choice (B) is correct. An aluminized barrier isn't one of the layers of turnout gear.

11. **C.** In the third paragraph, you find a description of a Level A hazmat suit. According to the passage, these suits fit loosely, and they have an internal breathing apparatus and a two-way radio.

12. **C.** According to the table, the two types of hoses that aren't reinforced are impregnated single-jacket hose and woven-jacket hose. Therefore, you can conclude that a 2-inch woven-jacket hose is the only listed hose that isn't reinforced. Choice (C) is correct.

13. **D.** Only booster hose matches the description in the question. The size of the hose, 1 inch, narrows the correct answer to either Choice (C) or Choice (D). The info about the reinforcement and the outer covering eliminates Choice (C). Choice (D) is correct.

14. **A.** According to the table, woven-jacket hose has a rubber lining.

15. **D.** According to the table, flexible noncollapsible intake hose and noncollapsible intake hose have the same size range, the same outer covering, and the same lining. However, flexible noncollapsible intake hose is fabric and plastic–reinforced, whereas noncollapsible intake hose is fabric and wire–reinforced. Therefore, Choice (D) is correct.

16. **D.** According to the passage, a firefighter wearing a black helmet with a green shield is part of a hazardous materials or marine unit, which makes Choice (D) a true statement. A white helmet with a red shield would represent the commanding officer of a ladder company, so Choice (A) is incorrect. A firefighter wearing an all-black helmet is part of an engine company, so Choice (B) is incorrect. An orange shield represents a probationary firefighter, so it's unlikely that a commanding officer would have an orange shield, so you can eliminate Choice (C), too.

17. **B.** The first sentence of the third paragraph states, "Unfortunately, not all departments use the same color-coding system to identify firefighter or company functions." Therefore, Choice (B) is correct. The fact that different departments use different color codes is a drawback.

18. **C.** In the scenario described in the question, the victim in the apartment building window would likely need to be rescued with a ladder truck. Therefore, the firefighter with the yellow shield (a squad company member) should look for a firefighter with a red shield on his helmet (a ladder company member). Choice (C) is correct.

19. **A.** The first paragraph states, "If firefighters need immediate assistance with something, they need to be able to find someone who knows how to help them as quickly as possible. For this reason, many fire departments across the United States color-code their helmets." Choice (A) is correct. Departments color-code helmets so firefighters can quickly find someone who can help them.

20. **C.** A marine unit would likely be involved in a river rescue, and according to the passage, firefighters in marine units wear black helmets with green shields on them.

21. **B.** This question asks you to identify the best title for the passage, which is similar to asking about the main idea. In this passage, the author describes several specific methods that firefighters use to create ventilation openings that allow heat and smoke to escape from fires. Therefore, Choice (B), "Ventilation Tactics," is the best title for the passage.

22. **C.** According to the passage, using a hose stream to force smoke and heat out a ventilation opening, such as a window or a door, is called *hydraulic ventilation.* Another clue is the word *hydraulic* itself. Words that include the root word *hydr-*, such as *hydroelectric* or *hydrant*, usually have something to do with water. Choice (C) is the best answer.

23. **A.** The first sentence of the passage states that when a fire produces a lot of heat or smoke, firefighters create openings that allow the heat or smoke to escape. The paragraph goes on to explain that firefighters create vents by opening windows or doors or by creating their own ventilation openings. Choice (A) is correct.

24. **D.** The fourth paragraph explains that auto- or self-ventilation occurs when a fire in an enclosed room produces so much heat and smoke that the room can no longer contain it. When this occurs, the fire may burn a hole in the ceiling or roof or cause windows to shatter. Choice (D) describes a scenario in which self-ventilation occurs.

25. **C.** To answer this question, you have to draw a conclusion based on the information provided in the passage. Hydraulic ventilation is often used when firefighters want to protect property, so this form of ventilation is probably the least destructive; therefore, you can eliminate Choice (A). Self-ventilation and creating a ventilation hole by cutting a hole in the ceiling both result in structural damage, so Choice (B) is incorrect. The author doesn't explain how effective opening a window or door or self-ventilation is, so you can eliminate Choice (D), too.

26. **D.** In the second paragraph, the author lists tools used during salvage operations, including floor runners, squeegees, and water vacuums. The author does not mention hoses, so Choice (D) is correct.

27. **A.** The purpose of salvage operations, as explained in the first paragraph, is to make sure that property owners do no lose their most valued possessions. Therefore, Choice (A), "protect property owners' possessions from damage," is the best answer.

28. **B.** This question is about a detail in the passage, which can be found in the third paragraph: "Then they wrap the entire pile with large salvage tarps to protect the property from water damage."

29. **D.** This question asks you to make an inference by combining your knowledge with information from the passage. According to the passage, firefighters use salvage covers to protect furniture from water damage, so Choice (A) is incorrect. Fire departments are not responsible for finding shelter for fire victims, nor would they completely replace the roof of a burned home, so you can eliminate Choices (B) and (C). However, firefighters may use roofing materials to temporarily patch a hole in the roof caused by the fire. Choice (D) is the best answer.

30. **A.** The passage mentions that fire can spread through walls, so you can conclude that the purpose of moving furniture to the middle of a room, and therefore away from the walls, is to keep it away from walls through which fire could spread. Choice (A) is the best answer. Choice (B) may seem like a good answer, but moving the furniture to the middle of the room wouldn't necessarily protect it from water damage. Tarps accomplish this task.

Part 2: Verbal Expression

31. **C.** The correct spelling is *access*. *Access* and *excess* are commonly confused words, but *access* means "to get at," and *excess* means "extra."

32. **D.** The correct spelling is *defibrillator*.

33. **B.** The correct spelling is *aerial*.

34. **C.** The correct spelling is *all-terrain*.

35. **A.** The correct spelling is *analysis*. Choice (D), *analyses,* is the plural of *analysis,* but you need the singular spelling in this sentence.

36. **B.** The correct spelling is *steering*.

37. **B.** This sentence needs a possessive adjective to be correct. The words *there, their,* and *they're* all sound the same, but only *their* is a possessive adjective, so Choice (B) is correct. *There* is an adverb used to point out location, *they're* is the contraction of *they are*, and *they* is a subject pronoun.

38. **B.** The verb form that correctly completes the sentence is *will visit*. The phrase "Next week" suggests that the action will take place in the future, and *will visit* is a future-tense verb. The other choices do not fit within the context of the sentence.

39. **C.** The verb form that correctly completes the sentence is *responded*. The phrase "Two hours ago" suggests that the action took place at a specific time in the past, and *responded* is a simple past-tense verb. Choice (C) is correct. Choice (D), *had responded*, is also a past-tense form — past perfect. However, past perfect tense is typically used to describe actions that happened *before* or *up to* a certain time in the past.

40. **D.** Though the executive board of the department may include several people, as a unit, *executive board* is a singular noun. For the sentence to be in agreement, it needs a singular possessive adjective. *Its* is a singular possessive adjective, so Choice (D) is correct.

41. **B.** The correct sentence reads, "Sometimes firefighters are the first to encounter an injured victim at an emergency scene; therefore, they are trained as both EMTs and paramedics." The original sentence contains two independent clauses separated by the conjunction *and*. For that version of the sentence to be correct, it would need a comma before the conjunction. With a semicolon, each independent clause stands on its own, and the transition word *therefore* establishes a cause and effect relationship between the two clauses.

42. **D.** The correct sentence says, "When firefighters respond to an emergency, they typically use active visual and audible warnings, such as lights and sirens, to warn other drivers." The original sentence repeats the word *firefighters,* which isn't grammatically incorrect, but replacing the second instance of the word with a pronoun avoids repetition, making the sentence less awkward and easier to read. Choice (D) is correct.

43. **C.** The correct sentence reads, "If fuel oil, gasoline, or jet fuel is on fire, firefighters should consider attacking the flames with foam rather than with water." In the original sentence, each element of the compound subject was separated with the conjunction *or*. The comma between elements eliminates extra words. Choice (C) is correct.

44. **B.** *Carefully* means *cautiously*. Firefighter Jeffries cautiously opens the cylinder valve to check the alarm on his self-contained breathing apparatus.

45. **A.** *Obstinacy* means *stubbornness*. A stubborn firefighter may be reprimanded for failing to take orders or see another's perspective.

46. **C.** *Colloquial* means *conversational*. The phrase "easy to talk to" suggests that Chief Duncan is someone who is very conversational.

47. **D.** *Incorporated* means *integrated*. Both *incorporated* and *integrated* mean *fit in*. Station 82 managed to fit a mandatory breakfast hour into the schedule.

48. **C.** *Wary* best completes this sentence. *Wary* means *distrustful,* and firefighters should certainly be distrustful of weakened floors or ceilings.

49. **A.** *Accurate* best completes this sentence. *Accurate* means *exact* or *correct*. Firefighters would certainly want a helicopter to hit the exact area that's on fire.

50. **B.** *Justify* is the best word choice. When you justify something, you give good reasons for it. The positive results that smoke jumpers get from their activities are good reasons for them to continue their risky work.

Part 3: Observation and Memory

51. **D.** The picture shows eight cars. The accident involves two cars. One car is traveling east on the one-way portion of First Street, and other car is traveling west on the two-way portion of First Street. Two cars are traveling south, and a third southbound car has pulled off the road. One car is traveling north. Choice (D) is the correct answer.

52. **B.** Only one car is traveling west. It's located to the far right of the picture. It appears to be traveling west on the two-way portion of First Street.

53. **B.** A total of seven people are visible in the picture, but only four people are in the cars involved in the accident. The eastbound car has one person in the back seat and another person who appears to have been thrown through the windshield. The southbound car appears to have one driver and one passenger in the front seat. Choice (B) is correct.

54. **C.** It appears to be snowy and icy in the picture. Snow is falling from the sky, snow banks are piled high along the road, and some snow has piled up on the branches of a tree. The road looks shiny, which suggests that it could be icy and slippery.

55. **C.** A total of seven people are visible in the picture, but only two have gotten out of their cars. One appears to have gotten out of the westbound car on First Street, and the other appears to have gotten out of the southbound car that has pulled off the road.

56. **C.** First Street runs from west to east. A one-way sign appears on First Street, to the west of the road that runs north to south. However, there is no one-way sign on First Street, to the east of the road that runs north to south. In addition, a car appears to be traveling west on First Street, and double (yellow) lines on that part of the road indicate two-way traffic. These clues suggest that First Street becomes a two-way street east of the road that runs north to south.

57. **A.** No electrical wires appear in the picture, so you can eliminate Choice (C). You can also eliminate Choice (D) because none of the cars near the scene of the accident are traveling north. The eastbound car appears to be smoking, but the southbound car is not on fire, so Choice (B) is incorrect. The best answer is Choice (A). One of the cars appears to be leaking some type of fluid.

58. **C.** The eastbound car holds two victims. One is in the back seat. The other appears to have been thrown through the windshield.

59. **D.** In the picture, cars traveling south have to stop at a stop sign. Cars traveling east do not have a stop sign. It's snowing outside, and the road looks like it could be icy. It appears that the southbound car may have slid through the stop sign into the intersection, where the eastbound car crashed into its side, pushing it into the northbound lane.

60. **B.** The accident has four victims. The victim who needs the most help is the one in the eastbound car, who appears to have gone through the windshield of the car. Because this person is (or was) in the front seat, you can assume that he or she was the driver of the car.

61. **A.** The first paragraph of the passage states that spraying water on a fire involving flammable liquids can cause the burning liquid to disperse, thereby spreading the flames.

62. **C.** Crude oil, jet fuel, and kerosene are all flammable liquids, according to the third paragraph of the passage, so you can eliminate Choices (A), (B), and (D). Only Choice (C), oxygen, is not a flammable liquid. Oxygen is usually a gas.

63. **C.** The passage explains that when a flammable liquid fire occurs near an elevated area, such as a wall or a sidewalk, firefighters use the bank-down method to extinguish the fire. With this method, they spray the foam on the elevated area, and it eventually spills over the side and gently lands on the pool of burning liquid. Because a curb and a sidewalk are similar, you can assume that firefighters would use the bank-down method in the scenario described in the question.

64. **D.** According to the passage, when firefighters use the roll-on method, they place the hose at the edge of the pool of burning liquid and allow the foam to slowly roll backward onto the fire. Choice (D) is the best description of the roll-on method.

65. **A.** According to the passage, polar solvents include alcohols, ketones, esters, acids, and acetone, so Choice (A) is correct. Benzene, gasoline, and fuel oil are not polar solvents.

66. **D.** The elements necessary for a fire to ignite and continue to burn are heat, fuel, and oxygen, so you can eliminate Choices (A), (B), and (C). Smoke is a byproduct of combustion, so Choice (D) is the correct answer.

67. **C.** The passage describes three methods for applying foam to fires involving flammable liquids: the roll-on, bank-down, and rain-down methods.

68. **D.** According to the passage, when the foam dissipates, it leaves behind water, which extinguishes any remaining embers. Choice (D) is correct.

69. **A.** The second-to-last paragraph explains that the rain-down method is a good way to apply foam to large fires. Choice (A) is the best answer.

70. **B.** Choices (A), (C), and (D) all describe actions that may or may not be used when applying foam to fires, depending on which application method firefighters use. However, the passage warns against shooting foam directly into a liquid-fueled fire, so Choice (B) is the correct answer.

Part 4: Spatial Orientation

71. **B.** You can eliminate Choices (A) and (C) because they require you travel the wrong way on Pine. Choice (D) requires a few extra turns than Choice (B), so Choice (B) is the most direct route to the deli.

72. **A.** The fire engine begins at the corner of Pine and First, facing east. Traveling two blocks east and turning left puts the fire engine on Main. Traveling north one block and turning left puts the fire engine on West Oak. Traveling southwest one block and turning right puts the engine on Third. Traveling north one block puts the engine at the corner of Third and Stanton, right near the hardware store. Choice (A) is correct.

73. **D.** Because of the special restrictions on West Oak, the fire engine cannot travel part of that street to get to Point 1. Therefore, the fastest route is to turn north on main, west on Stanton, south on Third, southwest on West Oak (the open part), and west on Oak. Choice (D) is the best answer.

74. **B.** The six houses are the only landmarks of note that border Willow, which narrows down the answer choices. After you home in on that area, you just have to double-check the other street names to make sure you're looking at the right spot.

75. **A.** Point 3 is closest to some apartments, but that's not an answer choice. Of the answer choices listed, Point 3 is closest to the hardware store.

76. **D.** The kitchen shares walls with the living room and the dining room, which means those two rooms are immediately exposed to the fire. Choice (D) is the best answer.

77. **B.** If the fire is in the kitchen and the dining room, the occupants of the living room should try to avoid those rooms when exiting the house. Choices (A), (C), and (D) all have the occupants of the living room passing through the burning rooms, so you can eliminate all three of them as correct answers.

78. **C.** You can eliminate Choice (D) immediately, because the curtains in the study are on fire, so passing through that window would be incredibly dangerous. Because the fire has spread to the hall, the door to bedroom 3 is likely blocked, which means that the occupants of bedroom 3 cannot reach the home's northern or southern doors, so you can eliminate Choices (A) and (B) as well. Choice (C) is the safest way to exit the house from bedroom 3.

79. **A.** Firefighter Swanson will encounter the following on her journey down the hall and back to the southern door: the door to bedroom 1, the door to the bathroom, the door to bedroom 2, the door to bedroom 3, the northern door, the northern window, the door to the study, the opening to the dining room, the opening to the living room, and the southern window. That makes 6 doors, 2 windows, and 2 openings, so Choice (A) is correct.

80. **A.** The southern side of the house has a big picture window to the left. To the right is a small window, a door, and another small window. In the answer choices, only Choice (A) has a big picture window to the left and a small window, a door, and another small window to the right.

81. **B.** The most direct route to Point 2 is to make a right on Sterling, a right on Fifth, a right on Joseph, a left on Sixth, and a left on River, so Choice (B) is the correct answer. Choices (A) and (C) would take the firefighters away from the fire at first. Choice (D) would require the firefighters to travel the wrong way on Fourth.

82. **D.** Trace the route. From Seventh, the firefighters turn right and travel west three blocks, which puts them at the corner of Joseph and Second. Turning right and traveling one block north puts them at the corner of Second and River. Turning right and traveling three blocks east puts them at the corner of River and Seventh. Turning right and traveling one block south puts them at Seventh and Joseph. Making a left followed by the next right puts them on Maple. Traveling south one block puts them at the corner of Maple and Sterling.

83. **B.** The convenience store is northwest of the school, southwest of the auto parts store, west of the church, and east of the drug store. Choice (B) is correct.

84. **A.** According to the key, apartment buildings are represented by rectangles. Three apartment buildings are located on Joseph: one near the bar on the corner of Joseph and Second, one at the corner of Joseph and Sixth, and one at the corner of Joseph and Seventh.

85. **C.** You can eliminate Choices (A), (B), and (D) because all three of these routes would take the engine away from the day care before taking them toward it.

86. **D.** Exposures are other rooms or structures that are in danger of igniting because of their proximity to the fire. In this case, a fire at the bar would place the southern wall of the hair salon and the eastern wall of the apartment building on Joseph in the most danger. These two walls face the burning building. Therefore, Choice (D) is correct.

87. **A.** Trace the route. If the engine leaves the station and travels south on Seventh, the first right is Joseph. Three blocks to the west and a right turn puts the engine on Second. One block north and a right turn will put the engine on River. Two blocks east and a left turn will put the engine on Sixth, to the east of the wooded area near Point 2.

88. **C.** Trace the route. Then count the number of houses, which are represented as small squares. Along this route, the fire engine passes 10 houses. The engine doesn't pass any houses until it gets to Sixth. On Sixth, it passes two houses. On River, it passes seven houses (four on the north side of River and three on the south side of River). On Seventh, the engine passes one more house on the corner of River and Seventh.

89. **B.** You can eliminate Choice (A) because it would take the driver directly through the blocked intersection. You can eliminate Choices (C) and (D) because they would require the driver to drive the wrong way on one-way streets. Choice (B) is the best answer.

90. **C.** The southwestern corner of the map features a day care, a baseball field, and a pizza parlor. The southeastern corner features a basketball court, a playground, and a school. It seems likely that these two areas would have a high concentration of children.

Part 5: Reasoning and Judgment

91. **A.** To answer this question, you must use your best judgment based on what you know. Firefighter Rigol does not know the elderly man. He has no way to know that the car in question even belongs to the elderly man. Therefore, you can eliminate Choices (B) and (D). Because Firefighter Rigol can't be certain of the man's intentions, he should know that breaking into the car is a poor idea. Ordering the man off the premises if he truly needs help is rather harsh, so you can eliminate Choice (C), too. Choice (A) is the best answer.

92. **C.** The passage specifically states that if two firefighters are present, they can use the seat lift/carry to move the victim to safety, so Choice (C) is the best answer. The passage

specifically mentions moving an unconscious victim, but it doesn't specify that you can use the seat lift/carry *only* when the victim is unconscious, so you can eliminate Choice (A). You can't do the seat lift/carry with only one person, so Choice (B) is incorrect. The victim doesn't have to be already seated to perform the seat lift/carry — you can raise the victim to a seated position — so Choice (D) is also incorrect.

93. **B.** Though you may not be familiar with the seat lift/carry, you can still determine the correct order of steps to perform the lift based on the information provided. You can't place your "free hand" under the victim's legs until your other arm is across the victim's back, so you know that Choice (D) comes after Choice (A). You can't lift the victim until you have your hands and arms in the correct positions, so you know that Choice (C) comes after Choices (A) and (D). Finally, you can't put your arms and hands in the right position until the victim has been placed in a seated position, so you know that Choice (B) comes before Choices (A) and (D).

94. **B.** The correct order in which to help the victims would be 5, 1, 4, 3, 2. You should first roll the victim onto his/her back and raise him/her to a seated position. Next, each firefighter should place an arm across the victim's back and then place his or her free hand under the victim's legs. The firefighters should then lift the victim at the same time and move the victim to safety. You should eliminate Choices (A) and (C) immediately, because it doesn't make sense to carry the victim to safety until you've correctly position the victim for carrying.

95. **C.** Firefighters' first responsibility at a fire scene is to protect life and then to protect property. You can eliminate Choice (B) because leaving Anderson and the victim behind would not protect life. You can also eliminate Choice (C) because protecting property is not the priority in this situation — protecting life is. Choice (A), searching the house for other victims, is a possibility, but with direct orders to hurry, it's probably best for Michaels to grab the victim's feet and help Anderson get him to safety. This will get the victim, as well as Anderson and Michaels, to safety as quickly as possible, thereby protecting three lives. Choice (C) is the best answer.

96. **C.** Using logic, you can determine how these two sets of words are related. *Flammable* and *noncombustible* are antonyms, which are words with opposite meanings. *Salvage* is an antonym of *destroy*. Choice (C) is correct.

97. **A.** A screwdriver is the tool used to put a screw in place. Similarly, a hammer is the tool used to put a nail in place, so Choice (A) is correct.

98. **C.** *Resolve* is a synonym, or a word with a similar meaning, of *determination*. *Truthfulness* is a synonym of *honesty,* so Choice (C) is correct.

99. **D.** A fire extinguisher can expel carbon dioxide to put out fires. A fire hydrant expels water to put out fires, so Choice (D) is correct.

100. **C.** Firefighters would be responsible for reporting fire-related hazards. An out-of-date extinguisher, a broken sprinkler head, and an electrical wire protruding from an exposed outlet all have the potential to cause fires, so you can eliminate Choices (A), (B), and (D). The mislabeled bag of medical waste, although a potential health hazard, is not firefighters' responsibility to report.

101. **C.** At an emergency scene, firefighters have to follow superior officers' orders and work in a coordinated effort with others to ensure that everyone remains safe. They also have a responsibility to protect life. Therefore, if Jenkins believes that Lucas needs immediate assistance, she should alert the chief that Lucas needs help while continuing to secure the scene. Choice (C) is correct. It will be up to the chief whether to allow Jenkins to stop securing the scene to assist Lucas or get another firefighter to help Lucas.

102. **A.** According to the scenario in the question, the chemical mixture is giving off a noxious vapor that has made workers feel ill. According to the passage, the only suit that protects against vapors is a Level A hazmat suit. Therefore, you can safely recommend that firefighters responding to this call should wear Level A hazmat suits. Choice (A) is correct.

103. **C.** According to the passage, if an identified substance doesn't pose a respiratory risk, firefighters can usually wear a Level C suit with a respirator that purifies the air. A Level A suit,

Choice (A), would be required only if the chemical gave off a gas, vapor, or mist, but the question describes the substance as a white powder. A Level B suit, Choice (B), is designed to protect against chemical spills and splashes, so it wouldn't be necessary when dealing with anthrax powder. A Level D suit, Choice (D), offers no breathing protection, so this type of suit wouldn't be recommended when dealing with anthrax, which can be dangerous if you breathe in a lot of it. Choice (C) is the best answer. Firefighters can wear a Level C suit with an air-purifying respirator, which will offer enough protection against anthrax spores.

104. **C.** To answer this question, you must use logic to determine the number sequence. In this sequence, numbers are alternately multiplied by 4 and divided by 2: $1 \times 4 = 4$, and $4 \div 2 = 2$; $2 \times 4 = 8$, and $8 \div 2 = 4$; $4 \times 4 = 16$, and $16 \div 2 = 8$; $8 \times 4 = 32$, and $32 \div 2 = 16$. Therefore, 8 is the missing number.

105. **B.** Determine the number sequence. In this sequence, each number is multiplied by a number that is 1 greater than the last multiplier: $1 \times 1 = 1$; $1 \times 2 = 2$; $2 \times 3 = 6$; $6 \times 4 = 24$; $24 \times 5 = 120$; $120 \times 6 = 720$; $720 \times 7 = 5,040$. Therefore, 120 is the missing number.

106. **B.** Determine the number sequence. In this sequence, each number is multiplied by 10, which is why the decimal point keeps moving one place to the right in the numbers before 1 and why an additional 0 is added to each number after 1. Choice (B) is correct.

107. **C.** To answer this question, you must review the correct order of the steps listed in the passage. According to the passage, after the male end of the hose coupling has been pressed into the ground, you should press one knee where the hose meets the female coupling's shank.

108. **D.** Firefighters' first responsibility is to protect life and then to protect property. Because the police are with the driver of the car, firefighters can focus on protecting property. In this scenario, that means trying to divert the water so that it stops pouring water onto a nearby lawn and driveway until the water company can arrive to replace or repair the hydrant. Choice (D) is the best answer.

109. **C.** To answer this question, use logic to determine the pattern. In the first part of the pattern, the circles are fully shaded, half-shaded on the bottom, and not shaded. If this pattern holds true for the squares, then the next part of the pattern should include squares that are fully shaded, half-shaded on the bottom, and not shaded. Because the last two squares are half-shaded on the bottom and not shaded, you can conclude that the missing shape is a fully shaded square.

110. **D.** Determine the pattern. If you look carefully at this pattern, you notice that the L-shaped arrows consistently make a quarter turn (90 degrees) counterclockwise. If this pattern holds true and the last image of the L-shaped arrows turns 90 degrees counterclockwise, the arrows will point up and to the left, just like the first image in the pattern.

Part 6: Performing Mathematical Calculations

111. **D.** A cubic foot is a unit of measurement that indicates volume. A rectangular portable water tank looks like a box, and to find the volume of a box, you have to multiply length, width, and height: $6 \times 4 \times 5 = 120$. The portable water tank can hold 120 cubic feet of water.

112. **A.** To convert an improper fraction into a mixed number, you have to divide the numerator (top number) by the denominator (bottom number) and place the remainder (if there is one) over the denominator. In this case, divide 17 by 5:

$$\begin{array}{r} 3 \\ 5\overline{)17} \\ \underline{-15} \\ 2 \end{array}$$

$$3\frac{2}{5}$$

113. **B.** To solve this equation, multiply the cost of one hoagie ($5) by the number of hoagies sold (387) to see how much money the fire department made: $5 × 387 = $1,935. Then subtract the amount the fire department made after expenses ($1,451.25) from the total amount they earned ($1,935.00) to find the amount they spent on ingredients: $1,935.00 − $1,451.25 = $483.75. The department spent $483.75 on ingredients.

114. **C.** To find the answer to this question, first solve for volume to determine how many cubic feet of water were pumped into the pool (remember that if the diameter of the pool is 24 feet, the radius is only 12 feet):

$$V = \pi r^2 h$$
$$V = \pi (12^2)4$$
$$V = \pi (144)(4)$$
$$V \approx (3.14)(576)$$
$$V \approx 1{,}808.64$$

Now divide the result by 3 (the number of hours it took to fill the pool) to determine how many cubic feet of water the department pumped into the pool per hour: 1,808.64 ÷ 3 = 602.88. The department pumped about 603 cubic feet of water into the pool each hour.

115. **C.** Because a square has four equal sides and Firefighter Thomas used 200 feet of caution tape to create the perimeter of the square, you can conclude that each side of the square is 50 feet long (200 ÷ 4 = 50). To determine the area, multiply length by width: 50 × 50 = 2,500. Therefore, the area of the accident scene is 2,500 square feet.

116. **A.** To add or subtract fractions, you must find the least common denominator. The least common denominator for 4 and 8 is 8. Convert the fractions and then subtract:

$$\frac{3}{4} - \frac{5}{8} = \frac{6}{8} - \frac{5}{8} = \frac{1}{8}$$

117. **B.** The ratio of males to females is 4:1. You know that 32 males are in the class, so you need to determine the number of females that would create a 4:1 ratio between males and females. Because the number of males is 4 times the number of females, divide the number of males by 4: 32 ÷ 4 = 8. The ratio 32:8 is equal to 4:1, so Choice (B), 8, is the correct answer.

118. **C.** Be careful with this problem. It provides the weight of 1 gallon of water in pounds, but it wants to know the weight of 3,500 gallons of water in tons. Remember, 1 ton is 2,000 pounds. To answer the question, multiply to find the total weight of the water in pounds: 3,500 × 8 = 28,000. Then divide by 2,000 to get the answer in tons: 28,000 ÷ 2,000 = 14. Therefore, 3,500 gallons of water adds 14 tons of extra weight to the tanker.

119. **B.** To convert a fraction to a decimal, divide the numerator (the top number) by the denominator (the bottom number). In this case, divide 3 by 5. The result is 0.6.

120. **D.** To solve for time, let *r* = rate of speed, *d* = distance, and *t* = time. Solve for *t*:

$$d = rt$$
$$7 = 35t$$
$$\frac{7}{35} = \frac{35t}{35}$$
$$\frac{1}{5} = t$$

It will take the engine $\frac{1}{5}$ of an hour, or 12 minutes (60 minutes ÷ 5), to reach the structure.

121. **C.** If the building is 220 feet tall and each story is 11 feet high, you can determine the number of stories by dividing the overall height by the height of each story: 220 ÷ 11 = 20. The building has 20 stories, so Choice (C) is correct.

122. **C.** From the image, you know that the base of the triangle is 25 feet and the height is 15 feet. To answer the question, use the formula to find the area of a triangle:

$$A = \frac{1}{2}bh$$
$$A = \frac{1}{2}(25)(15)$$
$$A = 187.5$$

The area of the triangle is 187.5 square feet. Choice (C) is correct.

123. **A.** To find the answer to this question, add 20% (the percentage collected at points around the city) to 5% (the percentage dropped off at the fire department): 20% + 5% = 25%. Therefore, 25% of the money collected came from these two sources. Now multiply $15,000 (the total collected) by 0.25: 15,000 × 0.25 = 3,750. The fire department collected $3,750 from these two sources. Choice (A) is correct.

124. **D.** To find the average length of each hose, simply divide the total length (975 feet) by the number of hoses (11): 975 ÷ 11 ≈ 88.6. Each hose was about 88.6 feet long.

125. **C.** Solve the problem for x:

$$18 + 8x^2 = 50$$
$$8x^2 = 32$$
$$\frac{8x^2}{8} = \frac{32}{8}$$
$$x^2 = 4$$
$$\sqrt{x^2} = \sqrt{4}$$
$$x = 2 \text{ or } -2$$

The correct answer is 2, so Choice (C) is correct.

126. **B.** To find the cubic footage of the tank, divide the total number of gallons (1,500) by the number of gallons equivalent to 1 cubic foot (7.5): 1,500 ÷ 7.5 = 200. The tank is 200 cubic feet.

127. **B.** To answer this question, use the formula provided. Fill in the known variables and solve for Q, the unknown:

$$FL = CQ^2L$$
$$1,500 = (25)(Q^2)(1)$$
$$\frac{1,500}{25} = \frac{25Q^2}{25}$$
$$60 = Q^2$$
$$\sqrt{60} = \sqrt{Q^2}$$

Finding the square root without a calculator is tough, so use logic to finish the problem: You know that $7^2 = 49$ and $8^2 = 64$, so you can reason that if $Q^2 = 60$, then Q has to be greater than 7 but less than 8. The only answer that fits is Choice (B), 7.7. Check your answer by multiplying: 7.7 × 7.7 = 59.29, which is close to 60.

128. **C.** Use the formula to find the volume of a cylinder:

$$V = \pi r^2 h$$
$$V = \pi(8^2)15$$
$$V = \pi(64)15$$
$$V \approx (3.14)(960)$$
$$V \approx 3,014.4$$

The volume is approximately 3,014 cubic feet. Choice (C) is correct.

129. **A.** When you square a number, you multiply the number by itself. When you multiply two fractions, you multiply the numerators (on top) and the denominators (on bottom). Therefore, the correct answer is $\left(\frac{1}{2}\right)^2 = \frac{1}{2} \times \frac{1}{2} = \frac{1}{4}$.

130. **B.** To answer this question, multiply the number of gallons (5) by the number of pounds per gallon (8) and add 2.5 (the weight of the tank): $5 \times 8 + 2.5 = 42.5$.

Part 7: Mechanical Aptitude

131. **A.** Gears that touch each other must spin in opposite directions. Therefore, if Gear 3 spins counterclockwise, then Gear 2 has to spin clockwise; if Gear 2 spins clockwise, then Gear 1 has to spin counterclockwise. Therefore, Choice (A) is correct.

132. **B.** When the teeth of gears fit together, smaller gears make more revolutions per minute than larger gears. Because Gear 2 is smaller than both Gear 1 and Gear 3, it must make more revolutions per minute than either of the other gears. Choice (B) is correct.

133. **C.** A chain saw, like other saws, is a cutting tool, which is one of the four types of forcible entry tools used by firefighters. The others include prying tools, pushing/pulling tools, and striking tools.

134. **A.** To answer this question, you can first determine the per-pound stretch of the spring ($8 \div 10$) and then multiply that answer by the number of pounds (15). But you can make the math a little easier if you use some logic: 15 and 10 are both multiples of 5, so you can figure out how much stretch you get for every 5 pounds. If you get 8 inches of stretch for every 10 pounds, then you get 4 inches of stretch for every 5 pounds. Because 15 pounds is 3 times 5 pounds, you can multiply the stretch by 3 to get the right answer: 3×4 inches = 12 inches. Therefore, the spring would stretch 12 inches under a pull of 15 pounds.

135. **C.** When the belt between two pulleys is crossed, it causes the wheels to spin in opposite directions. Therefore, if Wheel A spins clockwise, Wheel B must spin counterclockwise.

136. **B.** In a wheel-and-axle setup, the wheel moves a greater distance than the axle with less force. The axle moves a lesser distance than the wheel, Choice (B), and greater force is required to move it.

137. **D.** To figure out the force required to lift the box, remember the formula $w \times d_1 = f \times d_2$ (see Chapter 10). Plugging in the numbers, you get (50 pounds)(6 feet) = f(3 feet). You can solve for force by multiplying the weight of the box (50) by the distance in feet from the box to the fulcrum (6) and dividing by the distance from the fulcrum to the firefighter (3). Therefore, the force required to lift the box is 100 pounds.

138. **C.** By moving the fulcrum closer to the object you're trying to lift, you'll need to apply less force to lift the object. To figure out the force required to lift the box, remember the formula $w \times d_1 = f \times d_2$. Plugging in the numbers gives you (50 pounds)(4 feet) = f(5 feet). Solve for force by multiplying the weight of the box (50) by the distance in feet from the box to the fulcrum (now 4 feet) and dividing by the distance from the fulcrum to the firefighter (now 5 feet). The force required to lift the box is now 40 pounds.

139. **D.** To decrease the amount of force required to lift the box, the firefighter should move the fulcrum closer to the box. The closer the fulcrum is to the box, the less force the firefighter will have to apply to lift it. Choice (D) is the best answer.

140. **A.** An inclined plane, or ramp, allows you to use less force to move an object by increasing the distance over which you apply the force, Choice (A) is the best answer. Choice (B) describes a fastener. Choice (C) describes a lever (or a system of movable pulleys). Choice (D) describes a fixed pulley.

141. **A.** The steepness of an inclined plane affects how easy it is to move an object along it. The steeper the plane, the faster and easier it is to move the object down, and the slower and more difficult it is to move the object up. In this case, Ball A sits on a steeper plane than Ball B, which means it will move down the plane faster than Ball B. Choice (A) is correct.

142. **D.** The ratio between the sizes of the two wheels in the pulley system relates to the ratio between the rotations of the two wheels. Therefore, if Wheel A is twice as big as Wheel B, Wheel B will have to make twice as many rotations as Wheel A to keep up. If Wheel A makes 30 revolutions per minute, then Wheel B makes 60 revolutions per minute.

143. **B.** Two pulleys connected by a belt spin in the same direction, unless the belt is crossed, in which case they spin in opposite directions. In the illustration, the belt between the two pulleys is not crossed, which means that both pulleys move in the same direction.

144. **B.** The picture shows a coping saw, which has a handle and a thin, steel blade stretched between the ends of a C-shaped frame. It's often used in woodworking to make intricate cuts.

145. **C.** The picture shows a maul, which has a long handle and a dual-purpose head with one side that resembles a sledgehammer and one side that resembles an axe. Choice (C) is correct. A maul would be a good tool for splitting a log in half.

146. **D.** A blowtorch is a tool with a small cylinder of gas that produces a flame.

147. **A.** The key word in the question is *cut*. You need to find a cutting tool. A handsaw is definitely a cutting tool, and it would work well to cut through a wooden board.

148. **D.** The key word in the question is *cut*. You need to find a cutting tool. You can eliminate Choice (A), because it's not a cutting tool. A pair of wire cutters is a cutting tool, but you need something stronger to cut through a chain, so you can eliminate Choice (B). Choice (C) is incorrect as well; a circular saw is typically used to make precise cuts to materials that are clamped securely in place. Therefore, bolt cutters are the best choice.

149. **B.** The image shows a crowbar, which is a tool that firefighters often use for prying.

150. **D.** The image shows a sledgehammer, which is a tool that firefighters often use for striking.

Answer Key

Part 1: Reading Comprehension

1. C	7. B	13. D	19. A	25. C
2. C	8. A	14. A	20. C	26. D
3. D	9. C	15. D	21. B	27. A
4. A	10. B	16. D	22. C	28. B
5. B	11. C	17. B	23. A	29. D
6. D	12. C	18. C	24. D	30. A

Part 2: Verbal Expression

31. C	35. A	39. C	43. C	47. D
32. D	36. B	40. D	44. B	48. C
33. B	37. B	41. B	45. A	49. A
34. C	38. B	42. D	46. C	50. B

Part 3: Observation and Memory

51. D	55. C	59. D	63. C	67. C
52. B	56. C	60. B	64. D	68. D
53. B	57. A	61. A	65. A	69. A
54. C	58. C	62. C	66. D	70. B

Part 4: Spatial Orientation

71. B	75. A	79. A	83. B	87. A
72. A	76. D	80. A	84. A	88. C
73. D	77. B	81. B	85. C	89. B
74. B	78. C	82. B	86. D	90. C

Part 5: Reasoning and Judgment

91. A	95. C	99. D	103. C	107. C
92. C	96. C	100. C	104. C	108. D
93. B	97. A	101. C	105. B	109. C
94. B	98. C	102. A	106. B	110. D

Part 6: Performing Mathematical Calculations

111. D	115. C	119. B	123. A	127. B
112. A	116. A	120. D	124. D	128. C
113. B	117. B	121. C	125. C	129. A
114. C	118. C	122. C	126. B	130. B

Part 7: Mechanical Aptitude

131. A	135. C	139. D	143. B	147. A
132. B	136. B	140. A	144. B	148. D
133. C	137. D	141. A	145. C	149. B
134. A	138. C	142. D	146. D	150. D

Chapter 19

Practice Exam 3

• •

*T*his practice exam is similar to the written exam you'd encounter during the firefighter hiring process in New York City, New York. The exam is based on actual questions from real New York City tests. The questions on this test aren't organized into sections; you find a mix of different question types. However, the test begins with a memory part, which you should complete first.

To get the most out of this practice test, take it as you'd take the real written exam:

- ✔ Allow yourself 3 hours to complete the exam, and take the whole exam at one time, completing the memory section (questions 1 through 10) first.

- ✔ Take the test in a quiet place, such as a library or a private office, to avoid interruption.

- ✔ Bring a timer, because you need to time yourself during certain portions of the exam.

- ✔ Bring a pencil and some scratch paper. You may use a standard numeric calculator during the test. Other electronic devices are not permitted.

- ✔ Use the answer sheet that's provided.

After you complete the practice exam, check your answers against the answer explanations in Chapter 20. The purpose of this practice exam is to help you identify your strengths and weaknesses on the written exam so you know where to focus your studies. For example, if you have trouble memorizing a floor plan, you'll know that you need to brush up on your observation and memory skills.

Answer Sheet for Practice Exam 3

1 (A) (B) (C) (D)	41 (A) (B) (C) (D)	81 (A) (B) (C) (D)
2 (A) (B) (C) (D)	42 (A) (B) (C) (D)	82 (A) (B) (C) (D)
3 (A) (B) (C) (D)	43 (A) (B) (C) (D)	83 (A) (B) (C) (D)
4 (A) (B) (C) (D)	44 (A) (B) (C) (D)	84 (A) (B) (C) (D)
5 (A) (B) (C) (D)	45 (A) (B) (C) (D)	85 (A) (B) (C) (D)
6 (A) (B) (C) (D)	46 (A) (B) (C) (D)	86 (A) (B) (C) (D)
7 (A) (B) (C) (D)	47 (A) (B) (C) (D)	87 (A) (B) (C) (D)
8 (A) (B) (C) (D)	48 (A) (B) (C) (D)	88 (A) (B) (C) (D)
9 (A) (B) (C) (D)	49 (A) (B) (C) (D)	89 (A) (B) (C) (D)
10 (A) (B) (C) (D)	50 (A) (B) (C) (D)	90 (A) (B) (C) (D)
11 (A) (B) (C) (D)	51 (A) (B) (C) (D)	91 (A) (B) (C) (D)
12 (A) (B) (C) (D)	52 (A) (B) (C) (D)	92 (A) (B) (C) (D)
13 (A) (B) (C) (D)	53 (A) (B) (C) (D)	93 (A) (B) (C) (D)
14 (A) (B) (C) (D)	54 (A) (B) (C) (D)	94 (A) (B) (C) (D)
15 (A) (B) (C) (D)	55 (A) (B) (C) (D)	95 (A) (B) (C) (D)
16 (A) (B) (C) (D)	56 (A) (B) (C) (D)	96 (A) (B) (C) (D)
17 (A) (B) (C) (D)	57 (A) (B) (C) (D)	97 (A) (B) (C) (D)
18 (A) (B) (C) (D)	58 (A) (B) (C) (D)	98 (A) (B) (C) (D)
19 (A) (B) (C) (D)	59 (A) (B) (C) (D)	99 (A) (B) (C) (D)
20 (A) (B) (C) (D)	60 (A) (B) (C) (D)	100 (A) (B) (C) (D)
21 (A) (B) (C) (D)	61 (A) (B) (C) (D)	
22 (A) (B) (C) (D)	62 (A) (B) (C) (D)	
23 (A) (B) (C) (D)	63 (A) (B) (C) (D)	
24 (A) (B) (C) (D)	64 (A) (B) (C) (D)	
25 (A) (B) (C) (D)	65 (A) (B) (C) (D)	
26 (A) (B) (C) (D)	66 (A) (B) (C) (D)	
27 (A) (B) (C) (D)	67 (A) (B) (C) (D)	
28 (A) (B) (C) (D)	68 (A) (B) (C) (D)	
29 (A) (B) (C) (D)	69 (A) (B) (C) (D)	
30 (A) (B) (C) (D)	70 (A) (B) (C) (D)	
31 (A) (B) (C) (D)	71 (A) (B) (C) (D)	
32 (A) (B) (C) (D)	72 (A) (B) (C) (D)	
33 (A) (B) (C) (D)	73 (A) (B) (C) (D)	
34 (A) (B) (C) (D)	74 (A) (B) (C) (D)	
35 (A) (B) (C) (D)	75 (A) (B) (C) (D)	
36 (A) (B) (C) (D)	76 (A) (B) (C) (D)	
37 (A) (B) (C) (D)	77 (A) (B) (C) (D)	
38 (A) (B) (C) (D)	78 (A) (B) (C) (D)	
39 (A) (B) (C) (D)	79 (A) (B) (C) (D)	
40 (A) (B) (C) (D)	80 (A) (B) (C) (D)	

New York City Practice Exam

Time: 3 hours for 100 questions

Directions: Answer the memory questions (1 through 10) first and then move on to the other questions. Record your answers in the appropriate spaces on your answer sheet.

> *Firefighters often have to enter and exit buildings in conditions with limited or no visibility. For this reason, they must quickly and accurately memorize floor plans so they can safely enter and exit the building and help victims in need.*
>
> *You'll have 5 minutes to memorize the apartment floor plan that appears in the appendix. The apartment has an apartment on each side and a fire escape in the back. Then you'll have to answer some questions about it from memory. Use your timer to alert you when 5 minutes have passed, or ask a partner to time you. Begin when you are ready.*

STOP DO NOT TURN THE PAGE UNTIL TOLD TO DO SO.

1. A firefighter is rescuing a child from a room with only one means of escape. Which one of the following rooms is the firefighter in?

    (A) the master bedroom

    (B) bedroom 4

    (C) the kitchen

    (D) bedroom 2

2. A person wanting to use the fire escape to exit the apartment would be able to access the escape through the window of

    (A) the master bedroom.

    (B) bedroom 2.

    (C) bedroom 3.

    (D) the kitchen.

3. If Apartment B is on fire, people in Apartment C closest to the fire would be those spending time in

    (A) the master bedroom.

    (B) the kitchen.

    (C) bedroom 4.

    (D) bathroom 2.

4. Firefighters entering the apartment through the entrance door would enter into the

    (A) kitchen.

    (B) dining room.

    (C) office.

    (D) living room.

5. Of the following rooms in the apartment, which one does not have a door that closes?

    (A) the master bathroom

    (B) the office

    (C) bedroom 2

    (D) the dining room

6. After responding to a fire at this apartment, a firefighter complains about a room that cannot be accessed from the hallway. Which room is the firefighter referring to?

    (A) the kitchen

    (B) the master bathroom

    (C) the office

    (D) the living room

7. There is a fire in the apartment and the ladder of the fire truck in the street cannot be placed against the fire escape. The ladder should be raised from the street to reach a window in

    (A) the master bedroom.

    (B) bedroom 3.

    (C) bedroom 2.

    (D) the office.

8. If there is a fire in bedroom 2 and a firefighter is rescuing a young woman in bedroom 4, the safest and quickest means of escape would be through the

    (A) window of bedroom 4.

    (B) living room and the apartment entrance.

    (C) master bedroom.

    (D) master bathroom.

9. If a firefighter needs to enter the office but there is a fire in the hallway, which other room could the firefighter enter to gain access to the office?

    (A) the dining room

    (B) the kitchen

    (C) bedroom 2

    (D) the master bedroom

Go on to next page

10. Which of the following choices lists two rooms that have *no* windows?

    (A) bedroom 3 and bedroom 2

    (B) bedroom 4 and bathroom 2

    (C) bedroom 4 and the master bedroom

    (D) bathroom 2 and the master bedroom

For each question, choose the most correct answer (A, B, C, or D). Mark the space on your answer sheet that corresponds to the question number and the letter indicating your choice.

Use the information in the following passage to answer questions 11–13.

While arsonists intentionally set fires to produce a specific vengeful or monetary result, pyromaniacs are those who seek comfort and relief from starting fires. Pyromania is a recognized impulse-control disorder categorized by the frequent setting of fires, the experience of tension or frustration before setting fires, a deep interest and curiosity in fire equipment and paraphernalia, and the experience of relief or pleasure after a fire has been successfully started. Pyromaniacs do not set fires to cover up crimes, collect insurance, take a stand against the government, or seek revenge. They are also typically not depressed or under the influence of drugs or alcohol when they set fires. Pyromaniacs enjoy watching fires burn.

11. A pyromaniac is a person who sets fires

    (A) to cover up crimes or collect insurance.

    (B) for vengeance or money.

    (C) to feel comfort or relief.

    (D) because of depression or substance abuse.

12. A pyromaniac who is unable to start a fire may

    (A) experience frustration or increased stress.

    (B) attack those preventing him or her from starting a fire.

    (C) choose to smash windows or slit tires instead.

    (D) drink enough alcohol to settle his or her nerves.

13. To be diagnosed with pyromania is to be diagnosed with

    (A) a mild case of depression.

    (B) an impulse-control disorder.

    (C) an alcohol addiction.

    (D) an antisocial personality.

Go on to next page

Use the following passage and image to answer questions 14–20.

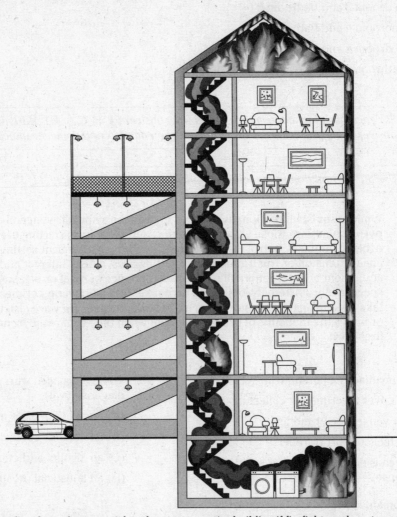

Basement fires have the potential to threaten an entire building if firefighters do not respond to them correctly. Although the fire may be on the lowest level of the house, smoke and burning embers can make their way up staircases leading from the basement to the attic, sparking additional fires and causing a large amount of smoke damage along the way. Smoke and embers can also sneak into a wall and spread through the height of the house, creating sparks, small fires, and damage in the wall as they move upward. If a building does not have fire-stops (small pieces of wood placed within the walls to stop smoke from spreading upward), smoke can easily travel throughout the home.

When responding to a basement fire, firefighters should be prepared to ventilate the area. If the basement does not have ground-level windows, firefighters cannot apply horizontal ventilation. Instead, they must ventilate vertically. The first way to ventilate a basement fire is to create a hole in the side of the house opposite the staircase on the first floor. Smoke will follow the open staircase from the basement to the first floor and then exit through the hole, sometimes with assistance from a fan facing the hole. To avoid moving the smoke up the staircase, firefighters can cut a hole in the ceiling of the basement directly above the fire, which will bring the smoke into the first floor. An additional hole in the side of the house will force the smoke outside. If ventilation cannot occur on the first floor, firefighters may make a hole in the roof. After the smoke and embers reach the attic, via staircase or walls, the smoke escapes out of the top of the house.

Firefighters should take care never to direct a stream of water into a hole created for ventilation.

Go on to next page

14. Which of the following statements about basement fires is most accurate?

   (A) A basement fire typically threatens only the basement of a building.

   (B) A basement fire is a threat to an entire building.

   (C) A basement fire always spreads through the walls of a building.

   (D) A basement fire rarely spreads to the attic of a building.

15. Basement fires use which of the following parts of a building to spread to additional floors?

   (A) garages

   (B) ceilings

   (C) staircases

   (D) doorways

16. Which of the following might prevent a fire from spreading through the walls of a building?

   (A) windows

   (B) staircases

   (C) insulation

   (D) fire-stops

17. When creating ventilation, firefighters should never

   (A) direct water into the hole.

   (B) make a hole in the ceiling above a fire.

   (C) make a hole in the roof of a building.

   (D) use horizontal ventilation techniques.

18. One way firefighters could ventilate the basement fire pictured in the image would be to

   (A) make a hole in floor above the fire and in the exterior wall of the living room on the first floor.

   (B) make a hole in the floor above the fire and open the doorway to the staircase on the first floor.

   (C) make a hole in the exterior basement wall under the staircase.

   (D) place a fan in the basement to direct the smoke up the staircase.

19. If firefighters cannot create a ventilation hole in the floor above the fire, another option for ventilation is to make a hole in the wall

   (A) on the same side of the building as the staircase.

   (B) opposite the staircase on the sixth floor.

   (C) opposite the staircase on the first floor.

   (D) on the second floor of the building.

20. Firefighters were unable to create a ventilation opening on the first floor, and smoke and fire have traveled through the walls and reached the attic of the building pictured in the diagram. Firefighters should

   (A) place a fan at the top of the staircase.

   (B) make a hole in the roof for vertical ventilation.

   (C) make a hole in the staircase on the sixth floor.

   (D) open all the windows throughout the building.

Go on to next page

Use the information in the following passage to answer questions 21–28.

When firefighters are called to the scene of a traffic accident, they should be prepared to encounter a victim trapped in one or more of the vehicles involved in the crash. As they arrive on the scene, firefighters should evaluate their surroundings. This includes noting how many vehicles were involved, additional traffic hazards, the potential for fires, and the presence of hazardous materials. While sizing up the scene, firefighters often use their trucks as roadblocks. They may park across lanes or only in the closest lane to the scene. Their goal is simple: to keep pedestrians and other drivers away from the potential for danger.

In an ideal situation, at least one firefighter is responsible for assessing each vehicle. In this case, all vehicles receive simultaneous and equal attention. After receiving their vehicle assignments, firefighters then search the area surrounding the vehicle for anything that may pose a threat to any victims or rescue personnel. This may include gas or fuel spills, small fires, or an unstable vehicle that can roll forward, backward, or onto its side. To ensure that a vehicle does not move while firefighters are attempting to rescue the victim from the car, firefighters typically place wooden cribbing (pieces of wood of various sizes) and wedges in front of or behind the tires to secure them in place. If the vehicle is on its side, firefighters crib the vehicle to stop it from flipping over. This may involve placing blocks of wood beneath the side of the vehicle that is on the ground.

If it is safe to approach the vehicle, a firefighter must then assess a victim. To assess and eventually remove the victim, emergency personnel must move pieces of the vehicle away from the victim. The doors, windows, gas pedals, seat belts, dashboard, and even steering wheel can be easily taken from the vehicle to provide better access to the victim. It is vital that firefighters take the car away from the victim before they attempt to take the victim out of the car. Firefighters should package the victim (dress and bandage wounds, splint broken bones, and immobilize the body) before removing him or her from the vehicle. After the victim is packaged, firefighters must cover all sharp edges — broken glass, splintered metal or plastic — with blankets or other cloths to ensure that the victim and rescue personnel do not receive cuts, scrapes, or other injuries while moving away from the vehicle.

21. When firefighters arrive on the scene of a traffic accident, they may use which of the following as road blocks?

   (A) damaged vehicles

   (B) piles of wood and cribbing

   (C) other firefighters

   (D) fire trucks

22. When firefighters crib a vehicle, they

   (A) remove parts of it.

   (B) keep it from moving.

   (C) cover all sharp edges.

   (D) clean up fuel spills.

23. Ideally, how many vehicles should a single firefighter assess at the scene of an accident?

   (A) 1

   (B) 2

   (C) 3

   (D) all vehicles involved

24. When firefighters package a victim, they

   (A) take the victim out of the vehicle.

   (B) cover up sharp edges in the vehicle.

   (C) take care of the victim's wounds.

   (D) take away parts of the vehicle.

Go on to next page

25. If firefighters want to secure a vehicle that they discovered on its side, they would

    (A) take the vehicle apart piece by piece.

    (B) turn the vehicle over so it sits on its tires.

    (C) place blocks of wood beneath the side on the ground.

    (D) place blocks of wood behind its front and back tires.

26. To assess an accident victim trapped inside a vehicle, firefighters should remove all of the following EXCEPT the

    (A) vehicle's doors.

    (B) steering wheel.

    (C) accident victim.

    (D) dashboard.

27. A firefighter wants to remove a trapped victim from a vehicle. Which of the following should the firefighter do LAST?

    (A) Cover the vehicle's sharp edges.

    (B) Dress and bandage the victim's wounds.

    (C) Assess the victim for injuries.

    (D) Immobilize the victim's body.

28. What should a firefighter do BEFORE assessing an accident victim?

    (A) Remove the victim from the vehicle.

    (B) Notify additional emergency personnel.

    (C) Cover all sharp edges in the vehicle.

    (D) Look around the vehicle for potential dangers.

Go on to next page

> *Use the information in the following passage to answer questions 29–32.*

When firefighters lecture groups about fire safety in their homes or at community/residential meetings, their main objective should be to convince their audience to embrace fire-safe practices in their everyday lives. Understanding the value of being prepared for a fire may persuade people to be more conscious of fire hazards in their homes. If people know how to act during a fire, they may be able to escape from the building before firefighters arrive on scene. The following safety rules and precautions may aid a person in safely escaping a fire:

- ✔ Install and ensure the proper operation of smoke detectors.
- ✔ Agree upon a meeting place outside the home if a fire occurs.
- ✔ Keep all bedroom doors closed while asleep.
- ✔ Ensure that all windows are operable.
- ✔ Ensure that every room has at least two unblocked fire exits.
- ✔ Keep a whistle or other noisemaker in all rooms to use as an alert of smoke or fire.
- ✔ Train all occupants in the proper use of the fire escape ladder.
- ✔ Roll out of bed and onto the floor when alerted to a fire. Do not sit or stand.
- ✔ Stay close to the floor, because extreme heat and smoke rise toward the ceiling.
- ✔ Crawl to the door and feel it with the back of your hand.
- ✔ If the door is warm, use a window for escape.
- ✔ Go to the established meeting place.
- ✔ Call the fire department to report the fire.

29. The main point of this passage is that people should

    (A) know to roll out of bed and onto the floor when alerted to a fire.

    (B) be aware of fire safety practices so they can escape a fire without injury.

    (C) remember to install properly operating fire alarms throughout their homes.

    (D) always go to bed with a whistle or other noisemaker close by.

30. Which of the following should you do first when you are alerted to a fire during the night?

    (A) Close the bedroom door.

    (B) Blow a whistle to alert others.

    (C) Call the fire department to report the fire.

    (D) Roll out of the bed and onto the floor.

31. All of the following steps should be performed before a fire takes place EXCEPT

    (A) training all occupants in the proper use of the fire escape.

    (B) ensuring that all windows can be opened easily.

    (C) calling the fire department to report the fire.

    (D) establishing a safe place to meet outside of the building.

32. This passage states that firefighters should

    (A) train the occupants of a house to use a fire escape ladder.

    (B) understand the value of being prepared for a fire.

    (C) use a window for escape in the event that a door feels warm.

    (D) convince their audience to embrace fire-safe practices.

Go on to next page

Use the information provided to answer questions 33–35.

33. While unloading the equipment from the back of the fire truck at the scene of a fire, a firefighter is approached by an older woman who tells him that one of the other firefighters in his company has just cursed at her for stepping in front of him while he was carrying a ladder. The firefighter should tell the woman to

(A) get over it because she was clearly in the way.

(B) talk to their supervisor after the fire is under control.

(C) find him after the fire, and he will get her an apology.

(D) find the offending firefighter an make him apologize immediately.

34. While finishing an inspection of a hospital, a firefighter takes the stairs to the ground floor. He notices papers, food wrappers, and cigarette butts on almost every landing. The papers are a fire hazard, and no one should be smoking in a hospital. The manager of the hospital tells him that neither personnel nor visitors use the stairway, so they do not clean it often. She also mentions that the last inspector did not say anything about the condition of that particular stairwell. What should the firefighter do FIRST?

(A) Tell the manager to instruct her custodial team to clean every stairway each night.

(B) Make a "NO SMOKING" sign to tape on the door to the stairwell and on all the landings.

(C) Request the name of the last firefighter who inspected the hospital and report him.

(D) Dismiss his own complaint because the last inspector did not think the trash was a violation.

35. A young man who appears to be intoxicated stumbles into the firehouse one night and approaches the first firefighter he sees. He tells him that he accidentally locked his keys in the car. He asks the firefighter to unlock the doors for him so he can go home. What should the firefighter do?

(A) Grab his tools and follow him to his car to unlock the doors and find his keys.

(B) Convince him to get in the nearest engine so the firefighter can take him home.

(C) Question him about how much he had to drink and which bar he has been in.

(D) Ask him for the location of the car and then call a tow truck for the car and a cab for him.

Go on to next page

Refer to the items pictured below to answer questions 36–43. Keep in mind that pictures are not drawn to scale. Each item is identified by a number. For each question, choose the answer that gives the number or numbers that most correctly answers the question.

Go on to next page

36. Which of the following should be placed beside a hole created for ventilation?

    (A) 9

    (B) 11

    (C) 15

    (D) 17

37. Which of the following pairs of tools can be used to enter a vehicle in which a victim is trapped?

    (A) 1 and 7

    (B) 6 and 20

    (C) 10 and 18

    (D) 8 and 14

38. Which of the following tools can a firefighter use to carry extra tools?

    (A) 16

    (B) 10

    (C) 11

    (D) 17

39. Which of the following should be connected to a fire hose to transfer water to the fire?

    (A) 2

    (B) 3

    (C) 14

    (D) 15

40. Which of the following pairs of tools can be used to create ventilation in the roof or wall of a building?

    (A) 1 and 5

    (B) 8 and 9

    (C) 10 and 13

    (D) 12 and 19

41. Which of the following items should be used to keep pedestrians or bystanders away from the scene of a fire or a traffic accident?

    (A) 2

    (B) 9

    (C) 11

    (D) 15

42. Which of the following items should be used to brush debris off the road after a motor vehicle accident?

    (A) 3

    (B) 9

    (C) 13

    (D) 14

43. Which of the following would a firefighter take into a burning building?

    (A) 7

    (B) 11

    (C) 13

    (D) 14

Go on to next page

> *Use the information in the following passage and illustration to answer questions 44 and 45.*

A fire company responds to a fire at the local middle school. While the engine company attacks the fire, members of the truck/rescue company enter the school to search for victims. As two firefighters make their way down the smoky hall, they come to the first classroom. Only one firefighter should enter a classroom at a time. Firefighter 1 enters the classroom. Below is an illustration of the current circumstances.

44. To make sure that Firefighter 1 is safe, what should Firefighter 2 do next?

(A) follow Firefighter 1 into the classroom

(B) remain in the hall and talk to Firefighter 1

(C) move down the hall to check another classroom

(D) call other members of the company for help

45. What is Firefighter 2 doing wrong?

(A) He should be crawling, not standing, to avoid the heat.

(B) He is not wearing appropriate footwear or headgear.

(C) He should be checking inside the lockers behind him for damage.

(D) He should be waiting for Firefighter 1 at the end of the hall.

Go on to next page

> *Use the information in the following passage to answer questions 46–49.*

According to multiple studies conducted in the United States, Great Britain, and Australia, the occupation of fighting fires brings with it a high risk of various cancers and heart disease. All who are familiar with firefighting expect that if a firefighter is injured at a scene, the injury is from burns, smoke inhalation, or possibly a fallen ceiling or structure. Although these events do occur, heart attacks cause more deaths than flames and smoke. Researchers have estimated that heart attacks contribute to approximately 52 percent of deaths that occur on the scenes of fires each year. Dealing with extreme heat, overexertion, toxic substances, and psychological stress makes firefighters 10 to 100 times more likely than the general public to have a heart attack. Firefighters' lack of physical fitness may also make them more vulnerable to heart disease. Unions in multiple countries have fought for years to make health and fitness programs mandatory for firefighters. In 2007, less than 30 percent of all departments in the United States had a mandatory program.

Firefighters are also more likely to be diagnosed with five types of cancers: prostate cancer, testicular cancer, Hodgkin's lymphoma, melanoma, and mesothelioma. Specialists have attributed the development and spread of these cancers to toxins in the air on the scenes of fires and to substandard gear. Unions have petitioned for better protective gear and government programs to support firefighters diagnosed with cancers linked to exposure of toxins, such as mesothelioma, which is linked to exposure to asbestos.

46. The main point of this passage is that a career in firefighting

(A) is stressful and will most likely result in death by cancer.

(B) does not guarantee that a firefighter will be physically fit.

(C) puts many firefighters at high risk for heart disease and cancers.

(D) is dangerous because certain protective gear is substandard.

47. According to this passage, 52 percent of personnel deaths that occur at the scene of an emergency each year are related to

(A) mesothelioma.

(B) heart attacks.

(C) toxic substances.

(D) psychological stress.

48. According to this passage, unions have petitioned for all of the following EXCEPT

(A) support for firefighters diagnosed with cancers.

(B) mandatory leave to combat stress.

(C) mandatory physical fitness programs.

(D) better protective gear.

49. Firefighters who are continuously exposed to asbestos, a toxin, are most likely to suffer

(A) Hodgkin's lymphoma.

(B) heart disease.

(C) melanoma.

(D) mesothelioma.

Go on to next page

Use the information provided to answer questions 50–54.

50. Firefighter Garcia must check the ladders at the beginning of each tour of duty. He must check each ladder to make sure that it is working, clean, and not in need of repair. If a ladder is in need of repair, he must put a tag on it and call the ladder repair technician. At the start of a new tour of duty, five ladders must be ready to use. If fewer than five are ready to use, Firefighter Garcia must alert the fire chief who will locate additional replacement ladders. After Firefighter Garcia inspects eight ladders, he finds that four are in need of repair. What is the minimum number of replacement ladders the fire chief must find?

(A) 1

(B) 2

(C) 3

(D) 4

51. When Company 75 arrives at the scene of a house fire, a woman hysterically yells at many of the crew's members for taking so long to respond to her call. She claims to have been waiting on her front lawn for almost 25 minutes, watching her belongings burn. The firefighters know that it took them only 7 minutes to get their gear and arrive at her house. What should the firefighters do?

(A) Ignore her and join their fellow firefighters in an attempt to gain control of the fire.

(B) Ask her what time she called and then prove to her that only 7 minutes have passed.

(C) Take their time putting out the fire because she had no right to speak to them angrily.

(D) While getting the hoses ready, explain to her the concept of time during an emergency.

52. Properly caring for a fire hose extends its life. Hose care includes washing and drying hoses as needed. Hard suction hose, rubber-jacket hose, and hard-rubber booster hose need only be rinsed with water, but it is permissible to add mild soap. Each time a woven-jacket hose is used, the dirt should be brushed off. Often, this is the only cleaning needed. However, if the dirt cannot be easily removed, woven-jacket hoses may be washed with water.

Of the following, the most accurate statement concerning washing fire hoses is that most should

(A) be washed with water as needed.

(B) have the dirt brushed off them after each use.

(C) be washed with water and mild soap after each use.

(D) have the dirt brushed off them occasionally.

53. On the scene of a chemical spill, a firefighter notices that a firefighter who is new to the company does not have the correct boots on to enter the premises. What should he do?

(A) Tell the new firefighter to change his boots and explain why.

(B) Report the new firefighter to the company's chief.

(C) Order the new firefighter to immediately change his boots.

(D) Say nothing and keep an eye on him as he enters the spill zone.

54. A house fire that was contained to the attic is almost out. The homeowners approach one of the truck company's members and ask if they may run into the foyer to grab coats for their children. What should the firefighter NOT do?

(A) Offer them a blanket to wrap around their children.

(B) Tell them to wait until the fire is completely out.

(C) Allow them to run in because the fire is only in the attic.

(D) Explain the dangers of entering a house full of smoke.

Go on to next page

Use the information in the following passage to answer questions 55–58.

When firefighters, investigators, or members of an arson squad arrive on the scene, they should be on the lookout for evidence of suspicious behavior. Even before they arrive, however, suspicions may arise. The time of day the fire began and even weather conditions may point firefighters in the direction of arson. For example, if firefighters respond to a house fire at 2 a.m., some, if not all, residents of the house will most likely be dressed in sleepwear. They should look as if they suddenly awoke due to smoke, heat, or the sound of a fire alarm. Firefighters should also consider weather. If it is winter, windows should not be open. If it is summer, it would be odd to find the furnace turned on. If called to a fire during a rainstorm or snowstorm, firefighters should be suspicious of how the fire began. Arsonists tend to use inclement weather in their favor, because it may take the company longer to respond to the call in snow or heavy rain.

55. Arsonists may set a fire during a snowstorm or rainstorm because

  (A) melting snow will put out the flames as it falls.

  (B) road conditions will make it difficult for a fire company to respond.

  (C) few witnesses will be outside during bad weather.

  (D) the snow will cover footprints and wash away fingerprints.

56. Members of a fire department's arson squad should begin looking for evidence of suspicious behavior

  (A) after an initial inspection.

  (B) on their way to the fire scene.

  (C) when they arrive on the scene.

  (D) after the fire has been contained.

57. If firefighters respond to a fire very late on a summer night, they may suspect arson if

  (A) the weather is warm and the air conditioning is on in the bedrooms.

  (B) the windows are open in the living room, dining room, and kitchen.

  (C) the homeowner is fully clothed in weather-appropriate attire.

  (D) the neighbors are gathered on the sidewalks and in driveways.

58. Of the following, which would NOT be an item that firefighters should be suspicious of when responding to a late-night fire?

  (A) open windows in the winter

  (B) a furnace on in the summer

  (C) a homeowner in her pajamas

  (D) a homeowner who has been on a walk

Go on to next page

Use the information in the following map to answer questions 59–63.

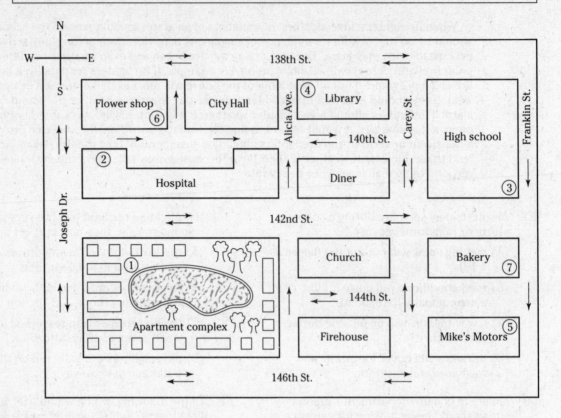

59. If members of an engine company enter the mapped area at the intersection of Joseph Drive and 138th Street and need to get to location 5, which of the following routes will get them there fastest?

(A) west on 138th Street, south on Franklin Street

(B) east on 138th Street, south on Franklin Street

(C) east on 138th Street, south on Alicia Avenue, east on 144th Street

(D) south on Joseph Drive, east on 142nd Street, south on Carey Street

60. While at the firehouse, firefighters are called to a fire drill at the local high school. The quickest route to the high school is

(A) north on Carey Street and east on 142nd Street.

(B) east on 146th Street and north on Franklin Street.

(C) north on Alicia Avenue and east on 140th Street.

(D) north on Alicia Avenue and east on 138th Street.

61. While visiting location 6, a firefighter overhears a delivery driver's request for directions to an apartment building on 142nd Street and Joseph Drive. The firefighter should suggest which of the following routes to the driver?

(A) west on 140th Street, south on Joseph Drive

(B) east on 140th Street, south on Alicia Avenue, west on 142nd Street

(C) north through the alley, west on 138th Street, south on Joseph Drive

(D) west on 140th Street, north on Alicia Avenue, west on 138th Street, south on Joseph Drive

Go on to next page

62. At location 7, a woman asks an off-duty fire-fighter for driving directions to location 6. He would be INCORRECT if he gave her which of the following directions?

    (A) south on Franklin Street, west on 146th Street, north on Carey Street, west on 140th Street

    (B) west on 144th Street, north on Carey Street, west on 138th Street, south on Joseph Drive, east on 140th Street

    (C) west on 144th Street, north on Alicia Avenue, west on 142nd Street, north on Joseph Drive, east on 140th Street

    (D) south on Franklin Street, west on 146th Street, north on Joseph Drive, east on 140th Street

63. Returning from assisting with a traffic accident in a neighboring county, an engine company enters the mapped area at the intersection of 138th Street and Franklin Street. The best route back to the fire house would be

    (A) east on 138th Street and south on Carey Street.

    (B) west on 138th Street and south on Alicia Avenue.

    (C) south on Franklin Street and east on 146th Street.

    (D) south on Franklin Street and west on 146th Street.

Use information in the following passage and illustration to answer questions 64–68.

Sometimes firefighters have to move an unconscious or injured victim to an ambulance to transport him or her to a hospital. To do this, they often use two or three rescuers to lift the victim swiftly and carefully from the original location to a gurney. When this occurs, one firefighter takes the lead and instructs the others while simultaneously assisting them with moving the victim. After the gurney has been placed near the victim, the firefighters kneel close to one side of the victim, all while keeping their backs straight. While the lead firefighter takes responsibility for supporting the victim's head and neck, the other two rescuers should slide their arms under the victim's back and legs. At the same time, all three rescuers should roll the victim toward their chests and stand. When the victim is above the gurney, rescuers should slowly roll the body away from them onto the gurney.

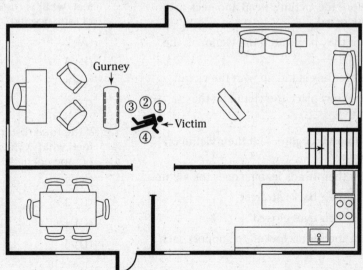

Go on to next page

64. Firefighters need to move this victim to safety. A gurney has been placed in the room. Which firefighter is NOT needed according to the preceding directions?

    (A) Firefighter 1

    (B) Firefighter 2

    (C) Firefighter 3

    (D) Firefighter 4

65. Which firefighter should ideally be responsible for giving orders?

    (A) Firefighter 1

    (B) Firefighter 2

    (C) Firefighter 3

    (D) Firefighter 4

66. Which firefighters should stand simultaneously to carefully lift the victim off the floor?

    (A) Firefighters 1 and 2 only

    (B) Firefighters 2 and 3 only

    (C) Firefighters 2, 3, and 4 only

    (D) Firefighters 1, 2, and 3 only

67. When should the firefighters lifting the victim roll the victim toward their chests?

    (A) before the victim's head and neck are supported

    (B) after they have lifted the victim off the floor

    (C) before they stand up with the victim

    (D) after they place the victim on the gurney

68. How should firefighters lift their victim off the ground?

    (A) with their heads leaning over the victim

    (B) with their backs straight

    (C) with their eyes closed

    (D) with their arms locked to support each other

> *Use the information in the following passage to answer questions 69–74.*

In an attempt to keep the scene of a fire safe for bystanders and firefighters alike, firefighters are responsible for putting up barricades around the affected area using yellow tape. The tape typically reads "FIRE LINE — DO NOT CROSS." Each roll contains approximately 1,500 feet of tape.

69. If the total distance to barricade the property is 1,375 feet, what is the minimum number of rolls of tape needed?

    (A) 1

    (B) 2

    (C) 3

    (D) 4

70. If the total distance to barricade is 7,500 feet, what is the minimum number of rolls of tape needed?

    (A) 3

    (B) 4

    (C) 5

    (D) 6

71. If the total distance to barricade is 5,250 feet, what is the minimum number of rolls of tape needed?

    (A) 2

    (B) 3

    (C) 4

    (D) 5

72. If the total distance to barricade is 3,750 feet, what is the minimum number of rolls of tape needed?

    (A) 2

    (B) 3

    (C) 4

    (D) 5

Go on to next page

73. If the total distance to barricade is 10,500 feet, what is the minimum number of rolls of tape needed?

    (A) 4

    (B) 5

    (C) 6

    (D) 7

74. If the total distance to barricade is 6,750 feet, what is the minimum number of rolls of tape needed?

    (A) 4

    (B) 5

    (C) 6

    (D) 7

Use the information in the following list to answer questions 75–79. These questions concern various teams that respond to fire emergencies. Listed below are four groups, numbered 1–4, to which these firefighters may belong. For each question, choose the team that would be responsible for performing the specified task.

1. **First-due engine company:** Establishes incident command, initiates fire attack, reports location and conditions to dispatch, requests additional support if needed

2. **Second-due engine company:** Makes sure water supply is adequate to continue to fight fire, lays additional hose if needed, assists first-due engine company

3. **Truck/rescue company:** Performs ventilation, conducts search and rescue, sets up lighting equipment if needed

4. **Rapid intervention crew:** Rescues trapped firefighters

75. If a firefighter's responsibilities include laying additional hose lines and ensuring a strong water supply, the firefighter is most likely a member of which of the following?

    (A) 1

    (B) 2

    (C) 3

    (D) 4

76. If a firefighter's responsibilities include rescuing a firefighter in distress, the firefighter is most likely a member of which of the following?

    (A) 1

    (B) 2

    (C) 3

    (D) 4

77. If a firefighter's responsibilities include initiating incident command and fire attack, the firefighter is most likely a member of which of the following?

    (A) 1

    (B) 2

    (C) 3

    (D) 4

78. If a firefighter's responsibilities include search and rescue and ventilation, the firefighter is most likely a member of which of the following?

    (A) 1

    (B) 2

    (C) 3

    (D) 4

79. If extra lighting is needed to attack the fire, firefighters from which of the following would most likely be contacted?

    (A) 1

    (B) 2

    (C) 3

    (D) 4

Go on to next page

Use the information provided to answer questions 80 and 81.

80. An elderly woman comes to the firehouse and tells the firefighters on duty that she is having terrible chest pain. Of the following, it would be best for firefighters to

(A) guide the woman to a chair and call for assistance.

(B) tell the woman to go to a nearby hospital.

(C) help her leave the firehouse because this is not a problem for firefighters.

(D) tell her she can use the phone in the firehouse to call for help.

81. Before firefighters can return to the fire station after responding to a small oven fire, the homeowner bursts out of the house and yells at the firefighters gathered around the engine. She accuses them of stealing a $20 bill she keeps on the side of her fridge for emergencies. What should the firefighters do?

(A) Chip in and offer her $20 to make up for the money she thinks they stole from her.

(B) Tell her they would not steal from her and ask her to report the theft to the supervisor.

(C) Tell her the side of a refrigerator is a stupid place to hang money; it could have fallen anytime.

(D) Empty their pockets in front of her to prove that they did not take her money.

Use the information in the following passage to answer question 82.

Taking care not to disrupt a fire's thermal balance is one of the most critical tasks firefighters perform while attacking a fire. Thermal layers are comprised of gases. The hottest gases, including smoke, rise to the ceiling of a room, and the cooler gases fall to the floor. Naturally, firefighters attack fires from the floor of the room, crouched on their knees by the doorway. If firefighters have not yet ventilated a room that has filled with smoke and if flames shoot upward toward the ceiling, it will disrupt the thermal balance of the room. The thermal gases will mix, and the firefighters in the room, regardless of their position on the ground, will find themselves in sudden extreme heat. If the thermal balance is interrupted, firefighters will need to resort to forced ventilation.

82. Which image depicts firefighters taking all precautions to maintain a thermal balance in the room?

(A)

(B)

(C)

(D)

Go on to next page

> *Use the information in the following passage to answer questions 83 and 84.*

      Firefighters use SCBAs (self-contained breathing apparatuses) to breathe during a fire. The mask enables a firefighter to breathe clean air, rather than air filled with smoke and particles from the fire, into his or her lungs. Before donning SCBA gear, a firefighter must ensure that his or her air cylinder is full and that the remote pressure gauge reads within 100 psi of the cylinder gauge.

83. Pictured below is an illustration of the gauges firefighters use to check how much air is in their cylinders. This particular gauge shows that the cylinder is

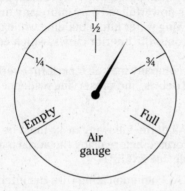

    (A) empty

    (B) full

    (C) less then ¼ full

    (D) more than ½ full

84. A typical cylinder holds 45 minutes' worth of air, measuring 4,500 psi. If the air cylinder contains 4,200 psi, which of the following gauges shows a safe measurement for the remote pressure gauge?

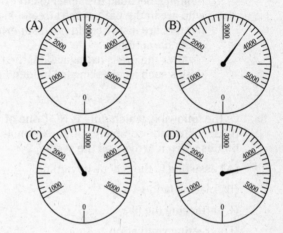

Go on to next page

> Use the information in the following passage to answer questions 85 and 86.

The truck/rescue company often arrives with the first-due engine company. While the engine company prepares to attack the flames, the truck/rescue company is responsible for entering the building to rescue victims, conduct salvage, ventilate, and place ladders where they are needed. Those members of the company who do not enter the building keep watch from outside, looking for victims who may not have escaped or watching to see whether the fire has spread to other sections of the building. They may set up lighting equipment and control other utilities.

If the fire is a challenge to the engine company, the truck/rescue company may be asked to assist with attacking the fire. After placing the necessary ladders and communicating with members of the interior team to ensure their safe exit from the building, members of the truck/rescue company raise the aerial master stream device to the height of the fire. It is crucial that the truck/rescue company contact any firefighters who may remain inside the building, because the aerial master device's aim is powerful and may injure any firefighters who are in the path of the stream. In addition, flowing water into a building while other firefighters are inside could push superheated gases onto the interior crews, which could seriously harm them.

After the fire is extinguished, the truck/rescue company may also perform overhaul duties such as checking for hidden fire, removing debris, and preserving evidence.

85. Of the following, which duty is NOT one of the truck/rescue company's first responsibilities when it arrives on the scene?

(A) assisting in the rescue of victims

(B) placing ladders

(C) attacking the fire

(D) creating ventilation

86. All of the following tasks must be performed before using the aerial master device EXCEPT

(A) communicating with the interior team.

(B) placing ladders.

(C) performing overhaul.

(D) rescuing victims.

Go on to next page

Use the information in the following passage and image to answer questions 87–90.

If the fire conditions inside a building or a room in a building are too extreme for firefighters to enter, firefighters often take an indirect approach to attacking the flames. From the entrance of the room or building, firefighters aim the nozzle at the ceiling above the burning area. The water attacks the heated gases atop the flames and then drips down onto the fire from above. Firefighters then shift their aim to the ground level where the fire is. They typically follow three patterns when altering their aim. These patterns resemble the letters T, Z, and O. The most commonly used pattern is O. This mixture of direct and indirect aiming is called a combination attack. It is imperative that firefighters ventilate the room before taking aim at any smoke, gases, or flames near the ceiling.

Illustration A

Illustration B

Go on to next page

87. The firefighters in Illustration A are attacking the fire using a(n)

    (A) indirect attack.

    (B) T pattern.

    (C) Z pattern.

    (D) O pattern.

88. The firefighters in Illustration B are attacking the fire using a(n)

    (A) indirect attack.

    (B) T pattern.

    (C) Z pattern.

    (D) O pattern.

89. In Illustration A and Illustration B, firefighters performed which of the following duties before attacking the fire?

    (A) aiming at the ceiling

    (B) ventilating the room

    (C) checking the heat levels

    (D) aiming at the floor

90. If a firefighter is using a combination attack to fight a fire, the firefighter is

    (A) alternating between foam and water.

    (B) alternating aim between the floor and the ceiling.

    (C) switching the type of hose nozzle every few minutes.

    (D) alternating between crouching and standing.

Use the information in the following passage to answer questions 91 and 92.

The most common emergency concerning elevators involves the elevator car's malfunctioning and becoming stuck between two floors. In this situation, passengers are trapped inside, but they should not suffer any physical injury. When responding to an elevator malfunction where people are trapped inside the car, the first thing firefighters should do is ensure that an elevator technician has also been alerted and is on the way to the scene. If the fire company arrives before the technician, firefighters should not attempt to move the elevator in any way. They should not apply pressure, play with the wires, or try to open the doors unless a medical emergency arises. Even then, only firefighters specially trained in performing elevator rescues should try to enter the car or remove someone from it.

Whether a medical emergency exists or not, a firefighter should remember to make continuous contact with the passengers who are stuck in the car. When a car is stuck but visible from an open set of doors, firefighters can attempt to speak or shout to those trapped, assuring them that help is on the way. If the car is too far from the doors or the doors are not yet open, firefighters can make contact using the emergency phone. They should inquire as to how many people are trapped and whether anyone is injured or has become ill. Firefighters may also keep the passengers updated on the status of the elevator technician.

91. If four people are trapped in an elevator and are not experiencing any medical emergencies, firefighters on the scene should do all of the following EXCEPT

    (A) call them on the emergency phone.

    (B) reassure them that they will be okay.

    (C) attempt to pull them from the elevator.

    (D) wait for an elevator technician to arrive.

92. When responding to an elevator emergency, it is critical that firefighters

    (A) do everything they can to remove those trapped from the elevator.

    (B) maintain constant communication with those trapped in the elevator.

    (C) pry open the doors as soon as they get there to check on those inside.

    (D) send at least one firefighter into the elevator to wait with the passengers.

Go on to next page

Use the information in the following passage to answer questions 93–96.

If an investigator or member of an arson team is not on the scene when firefighters discover an item that they think is evidence of a crime, firefighters should do what they must to protect and preserve the area. While attacking a fire, firefighters should be careful not to step on or wash away any evidence. They should leave all burned papers in trash cans and fireplaces for the arson team to investigate. Firefighters should touch or move evidence only when removal of the evidence is essential to extinguishing the fire or if conditions of the area in which the evidence was found may eventually result in destruction of the evidence. Upon moving evidence, firefighters should document their actions in a detailed report. If the evidence is in a secure location, firefighters should set up a protective barrier around the item in question or should stand guard so other firefighters and investigators do not disturb the area.

Typically, departments or companies would like their firefighters not to touch evidence in an arson case. After a firefighter moves the evidence, the firefighter becomes responsible for it and may need to appear in court to testify as to what item was found and where it was found. Not only is appearing in court expensive, but it may also keep a firefighter from working with the station for several days.

93. If a firefighter has no choice but to move evidence from its original location, the firefighter should do all of the following EXCEPT

(A) pass the evidence on to others for an opinion.

(B) write a report detailing what he or she did.

(C) attend a trial if he or she is needed to testify.

(D) stand guard to ensure that it is not disturbed.

94. Based on the passage, fire supervisors do not like their firefighters to touch evidence they find at the scene of an arson fire because fire supervisors know that firefighters may

(A) come to the wrong conclusions about what they find.

(B) have to appear at a trial, which costs both time and money.

(C) be accused of planting the evidence.

(D) accidentally destroy the evidence, making arson hard to prove.

95. Firefighters discover what they believe to be crucial evidence in a trash can of an office that has been damaged by a fire. The firefighters should do which of the following?

(A) Remove the trash can from the office and take it outside for the arson squad.

(B) Remove the suspicious items from the trash can and show them to an investigator.

(C) Leave the trash and the trash can in their original location and continue overhauling.

(D) Leave the trash and the trash can in their original location and notify an investigator.

96. If a firefighter suspects that a door in a room his team is overhauling shows signs of forced entry, he should

(A) make a note of it and discuss the evidence with his supervisor.

(B) set up a protective barrier around the doorway to preserve any evidence.

(C) tie a red flag on the door handle to alert investigators.

(D) do nothing but remember to notify the investigators later on.

Go on to next page

Use the information in the following passage to answer questions 97 and 98.

Because firefighters work with water, they should be knowledgeable of water pressure in fire hydrants. Pressure is measured in psi (pounds per square inch). Four types of water pressure directly affect the fire service: static pressure, normal operating pressure, residual pressure, and flow pressure. The pressure in hydrants before use is *static,* or unmoving, pressure. Taking measurements of *normal operating pressure* must occur during a time of day when an average amount of water in a neighborhood is in use. The water pressure that is not in use by fire hoses, adapters, or fittings is called *residual pressure. Flow pressure* is measured when water is released from a hydrant.

97. The measurement of normal operating pressure depends on

(A) how many people are taking the measurement.

(B) the location of the hydrant in the neighborhood.

(C) the time of day the measurement is taken.

(D) the season in which the measurement is taken.

98. According to the passage, the measurement of the pressure in the hydrant before use is

(A) residual pressure.

(B) static pressure.

(C) normal operating pressure.

(D) flow pressure.

99. A second-grade class takes a field trip to the local firehouse. At the station, the students receive a tour of the house, and the firefighters show them the equipment they use while fighting fires or rescuing victims. Allowing schools to take field trips to fire stations is

(A) good, because it gives firefighters something to do when they are not on a call.

(B) bad, because firefighters should be resting when they are not working.

(C) good, because it allows firefighters to teach young children about fire safety.

(D) bad, because the children may break the equipment if they try to play with it.

100. While putting the hose away after successfully attacking a fire, a firefighter's superior tells her to use a reverse horseshoe finish instead of the triple layer load she had started. However, the firefighter feels that her method would be the most effective and efficient. In this situation, the firefighter should

(A) follow her superior's directions and then ask her for an explanation later.

(B) explain to her superior why she is using the triple layer load instead.

(C) wait until her superior walks away and continue to use her preferred technique.

(D) demand an explanation as to why she should use the reverse horseshoe finish.

Chapter 20

Practice Exam 3: Answers and Explanations

. . . .

*I*f you've finished the New York City practice exam from Chapter 19, you're probably curious to see how you did. Read the answers and explanations in this chapter, or use the Answer Key at the end of this chapter to quickly see how well you performed. Remember, the practice exam can help you determine where you need to focus your studies for the real written firefighter exam.

Answers and Explanations

1. **D.** You have to answer this question from memory, so check your mental picture before looking at the answer choices. The master bathroom, bathroom 2, and bedroom 2 each have only one door through which escape is possible. Of the answer choices, only bedroom 2, Choice (D), is on the list.

2. **C.** Recall the floor plan of the apartment. The apartment's only fire escape can be accessed through the windows in bedroom 3 and bedroom 4, so Choice (C) is the right answer.

3. **D.** Think about the floor plan before viewing the answer choices. Rooms positioned along the side of the apartment closest to Apartment B include bedroom 3, bathroom 2, bedroom 2, the office, and the dining room. Out of those, bedroom 2, Choice (D), is the only one that appears in the answer choices.

4. **D.** To answer this question, picture the floor plan of the apartment. The apartment's entrance door is at the bottom of the picture, and it leads into the living room.

5. **D.** Recall the floor plan. The dining room, living room, and kitchen do not have doorways that close. The right answer is Choice (D), dining room.

6. **B.** Visualize the floor plan before you look at the answer choices. The only way to get in and out of the master bathroom is through a doorway in the master bedroom. The master bathroom doesn't open to the hallway, so Choice (B) is correct.

7. **B.** Try to remember which rooms have windows. Bedrooms 3 and 4, at the top of the floor plan, are the only rooms in the apartment that do. Choice (B) is correct.

8. **A.** Check your mental picture of the apartment before looking at the answer choices. If the firefighter is already in bedroom 4, he or she should use the fire escape located outside bedroom 4's window. Choice (A) is correct.

9. **A.** Recall the floor plan. The office can be accessed from the hallway or through the dining room. Because the hallway is blocked, the only access is through the dining room.

10. **D.** The question asks for rooms without windows. Think about the floor plan. Bedrooms 3 and 4 have access to the fire escape and additional windows that firefighters can enter, so you can eliminate Choices (A), (B), and (C). The correct answer is Choice (D) — bathroom 2 and the master bedroom have no windows.

11. **C.** Pyromaniacs typically experience joy, relief, or comfort from setting fires and watching them burn. They do not usually want to destroy property or harm others.

12. **A.** A pyromaniac typically feels frustration or tension before igniting a fire. If he or she is unable to start a fire, these feelings wouldn't be resolved and would likely worsen. The passage doesn't mention anything about attacking those who want to prevent a fire or engaging in other criminal acts, so you can eliminate Choices (B) and (C). The passage also mentions that pyromaniacs aren't typically under the influence of alcohol when they start fires; rather, their relief comes from the fire. Therefore, Choice (D) is also incorrect. The right answer is Choice (A).

13. **B.** The passage notes that pyromania is an impulse-control disorder. Pyromania is categorized as an impulse-control disorder in the DSM-IV (*Diagnostic and Statistical Manual of Mental Disorders,* 4th edition).

14. **B.** Smoke and embers from a basement fire can travel throughout the entire structure via staircases and walls. Smoke and embers may then move into the attic, thus threatening the entire structure.

15. **C.** Because stairways are typically continuous and open in larger buildings (such as the apartment building in the image provided), smoke and embers may use them to travel to the top of a building.

16. **D.** According to the passage, fire-stops are small pieces of wood placed within the walls to stop smoke from spreading upward.

17. **A.** The very last sentence of the passage states that firefighters should never direct a water stream through a ventilation hole. The water could actually stop the ventilation process and seriously threaten any firefighters inside the building.

18. **A.** One way to ventilate the basement fire is to cut one hole above the flames in the basement and an additional hole in the exterior wall of the living room. This will move the smoke outdoors instead of through the rest of the building.

19. **C.** According to the passage, cutting a hole in the side of the house opposite the staircase would allow smoke to follow the open staircase from the basement to the first floor and then move out the hole.

20. **B.** If smoke and fire have reached the top floor of the building (as a result of not being able to create ventilation on the first floor), firefighters should cut a hole in the roof to vent smoke and heat from the top of the building. The longer the fire burns in the attic, the more damage it will cause in the attic and the greater the chance another fire will ignite somewhere in the building.

21. **D.** While sizing up the scene, firefighters often use their trucks as roadblocks. They may park across lanes or only in the lane closest to the scene.

22. **B.** When firefighters *crib* a vehicle, they place wooden *cribbing* (pieces of wood of various sizes) and wedges in front or behind the tires to keep the vehicle from moving. If the vehicle is on its side, they place cribbing beneath the side of the vehicle that is on the ground.

23. **A.** In an ideal situation, at least one firefighter would be responsible for assessing each vehicle, resulting in all vehicles' receiving simultaneous and equal attention.

24. **C.** When firefighters *package* a victim, they dress and bandage the victim's wounds, splint broken bones, and immobilize the body.

25. **C.** If the vehicle is on its side, they would crib the vehicle to stop it from flipping over by placing blocks of wood beneath the side of the vehicle that is closest to the ground.

26. **C.** Firefighters should take pieces of the vehicle away from the victim instead of immediately removing the victim from the vehicle. This ensures that the victim is not injured by any piece of the vehicle during extrication.

27. **A.** According to the passage, the last thing firefighters should do before removing a victim from a car is ensure that all sharp edges are covered with cloth or other soft materials. Doing so keeps both the victim and rescue personnel from being cut, scraped, or bruised while moving away from the vehicle.

28. **D.** According to the passage, the first thing firefighters should do when they arrive on scene is evaluate their surroundings, noting the number of vehicles involved, traffic hazards, the potential for fires, and hazardous materials. Therefore, looking around the vehicle for potential dangers, Choice (D), should be done before firefighters begin to assess the victim.

29. **B.** The main point of this passage is that people should always be aware of safe practices that will help them escape their home or other buildings in the event of a fire.

30. **D.** If you waken at night and your home is on fire, you should roll out of bed and onto the floor. This ensures that you're away from any smoke or heat that may rise to the ceiling.

31. **C.** The fire department should not be called unless a fire is actually taking place; false alarms can distract or prevent firefighters from responding to real fires.

32. **D.** When speaking at a school, home, or meeting, firefighters should stress the importance of everyone's being prepared to handle a fire.

33. **B.** Rescuing victims and attacking the fire is the main priority at the scene of a fire. If any bystanders approach a firefighter in the midst of fighting a fire, he or she should tell the bystander to speak to the department's supervisor after the fire is under control.

34. **A.** In the event of a fire, all visitors and hospital personnel will be instructed to use the stairs instead of the elevators. A staircase containing papers, trash, and other items creates additional danger if people are trying to escape a burning building. The firefighter should insist that the manager instruct her custodial team to clean every stairway each night.

35. **D.** A firefighter's job does not include retrieving keys from locked cars or escorting drunken people home at the end of the night. Firefighters should also never hand the keys to a vehicle to an intoxicated person. The best thing to do in this situation would be to call a tow truck and a cab.

36. **C.** Illustration 15 shows a ventilation fan, which can be placed alongside a ventilation hole to draw smoke out of a structure. Choice (A) is a fire ladder, Choice (B) is a roll of caution tape, and Choice (D) is a portable water tank.

37. **B.** The items in illustrations 6 and 20 are a window punch and a crowbar, both of which can be used to enter a vehicle in which a victim is trapped. The items in Choice (A) are a bullhorn and a seatbelt cutter; in Choice (C), a pair of gloves and a saw; and Choice (D), a screwdriver and a self-contained breathing apparatus (SCBA).

38. **A.** Illustration 16 shows a tool strap, which firefighters use to carry tools. Choice (B) is a pair of gloves, Choice (C) is a roll of caution tape, and Choice (D) is a portable water tank.

39. **B.** A fire hose should be connected to a fire hydrant, illustration 3, to transfer water from the source to the fire. The item in Choice (A) is a first aid kit. Choice (C) shows a self-contained breathing apparatus, and Choice (D) is a ventilation fan.

40. **D.** The items in illustrations 12 and 19 are a pick-head axe and a ventilation saw, which firefighters use to cut or make ventilation holes in the roof or wall of a building. The items in Choice (A) are a megaphone and a wrench; in Choice (B), a screwdriver and a ladder; and in Choice (C), gloves and a push broom.

41. **C.** Illustration 11 shows a roll of caution tape, which is used to keep bystanders away from the scene of a fire or an accident. Choice (A) is a first aid kit, Choice (B) is a ladder, and Choice (D) is a ventilation fan.

42. **C.** Illustration 13 shows a push broom, which is used to clear debris off the road at the scene of a motor vehicle accident. Choice (A) is a fire hydrant, Choice (B) is a ladder, and Choice (D) is a self-contained breathing apparatus.

43. **D.** Illustration 14 shows a self-contained breathing apparatus, which a firefighter would take into a burning building. Choice (A) is a seat-belt cutter, Choice (B) is a roll of caution tape, and Choice (C) is a push broom.

44. **B.** Firefighter 2 should remain in the hall and hold constant conversation with Firefighter 1 as Firefighter 1 searches the room. The conversation will keep Firefighter 1 oriented as he reports his findings to Firefighter 2, who is keeping watch in the hall.

45. **A.** Firefighter 1 should be crawling close to the floor to avoid the extreme heat and smoke that is gathering near the ceiling.

46. **C.** Studies in the United States, Great Britain, and Australia have found that firefighters have a greater risk of experiencing a heart attack and five specific types of cancer than nonfirefighters.

47. **B.** Researchers have estimated that heart attacks contribute to approximately 52 percent of deaths that occur on the scenes of fires each year.

48. **B.** According to the passage, unions have petitioned for mandatory physical fitness programs, better protective gear, and government aid for firefighters diagnosed with cancers related to toxins found at the scene of fires. The passage does not say that they petitioned for mandatory leave to combat stress.

49. **D.** Scientists have linked mesothelioma to the long-term exposure of asbestos.

50. **A.** There must be five ladders that are ready to use, and the company has eight ladders. Officer Garcia discovers that four of them are in need of repair, so the other four are ready to use. Therefore, the fire chief must find one replacement ladder to meet the requirement of having five ready-to-use ladders.

51. **A.** The firefighters' main objective is to put out the fire in a timely manner so that there is little property damage. Choice (D) may seem like a good choice, because the firefighters are getting the hoses ready as they explain to the woman how quickly time passes in a frightening situation; however, the firefighters should be focusing on the fire.

52. **A.** The question says that hard suction hose, rubber-jacket hose, and hard-rubber hose need only be rinsed with water and that woven-jacket hose should be washed with water only when the dirt cannot be brushed. Therefore, most fire hoses should be washed with water as needed.

53. **A.** The experienced firefighter should tell the new firefighter to change his footwear and explain why he needs a particular set of boots to enter the premises. The next time the new firefighter responds to a chemical spill, he will know to wear different footwear.

54. **C.** Firefighters should never allow anyone to enter a burning building for any reason, even if the fire is on the opposite end of where the person requests to enter.

55. **B.** Arsonists tend to use inclement weather that may cause poor road conditions or visibility to assist them in their task of destroying property. A snowstorm may make it difficult for a fire company to get to the scene of a fire.

56. **B.** The passage states, "Even before they arrive, however, suspicions may arise. For example, the time of day the fire began and even weather conditions may point firefighters in the direction of arson." Therefore, members of the arson squad can start gathering evidence on their way to the fire scene. Choice (B) is correct.

57. **C.** When responding to a fire in the middle of the night, firefighters should be suspicious of a homeowner who is fully clothed and alert to what is going on around him or her. Typically, people are sleeping and disheveled when a fire occurs unexpectedly at night.

58. **C.** When responding to a fire in the middle of the night, firefighters should not be suspicious of a homeowner in pajamas. Typically, people are asleep when a fire occurs unexpectedly at night.

59. **B.** The shortest route to location 5 (Mike's Motors) from the intersection of Joseph Drive and 138th Street, without illegally traveling on any one-way streets, is east on 138th Street and south on Franklin Street.

60. **A.** The shortest route to the local high school from the firehouse, without illegally traveling on any one-way streets, is north on Carey Street and east on 142nd Street.

61. **C.** The firefighter should suggest that the delivery man, who is driving and cannot travel illegally on one-way streets, should turn north on the alley beside the Flower Shop. He should then go west on 138th Street and south on Joseph Drive.

62. **A.** The firefighter would be incorrect if he gave the woman driving directions that included traveling west on 140th Street. City Hall and the Flower Shop are located on a one-way section of 140th Street that requires traveling east in a vehicle.

63. **D.** The best route back to the fire house would include traveling south on Franklin Street and west on 146th Street.

64. **D.** Typically, only two to three firefighters are needed to lift/carry a victim from the floor to a gurney. All the firefighters should be on one side of the victim's body, so Firefighter 4 is not needed.

65. **A.** The firefighter positioned at the head/neck of the victim should be the one who instructs the other two firefighters; in this case, Firefighter 1 should perform these duties.

66. **D.** All firefighters should lift the victim and stand at the same time. In this case, Firefighters 1, 2, and 3 should perform these actions together.

67. **C.** The firefighters should roll the victim toward their chests before they lift the victim from the floor. This ensures that they have a strong hold on the victim.

68. **B.** The firefighters should keep their backs straight while lifting a victim off the floor; this helps properly support the victim's weight.

69. **A.** Each roll of tape is 1,500 feet; therefore, only 1 roll of tape is required.

70. **C.** Divide the distance to barricade by the length of a single roll of tape to find the number of rolls: 7,500 ÷ 1,500 = 5. Therefore, you need 5 rolls of tape.

71. **C.** Divide the distance to barricade by the length of a single roll of tape to find the number of rolls: 5,250 ÷ 1,500 = 3.5. Three full rolls of tape won't complete the barricade, so you'll have to use a fourth roll. Choice (C) is correct.

72. **B.** Divide the distance to barricade by the length of a single roll of tape to find the number of rolls: 3,750 ÷ 1,500 = 2.5. Two full rolls of tape won't complete the barricade, so you'll have to use a third roll. Choice (B) is correct.

73. **D.** Divide the distance to barricade by the length of a single roll of tape to find the number of rolls: 10,500 ÷ 1,500 = 7. Therefore, you need 7 rolls of tape.

74. **B.** Divide the distance to barricade by the length of a single roll of tape to find the number of rolls: 6,750 ÷ 1,500 = 4.5. Four full rolls of tape won't complete the barricade, so you'll have to use a fifth roll. Choice (B) is correct.

75. **B.** The second-due engine company is typically responsible for laying additional hose lines and ensuring a strong water supply.

76. **D.** The rapid intervention crew is typically responsible for rescuing distressed firefighters.

77. **A.** The first-due engine company initiates incident command and fire attack.

78. **C.** The truck/rescue company engages in search and rescue and performs ventilation.

79. **C.** Additional lighting is usually the responsibility of the truck/rescue company.

80. **A.** Although firefighters may not be trained to assist the woman, they should definitely help her. Guiding her to a chair and calling an ambulance is the best way to help.

81. **B.** Firefighters accused of any crimes, including theft, at the scene of a fire should always have the accuser/victim report the perceived crime to their department supervisor.

82. **C.** The firefighter in Choice (C) has taken all necessary precautions to avoid disrupting the thermal balance of the room; he has created ventilation in the roof, he is on his knees away from the fire, and he is directing the stream of water toward the bottom of the flames. In Choice (A), the firefighter is standing; in Choice (B), the firefighter has not ventilated the room; and in Choice (D), the firefighter is directing the water toward the thermal gases near the ceiling.

83. **D.** The arrow indicates that the cylinder is between ½ and ¾ of the way full; thus, the cylinder is more than ½ full.

84. **D.** The arrow on this gauge points to an area between 4,000 and 4,500 psi; therefore, it is closest to 4,200 psi. In Choice (A), the gauge shows 3,000 psi; in Choice (B), it shows 3,500 psi; and in Choice (C), it shows 2,500 psi.

85. **C.** The truck/rescue company assists in attacking the fire only when the first-due and second-due companies request its assistance. Otherwise, members of this company are responsible for other duties, such as rescuing victims, conducting salvage, ventilation, and placing ladders.

86. **C.** Firefighters perform overhaul duties after the fire is controlled or completely out, not in the midst of fighting a fire that has recently grown in size or strength.

87. **A.** Firefighters in Illustration A are using a nonspecific indirect approach to fight the fire. They are aiming the stream at the ceiling and allowing the water to drip carefully onto the flames below.

88. **D.** Firefighters in Illustration B are using an indirect approach with an O pattern. This means that the stream of water is repeatedly hitting the flames on the ground directly and then mixing with the heat and gases toward the ceiling.

89. **B.** Illustrations A and B show the room has been ventilated by breaking the window. Firefighters must ventilate the room before taking aim at any smoke, gases, or flames near the ceiling.

90. **B.** When a firefighter uses a mixture of direct (aiming at the floor/flames) and indirect (aiming at the ceiling/heat/gases) methods to attack a fire, he or she is using a combination attack.

91. **C.** Firefighters should never attempt to remove people from an elevator unless there is a medical emergency and the firefighters are specially trained for an elevator rescue.

92. **B.** Firefighters should make continuous contact with the passengers who are stuck in the car. When a car is stuck but visible from an open set of doors, firefighters can attempt to speak or shout to those trapped, assuring them that help is on the way.

93. **A.** If a firefighter must move evidence, he or she should move it as little as possible. The firefighter should attempt to preserve its original state and should not allow it to pass through multiple hands until the arson squad or investigators say it is appropriate to do so.

94. **B.** Because department superiors know that appearing in court is expensive and that it may keep a firefighter from work for several days, they encourage their firefighters to avoid touching or moving evidence if possible. Choice (D) is also a good answer, but the question uses the specific wording "based on the passage," and the last three sentences make it clear that supervisors worry about costly court trials and firefighters missing work.

95. **D.** If there is no threat to the trash can or any evidence inside, the firefighters should leave all burned papers in trash can for the arson team to investigate.

96. **B.** The firefighter should set up a barrier or stand guard at the doorway until he can show an investigator or member of an arson squad what he has found. Tampering with the door in any way may lead to the loss of crucial evidence.

97. **C.** According to the passage, the measurement of normal operating pressure should be taken during a time of day when an average amount of water in a neighborhood is in use. Therefore, the pressure depends on the time of day. Choice (C) is correct.

98. **B.** The pressure in hydrants before use is static, or unmoving, pressure.

99. **C.** While touring a fire station, firefighters can show children the equipment and methods used to keep safe during a fire. Firefighters can use the tour as an opportunity to teach children about fire safety. Choice (C) is correct.

100. **A.** Firefighters always respect their superiors, even if they don't agree with them. After the task has been completed according to the superior's specifications, the firefighter can then ask why the technique her superior requested was the correct one to use.

Answer Key

1. D	21. D	41. C	61. C	81. B
2. C	22. B	42. C	62. A	82. C
3. D	23. A	43. D	63. D	83. D
4. D	24. C	44. B	64. D	84. D
5. D	25. C	45. A	65. A	85. C
6. B	26. C	46. C	66. D	86. C
7. B	27. A	47. B	67. C	87. A
8. A	28. D	48. B	68. B	88. D
9. A	29. B	49. D	69. A	89. B
10. D	30. D	50. A	70. C	90. B
11. C	31. C	51. A	71. C	91. C
12. A	32. D	52. A	72. B	92. B
13. B	33. B	53. A	73. D	93. A
14. B	34. A	54. C	74. B	94. B
15. C	35. D	55. B	75. B	95. D
16. D	36. C	56. B	76. D	96. B
17. A	37. B	57. C	77. A	97. C
18. A	38. A	58. C	78. C	98. B
19. C	39. B	59. B	79. C	99. C
20. B	40. D	60. A	80. A	100. A

Chapter 21

Practice Exam 4: The National Firefighter Selection Inventory (NFSI)

● ●

*T*his practice test is based on the National Firefighter Selection Inventory (NFSI). The NFSI is a written firefighter exam developed by a group of experts from firefighting agencies throughout the United States. The test includes 105 cognitive-ability questions and 50 personality-attribute questions. Candidates have 150 minutes (2.5 hours) to complete the entire test. Cognitive-ability questions on the NFSI test fall into the following areas: verbal comprehension, verbal expression, problem sensitivity, deductive reasoning, inductive reasoning, information ordering, mathematical reasoning, and number facility. Personality-attribute questions on the NFSI test fall into the following areas: stress tolerance, team orientation, and motivation/attitude.

To get the most out of this practice test, take it like you'd take the real written exam:

- ✔ Allow yourself 120 minutes (2 hours) to complete the exam, and take the whole exam at one time. *Note:* Because personality-attribute questions have no right or wrong answers, we've omitted them from this practice test and included only 105 cognitive-ability questions, so we shortened the time frame.

- ✔ Take the test in a quiet place, such as a library or a private office, to avoid interruption.

- ✔ Bring a pencil and some scratch paper.

- ✔ Use the answer sheet that's provided.

After you complete the practice exam, check your answers against the answer explanations in Chapter 22. The purpose of this practice exam is to help you identify your strengths and weaknesses on the NFSI exam so you know where to focus your studies.

Answer Sheet for Practice Test 4

1 (A) (B) (C) (D) (E)	41 (A) (B) (C) (D) (E)	81 (A) (B) (C) (D) (E)
2 (A) (B) (C) (D) (E)	42 (A) (B) (C) (D) (E)	82 (A) (B) (C) (D) (E)
3 (A) (B) (C) (D) (E)	43 (A) (B) (C) (D) (E)	83 (A) (B) (C) (D) (E)
4 (A) (B) (C) (D) (E)	44 (A) (B) (C) (D) (E)	84 (A) (B) (C) (D) (E)
5 (A) (B) (C) (D) (E)	45 (A) (B) (C) (D) (E)	85 (A) (B) (C) (D) (E)
6 (A) (B) (C) (D) (E)	46 (A) (B) (C) (D) (E)	86 (A) (B) (C) (D) (E)
7 (A) (B) (C) (D) (E)	47 (A) (B) (C) (D) (E)	87 (A) (B) (C) (D) (E)
8 (A) (B) (C) (D) (E)	48 (A) (B) (C) (D) (E)	88 (A) (B) (C) (D) (E)
9 (A) (B) (C) (D) (E)	49 (A) (B) (C) (D) (E)	89 (A) (B) (C) (D) (E)
10 (A) (B) (C) (D) (E)	50 (A) (B) (C) (D) (E)	90 (A) (B) (C) (D) (E)
11 (A) (B) (C) (D) (E)	51 (A) (B) (C) (D) (E)	91 (A) (B) (C) (D) (E)
12 (A) (B) (C) (D) (E)	52 (A) (B) (C) (D) (E)	92 (A) (B) (C) (D) (E)
13 (A) (B) (C) (D) (E)	53 (A) (B) (C) (D) (E)	93 (A) (B) (C) (D) (E)
14 (A) (B) (C) (D) (E)	54 (A) (B) (C) (D) (E)	94 (A) (B) (C) (D) (E)
15 (A) (B) (C) (D) (E)	55 (A) (B) (C) (D) (E)	95 (A) (B) (C) (D) (E)
16 (A) (B) (C) (D) (E)	56 (A) (B) (C) (D) (E)	96 (A) (B) (C) (D) (E)
17 (A) (B) (C) (D) (E)	57 (A) (B) (C) (D) (E)	97 (A) (B) (C) (D) (E)
18 (A) (B) (C) (D) (E)	58 (A) (B) (C) (D) (E)	98 (A) (B) (C) (D) (E)
19 (A) (B) (C) (D) (E)	59 (A) (B) (C) (D) (E)	99 (A) (B) (C) (D) (E)
20 (A) (B) (C) (D) (E)	60 (A) (B) (C) (D) (E)	100 (A) (B) (C) (D) (E)
21 (A) (B) (C) (D) (E)	61 (A) (B) (C) (D) (E)	101 (A) (B) (C) (D) (E)
22 (A) (B) (C) (D) (E)	62 (A) (B) (C) (D) (E)	102 (A) (B) (C) (D) (E)
23 (A) (B) (C) (D) (E)	63 (A) (B) (C) (D) (E)	103 (A) (B) (C) (D) (E)
24 (A) (B) (C) (D) (E)	64 (A) (B) (C) (D) (E)	104 (A) (B) (C) (D) (E)
25 (A) (B) (C) (D) (E)	65 (A) (B) (C) (D) (E)	105 (A) (B) (C) (D) (E)
26 (A) (B) (C) (D) (E)	66 (A) (B) (C) (D) (E)	
27 (A) (B) (C) (D) (E)	67 (A) (B) (C) (D) (E)	
28 (A) (B) (C) (D) (E)	68 (A) (B) (C) (D) (E)	
29 (A) (B) (C) (D) (E)	69 (A) (B) (C) (D) (E)	
30 (A) (B) (C) (D) (E)	70 (A) (B) (C) (D) (E)	
31 (A) (B) (C) (D) (E)	71 (A) (B) (C) (D) (E)	
32 (A) (B) (C) (D) (E)	72 (A) (B) (C) (D) (E)	
33 (A) (B) (C) (D) (E)	73 (A) (B) (C) (D) (E)	
34 (A) (B) (C) (D) (E)	74 (A) (B) (C) (D) (E)	
35 (A) (B) (C) (D) (E)	75 (A) (B) (C) (D) (E)	
36 (A) (B) (C) (D) (E)	76 (A) (B) (C) (D) (E)	
37 (A) (B) (C) (D) (E)	77 (A) (B) (C) (D) (E)	
38 (A) (B) (C) (D) (E)	78 (A) (B) (C) (D) (E)	
39 (A) (B) (C) (D) (E)	79 (A) (B) (C) (D) (E)	
40 (A) (B) (C) (D) (E)	80 (A) (B) (C) (D) (E)	

NFSI Practice Test

Time: 120 minutes for 105 questions

Directions: Complete the following practice exam. Carefully read the directions that precede each passage or question set. Select the answer choice that most correctly answers each question. Mark the space on your answer sheet that corresponds to the question number and the letter indicating your choice.

Questions 1–3 are based on the following passage.

Engine 8 is dispatched at 8:46 p.m. to the scene of a car accident on Grove. Firefighters arrive at the scene at 8:59 p.m. and find that a Jeep swerved to miss a deer and hit a midsize car head on. A passenger in the midsize car, a male in his twenties, is trapped in the car.

Firefighters Sanchez and O'Rourke extricate the passenger from the vehicle. Firefighter Kane checks on the driver of the midsize car, a female in her twenties. She is sitting on the curb and appears dazed but uninjured. Firefighter Harris checks on the driver of the Jeep, a female in her forties.

The police arrive at the accident scene at 9:08 p.m., and an ambulance arrives at 9:12 p.m. Firefighters Sanchez and O'Rourke remove the passenger side door from the midsize car and successfully free the passenger by 9:20 p.m.

The passenger in the midsize car is loaded into the ambulance at 9:21 p.m. and arrives at St. Johns Hospital at 9:32 p.m. He is admitted. Neither the driver of the midsize car nor the driver of the Jeep suffered any injuries.

1. How much time elapsed between the time that Engine 8 arrived at the scene and the time that the passenger of the midsize car was loaded into the ambulance?

    (A) 19 minutes

    (B) 20 minutes

    (C) 21 minutes

    (D) 22 minutes

    (E) 23 minutes

2. Who checked on the driver of the Jeep?

    (A) Firefighter Harris

    (B) Firefighter Kane

    (C) Firefighter O'Rourke

    (D) Firefighter St. Johns

    (E) Firefighter Sanchez

3. At what time did the ambulance arrive at the scene?

    (A) 8:59 p.m.

    (B) 9:08 p.m.

    (C) 9:12 p.m.

    (D) 9:20 p.m.

    (E) 9:21 p.m.

Go on to next page

Question 4 is based on the following passage.

Firefighters were called to the scene of a brush fire on East Mountain this morning. The fire had spread to only a few acres when crews with the Department of Conservation began dropping water onto the flames from helicopters. However, despite their efforts, by noon the fire had spread to nearly 100 acres, and firefighters are still working to contain it.

Businesses in the area, including a mall with more than 50 stores, were concerned that the heavy smoke might damage merchandise and drive away customers. The fire marshal suggested that the stores change filters in air conditioning and heating units to prevent problems indoors.

The cause of the fire is under investigation. Firefighter Martin spoke to a motorist traveling in an SUV near East Mountain around the time the fire started. The motorist reported seeing smoke from a campfire before the flames erupted.

4. How did the fire most likely start?

(A) A group of campers intentionally started the fire.

(B) A group of campers failed to properly extinguish their campfire.

(C) A group of store owners did not change filters in heating units.

(D) A motorist in an SUV accidentally started the fire.

(E) There is no apparent cause for the fire.

Use the information in the following passage to answer questions 5–9.

The driver of a blue pickup truck is weaving in and out of his lane on an interstate. He tailgates the car in front of him and then dangerously passes the car. He then collides with a car in the right lane, a black Volkswagen. Several drivers who witness the accident pull over to assist those involved in the accident. A young man in his late teens uses his cell phone to call 911.

Firefighters arrive at the scene and assess the situation. They find the driver of the pickup truck, a man in his early fifties, unconscious and bleeding. He smells like alcohol. The driver of the Volkswagen, a woman in her late thirties, is conscious but is bleeding and complaining of head pain. The driver-side window is smashed, and she is covered in small pieces of glass. A passenger in the car, a woman in her late twenties, appears uninjured and has exited the vehicle.

The firefighters determine that the driver of the Volkswagen must be extricated so that her injuries can be assessed and treated. They cautiously remove the driver and discover that she has several deep cuts on her face and head.

Shortly after firefighters assess the driver of the Volkswagen, the driver of the pickup truck regains consciousness and is able to communicate how he feels. He staggers when he walks, and his speech is slurred. He appears to have broken his right arm. Firefighters monitor his condition until an ambulance arrives.

Both drivers are transported to the hospital. The driver of the pickup truck is treated and released. The driver of the Volkswagen is treated and admitted for observation.

Go on to next page

5. Which is an accurate description of the driver of the Volkswagen?

(A) a man in his early fifties

(B) a young man in his late teens

(C) a woman in her late twenties

(D) a woman in her late thirties

(E) a woman in her early forties

6. What is the MOST likely reason that the driver of the pickup truck collided with the Volkswagen?

(A) He was on his cell phone.

(B) He fell asleep.

(C) He was speeding.

(D) He hit the median.

(E) He was drunk.

7. What injury did the driver of the pickup truck suffer?

(A) several deep cuts on his head.

(B) several deep cuts on his face

(C) a broken left arm

(D) a broken right arm

(E) an abdominal injury

8. What is MOST likely to have caused the Volkswagen driver's injuries?

(A) the steering wheel

(B) the driver's side window

(C) the airbag

(D) the driver's side door

(E) the dashboard

9. What is an appropriate title for this passage?

(A) "The Dangers of Passing"

(B) "The Dangers of Speeding"

(C) "Assessing Accident Victims' Injuries"

(D) "The Dangers of Driving Drunk"

(E) "Witnesses Can Save Lives"

Use the information in the following passage to answer questions 10–12.

Portable fire extinguishers are classified into five categories based on their intended use. The following is a description of each category.

✔ **Class A:** Class A fire extinguishers are used on fires involving common combustibles such as paper, wood, cardboard, and cloth. These fire extinguishers have a numerical rating of 1-A, 2-A, 3-A, 4-A, 6-A, 10-A, 20-A, 30-A, and 40-A. The higher the number, the more square feet of fire the extinguisher can extinguish.

✔ **Class B:** This type of fire extinguisher is used to fight flammable or combustible liquids, greases, and gases, including gasoline, kerosene, and oil. Class B fire extinguishers have a numerical rating, which can be 1-B, 2-B, 5-B, 10-B, 20-B, 30-B, 40-B, or any number up to 640-B. The higher the number, the more square feet of fire the extinguisher can extinguish.

✔ **Class C:** Class C fire extinguishers are used to fight fire involving electrical equipment, such as appliances and computers. They should be used to fight electrical fires involving wires, outlets, and circuit breakers. Water can't be used to fight such fires because of the risk of shock. Class C fire extinguishers don't have a numerical rating.

Go on to next page

✔ **Class D:** These fire extinguishers are used to fight metal fires. The agent inside the extinguisher depends on the metal for which it was designed. Before using a Class D fire extinguisher, check the faceplate to see which type of metal the extinguisher should be used for. Class D fire extinguishers are commonly kept in chemical laboratories and are used to fight fires involving metals such as magnesium, sodium, titanium, and potassium. These fire extinguishers do not have a numerical rating.

✔ **Class K:** Class K extinguishers are used to fight fires involving cooking oil. These extinguishers are designed for use on products found in kitchens, such as peanut oil and canola oil. Although a Class B extinguisher can be used, a Class K extinguisher is more effective for these types of fires.

10. Firefighters are called to a fire in a house. The fire began in the kitchen, where the homeowner was cooking. When the food on the stove caught fire, the homeowner tried to put out the fire with water, which made the fire spread. Which type of fire extinguisher should the homeowner have used?

(A) Class A
(B) Class B
(C) Class C
(D) Class D
(E) Class K

11. Firefighters are called to a fire in a large warehouse filled with crates of paper. Which fire extinguisher rating would be best to fight this fire?

(A) 2-A
(B) 10-A
(C) 40-A
(D) 40-B
(E) 640-B

12. Firefighters are called to a fire in a chemical laboratory involving magnesium. Firefighter Ross grabs a Class D fire extinguisher. What should he do before using it?

(A) read the faceplate
(B) check the numerical rating
(C) make sure it is the right size
(D) see whether it contains water
(E) find the square footage

Go on to next page

Use the following table to answer questions 13 and 14.

Toxic Atmospheres Associated with Fire

Toxic Atmosphere	Traits	Cause	Effect
Carbon monoxide	Colorless; odorless	Incomplete combustion	Cause of most fire-related deaths
Hydrogen chloride	Slightly yellow; strong odor	Burning plastics	Irritated eyes and respiratory tract
Hydrogen cyanide	Colorless; bitter odor	Burning of rubber, foam, and paper	Difficulty breathing
Nitrogen dioxide	Reddish-brown; strong odor	Burning of grains	Irritated nose and throat

13. Firefighters respond to a fire near a silo on a farm. There is a strong odor. They find a man who says his throat is burning. What toxic atmosphere might he have been exposed to?

(A) carbon monoxide

(B) hydrogen chloride

(C) hydrogen cyanide

(D) nitrogen dioxide

(E) none of the above

14. Firefighters respond to a fire at a carpet factory. Several employees are finding it difficult to breathe. What toxic atmosphere might they have been exposed to?

(A) carbon monoxide

(B) hydrogen chloride

(C) hydrogen cyanide

(D) nitrogen dioxide

(E) none of the above

Use the information in the following passage to answer questions 15–19.

Firefighters must know how to operate and control a hose line to fight fires effectively. When firefighters use a large-size attack line, they have several methods to choose from in terms of operation.

Although it is strongly recommended that two or three firefighters work together to control a large-size attack line, sometimes this is not an option and a single firefighter must accomplish the task. When this is the case, the firefighter should follow the one-firefighter method of operation. The firefighter secures slack from the line and uses the slack to create a circle with the nozzle at one end and the line extending to the truck at the other end. The firefighter then sits on the part where the nozzle crosses the line extending to the truck. The firefighter has control of the line this way but only limited control of the nozzle.

The two-firefighter method is a better way to maintain control of the nozzle. When using this method, one firefighter holds the nozzle in one hand and holds the hose behind the nozzle in the other hand. This firefighter may rest the hose line against the waist and across the hip. The second firefighter gets into position about 3 feet behind the first. This firefighter places one knee on the line and both hands on the hose line.

The three-firefighter method is the best method to use when operating a large-size attack line. When using this method, the first firefighter holds the nozzle in the position described in the two-firefighter method. The second firefighter, called the backup firefighter, stands behind the first and holds the hose in both hands. The third firefighter kneels on the hose and holds it in both hands. Some departments prefer all three firefighters to use hose straps and remain standing, an option that offers better mobility.

Go on to next page

15. According to the two-firefighter method, the first firefighter places one hand on the _____ and the other hand on the hose. The second firefighter stands about _____ feet behind the first firefighter.

    (A) nozzle; 2

    (B) nozzle; 3

    (C) knee; 3

    (D) line; 2

    (E) line; 3

16. What is the best title for this passage?

    (A) "Methods for Using a Large-Size Attack Line"

    (B) "Why the Three-Person Firefighter Method Is Best"

    (C) "How to Hold the Nozzle"

    (D) "Firefighting Techniques"

    (E) "Gaining Control of the Attack Line"

17. Which of the following was NOT a method described for using a fire hose?

    (A) the one-firefighter method

    (B) the two-firefighter method

    (C) the three-firefighter method without hose straps

    (D) the three-firefighter method with hose straps

    (E) the four-firefighter method

18. Which firefighter would most likely kneel on the hose line?

    (A) a firefighter using the one-firefighter method

    (B) the first firefighter in the two-firefighter method

    (C) the second firefighter in the two-firefighter method

    (D) the first firefighter in the three-firefighter method

    (E) the second firefighter in the three-firefighter method

19. Which method should a firefighter use if he needs to have good control of the hose and needs to move from place to place?

    (A) the one-firefighter method

    (B) the two-firefighter method

    (C) the two-firefighter method with hose straps

    (D) the three-firefighter method without hose straps

    (E) the three-firefighter method with hose straps

Use the information in the following passage to answer questions 20–23.

Engine Company 10 was dispatched to a fire at 9:25 a.m. at an elementary school. A teacher in the parking lot called 911 and reported that he saw smoke pouring from some windows. The elementary school is located on Spring Street. Because class isn't in session yet, no children were in the building at the time.

Engine Company 10 arrived at the scene about 9:38 a.m. Firefighters saw the smoke and determined that it was coming from the windows of the teachers' lounge. The teachers and secretaries in the lounge had already evacuated the building. The firefighters proceeded into the building to look for the source of the smoke. They found a small fire inside a microwave in the teachers' lounge.

The firefighters were able to quickly put out the fire in the microwave using a handheld fire extinguisher in the lounge. The fire was out by 9:45 a.m.

Firefighter Rollins spoke to the teachers and secretaries who were in the lounge when the fire started. One of the teachers explained that she tried to heat food in an aluminum container. Before she knew it, flames were shooting from the microwave. She was unable to get close enough to the microwave to pull out the plug. Engine Company 10 left the elementary school and returned to the station at 11:03 p.m.

Go on to next page ⟶

20. Who reported the fire?

    (A) a teacher in the parking lot

    (B) a secretary of the school

    (C) the principal of the school

    (D) a student in the parking lot

    (E) a secretary in the parking lot

21. What did the firefighters do BEFORE they entered the building?

    (A) put out the fire in the microwave

    (B) determined the location of the fire

    (C) talked to the teachers who were in the lounge

    (D) extinguished the flames

    (E) looked for the microwave

22. What time did the firefighters extinguish the fire?

    (A) 9:25 a.m.

    (B) 9:38 a.m.

    (C) 9:45 a.m.

    (D) 10:02 a.m.

    (E) 11:03 p.m.

23. How much time elapsed from the time the firefighters were dispatched to the fire and the time they arrived at the scene?

    (A) 3 minutes

    (B) 12 minutes

    (C) 13 minutes

    (D) 20 minutes

    (E) 23 minutes

Use the information in the following passage to answer questions 24–27.

Firefighters use rope to haul tools, support rescuers, and rescue fire victims. The four common types of rope used by firefighters are laid, braided, braid-on-braid, and kernmantle. Here is a description of each of these types.

✔ **Laid rope:** This type of rope is made of strands of yarn, usually three, that are twisted together to create rope strands. It is flexible, stretchy, easy to splice, and inexpensive. However, because the strands are exposed, laid rope is subject to abrasion and is easily damaged. Laid rope is used primarily as utility rope.

✔ **Braided rope:** Braided rope is usually made of synthetic fibers that are intertwined or braided together. Braided rope is harder to splice than laid rope and is more expensive. It is less stretchy and is less likely to tangle than laid rope. Like laid rope, braided rope is typically used as utility rope.

✔ **Braid-on-braid rope:** This type of rope is also called *double-braided rope.* It has an outer sheath and an inner core, and both the sheath and the core are braided, which makes the rope strong. It does not stretch, but the sheath and core have a tendency to slide. Firefighters usually use braid-on-braid rope for utility applications.

✔ **Kernmantle rope:** Kernmantle rope is a jacketed rope, which means it has a covering over the load-bearing strands. The outer jacket is called the *sheath,* and the load-bearing strands are called the *kern.* Kernmantle is the strongest type of rope and is not susceptible to abrasion. Dynamic kernmantle rope stretches, whereas static kernmantle rope doesn't. Fire departments frequently use static kernmantle rope for rescue operations.

Go on to next page

24. Firefighters are fighting a fire in a four-story apartment building. They need an extremely strong rope that does not stretch to rescue a burn victim. What type of rope will they most likely use?

    (A) static kernmantle

    (B) braided

    (C) dynamic kernmantle

    (D) braid-on-braid

    (E) laid

25. At the fire station, firefighters use an inexpensive rope that is easy to splice so they can attach it to hooks. What type of rope do they most likely use?

    (A) static kernmantle

    (B) braided

    (C) dynamic kernmantle

    (D) braid on braid

    (E) laid

26. Braid-on-braid rope has an outer braid called a(n) _____ and an inner braid called a(n) _____.

    (A) jacket; kern

    (B) jacket; core

    (C) sheath; core

    (D) outer; inner

    (E) sheath; kern

27. Firefighters are using braid-on-braid rope to lift tools to the upper story of a building. What is the primary concern in using this type of rope?

    (A) It will splice.

    (B) It will tangle.

    (C) It will stretch.

    (D) It will slide.

    (E) It will abrade.

Use the information in the following passage to answer questions 28–30.

Firefighters spend a great deal of time at the fire station waiting to be dispatched to fires. It is important that they minimize or eliminate safety hazards at the fire station, both for their own safety and the safety of visitors.

They should make every effort to eliminate conditions that could cause trips, slips, and falls. Firefighters should take care to eliminate slippery surfaces by cleaning up spills as soon as they occur. This also holds true for water tracked in by visitors. Firefighters should mop up water right away. They should keep floors clean and pick up and put away loose items. They should ensure that aisles and stairways are unobstructed and that stairs and hallways are well lit. They should inspect hand rails, slide poles, and slides to make sure that they are clean and in good condition.

Firefighters should take extra care when cleaning and maintaining tools and equipment. They should always use appropriate personal protective equipment (PPE) and remove jewelry, such as watches and rings, at the start of each shift. They should inspect tools before using them to make sure they are in good working condition.

Back strains are a common injury among firefighters and are most often caused by improper lifting. Firefighter should learn how to lift equipment correctly at the fire station. They should not attempt to lift heavy equipment alone. In addition to injuring themselves, they risk dropping and breaking expensive equipment.

Go on to next page

28. What would be the most appropriate title for the preceding passage?

    (A) "Problems at the Fire Station"

    (B) "Keeping the Fire Station Clean"

    (C) "Preparing for Visitors at the Station"

    (D) "Avoiding Back Strain at the Fire Station"

    (E) "Minimizing Safety Hazards at the Station"

29. Which is NOT discussed as a safety concern at the fire station?

    (A) taking care when cleaning equipment

    (B) keeping floors clean and dry

    (C) lifting equipment correctly

    (D) walking, not running, on floors

    (E) inspecting hand rails, slide poles, and slides

30. Why is it important for firefighters to learn how to lift equipment correctly?

    (A) because if they lift something incorrectly, they might injure their backs

    (B) because they must often lift equipment alone

    (C) because if they lift something incorrectly, they might drop and break equipment

    (D) both A and B

    (E) both A and C

Use the information in the following passage to answer questions 31–33.

To avoid becoming trapped in a collapsed building, firefighters must understand how buildings are constructed. Houses and buildings are built to withstand weather conditions, such as wind, snow, and rain. These extra weather-resistant materials make the building heavy. The intended use of the building can also weigh it down. For example, an office building might be filled with heavy furniture, equipment, and many people. These factors all create stress on the building's ability to resist gravity and collapse. This stress is called *building load.*

Load is divided into two broad types: dead load and live load. *Dead load* refers to the weight of building materials and any equipment permanently attached to the building. *Live load* includes movable equipment, furniture, people — anything not attached to the structure.

Dead and live load can be further broken down into these categories: distributed load, concentrated load, and impact load. *Distributed load,* such as snow on a roof, is a load that is applied equally to a large area. *Concentrated load* is a load applied to a small area. An air-conditioning unit on a roof is an example of a concentrated load. *Impact load* is load that is in motion, such as people moving in an office building.

31. Load that refers to the weight of building materials along with equipment that is permanently attached to the building is called _____ load.

    (A) live

    (B) distributed

    (C) concentrated

    (D) impact

    (E) dead

32. A fire chief is concerned that part of a building that is on fire might collapse. This part of the building has a heavy heating unit on a top floor that is not permanently attached to the building. What type of load is this?

    (A) building

    (B) dead

    (C) distributed

    (D) concentrated

    (E) impact

Go on to next page

33. Which is an example of a live load?

    (A) office furniture in a building

    (B) a wind gust hitting a building

    (C) a house's roof

    (D) a house's windows

    (E) people outside the building

Use the following passage to answer questions 34–35.

> Firefighters sometimes have to break a glass panel in a door to unlock the door and enter a home to fight a fire. Here are the steps for breaking a glass door panel in no particular order.
>
> 1. Use the tool to clear away the broken glass in the doorframe.
>
> 2. Stand to the side of the glass panel that you need to break.
>
> 3. Choose the most appropriate tool to break the glass.
>
> 4. Using a gloved hand, reach inside and unlock the door.
>
> 5. Strike the glass as close to the top of the pane as you can.

34. What is the logical order of the above statements?

    (A) 3, 2, 5, 1, 4

    (B) 2, 4, 1, 5, 3

    (C) 4, 3, 5, 1, 4

    (D) 3, 5, 2, 4, 1

    (E) 2, 3, 1, 5, 4

35. According to the above statements, what should firefighters do after they clear away the broken glass?

    (A) choose the correct tool

    (B) unlock the door

    (C) strike the glass close to the top of the pane

    (D) break the glass

    (E) stand to the side of the glass pane

Go on to next page →

Use the information in the table to answer questions 36–39.

Classification of Flammable and Combustible Liquids

Classification	Term	Flash Point*; Boiling Point	Examples
Class IA	Flammable	Below 73°F; Below 100°F	Ethyl ether, ethyl chloride, petroleum ether
Class IB	Flammable	Below 73°F; Above 100°F	Acetone, ethyl alcohol, gasoline
Class IC	Flammable	Above 73°F; Below 100°F	Turpentine, methyl alcohol, isopropanol
Class II	Combustible	At or above 100°F; NA	Kerosene, Camphor oil, acetic acid
Class IIIA	Combustible	At or above 140°F; NA	Naphthalene, octyl alcohol
Class IIIB	Combustible	At or above 200°F; NA	Glycerine, propylene glycol

*Flash point is the minimum temperature at which a liquid gives off a vapor that can ignite.

36. Which of the following classifications has a flash point below 73°F?

    (A) Class IB
    (B) Class IC
    (C) Class II
    (D) Class IIIA
    (E) Class IIIB

37. Which of the following liquids will boil at a temperature below 100°F?

    (A) kerosene
    (B) acetic acid
    (C) turpentine
    (D) camphor oil
    (E) glycerine

38. Firefighters may use aqueous film forming foam, called AFFF/Class B, to attack flammable liquid fires. Which of the following is considered a flammable liquid?

    (A) petroleum ether
    (B) kerosene
    (C) octyl alcohol
    (D) naphthalene
    (E) acetic acid

39. Firefighters are called to the scene of an overturned tanker truck on an interstate that has resulted in a gasoline spill. At what temperature will the gasoline start to boil?

    (A) 70°F
    (B) 75°F
    (C) 80°F
    (D) 95°F
    (E) 105°F

Go on to next page

Use the information in the following passage to answer question 40.

Firefighter Torres is concerned with the odd behavior of Firefighter Hogan. Although Firefighter Hogan has been a responsible employee in the past, his behavior has changed. He is often late to work and looks ill. He says he is going home after his shift, but then his wife calls looking for him. Firefighter Torres knows that his wife has threatened to leave him if he doesn't stop drinking, but Firefighter Hogan says he only drinks occasionally.

40. Based on the information given in the passage, what is most likely the reason for Firefighter Hogan's behavior?

(A) financial problems

(B) marital problems

(C) alcohol problems

(D) physical illness

(E) boredom

Use the information in the following passage to answer questions 41–43.

There have been a large number of fires in the area recently. The following are descriptions of each fire:

✔ **Multifamily dwelling:** (February 10) The cause of the fire was determined to be a portable heater that was left on near newspapers and magazines. There was some damage to three apartments. Two other apartments suffered smoke and water damage.

✔ **House 1:** (February 15) The cause of the fire was determined to be soot buildup in the chimney. Damage was limited to the living and dining rooms because firefighters were able to contain the fire.

✔ **Office building:** (February 23) The cause of the fire has not yet been determined. Much of the office furniture and electronic equipment was destroyed, but the building structure remains intact.

✔ **House 2:** (February 24) The cause of the fire is believed to be faulty wiring. The house and its contents were destroyed because the fire spread very quickly and the house was engulfed before firefighters arrived. The fire also spread to a nearby double-block, destroying one side. The second side suffered smoke and water damage.

✔ **Restaurant:** (March 1) The cause of the fire was determined to be grease in the kitchen. Only the kitchen sustained damage because the manager put out the fire with a hand-held extinguisher. The fire was out before firefighters arrived at the scene.

Go on to next page

41. Which fire caused the most damage?

    (A) multifamily dwelling

    (B) house 1

    (C) office building

    (D) house 2

    (E) restaurant

42. What was the cause of the fire in House 2?

    (A) grease in the kitchen

    (B) soot buildup in the chimney

    (C) faulty wiring

    (D) a portable heater

    (E) the cause has not yet been determined

43. Which fire was put out before firefighters arrived?

    (A) multifamily dwelling

    (B) house 1

    (C) office building

    (D) house 2

    (E) restaurant

Use the information in the following passage to answer questions 44–46.

When attacking a fire, firefighters should be aware of the type of materials used to construct the building. Knowing this can help them stay safe and effectively fight the fire.

Most structures contain wood. The way in which wood reacts to fire depends on the size of the wood and the amount of moisture it contains. Smaller pieces of wood burn much more quickly than larger pieces, such as wooden beams. It is not uncommon for wooden beams to retain their shape during a fire. Wood that contains a great deal of moisture burns more slowly than very dry wood. Wood sometimes contains fire retardants designed to slow burning.

Concrete, brick, and stone are referred to as *masonry*. Masonry usually retains its form, even when exposed to fire for many hours. This is why masonry is used to build *firewalls*, structures designed to stop the spread of fire. Although concrete blocks and bricks may crack, they usually retain their structure and continue to provide support.

Most modern buildings have steel supports. Steel elongates in high temperatures. At about 900°F, steel weakens, and at 1,100°F it completely fails. Different types of steel react differently to fire, however, so firefighters should find out which type of steel was used in a structure. Firefighters can also use water to cool the steel and keep it from expanding and possibly collapsing.

44. What is the main advantage of masonry in a fire?

    (A) It can be cooled with water.

    (B) It expands but continues to support.

    (C) It retains its form in high temperatures.

    (D) It contains a great deal of moisture.

    (E) It contains fire retardants.

45. What is a disadvantage of steel in a fire?

    (A) It will fail at high temperatures.

    (B) It often cracks and breaks.

    (C) It needs moisture not to burn.

    (D) Small pieces burn very quickly.

    (E) Large pieces lose their shape.

46. What influences the speed at which a fire in a wooden structure spreads?

    (A) the age of the wood

    (B) the shape of the wood

    (C) the type of wood

    (D) the color of the wood

    (E) the moisture content of the wood

Go on to next page

> *Choose the word that is spelled correctly to complete the following sentences.*

47. Tools and _____ are vital to a firefighter's job.

    (A) equiptment

    (B) equitment

    (C) equipment

    (D) equipmint

    (E) equiptmant

48. The road was closed to _____ fire crews.

    (A) accommodate

    (B) acommodate

    (C) accomodate

    (D) accommadate

    (E) acomodate

49. Becoming physically fit requires _____ and determination.

    (A) dicipline

    (B) dicspline

    (C) disipline

    (D) discipline

    (E) discapline

50. It takes practice to _____ a fire hose effectively.

    (A) meneuver

    (B) maneuver

    (C) manuver

    (D) maneuvar

    (E) meneuvar

51. A Class C fire _____ is designed to put out an energized electrical fire.

    (A) extinguasher

    (B) extinguisher

    (C) extiguisher

    (D) ecstingwisher

    (E) extinguicher

52. When inspecting a self-contained breathing apparatus, you should always make sure that the air _____ is full.

    (A) cilinder

    (B) sylinder

    (C) cylinder

    (D) silinder

    (E) cylander

53. The bowline is a _____ knot that can serve many functions during fire operations.

    (A) versatile

    (B) versatal

    (C) versatel

    (D) versetal

    (E) versatle

54. Vertical _____ allows gases, smoke, and heat to escape from a point above a fire.

    (A) ventalation

    (B) ventalashun

    (C) ventilasion

    (D) ventelation

    (E) ventilation

> *For questions 55–56, please identify which one of the underline words is spelled incorrectly.*

55. The <u>transmission</u> of heat from one <u>area</u> to another can occur via three <u>mechanisms</u>: <u>conducsion</u>, convection, or <u>radiation</u>.

    (A) transmission

    (B) area

    (C) mechanisms

    (D) conducsion

    (E) radiation

56. Some common <u>elements</u> of a firefighter's personal protective <u>equipment</u> are a helmet, a <u>spesially</u> <u>designed</u> coat and pants, gloves, and a self-contained breathing <u>apparatus</u>.

    (A) elements

    (B) equipment

    (C) spesially

    (D) designed

    (E) apparatus

Go on to next page

> *Choose the appropriate word or phrase to complete the following sentences.*

57. Forward, reverse, and split _____ three basic types of supply hose lays.

    (A) is

    (B) are

    (C) was

    (D) has

    (E) am

58. After climbing a ladder to the second story, the firefighter _____ the window so he could enter the home and rescue the child.

    (A) broke

    (B) break

    (C) broken

    (D) breaked

    (E) broked

59. The firefighters developed a program about fire safety and prevention, which they plan to present _____ local elementary school students.

    (A) from

    (B) by

    (C) to

    (D) of

    (E) at

60. The second fire engine _____ more hard-suction hose, so now we have enough to reach the creek at the bottom the embankment and draft some water.

    (A) has brung

    (B) brang

    (C) has brought

    (D) bring

    (E) has brang

61. After the fire was extinguished, the firefighters _____ to the fire station.

    (A) will return

    (B) returned

    (C) return

    (D) is returned

    (E) are returning

62. Dried wood burns _____ than wood with a high moisture content does.

    (A) quicklier

    (B) quickly

    (C) quickest

    (D) more quickly

    (E) most quickly

63. Victor changed _____ mind about switching from a ladder company to an engine company.

    (A) their

    (B) its

    (C) he

    (D) his

    (E) him

64. The cause of the fire that destroyed the home _____ faulty wiring.

    (A) be

    (B) are

    (C) was

    (D) were

    (E) will be

65. The siren on the fire truck _____ drivers, who pulled to the side of the road and allowed the truck to pass.

    (A) alerted

    (B) will have alerted

    (C) will alert

    (D) will have been alerting

    (E) is alerting

Go on to next page

66. The abandoned warehouse began to
   _____ early in the morning.

   (A) burning

   (B) burned

   (C) burnt

   (D) burns

   (E) burn

67. The larger brush truck could maneuver the
   rough terrain better _____ the smaller
   brush truck could.

   (A) that

   (B) from

   (C) then

   (D) for

   (E) than

68. The wind _____ from the west all
   evening, which caused the wildland fire
   to spread ever farther.

   (A) blew

   (B) blown

   (C) blow

   (D) blowed

   (E) blue

69. The chief arrived at the fire faster than
   _____.

   (A) us

   (B) them

   (C) me

   (D) I

   (E) him

70. Chief Samuels leads tours for the children
   who visit the fire station on field trips
   because he is _____ than the other
   firefighters.

   (A) more friendlier

   (B) friendly

   (C) most friendly

   (D) friendlier

   (E) friendliest

71. The city council finished _____ budget,
   which includes a grant to the three local
   fire stations.

   (A) their

   (B) its

   (C) there

   (D) they're

   (E) it's

72. The jacket of the 1-inch woven-jacket hose
   was _____, so the hose had to be
   replaced.

   (A) been torn

   (B) torn

   (C) tear

   (D) tore

   (E) tears

*Please calculate the correct answers to the fol-
lowing questions.*

73. A tanker truck responds to a barn fire in a
   farmer's field. The truck travels at an average speed of 40 mph. It will take the truck
   15 minutes to reach the fire. How far away
   is the barn?

   (A) 5 miles

   (B) 7 miles

   (C) 10 miles

   (D) 12 miles

   (E) 14 miles

74. What is the square root of 1,600?

   (A) 20

   (B) 25

   (C) 30

   (D) 35

   (E) 40

Go on to next page

75. A fire has damaged part of a one-bedroom apartment. The apartment has a living room that is 10 feet by 12 feet, a bedroom that is 10 feet by 16 feet, a bathroom that is 6 feet by 6 feet, a kitchen that is 8 feet by 10 feet, and a dining room that is 6 feet by 6 feet. Firefighters contained the fire, so the smoke and water damaged only the kitchen and the dining room. How many square feet of the house were damaged?

    (A) 90 square feet

    (B) 116 square feet

    (C) 152 square feet

    (D) 312 square feet

    (E) 432 square feet

76. A fire department is dispatched to a car accident 5 miles from the fire station. The fire truck can travel to the accident scene at an average speed of 30 mph. What is the minimum amount of time it will take the fire truck to reach the car accident?

    (A) 10 minutes

    (B) 12 minutes

    (C) 16 minutes

    (D) 20 minutes

    (E) 25 minutes

77. Firefighters respond to a fire in a garage. The garage is 16 feet long by 20 feet wide. What is the area of the garage?

    (A) 36 square feet

    (B) 48 square feet

    (C) 72 square feet

    (D) 120 square feet

    (E) 320 square feet

78. Firefighters request a ladder truck at a fire in an apartment complex. The apartment complex has 12 stories. Each story has a height of 15 feet. How tall is the apartment complex?

    (A) 70 feet

    (B) 100 feet

    (C) 180 feet

    (D) 215 feet

    (E) 265 feet

79. During a training exercise, a firefighter must climb eight flights of steps in full bunker gear. Each flight has 12 steps. How many total steps must the firefighter climb to complete the training exercise?

    (A) 60

    (B) 72

    (C) 84

    (D) 96

    (E) 108

80. Your fire engine includes six hoses that are 125 feet long, two hoses that are 75 feet long, and one hose that is 150 feet long. If you attach all these hoses together, what would the total length of the hose be?

    (A) 325 feet

    (B) 425 feet

    (C) 975 feet

    (D) 1,050 feet

    (E) 1,200 feet

81. A fire alarm is tripped at the movie theater on the opposite end of town, which is 12 miles away. The fire engine arrives at the movie theater 20 minutes after leaving the station. What is the average speed the engine traveled between the station and the movie theater?

    (A) 25 mph

    (B) 30 mph

    (C) 32 mph

    (D) 34 mph

    (E) 36 mph

82. For ladders that are 35 feet in length or less, the ladder's reach is about 1 foot less than the overall length. For ladders that are more than 35 feet in length, the ladder's reach is about 2 feet less than the overall length. What is the reach of a ladder that has a length of 40 feet?

    (A) 38 feet

    (B) 39 feet

    (C) 40 feet

    (D) 41 feet

    (E) 42 feet

Go on to next page ⟶

83. The hose dryer at your fire station is drying several lengths of hose. Four of the hoses are 125 feet long, two of the hoses are 150 feet long, and one of the hoses is 175 feet long. What is the approximate average length of the hoses?

    (A) 64 feet

    (B) 116 feet

    (C) 139 feet

    (D) 150 feet

    (E) 161 feet

84. A fire alarm awoke a sleeping family at 2:43 a.m. At 2:47 a.m., the fire department was dispatched to the residence to put out a chimney fire. At 2:51 a.m., the fire engine left the station to respond to the call. The engine arrived at the home by 2:58 a.m. By 3:37 a.m., the fire department had successfully extinguished the fire. How much time elapsed between the time the fire engine left the station and the time the fire department extinguished the fire?

    (A) 39 minutes

    (B) 46 minutes

    (C) 50 minutes

    (D) 54 minutes

    (E) 57 minutes

Use the following information to answer questions 85–86.

Lieutenant Hernandez has to order items to distribute to children at the local elementary school during Fire Safety Week. The following is a list of items that Lieutenant Hernandez wants to order, along with the price for each item.

Item	Price
Reflective stickers (500 count)	$125.00
Plastic fire helmets (100 count)	$550.00
Lollipops with department logo (500 count)	$375.00
Fire safety coloring books (100 count)	$435.00
Fire safety DVD	$22.00

85. Based on the information provided in the table, what is the total cost for all of the items Lieutenant Hernandez wants to order?

    (A) $1,485.00

    (B) $1,507.00

    (C) $1,529.00

    (D) $1,550.00

    (E) $1,557.00

86. After making some calculations, Lieutenant Hernandez determines that the department does not have enough money to order all these items. He decides to order everything except the plastic fire helmets and the fire safety DVD. What is the total cost of his order?

    (A) $935.00

    (B) $957.00

    (C) $1,050.00

    (D) $1,110.00

    (E) $1,485.00

Go on to next page

Please calculate the correct answers to the following questions.

87. $\sqrt{289} + 87 - 26 =$

(A) 61

(B) 78

(C) 89

(D) 176

(E) 350

88. Firefighter Marshall has loaded five lengths of 75-foot hose on the fire engine. The hoses are connected by four couplings, each of which is 4 inches long. He wants the engine to carry 500 feet of hose. Approximately how much more hose does he need?

(A) 109.0 feet

(B) 116.4 feet

(C) 123.7 feet

(D) 125.0 feet

(E) 127.3 feet

Use the following table to answer questions 89–91.

Types of Fire Call by Year

Type of Fire Call	2007	2008	2009
Structure fire	13	6	9
Wildland fire	27	44	21
Vehicle fire	10	?	11
Vehicle accident	35	28	41
Total	85	87	?

89. How many vehicle fires occurred in 2008?

(A) 7

(B) 9

(C) 11

(D) 14

(E) 17

90. What was the total number of fire calls in 2009?

(A) 73

(B) 77

(C) 82

(D) 85

(E) 87

91. Approximately what percentage of the total fires in 2007 were wildland fires?

(A) 12 percent

(B) 15 percent

(C) 27 percent

(D) 32 percent

(E) 41 percent

Please calculate the correct answers to the following questions.

92. Methane has an upper flammable limit that is five times less than the upper flammable limit for hydrogen. If hydrogen's upper flammable limit is 75.0, what is the upper flammable limit for methane?

(A) 5.0

(B) 7.5

(C) 15.0

(D) 25.0

(E) 27.5

93. 0.375 is equivalent to what fraction?

(A) $\frac{3}{4}$

(B) $\frac{2}{3}$

(C) $\frac{1}{4}$

(D) $\frac{3}{5}$

(E) $\frac{3}{8}$

Go on to next page

94. The maximum heat release rate for an upholstered sofa is 3,033.0 BTUs. The maximum heat release rate for a mattress is 37.9 BTUs. Approximately how many times greater is the maximum heat release rate for an upholstered sofa than for a mattress?

    (A) 80.0

    (B) 85.4

    (C) 87.3

    (D) 90.0

    (E) 91.3

95. Use the table below to determine which statement most accurately describes the relationship between the number of hours a wildland fire burns and the number of acres the fire consumes.

Number of Hours	Number of Acres Burned
1	25
2	27.5
3	30.25
4	33.275

    (A) As the number of hours increases by 1, the number of acres burned doubles.

    (B) As the number of hours increases by 1, the number of acres burned increases by 10 percent.

    (C) As the number of hours increases, the number of acres burned decreases.

    (D) As the number of hours increases, the number of acres burned decreases by half.

    (E) As the number of hours increases, the number of acres burned increases by 25 percent.

Use the following table to answer questions 96–98.

Information from the table has been purposefully omitted. Please calculate the missing information, if needed, to answer the questions.

The fire department keeps records of the number of students in each type of school in its coverage area and uses this information to plan for fire safety programs such as fire drills and fire prevention week. Recently the number of students in all types of schools has decreased.

School Type	2008	2009	Decrease
Daycare/preschool	137	127	10
Elementary school	1,263	?	196
Middle school	1,971	1,726	245
High school	2,807	2,688	119
Vocational school	216	192	24

Go on to next page

96. Which type of school had the greatest percentage of decrease?

    (A) Daycare/preschool

    (B) Elementary school

    (C) Middle school

    (D) High school

    (E) Vocational school

97. How many elementary school students were there in 2009?

    (A) 1,067

    (B) 1,113

    (C) 1,208

    (D) 1,317

    (E) 1,459

98. In 2009, what was the ratio of students in vocational schools to students in high schools?

    (A) 1:5

    (B) 1:3

    (C) 5:17

    (D) 1:20

    (E) 1:14

> *Please calculate the correct answers to the following questions.*

99. Your department has a set amount of money that it spends on fuel for each of five trucks: a small brush truck, a heavy brush truck, a ladder truck, a fire engine, and a cascade unit. Last year, 17 percent of that budget paid for fuel in the small brush truck; 22 percent paid for fuel in the heavy brush truck; 13 percent paid for fuel in the ladder truck; 36 percent paid for fuel in the engine. What percentage paid for fuel in the cascade unit?

    (A) 12 percent

    (B) 14 percent

    (C) 17 percent

    (D) 18 percent

    (E) 20 percent

100. You inspect an office building with a floor area of 42,000 square feet. According to the fire code, the office building should have one 10-pound ABC dry chemical fire extinguisher for every 6,000 square feet of floor area. The office building currently has four fire extinguishers. How many more must it purchase?

    (A) 2

    (B) 3

    (C) 4

    (D) 5

    (E) none

101. Use the table below to determine which statement most accurately describes the relationship between the number of hoses firefighters load onto a truck and the time required to load them.

Number of Hoses	Total Time
1	34 seconds
2	1 minute, 8 seconds
3	1 minute, 42 seconds
4	2 minutes, 16 seconds

(A) As the time increases by 34 seconds, firefighters are able to load an additional hose onto the truck.

(B) As the time increases by 34 seconds, firefighters are able to double the number of hoses they load onto the truck.

(C) As the number of hoses increases by 1, the time required to load them doubles.

(D) As the number of hoses increases by 1, the time required to load them decreases.

(E) As the number of hoses increases by 1, the time required to load them triples.

Go on to next page

102. Use the table below to determine which statement most accurately describes the relationship between the distance from a heavy load to the pivot point of a lever (in feet) and the force required to lift the load (in pounds).

Distance from Load to Pivot Point	Force Required to Lift Load
1 foot	40 pounds
2 feet	100 pounds
3 feet	200 pounds
4 feet	400 pounds

(A) After the first foot, as the number of feet increases by 1, the force required to lift the load triples.

(B) After the first foot, as the number of feet increases by 1, the force required to lift the load decreases.

(C) After the first foot, as the number of feet increases by 1, the force required to lift the load increases by half.

(D) After the first foot, as the number of feet increases by 1, the force required to lift the load doubles.

(E) After the first foot, as the number of feet increases by 1, the force required to lift the load increases by 75 percent.

103. Canonburg Fire Department responded to 55 calls in January, 47 calls in February, 53 calls in March, and 49 calls in April. Based on the department's average number of calls each month, about how many calls can Canonburg Fire Department expect in May?

(A) 41

(B) 43

(C) 48

(D) 51

(E) 58

104. Firefighter O'Hare responded to 48 fires last month. At 12 fires, he manned the nozzle. At 27 fires, he conducted search and rescue operations. At 9 fires, he created ventilation. At what percentage of the fires did Firefighter O'Hare perform tasks other than manning the nozzle?

(A) 9 percent

(B) 25 percent

(C) 36 percent

(D) 55 percent

(E) 75 percent

105. Nylon rope will melt at 480°F. Polyethylene rope will melt at 275°F. How many times hotter must the temperature be for a nylon rope to melt than for a polyethylene rope to melt? Round your answer to the nearest tenth.

(A) 0.4

(B) 0.6

(C) 1.6

(D) 1.7

(E) 2.7

Chapter 22

Practice Exam 4: Answers and Explanations

• •

1 f you've finished the NFSI practice exam (Chapter 21), you're probably curious to see how you did. Use the answers and explanations in this chapter to see how well you performed and to get info on answering any problems you missed. Remember, the practice exam can help you determine where you need to focus your studies for the real NFSI exam. To quickly score your test without reading the answer explanations, flip to the "Answer Key" at the end of the chapter.

Answers and Explanations

1. **D.** According to the passage, Engine 8 arrived at the scene at 8:59 p.m., and the passenger in the midsize car was loaded into the ambulance at 9:21 p.m. This is a difference of 22 minutes.

2. **A.** The passage says that Firefighter Harris checked on the driver of the Jeep and that Firefighter Kane checked on the driver of the midsize car. The question refers to the Jeep, so Choice (A) is correct.

3. **C.** The ambulance arrived at the scene at 9:12 p.m. Don't confuse the time of the ambulance's arrival with the time the passenger in the midsize car was loaded into the ambulance (9:32 p.m.).

4. **B.** The motorist at the scene right before the fire reported seeing smoke from a campfire on the mountain. Although the campers may have intentionally started the fire, Choice (A), it's more likely that the campers failed to properly extinguish their campfire. Choice (B) is the best answer.

5. **D.** The second paragraph of the passage says that the driver of the Volkswagen was a woman in her late thirties. The woman in her late twenties was a passenger, not the driver. Therefore, Choice (D) is correct.

6. **E.** The passage says that the driver of the pickup truck was weaving in and out of his lane and tailgating the car in front of him. Later, the passage reveals that he smelled like alcohol, that he staggered when he walked, and that his speech was slurred. These are all clues that he was driving under the influence. Choice (E) is correct.

7. **D.** The fourth paragraph of the passage says that the driver of the pickup truck appeared to have broken his right arm. Choice (D) is correct.

8. **B.** Look for clues in the passage and draw a conclusion. The passage says that the driver of the Volkswagen complained of head pain and was covered in small pieces of glass. The passage also says that the driver-side window of her car was smashed. These clues lead you to conclude that the driver-side window caused her injuries.

9. **D.** When you choose the best title for a passage, you find the main idea. The accident in the passage happened because the driver of the pickup truck was drunk. Choice (D) is the best answer. Although he did try to pass a car, Choice (A), this is not the main reason for the accident; speeding, Choice (D), is also not the main reason for the accident.

10. **E.** The fire started in the kitchen where the homeowner was cooking, and attempting to put out the fire with water made it worse. This tells you that the fire was probably a grease fire. According to the passage, the homeowner should've used a Class (K) fire extinguisher.

11. **C.** You can use deductive reasoning to answer this question. The fire is in a warehouse filled with crates of paper, so a Class A fire extinguisher should be used to put out the fire. The passage tells you that the higher the numerical rating, the greater the square footage the extinguisher can handle. Because the warehouse is large, you should choose the extinguisher with the highest number. Choice (C) is the correct answer.

12. **A.** The passage says that a Class D fire extinguisher is used to put out metal fires, but the agent inside the extinguisher depends on the metal it was designed to fight. This information is printed on the faceplate, which Firefighter Ross should read before he uses the extinguisher. Choice (A) is correct.

13. **D.** The question says the fire is near a silo on a farm, and grain is kept in a silo. The question also says that there's a strong odor and a man there complains of his throat burning. This information matches the traits, cause, and effect of nitrogen dioxide.

14. **C.** The question explains that the fire is at a carpet factory, which means the fire is fueled in part by rubber and foam. The employees are having trouble breathing. This information matches the traits, causes, and effect of exposure to hydrogen cyanide.

15. **B.** The third paragraph of the passage says that when using the two-firefighter method, the first firefighter places one hand on the nozzle and one hand on the hose. The second firefighter stands about 3 feet behind the first and places one knee and both hands on the line. Choice (B) is the correct answer.

16. **A.** To choose the best title, you have to find the main idea of the passage. This passage discusses methods firefighters may use when operating a large-size attack hose or line. Therefore, Choice (A) is the best answer. Although Choice (E) may also seem like a good answer, the methods discussed in this passage are specifically for a large-size attack line; methods differ for small- and medium-size attack lines.

17. **E.** A four-firefighter method is not discussed in this passage. Choice (E) is correct.

18. **C.** The firefighter who would most likely kneel on the hose line is the second firefighter in a two-firefighter method. The third firefighter in a three-firefighter method also kneels, but this is not an answer option. In the one-firefighter method, the firefighter sits rather than kneels.

19. **E.** The passage says that the three-firefighter method is the best method to use when operating a large-size attack line and that some departments prefer the firefighters to use hose straps because doing so offers the greatest mobility. Therefore, Choice (E) is correct.

20. **A.** The first paragraph of the passage says that a teacher in the parking lot called 911 and reported the fire. Choice (A) is correct.

21. **B.** The second paragraph of the passage says that firefighters determined that the smoke was coming from the windows of the teachers' lounge and then proceeded into the building to look for the source of the smoke. Choice (B) is correct.

22. **C.** The third paragraph of the passage says that the fire was out by 9:45 a.m. This is the time firefighters extinguished the fire.

23. **C.** Firefighters were dispatched to the fire at 9:25 a.m. and arrived at the scene at 9:38 a.m. This is a difference of 13 minutes.

24. **A.** Static kernmantle rope does not stretch and is commonly used in rescues. Choice (A) is correct.

25. **E.** Laid rope is the easiest to splice and is inexpensive, so Choice (E) is the best answer.

26. **C.** The passage says that the braid-on-braid rope "has an outer sheath and an inner core." Choice (C) is the correct answer.

27. **D.** Splicing, tangling, stretching, and abrading are all concerns when working with laid rope, not braid-on-braid rope, so you can eliminate Choices (A), (B), (C), and (E). The sheath and the core of braid-on-braid sometimes slide, however, so Choice (D) is correct.

28. **E.** This passage discusses cleaning spills, clearing away clutter, maintaining equipment, and avoiding back strain, all of which are ways to minimize risk at a fire station, so Choice (E) is the best answer. Although Choices (B), (C), and (D) are mentioned in this passage, they are not the main idea of the entire passage.

29. **D.** The passage does not mention that firefighters should walk rather than run in a fire station. Choice (D) is the correct answer.

30. **E.** The passage explains that firefighters need to know how to lift equipment correctly so that they don't strain their backs or break the equipment by dropping it. Both Choices (A) and (C) are correct, which is the answer option in Choice (E).

31. **E.** *Dead load* refers to the weight of building materials and equipment that is permanently attached to the building.

32. **D.** Because the heating unit is in only one part of the building, it is a concentrated load.

33. **A.** A *live load* is anything inside the building that is not attached. Office furniture is a live load. A wind gust hitting the building, Choice (B), is an impact load, and a house's roof, Choice (C), and windows, Choice (D), are dead loads. People outside the building, Choice (D) are not part of a building's load.

34. **A.** This question asks you to choose the correct order of the steps. Before a firefighter can break a glass plane, he or she would choose the correct tool (3). Then, the firefighter would stand next to the plane he or she intends to break (2). Then the firefighter would strike the plane (5). After this, the firefighter would clear away the broken glass (1). Lastly, the firefighter would unlock the door (4).

35. **B.** After the firefighter clears away the broken glass, the firefighter should unlock the door.

36. **A.** Liquids classified as Class IB have a flash point below 73°F (as do liquids in Class IA, but that isn't an answer option). Choice (A) is the correct answer.

37. **C.** Class IA and Class IC liquids boil below 100°F. Turpentine is a Class IC liquid, so Choice (C) is correct.

38. **A.** Liquids in Class IA, IB, and IC are all flammable. Petroleum ether is a Class IA liquid, so it's flammable. Choice (A) is correct.

39. **E.** To answer this question, find gasoline in the fourth column of the table. Then find the boiling point of liquids in this category. It is above 100°F. Choice (E) is correct.

40. **C.** The passage says that Firefighter Hogan does not go home after his shift, comes in late, and looks ill. It also says that his wife has threatened to leave him if he does not stop drinking. Firefighter Hogan's marital problems and ill appearance seem to stem from his alcohol abuse, so you can eliminate Choices (B) and (D). It's more likely that he has a drinking problem.

41. **D.** The House 2 fire caused the most damage. The passage says that the house and its contents were destroyed and that a nearby house was also damaged.

42. **C.** The cause of the fire in House 2 was faulty wiring. Choice (C) is correct.

43. **E.** The restaurant fire was put out before firefighters arrived.

44. **C.** The main advantage of masonry in a fire is that it retains its structure and is not easily damaged. This is why masonry is used to build firewalls.

45. **A.** The passage explains that steel fails at high temperatures, so a disadvantage of steel in a fire is that it could fail and cause the building to collapse.

46. **E.** According to the passage, wood that contains a lot of moisture burns more slowly than dry wood. Choice (E) is correct.

47. **C.** The correct spelling is *equipment*.

48. **A.** The correct spelling is *accommodate*. The word has a double *c* and a double *m*.

49. **D.** The correct spelling is *discipline*. The word has both an *s* and a *c*.

50. **B.** The correct spelling is *maneuver*.

51. **B.** The correct spelling is *extinguisher*. The *w* sound after the *g* is created by a combination of the letters *ui*.

52. **C.** The correct spelling is *cylinder*. The *s* sound at the beginning is created by the letter *c*, and the first short *i* sound is created by the letter *y*.

53. **A.** The correct spelling is *versatile*.

54. **E.** The correct spelling is *ventilation*. The *sh* sound is created by a combination of the letters *ti*.

55. **D.** The misspelled word in this sentence is *conducsion*. The correct spelling is *conduction*. Although both *si* and *ti* can create the *sh* sound in words (for example, *mission* or *nation*), *ti* is the correct combination in this word.

56. **C.** The misspelled word in this sentence is *spesially*. The correct spelling is *specially*.

57. **B.** The subject in this sentence is three types of hose lays: forward, reverse, and split. Because the subject is plural, the sentence needs a plural verb to be correct. *Is, was, has,* and *am* are all singular verbs. *Are* is a plural verb, so Choice (B) is correct.

58. **A.** The context of the sentence hints that you're looking for a past tense verb to make the sentence complete. The past tense of the verb *break* is *broke*, so Choice (A) is correct.

59. **C.** The word that best completes the sentence is *to*.

60. **C.** The word or phrase that best completes the sentence is *has brought*. This sentence needs a verb in the present perfect tense to make it complete. The present perfect tense is often used when the time period is not finished. In this case, you know the time is ongoing because the second half of the sentence states, "now we have," which indicates that the action is still occurring. To create the present perfect tense, you combine a present-tense form of *to have* (in this case, *has*) with the past participle of a verb (in this case, the past participle of *bring,* which is *brought*). *Brang* and *brung* aren't real words, so the correct answer is Choice (C).

61. **B.** The word or phrase that best completes the sentence is *returned*. This sentence needs a verb in the simple past tense to make it complete. Verbs in simple past tense indicate actions that started and finished at some point in the past. In this case, the firefighters started and finished returning after the fire was extinguished.

62. **D.** To create the comparative form of adverbs that end in *-ly* — in this case, *quickly* — you use the word *more*. You use the comparative form when a sentence compares two things. In this sentence, the comparison is between dry wood and wood with a high moisture content.

63. **D.** This sentence needs a possessive adjective to make it complete. Victor changed *Victor's* mind about switching from a ladder company to a truck company. The adjective *his* correctly replaces *Victor's* in the sentence, so Choice (D) is correct.

64. **C.** The subject of the sentence — *cause* — is singular, so the verb must also be singular. In addition, the word *destroyed* suggests that the action took place in the past. Therefore, you're looking for a singular verb in the past tense. The verb *was* is a singular, past tense verb, so Choice (C) is correct.

65. **A.** The words *pulled* and *allowed* in this sentence suggest that the action took place in the past, which means you're looking for a past tense verb. *Alerted* is a verb in the past tense, so Choice (A) is correct.

66. **E.** The verb in this sentence is *began*. The word *to* before the blank suggests that you're looking for an *infinitive*, which is a combination of the word *to* and the simple form of a verb. The word that correctly completes the sentence is *burn*.

67. **E.** This sentence compares two things: a large brush truck and a small brush truck. The word *than* correctly completes the sentence. Don't confuse *than* with *then*. *Than* is a conjunction used to make comparisons. *Then* is an adverb that refers to time.

68. **A.** To correctly complete this sentence, you need a verb in the simple past tense. The verb *blow* is irregular, which means that its spelling changes with its tense. In the simple past tense, the verb is spelled *blew,* so the correct answer is (A).

69. **D.** The word *than* is a hint that you need a subject pronoun to complete the sentence. Try to complete the sentence mentally: "The chief arrived at the fire faster than *I arrived.*" *I* correctly completes the sentence, so Choice (D) is correct.

70. **D.** The word *than* is a hint that this sentence makes a comparison between two things: the chief and the other firefighters (as a group). To create the comparative form of an adjective with two syllables, you have two options: add the word *more* before it or add *-er* to the end of it. You should never do both, however. Correct options in this sentence are *more friendly* or *friendlier*. Because *more friendly* is not an option, Choice (D), *friendlier,* is correct.

71. **B.** This sentence needs a possessive adjective to make it complete. The possessive adjective takes the place of what would be a possessive noun: The city council finished *the city council's* budget, which includes a grant to the three local fire stations. *City council* is singular, so the pronoun *its* correctly replaces *the city council's* in the sentence.

72. **B.** The missing verb and the presence of the word *was* in this sentence are hints that this sentence is written in passive voice. Passive voice is created by a form of the verb *to be* (*am, is, are, was, were,* and so on) and the past participle of a verb. The past participle of the verb *tear* is *torn,* so Choice (B) is correct.

73. **C.** Distance equals the rate of speed multiplied by time, or $d = rt$. The tanker truck is traveling at an average speed of 40 mph. The rate is in miles per hour, so to use the formula, you need the time to be in hours rather than minutes. An hour is divided into four 15-minute intervals, so 15 minutes is ¼ of an hour: $d = 40 \times ¼$. To figure out the distance, divide the speed by four. The barn is 10 miles away.

74. **E.** The square root of a number is a factor of a number that, when squared — or multiplied by itself — gives you the number. The square root of 1,600 is 40: $40^2 = 40 \times 40 = 1,600$.

75. **B.** *Area* and *square footage* are the same thing, and area = length × width. In this problem, you need to find the areas of both the kitchen and the dining room and then add them together. The area of the kitchen is 8 feet × 10 feet, or 80 square feet. The area of the dining room is 6 feet × 6 feet, or 36 square feet. Combined, the area of the kitchen and the dining room is 80 square feet + 36 square feet, or 116 square feet.

76. **A.** Distance equals the rate of speed multiplied by time, or $d = rt$. You know that the speed is 30 mph and the distance is 5 miles, so you have to solve for time *(t):*

$$d = rt$$
$$5 = 30t$$
$$\frac{5}{30} = \frac{30t}{30}$$
$$\frac{1}{6} = t$$

The time is equivalent to ⅙ of an hour, or 10 minutes.

77. **E.** Area = length × width. To find the area of the garage, multiply its length, 16 feet, by its width, 20 feet: 16 feet × 20 feet = 320 square feet.

78. **C.** To find the height of the apartment complex, you have to multiply the total number of stories by the height of each story. The apartment has 12 stories, each at a height of 15 feet: 12 stories × 15 feet/story = 180 feet. The building is 180 feet tall.

79. **D.** To find the answer, multiply the number of flights by the number of steps in each flight: 8 flights × 12 steps/flight = 96 steps.

80. **D.** To find the answer, first do some multiplication. To determine how many feet of 125-foot hose you have, multiply 6 hoses by 125 feet in each hose ($6 \times 125 = 750$). To determine how many feet of 75-foot hose you have, multiply 2 hoses by 75 feet in each hose ($2 \times 75 = 150$). Now add all lengths of hose together (don't forget about the one 150-foot hose): $750 + 150 + 150 = 1,050$.

81. **E.** The fire engine takes 20 minutes to travel 12 miles. Twenty minutes is equivalent to ⅓ of an hour. So to find the number of miles you could travel in one hour, multiply the distance by 3: $12 \times 3 = 36$. The engine averaged 36 mph on the way to the theater.

82. **A.** The question tells you that a ladder greater than 35 feet in length has a reach that is 2 feet less than the overall length. Therefore, a ladder that is 40 feet long overall would reach to 38 feet ($40 - 2 = 38$).

83. **C.** To determine how much 125-foot hose is in the dryer, multiply four hoses by 125 feet in each hose ($4 \times 125 = 500$). To determine the amount of 150-foot hose, multiply two hoses by 150 feet ($2 \times 150 = 300$). Now add all the lengths together (don't forget about the one 175-foot hose): $500 + 300 + 175 = 975$. To find the average length of hose, divide this total by the total number of hoses: $975 \div 7$. The result is approximately 139 feet.

84. **B.** This problem is loaded with times, but you need only to pinpoint two: the time the engine left the station (2:51 a.m.) and the time the fire was extinguished (3:37 a.m.). The first time is 9 minutes before 3:00 a.m., and the second is 37 minutes after 3:00, so the time elapsed is $9 + 37 = 46$ minutes.

85. **B.** This is a simple addition problem. Simply add up the prices for all of the items: $\$125 + \$550 + \$375 + \$435 + \$22 = \$1,507$.

86. **A.** To determine the answer, add up the costs for all of the items except the plastic fire helmets and the DVD: $\$125 + \$375 + 435 = \$935$.

87. **B.** Tackle this problem by dividing it into parts. First, determine the square root of 289. The square root of a number is a factor of a number that, when squared — or multiplied by itself — gives you the number. The square root of 289 is 17. Then just use basic addition and subtraction: $17 + 87 - 26 = 78$.

88. **C.** This question is tricky. It presents measurements in both inches and feet, and it requires multiple steps. Because the answers are given in feet, first convert all measurements to feet. To determine the length of five lengths of 75-foot hose, multiply: 5×75 feet = 375 feet. The four hose couplings are each 4 inches long: 4×4 inches = 16 inches. There are 12 inches in 1 foot, so 16 inches is about 1.3 feet. Now add the numbers together: 375 feet + 1.3 feet = 376.3 feet. Now subtract 376.3 from 500 to see how many more feet of hose Firefighter Marshall needs: $500 - 376.3 = 123.7$.

89. **B.** To determine how many vehicle fires occurred, subtract the number of other calls from the total: $87 - 6 - 44 - 28 = 9$. This is the number of vehicle fires that occurred in 2008.

90. **C.** To determine the total number of fire calls in 2009, add together all of the types of calls from 2009: $9 + 21 + 11 + 41 = 82$. There were 82 calls in 2009.

91. **D.** To determine percentages, divide the part by the whole. In this case, divide the number of wildland fires by the overall number of calls in 2007: $27 \div 85 \approx 0.32$. Then, multiply by 100: $0.32 \times 100 = 32$. Wildland fires made up 32 percent of the calls in 2007.

92. **C.** The upper flammable limit for hydrogen is 75.0. Methane's upper flammable limit is five times less than that, so to find the answer, divide 75.0 by 5: $75.0 \div 5 = 15.0$. The upper flammable limit of methane is 15.0.

93. **E.** The decimal 0.375 is equivalent to ⅜. If you divide 3 by 8, the result is 0.375.

94. **A.** The maximum heat release rate for the sofa is 3,033 BTUs. For the mattress, it's 37.9 BTUs. To determine how many times greater the maximum heat release rate for the sofa is than for the mattress, divide 3,033 by 37.9: $3,033 \div 37.9 \approx 80.0$. The sofa's maximum heat release rate is about 80 times greater than the mattress's heat release rate.

95. **B.** This problem involves mathematical reasoning. The first number in the Number of Acres Burned column is 25, and the second is 27.5, for an increase of 2.5 acres; 2.5 is 10 percent of 25, so you know that after two hours, the number of acres burned increased by 10 percent. Ten percent of 27.5 is 2.75, which, when added to 27.5, is equal to 30.25. Again, the table shows an increase of 10 percent after another hour. The statement that most accurately describes the relationship between the number of hours a wildland fire burns and the number of acres burned is Choice (B). As the number of hours increases by 1, the number of acres burned increases by 10 percent.

96. **B.** To find the percentage decrease, divide the number in the Decrease column by the original 2008 number for each type of school and multiply the result by 100. The number of elementary school students showed the sharpest decrease at 15.5%.

97. **A.** To find the number of elementary school students in 2009, subtract the *decrease* number from the 2008 number: 1,263 − 196 = 1,067.

98. **E.** A ratio is the relationship in quantity or size between two or more things. In this case, the ratio is between the number of vocational students (192) and the number of high school students in 2009 (2,688). This can be expressed as 192:2,688. However, 192 is a factor of 2,688. If you divide both numbers by 192, you can express the ratio as 1:14.

99. **A.** The total budget is represented as 100 percent. To find how much of this money was spent on the cascade unit, simply subtract how much was spent on each of the other trucks from 100: 100 − 17 − 22 − 13 − 36 = 12. The cascade unit received 12 percent of the fuel money.

100. **B.** To determine how many extinguishers you need, divide the total square footage (42,000) by the number of square feet covered by each extinguisher (6,000): 42,000 ÷ 6,000 = 7. Because the office building already has four extinguishers, it needs three more to comply with the fire code.

101. **A.** By looking at the times in the Total Time column, you can determine that the time increases by 34 seconds for each additional hose. Therefore, Choice (A) is correct. To help you see this pattern, you may want to convert all the hose-loading times to seconds: One hose takes 34 seconds, two take 68 seconds, three take 102 seconds, and four take 136 seconds.

102. **D.** In the Force Required to Lift Load column, you can see that after the first foot, the force doubles from 100 to 200 and from 200 to 400. As the force doubles, the distance between the heavy load and the pivot point increases by 1 foot.

103. **D.** To determine the average number of calls Canonburg Fire Department runs each month, add together number of calls in January, February, March, and April and divide by 4: 55 + 47 + 53 + 49 = 204, and 204 ÷ 4 = 51. Therefore, the fire department averages 51 calls per month and can expect about that many calls in May.

104. **E.** Firefighter O'Hare responded to 48 calls. He was not manning the nozzle during 36 of those calls (48 total calls − 12 calls manning the nozzle), so you can set up a proportion problem and cross-multiply to solve for *x*:

$$\frac{36}{48} = \frac{x}{100}$$

$$\frac{\cancel{48}x}{\cancel{48}} = \frac{3,600}{48}$$

$$x = 75$$

During 75 percent of the calls Firefighter O'Hare ran, he was not manning the nozzle.

105. **D.** To find the answer, simply divide to see 480 by 275 to see how many times greater 480 is than 275. The result, rounded to the nearest tenth, is 1.7. Therefore, the temperature at which nylon rope melts is about 1.7 times greater than the temperature at which polyethylene rope melts.

Answer Key

1. D	22. C	43. E	64. C	85. B
2. A	23. C	44. C	65. A	86. A
3. C	24. A	45. A	66. E	87. B
4. B	25. E	46. E	67. E	88. C
5. D	26. C	47. C	68. A	89. B
6. E	27. D	48. A	69. D	90. C
7. D	28. E	49. D	70. D	91. D
8. B	29. D	50. B	71. B	92. C
9. D	30. E	51. B	72. B	93. E
10. E	31. E	52. C	73. C	94. A
11. C	32. D	53. A	74. E	95. B
12. A	33. A	54. E	75. B	96. B
13. D	34. A	55. D	76. A	97. A
14. C	35. B	56. C	77. E	98. E
15. B	36. A	57. B	78. C	99. A
16. A	37. C	58. A	79. D	100. B
17. E	38. A	59. C	80. D	101. A
18. C	39. E	60. C	81. E	102. D
19. E	40. C	61. B	82. A	103. D
20. A	41. D	62. D	83. C	104. E
21. B	42. C	63. D	84. B	105. D

Part V
The Part of Tens

The 5th Wave   By Rich Tennant

"Here's one. What is the appropriate ring tone for your cell phone? 'Put Out the Fire,' 'Ring the Alarm,' or 'Smoke Gets In Your Eyes'?"

In this part . . .

No *For Dummies* book is complete without the Part of Tens. Part V includes our firefighter exam top-ten lists. The first list includes our "best of the best" advice to prepare for each of the exams in the hiring process — including the written exam, the physical ability test, the oral interview, the medical exam, and the psychological evaluation — and help turn you into a top candidate. The second list covers some basics that every firefighter needs to know. The chapters in this part are short and cut right to the chase, so give 'em a quick read and get on your way.

Chapter 23

Ten Ways to Improve Your Chances of Getting Hired

. . . .

In This Chapter
▶ Getting to know firefighters and what they do
▶ Being respectful and responsible
▶ Applying for firefighting positions
▶ Having a successful firefighter exam experience

. . . .

This chapter can help you every step of the way throughout the hiring process. Whether you're taking the written exam for the first time or preparing for your oral interview, these ten tips lead you in the right direction. If you keep our advice in mind, you'll increase your chances for success and you'll be well on your way toward becoming a firefighter.

Be Prepared

This may seem obvious, but you can never be too prepared. Arm yourself by gathering information about each step in the hiring process. Do some research on the Internet or talk to career firefighters. The more you know about the exams, the more comfortable you'll feel in each step of the process.

For each exam, be sure to check and double-check the time, date, and testing location. Arrive a bit early and make sure you have everything you need: pencils and scratch paper for the written exam, comfortable clothes and sneakers for the physical ability test, and so on.

Visit Local Fire Departments

What better way to apply our first tip ("Be Prepared") than by talking to the men and women who have already successfully completed the process? Career firefighters can point you in the right direction and give you tips to succeed. Some departments even offer ride-along programs that allow you to see firefighters in action and give you a taste for exactly what firefighters do.

Volunteer

Not only is volunteering with a local fire department a good way to give back to the community, but it's also a good way to get some hands-on firefighting experience. Volunteering allows you the opportunity to familiarize yourself with firefighting equipment, departmental hierarchy — that is, who's in charge — and emergency situations. Because volunteer departments sometimes work side by side with paid departments, you'll likely meet other firefighters who can give you training and offer you help and advice.

You may also consider volunteering elsewhere in the community. For example, volunteering with organizations such as Habitat for Humanity or Big Brothers Big Sisters shows that you like being involved in the community and enjoy helping others.

Maintain a Clean Background

If you know that you want to become a firefighter someday, keep in mind that a background investigation is part of the process. Avoid putting yourself in situations that could raise red flags later. Background investigators may talk to former employers, teachers, neighbors, family members, and spouses, and they'll likely check to see whether you have a police record. If you want your background check to come back clean, try to live your life in a respectful and responsible way. The following are some tips:

- ✔ Always be respectful toward your superiors — teachers, employers, elders, and so on.

- ✔ Always arrive on time for school, work, and other important engagements.

- ✔ Always do your best. Don't take shortcuts to get the job done faster. Do it right and take your time.

- ✔ Avoid brushes with the law. Follow the rules and steer clear of situations that could put you or others at risk.

These tips may seem trivial or obvious, but during the hiring process, someone may check with teachers to see whether you cut class or talk to employers about your work ethic. And you can expect that they'll check to see whether you have a criminal record. When hiring firefighters, departments look for honest, reliable, trustworthy candidates, and you'll likely have to answer questions about anything in your past that is cause for concern.

Be careful of what you — and your friends — post on social networking Web sites, such as Facebook and MySpace. Many fire departments look at these sites as part of the background check. In addition, many have policies regarding what's posted after the candidate is employed. Consider what a post or photo may look like to the fire department and general public before you put it out there for the world to see.

Enroll in Some Firefighting Classes

You can improve your chances on the exams by enrolling in some firefighting classes. It never hurts to further your education and increase your knowledge. Although the written firefighter exam doesn't require prior knowledge of firefighting, having prior knowledge of the fire service certainly won't hurt your chances and may even give you an edge further down the line.

Many fire departments, even volunteer ones, sponsor firefighting classes and hold trainings on a regular basis. Contact a local fire department to find out whether you can sign up for these classes. Classes may teach skills such as first aid, CPR, emergency vehicle operations, or wildland firefighting. Others may focus on building construction or hazardous materials. Local colleges or universities may also offer two- or four-year degrees in areas such as fire science or fire protection engineering.

Identify Where You Want to Work

Conduct some research on the fire departments where you want to work. Big cities are likely to have more available positions than small municipal fire departments, but you're also likely to encounter more competition for jobs. If necessary, broaden your search beyond your hometown.

Keep in mind that firefighters work in both the public sector and the private sector. Although many fire departments work for city or county governments, some businesses hire specially trained industrial firefighters who work to protect companies, factories, products, and employees.

 After you identify where you want to work, check the employment pages on those departments' Web sites and keep tabs to find out when those departments are hiring and testing candidates. When you see a job opening or an exam announcement, find out how to apply and get the ball rolling.

A great way to stay informed about national firefighter opportunities is to search online. Many Web sites help connect applicants with fire departments that are recruiting. Some charge a fee, but it's worth the price to receive notifications from hundreds of fire departments. The following are some excellent sites:

  ✔ www.NationalFireSelect.com
  ✔ www.FireRecruit.com

Apply at Multiple Locations

Hand-in-hand with identifying the departments where you want to work is applying at multiple locations. The more places you apply, the better chance you have of landing a job. Remember, the competition for firefighting jobs is fierce. Hundreds of applicants will square off for just a few available positions, so you have to do whatever you can to place the odds in your favor. Applying at multiple locations is a good way to ensure that you'll land a job somewhere.

Practice for Perfection

The old saying goes, "Practice makes perfect." You can apply this saying to every step of the firefighter hiring process. The following are some ways to practice:

  ✔ **Written exam:** Practice for the written exam by buying a study guide (like this one — see, you're already ahead of the curve!) and taking practice tests (see Chapters 15 through 22 of this book). You can find additional study tips and practice exams online.

  ✔ **Physical exam:** Practice for the physical exam by finding out exactly what your department will expect you to do. Create a workout regimen to whip your body into shape and stay in shape as you prepare to enter a training academy. Try a combination of exercises that target both your lower and upper body. Running, weight lifting, sit-ups, and push-ups are a few basic exercises that will help you prepare for the physical ability test. For guidance on putting a training program together, see Chapter 12.

  ✔ **Oral interview:** Practice for the oral interview by reviewing common interview questions and considering how you would answer each one. Have a friend or relative ask you questions so you can practice your responses aloud in front of others. Also, review your background information, because interviewers will likely have questions about your past. We offer interview tips in Chapter 13.

The more you practice for each step in the hiring process, the more likely you'll be to succeed and move on.

Take the Exam More than Once

Don't be afraid to take the exam multiple times. Maybe the first time around you passed the written exam but not the physical ability test. No problem. Next time you'll spend more time improving your physical fitness. The mechanical aptitude questions threw you for a loop? Before the next test, brush up on your knowledge of tools and simple machines. We're going to throw another cliché at you here: If at first you don't succeed, try, try again.

If you apply at multiple locations, you'll likely have to take these tests more than once anyway. You can expect each department to require the completion of each step in the hiring process. The more you take these exams, the more familiar you'll become with each one, and the more comfortable you'll feel with the entire process.

Stay Focused

The bottom line is that the firefighter hiring process takes a long time. You have to take several different exams, each of which has the potential to disqualify you as a candidate. Weeks, even months, may pass between the time you first apply and the date of the written exam, the physical ability test, or the oral interview. Therefore, it's important to maintain your focus. Keep your eye on the prize and never stop working toward your ultimate goal — a career as a firefighter.

Chapter 24

Ten Things Every Firefighter Should Do

In This Chapter

▶ Understanding how to succeed as a firefighter

▶ Preparing for a career in the fire service

Okay, we know you're not a firefighter yet, but if you use this guide and continue to pursue your goals, we know that you will be someday. For that reason, we want to share some practical, on-the-job advice with you. These actions help prepare you for a firefighting career and help you understand the traits of a successful firefighter.

Show Respect for the Job

Firefighting is a rewarding and honorable occupation. It's also an occupation that involves risk and danger. As a firefighter, give the job the respect, the time, and the dedication it deserves. For example, never take shortcuts, and remember that "good enough" is simply unacceptable. Listen to your superiors' orders and take their opinions to heart. Avoid becoming labeled an "IDI" — for having an "I deserve it" attitude.

Demonstrate Integrity

As a firefighter, you are a representative of both your department and the firefighting profession in general. Your actions affect the public's perception of firefighters. Therefore, it's important that you're honest and that you act in a responsible, trustworthy manner. Firefighters protect the community and its residents, and citizens look up to firefighters for that reason. You can't let them down — even when you're not on duty or in uniform.

Be a Team Player

Firefighting is all about teamwork. Each member of the team has a task to complete, and all members of the team depend on each other to get the whole job done. The failure of just one person to do his or her job correctly can put the entire team at risk. If that means asking for help, do it. Don't let your ego get in the way, and respect the chain of command.

Check Your Gear

A firefighter's personal protective equipment (PPE) and self-contained breathing apparatus (SCBA) are designed to protect him or her from smoke, heat, and flames. As a firefighter, your gear can literally help save your life, so check it thoroughly and check it often — preferably after each call so you know it's ready for the next one. For example, check your helmet for cracks, your boots for holes or melted soles, and your turnout coat and pants for tears or holes. Make sure your SCBA is in proper working order and that you have a full cylinder of air ready to go. In addition, make sure any equipment, gear, and tools that you share with other firefighters are also ready for the next call — their safety depends on it, too.

Display Leadership Qualities

Just because you're not the top dog in the department doesn't mean that you can't lead by example. During each shift you work, do your job to the best of your ability. Others will admire your dedication and skill, and they'll strive to do the same.

Find a Work/Home Balance

Firefighting is a stressful job, and firefighters see things that many people can't handle. We know that you don't want to upset your family with the stress and trauma of your day, but it's also important not to shut down or completely avoid communicating; doing so could lead to problems in your relationships. Don't be afraid to talk to your spouse or partner. In addition, try to focus on your children's smiles or the home-cooked meal on the table. When you enter the fire station, check family problems at the door. When you're on duty, you need to stay focused on the task at hand.

Ask Questions

As a firefighter, you're responsible for your own life and the lives of others. If you don't understand an order, get clarification. If you have a question, ask it. It's better to ask now than to regret not asking later.

Respect Your Superiors

As a firefighter, you have to listen to senior officers and follow orders. Understand that they're in charge for a reason. Senior officers are a wealth of knowledge and information, and you can learn a lot from them. Don't be afraid to sit down with them and ask questions.

Be Flexible

We're not talking about muscles and stretching here (although that type of flexibility is important, too!). Rather, we mean that you have to be ready for a call at a moment's notice, adapt to rapidly changing conditions, and work with diverse groups of people. In other words, go with the flow; there's no time to be picky.

Have Fun

Finally, have fun. As a career firefighter, you'll be doing a job you love with others who enjoy the same type of work. Sure, you're going to have to work some long days, and you'll have some days that you'll wish you could forget. But for the most part, if you enjoy what you do, you'll make your working environment a friendly, welcoming place for everyone, and you'll enjoy walking through the doors of the station each and every day.

Appendix

Observation and Memory Exercises

• •

The reading passages and illustrations in this appendix help test your observation and memory. They go with the practice exams in Part IV of this book, so if you plan to take any of those exams, resist the urge to look at these pages until an exam directs you to do so.

Memory Materials for Practice Exam 1

The following sections correspond to the Observation and Memory section in Part 3 of Practice Exam 1 (Chapter 15).

Listening and memory (Chapter 15)

Directions for questions 51–60: In this part, you'll be tested on your listening and memory skills, including your ability to hear, understand, and interpret information. Ask a partner to read aloud the following passage. DO NOT READ THE PASSAGE YOURSELF. DO NOT TAKE NOTES DURING THE READING. Immediately after your partner has finished reading, answer questions 51–60 based only on what you can remember from the reading. Choose the answer that *most correctly* answers each question. You may look at the passage only when checking your answers at the completion of Practice Exam 1.

Instructions to the reader: Carefully read the following passage aloud. After you begin, read the entire passage, pausing only between paragraphs. You may not answer questions about the passage or otherwise assist the test-taker. When you have finished reading, your task is complete, and you may leave the test-taker to allow him or her time to finish the test.

Water emergencies

Firefighters respond to all manner of emergencies — motor vehicle accidents, wildland fires, and structure fires, just to name a few. Sometimes they assist ambulance personnel or police officers in transporting patients or directing traffic. Often they must rescue victims from dangerous situations, such as a burning building or a crushed vehicle. At many of these emergency scenes, firefighters use water from hoses to douse flames or to wash debris from a roadway. But what if you're called to respond to an emergency *in* the water?

Water emergencies can occur anywhere. Don't think that just because you live in a relatively dry area that you don't have to worry about water rescues. Water emergencies can occur in rivers, lakes, streams, ponds, and even swimming pools. Because fire departments may be dispatched to respond to a wide variety of water emergencies, it's important to understand the different types of emergencies and the variety of methods you can use to help victims.

Two types of water emergencies are rescues and recoveries. A *rescue* typically involves a live victim — someone who is struggling in the water and needs help. A person who cannot swim and has fallen from a boat into a river is an example of a victim in need of a water rescue. A toddler who has fallen into a swimming pool is another example. The term *recovery* usually applies when firefighters must retrieve the remains of a person who has died as the result of a water emergency.

When participating in water rescues, you'll need to wear the proper equipment. Standard personal protective equipment, or PPE, is much too bulky to wear in the water. Rather, you'll need to wear a helmet specifically designed for water rescues and a personal flotation device, or PFD. In addition, your department may require that you wear a thermal protective suit, called a dry suit, which protects your entire body except for your head and sometimes your feet when working in the water. It's especially important to wear such a suit when working in or around cold water and ice, because it can prevent hypothermia. Hypothermia refers to a significant drop in body temperature.

Firefighters use several methods to rescue victims from the water, depending on the conditions of the emergency. These methods (in order of preference) are as follows: *reach, throw, row,* and *go*. In the reach method, you extend a tool with a long handle, such as a pike pole or even the pole of a rake, toward a victim in need of rescue. If the victim is able, he or she can grab the pole, and you can pull him or her to safety. The *reach method* typically works only when the victim is close. In the *throw method,* you toss a flotation device with an attached rope, such as a life preserver or an inner tube, to the victim. If the victim is able, he or she can hold on to the flotation device and keep his or her head above water as you use the rope to pull him or her to safety.

As you might have guessed, the *row method* involves a boat, though not necessarily a rowboat. With this method, you maneuver a boat to the victim. When you reach the victim, you pull him or her into the boat and return safely to shore.

The last method is the *go method*. The go method requires you to swim to the victim's aid. You hold on to the victim and try to keep his or her head above water as you swim back to shore, dragging the victim with you. Firefighters resort to the go method only when another method won't work, because it has the potential to result in two drowning victims: the original victim and the rescuer.

Visual memory (Chapter 15)

Directions for questions 61–70: In this part, you'll be tested on your observational and memory skills, including your ability to see, understand, and interpret information. Study the following image for 5 minutes. DO NOT TAKE NOTES ABOUT THE IMAGE AS YOU STUDY IT. At the end of 5 minutes, answer questions 61–70 based only on what you can remember from the image. DO NOT LOOK AT THE IMAGE AS YOU ANSWER THE QUESTIONS. Choose the answer that *most correctly* answers each question. You may look at the image only when checking your answers at the completion of Practice Exam 1.

Set your timer for 5 minutes and begin studying the image.

Davis Street fire scene

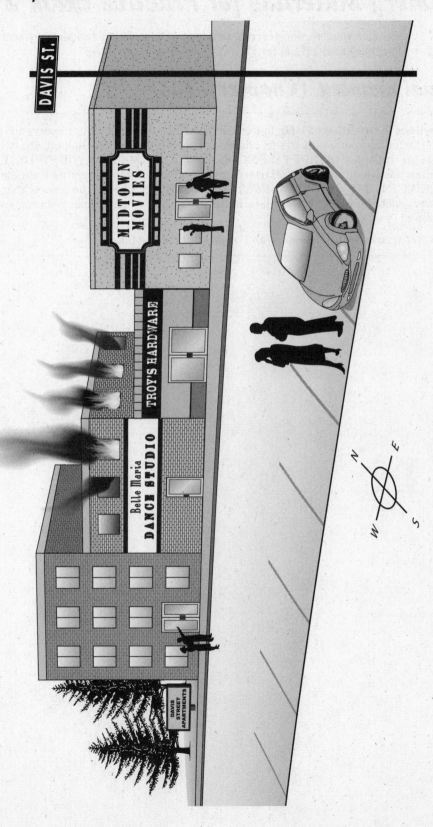

Memory Materials for Practice Exam 2

The following sections correspond to the Observation and Memory section in Part 3 of Practice Exam 2 (Chapter 17).

Visual memory (Chapter 17)

Directions for questions 51–60: In this part, you'll be tested on your observational and memory skills, including your ability to see, understand, and interpret information. Study the following image for 5 minutes. DO NOT TAKE NOTES ABOUT THE IMAGE AS YOU STUDY IT. At the end of 5 minutes, answer questions 51–60 based only on what you can remember from the image. DO NOT LOOK AT THE IMAGE AS YOU ANSWER THE QUESTIONS. Choose the answer that *most correctly* answers each question. You may look at the image only when checking your answers at the completion of Practice Exam 1.

Now, set your timer for 5 minutes and begin studying the image.

Snowy crash scene

Listening and memory (Chapter 17)

Directions for questions 61–70: In this part, you'll be tested on your listening and memory skills, including your ability to hear, understand, and interpret information. Ask a partner to read aloud the following passage. DO NOT READ THE PASSAGE YOURSELF. DO NOT TAKE NOTES DURING THE READING. Immediately after your partner has finished reading, answer questions 61–70 based only on what you can remember from the reading. Choose the answer that *most correctly* answers each question. You may look at the passage only when checking your answers at the completion of Practice Exam 2.

Instructions to reader: Carefully read the following passage aloud. After you begin, read the entire passage, pausing only between paragraphs. You may not answer questions about the passage or otherwise assist the test-taker. When you have finished reading, your task is complete, and you may leave the test-taker to allow him or her time to finish the test.

Flammable liquids

When firefighters attack a fire involving flammable liquids, such as gasoline or kerosene, they should know that water is probably not the best choice to use as an extinguishing agent. Although water works on some fires, it can actually cause some flammable liquids to disperse, thereby spreading the flames. Instead, firefighters will find that using foam is a better option.

For a fire to ignite and continue to burn, three elements must be present — fuel, heat, and a supply of oxygen. Firefighting foam forms a barrier over fire, which prevents oxygen from reaching the flames. Without oxygen, the fire cannot continue to burn, and the flames die down. As the foam dissipates, it leaves behind water to extinguish any remaining embers. Foam is successful on fires caused by flammable liquids because it separates the fire from its oxygen supply. When this division takes place, the temperature of the fuel and the area around it decreases. The foam continues to smother the area as it becomes water, which prevents flammable vapors from escaping and reduces the chance that the fire will reignite.

It's best to use foam when dealing with flammable liquids such as crude and fuel oil, gasoline, benzene, jet fuel, and kerosene. These hydrocarbons are difficult to fight with water because they tend to float on water. Because foam floats, too, it can smother the hydrocarbons on the surface and easily combat the flames. Foam is also useful when dealing with polar solvents such as alcohols, ketones, esters, acids, and acetone.

Firefighters may use a number of different techniques to apply foam to a fire. The technique that firefighters use depends entirely on the type and location of the fire. If firefighters use the wrong technique, however, the foam may not achieve the desired effect and the fire may continue to burn. The three main techniques that firefighters use to apply foam to fires involving flammable liquids are the roll-on method, the bank-down method, and the rain-down method.

Firefighters should use the roll-on method when the fire involves a pool of flammable liquid on the ground. It is best to aim the hose at the edge of the burning liquid pool. By keeping the hose stationary, the foam will push, or roll, backward onto the fire. Firefighters should distribute the foam continuously until they have covered the entire surface of the fuel. If necessary, firefighters may move to other spots along the edge of the spill to reach other burning areas.

When flammable liquid fires occur near sidewalks, walls, vehicles, or other raised surfaces, firefighters can use the bank-down technique to apply foam. In this method, firefighters aim the hose at the top of the elevated area. Eventually, the foam spills over the side of the elevated area and gently lands on the burning fuel on the ground below. Firefighters use this method when trucks overturn and spill oil or fuel or when they fight fires situated on hills.

If the burning liquid is not near a raised area or if the fire is too large to manage with the roll-on method, firefighters can use the rain-down method to apply foam. This technique involves directing the foam into the air above the burning fuel or oil. As the firefighters shoot the foam into the air, it falls softly onto the flames, like rain, forming a barrier and suffocating the flames. For smaller fires, firefighters may slowly move the hose from left to right. For large fires, firefighters should hold their aim above one specific area until those flames have been extinguished and then move on to the next area. One important thing for firefighters to remember when using foam is to avoid shooting foam directly into a liquid-fueled fire.

Firefighters should exercise caution when using foam. Skin contact with foam is not life-threatening, but foams can irritate the skin and eyes. Flushing with water will reduce any negative effects. In addition, firefighters should be careful to avoid ingesting or inhaling foam.

Memory Materials for Practice Exam 3

The following apartment floor plan is used to answer questions 1–10 in Practice Exam 3 (Chapter 19).

Directions: Look at this floor plan of an apartment. It has an apartment on each side and a fire escape in the back.

You will have 5 minutes to memorize this floor plan. Then you'll have to answer some questions about it from memory. Use your timer to alert you when 5 minutes has passed, or ask a partner to time you. Begin when you are ready.

Apartment floor plan

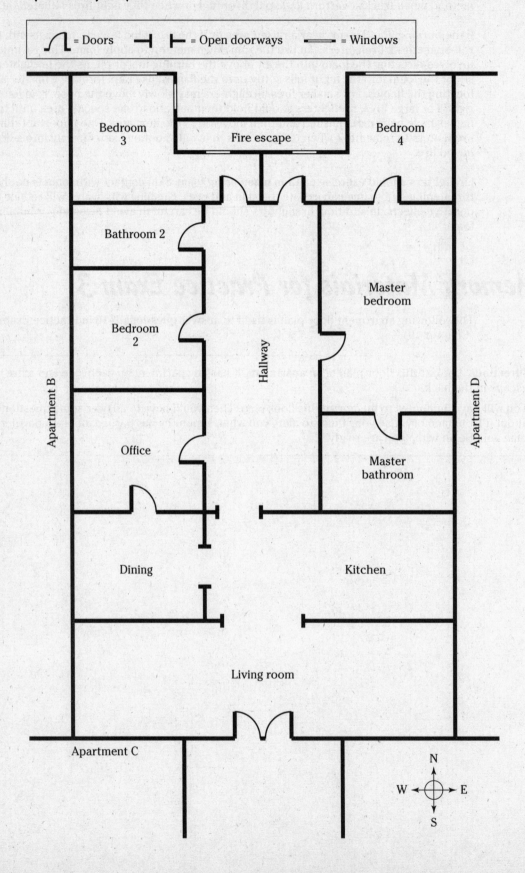

Index

Notes

Notes